King Henry V

ARDEN EARLY MODERN DRAMA GUIDES

Series Editors:
Andrew Hiscock, University of Wales, Bangor, UK and
Lisa Hopkins, Sheffield Hallam University, UK

Arden Early Modern Drama Guides offer practical and accessible introductions to the critical and performative contexts of key Elizabethan and Jacobean plays. Each guide introduces the text's critical and performance history, but also provides students with an invaluable insight into the landscape of current scholarly research, through a keynote essay on the state of the art and newly commissioned essays of fresh research from different critical perspectives.

A Midsummer Night's Dream, edited by Regina Buccola
Doctor Faustus, edited by Sarah Munson Deats
King Lear, edited by Andrew Hiscock and Lisa Hopkins
Henry IV, Part 1, edited by Stephen Longstaffe
'Tis Pity She's a Whore, edited by Lisa Hopkins
Women Beware Women, edited by Andrew Hiscock
Volpone, edited by Matthew Steggle
The Duchess of Malfi, edited by Christina Luckyj
The Alchemist, edited by Erin Julian and Helen Ostovich
The Jew of Malta, edited by Robert A. Logan
Macbeth, edited by John Drakakis and Dale Townshend
Richard III, edited by Annaliese Connolly
Twelfth Night, edited by Alison Findlay and Liz Oakley-Brown
The Tempest, edited by Alden T. Vaughan and
Virginia Mason Vaughan
Romeo and Juliet, edited by Julia Reinhard Lupton
Julius Caesar, edited by Andrew James Hartley
The Revenger's Tragedy, edited by Brian Walsh
The White Devil, edited by Paul Frazer and Adam Hansen
Edward III, edited by Kirk Melnikoff
Much Ado About Nothing, edited by Deborah Cartmell
and Peter J. Smith

Further titles are in preparation.

King Henry V

A Critical Reader

*Edited by Karen Britland
and Line Cottegnies*

THE ARDEN SHAKESPEARE
LONDON · NEW YORK · OXFORD · NEW DELHI · SYDNEY

THE ARDEN SHAKESPEARE
Bloomsbury Publishing Plc
50 Bedford Square, London, WC1B 3DP, UK
1385 Broadway, New York, NY 10018, USA

BLOOMSBURY, THE ARDEN SHAKESPEARE and the Arden Shakespeare logo are trademarks of Bloomsbury Publishing Plc

First published in Great Britain 2019
Paperback edition published 2020

Copyright © Karen Britland, Line Cottegnies and contributors, 2019

Karen Britland, Line Cottegnies and contributors have asserted their right under the Copyright, Designs and Patents Act, 1988, to be identified as authors of this work.

Cover design: Irene Martinez Costa
Cover image taken from the 1615 title page of *The Spanish Tragedy* by Thomas Kyd

All rights reserved. No part of this publication may be reproduced or transmitted in any form or by any means, electronic or mechanical, including photocopying, recording, or any information storage or retrieval system, without prior permission in writing from the publishers.

Bloomsbury Publishing Plc does not have any control over, or responsibility for, any third-party websites referred to in this book. All internet addresses given in this book were correct at the time of going to press. The author and publisher regret any inconvenience caused if addresses have changed or sites have ceased to exist, but can accept no responsibility for any such changes.

A catalogue record for this book is available from the British Library.

Library of Congress Cataloging-in-Publication Data
Names: Britland, Karen, 1970- author. | Cottegnies, Line, author.
Title: King Henry V : a critical reader / Karen Britland and Line Cottegnies.
Description: London; New York, NY : Bloomsbury Publishing, 2019. | Series: Arden Early Modern drama guides | Includes bibliographical references and index.
Identifiers: LCCN 2018024006 (print) | LCCN 2018024139 (ebook) | ISBN 9781474280112 (ePub) | ISBN 9781474280129 (ePDF) | ISBN 9781474280105 (hardback)
Subjects: LCSH: Shakespeare, William, 1564-1616. Henry V. | Shakespeare, William, 1564-1616—Study and teaching. | Henry V, King of England, 1387–1422—In literature. | Kings and rulers in literature. | Great Britain—History—Henry V, 1413-1422—Historiography.
Classification: LCC PR2812 (ebook) | LCC PR2812 .B75 2019 (print) | DDC 822.3/3—dc23
LC record available at https://lccn.loc.gov/2018024006

ISBN:	HB:	978-1-4742-8010-5
	PB:	978-1-3501-6479-6
	ePDF:	978-1-4742-8012-9
	eBook:	978-1-4742-8011-2

Series: Arden Early Modern Drama Guides

Typeset by RefineCatch Limited, Bungay, Suffolk

To find out more about our authors and books visit www.bloomsbury.com and sign up for our newsletters.

CONTENTS

Series Introduction vii
Notes on Contributors viii
Timeline xii

    Introduction 1
    Karen Britland and Line Cottegnies

1 The Critical Backstory 19
   James D. Mardock

2 Performance History 47
   Anne-Marie Miller-Blaise and Gisèle Venet

3 The State of the Art 75
   Emma Smith

4 *Henry V* on Screen 102
   Sarah Hatchuel

5 New Directions: Shakespeare's *Henry V* and Religion 126
   John Drakakis

6 New Directions: Making and Remaking the British Kingdoms – *Henry V*, Then and Now 156
   Christopher Ivic

7 New Directions: 'His Bruised Helmet and his Bended Sword' – The Politics of Criminality and Heroism in *Henry V*   180
Christine Sukic

8 New Directions: Agincourt and After – The Adversary's Perspective   201
Elizabeth Pentland

9 Learning and Teaching Resources   221
Gillian Woods, with Laura Seymour

Notes 247
Bibliography 297
Index 322

SERIES INTRODUCTION

The drama of Shakespeare and his contemporaries has remained at the very heart of English curricula internationally and the pedagogic needs surrounding this body of literature have grown increasingly complex as more sophisticated resources become available to scholars, tutors and students. This series aims to offer a clear picture of the critical and performative contexts of a range of chosen texts. In addition, each volume furnishes readers with invaluable insights into the landscape of current scholarly research as well as including new pieces of research by leading critics.

This series is designed to respond to the clearly identified needs of scholars, tutors and students for volumes which will bridge the gap between accounts of previous critical developments and performance history and an acquaintance with new research initiatives related to the chosen plays. Thus, our ambition is to offer innovative and challenging guides that will provide practical, accessible and thought-provoking analyses of early modern drama. Each volume is organized according to a progressive reading strategy involving introductory discussion, critical review and cutting-edge scholarly debate. It has been an enormous pleasure to work with so many dedicated scholars of early modern drama and we are sure that this series will encourage you to read 400-year-old play texts with fresh eyes.

Andrew Hiscock and Lisa Hopkins

NOTES ON CONTRIBUTORS

Karen Britland is Professor of Early Modern English Literature at the University of Wisconsin-Madison. She has just edited John Marston's tragicomedy, *The Dutch Courtesan*, for Arden Early Modern Drama and is currently working on an edition of *The Duchess of Malfi* for New Mermaids. She has also edited Elizabeth Cary's *The Tragedy of Mariam* (New Mermaids, 2010) and James Shirley's *The Imposture* (forthcoming). She is the author of a monograph on Queen Henrietta Maria's French heritage and theatrical interests, *Drama at the Courts of Queen Henrietta Maria* (2006), and is currently working on a project about the English Revolution.

Line Cottegnies is Professor of Early Modern English Literature at Sorbonne Université. She is the author of a monograph on the politics and poetics of wonder in Caroline poetry (1997) and has co-edited several collections, including *Authorial Conquests: Essays on Genre in the Writings of Margaret Cavendish* (2003), with N. Weitz, and *Women and Curiosity in Early Modern England and France*, with S. Parageau (2016). She had edited fifteen plays for the Gallimard edition of Shakespeare's works (2002–16), and *2 Henry IV* for Norton 3 (2016). She has translated the three parts of *Henry VI* – which led to an award-winning production directed by Thomas Jolly at the Avignon Festival in 2014. Her most recent publication is *Robert Garnier in Elizabethan England*, co-edited with M.-A. Belle (MHRA Tudor and Stuart Translations Series, 2017). She is currently working on a book project on Shakespeare's histories and the use of props.

John Drakakis is Emeritus Professor of English Studies at the University of Stirling and visiting professor at the University of

Lincoln. He is the editor of *Alternative Shakespeares* and the Arden 3 series edition of *The Merchant of Venice*. Professor Drakakis has published widely in the area of Shakespeare Studies and is the general and contributing editor of the revision of Geoffrey Bullough's *Narrative and Dramatic Sources of Shakespeare*. He is a member of the editorial boards of a number of scholarly journals and is the general editor of the Routledge New Critical Idiom series. Professor Drakakis is currently completing a book on *Shakespeare's Resources*. He holds an honorary D.Litt. from the University of Clermont-Auvergne, and an Honorary Fellowship from Wrexham Glyndwr University. He is an elected Fellow of the English Association and a member of the Academia Europoea.

Sarah Hatchuel is Professor of English Literature and Film at the University of Le Havre Normandie (France), President of the Société Française Shakespeare and head of the 'Groupe de recherche Identités et Cultures'. She has written extensively on adaptations of Shakespeare's plays (*Shakespeare and the Cleopatra/Caesar Intertext: Sequel, Conflation, Remake*, 2011; *Shakespeare, from Stage to Screen*, 2004; *A Companion to the Shakespearean Films of Kenneth Branagh*, 2000) and on TV series (*Lost: Fiction vitale*, 2013; *Rêves et series américaines: la fabrique d'autres mondes*, 2015). Professor Hatchuel is general editor of the Cambridge University Press *Shakespeare on Screen* collection (with Nathalie Vienne-Guerrin) and of the online journal *TV/Series* (with Ariane Hudelet)

Christopher Ivic is Senior Lecturer (Associate Professor) in English at Bath Spa University. His work has appeared in edited collections such as *British Identities and English Renaissance Literature* (2002), *Archipelagic Identities: Literature and Identity in the Atlantic Archipelago, 1550–1800* (2004), *Ars Reminiscendi: Mind and Memory in Renaissance Culture* (2009), *Memory Ireland: Explorations in Irish Cultural Memory* (2010), *Shakespeare and Wales: From the Marches to the Assembly* (2010), *Teaching Early Modern English Prose* (2010), *Celtic Shakespeare: The Bard and the Borderers* (2013) and *Staged Transgression in Shakespeare's England* (2013). With Grant Williams, he co-edited *Forgetting in Early Modern English Literature and Culture: Lethe's Legacies* (2004). He is also the author of *Shakespeare and National Identity: A Dictionary* (2017).

James D. Mardock is an Associate Professor of English at the University of Nevada, sometime dramaturg for the Lake Tahoe Shakespeare Festival, Coordinating Textual Editor of the Internet Shakespeare Editions (ISE), and the editor of the ISE *Henry V*. He has published articles on Shakespeare, Spenser, Jonson and John Taylor, and a monograph on Jonson's London. He is now at work on the ISE *Measure for Measure* and a book on Calvinism and metatheatre in early modern drama.

Anne-Marie Miller-Blaise is Associate Professor in Early Modern Literature and Cultural Studies at the Université Sorbonne Nouvelle. She is the author of *Le Verbe fait image*, which analyses George Herbert's poetry in the light of Reformation iconoclasm. She is currently finishing a book project, *Pandora's Basket: Poetic Objects and the Worth of Things*, which includes a reading of Shakespeare's sonnets, and is co-editing a journal issue on the profane quality of Shakespeare's theatre.

Elizabeth Pentland is Associate Professor of English at York University in Toronto and Coordinating Performance Editor for the Internet Shakespeare Editions (ISE). Her research focuses on England's literary and political relations with France during the period of the French civil wars. Her published work includes essays on Shakespeare, Marlowe, Mary Sidney and contemporary British playwright Tom Stoppard.

Laura Seymour is an Associate Lecturer in English at Bath Spa University. Her 2015 PhD thesis used cognitive theory to explore gesture in Shakespeare's plays. She is currently working on a Wellcome Trust funded project on Nonconformist gestures in Quaker writings.

Emma Smith is Professor of Shakespeare Studies at Hertford College, Oxford. Her research focuses on the reception of Shakespeare in performance, editing and criticism. She wrote the volume on *King Henry V* in the Shakespeare in Production series (2002). Her most recent work is *Shakespeare's First Folio: Four Centuries of an Iconic Book* (paperback 2018). Professor Smith is now working on a book about books.

Christine Sukic is Professor of Early Modern English Literature and Culture at the University of Reims Champagne-Ardenne, France. Her research interests focus on the heroic body and representations of the immaterial, and she has published on Shakespeare, George Chapman and Samuel Daniel. She is the chief editor of the scholarly online journal *Études Épistémè*. Her forthcoming monograph is entitled *Heroic Bodies on the Early Modern Stage: A Poetics of the Ineffable*.

Gisèle Venet is Emerita Professor at the Université Sorbonne Nouvelle. She has worked on the Mannerist and Baroque in relation to the early modern period and is the author of *Temps et vision tragique. Shakespeare et ses contemporains* (1985, 2002). She has published numerous critical editions of John Webster, John Ford, Robert Burton and William Shakespeare. Professor Venet is the co-editor, with J.-M. Déprats, of Shakespeare's eight-volume, bilingual, complete works published by Gallimard (Bibliothèque de la Pléiade Series). She is currently working on a French translation of Shakespeare's *Sonnets*.

Gillian Woods is a Senior Lecturer (Associate Professor) in Renaissance Literature and Theatre at Birkbeck, University of London. She is the author of *Shakespeare's Unreformed Fictions* (2013; joint winner of the Shakespeare's Globe Book Award), *A Reader's Guide to Essential Criticism: Romeo and Juliet* (2013) and articles on a range of Renaissance drama. Having recently co-edited *Stage Directions and Shakespearean Theatre* (2018), she is currently writing a monograph on Renaissance theatricalities.

TIMELINE

1337–1453	Hundred Years' War between England and France.
1337	The English king Edward III asserts his rights over France.
1377	Edward III dies; Richard II (son to the late Black Prince, Edward III's eldest son) becomes king of England.
1387	The future Henry V is born at Monmouth to Henry Bolingbroke (later Henry IV) and Mary de Bohun.
1398	Henry Bolingbroke is exiled. His son Henry is raised at the court of Richard II.
1399	Richard II is deposed. Henry Bolingbroke is crowned Henry IV.
1403	Henry IV and his son fight the rebellious Henry Percy (Harry Hotspur) at the Battle of Shrewsbury. Hotspur is killed.
1413	Henry IV sickens and dies. Henry V succeeds to the throne.
1415	Henry V embarks on a war with France. The Southampton Plotters (including Henry, 3rd Baron Scrope, and Richard, Earl of Cambridge) try to unseat Henry and are defeated. Henry successfully besieges Harfleur. Henry is victorious at the Battle of Agincourt.
1419	Henry is successful at the siege of Rouen.
1420	The Treaty of Troyes recognizes Henry as heir and regent of France. He marries Catherine de Valois, daughter of the French king, Charles VI.

TIMELINE

1421	Henry V's son, Henry (the future Henry VI), is born at Windsor Castle.
1422	Henry V dies at the Château de Vincennes, aged 36, and is buried in Westminster Abbey. Charles VI (king of France) dies.
1429	Joan of Arc supports the claim to the French throne of Charles, son of Charles VI. Her army is victorious at Orléans; Charles is crowned Charles VII of France in Reims.
1430	Joan of Arc is captured by the Duke of Burgundy's troops at the siege of Compiègne and sold to the English.
1431	Trial and execution of Joan of Arc in Rouen.
1437	Charles VII's French troops recapture Paris from the English.
1450	The French recapture Normandy.
1453	The French recapture Guyenne.
1455–c.1485	The Wars of the Roses (fought between the Houses of York and Lancaster) break out after Richard of York, the future Richard III, accedes to the English throne on the death of Henry VI (son of Henry V). In 1485, Henry Tudor, Earl of Richmond, from the House of Lancaster, finally secures the English crown.
1485	Henry Tudor is crowned in England as Henry VII, beginning the Tudor dynasty that will end with the death of Shakespeare's Queen Elizabeth I in 1603.
1509	Henry VIII becomes king of England.
1531	Sir Thomas Elyot first tells the story of Henry V's quarrel with the Chief Justice (for which there is no earlier historical authority).
1558	Elizabeth Tudor, Henry VII's granddaughter, becomes Queen Elizabeth I of England.
1564	William Shakespeare born in Stratford-upon-Avon.
1582	Shakespeare marries Anne Hathaway.

TIMELINE

1583	Shakespeare's daughter, Susanna, born.
1585	Shakespeare's twins, Hamnet and Judith, born.
1594	The anonymous play *The Famous Victories of Henry V*, thought to be a source for Shakespeare's play, is entered in the Stationers' Register. The first edition of the play is dated 1598.
1595	Probable date of composition for Shakespeare's *Richard II* (published 1597).
1596	Death of Shakespeare's son Hamnet.
1596–7	Shakespeare writes *1 Henry IV* (published 1598).
1596–9	Shakespeare writes *2 Henry IV* (published 1600).
1599	Globe theatre built in Southwark.
1599	Shakespeare writes *Henry V* (published in 1600). With *Julius Caesar*, the play shares the reputation of probably being Shakespeare's first Globe play.
1600	Publication of the first Quarto of *Henry V*, entitled *The Cronicle History of Henry the fift, With his battell fought at Agin Court in France. Togither with Auntient Pistoll.*
1601	Death of Shakespeare's father, John. Shakespeare probably writes *Hamlet*.
1603	Death of Queen Elizabeth I. King James VI of Scotland accedes to the English throne as James I of England.
1605	7 January: *Henry V* performed at the court of King James I.
1613	Globe theatre destroyed by fire. It is rebuilt in 1614.
1616	Death of Shakespeare.
1623	Publication of the first Folio, *Mr William Shakespeares Comedies, Histories, & Tragedies* (F).
1664	Roger Boyle's adaptation of *The History of Henry the Fifth* performed.
1723	After a period of neglect in the seventeenth century, *Henry V* is newly adapted for the London stage by Aaron Hill.

TIMELINE

1738	Shakespeare's *Henry V* is revived at Covent Garden.
1747	Shakespeare's *Henry V* is performed at Drury Lane, with David Garrick as the Prologue.
***c.* 1780**	Henry Fuseli paints *Discovering the Conspirators*, an illustration of Act 2, Scene 2 of *Henry V*, for the Boydell Shakespeare Gallery.
1781	First French translation of *Henry V* in *Théâtre de Shakespeare* (20 vols, 1776–83), by Pierre Le Tourneur.
1789–1811	J. P. Kemble plays Henry V at Drury Lane and then Covent Garden.
1801	Schlegel's translation of *Henry V* into German.
1859	Charles Kean produces the play, interpolating a great pageant of Henry's entry into London after Agincourt.
1873	François-Victor Hugo translates *Henry V* into French (in *Œuvres complètes de Shakspeare*).
1944	Laurence Olivier's screen version of the play is filmed as British and Allied troops are preparing to invade Normandy during the Second World War.
1958	*Henry V* is performed at the inaugural Shakespeare Festival in Stratford, Ontario, directed by Michael Langham, with Christopher Plummer as Henry and with French Canadian actors in the French roles.
1965	The African American actor Robert Hooks plays Henry in the Mobile Theater Company's production of *Henry V* at the New York Shakespeare Festival, alongside Ellen Holly as Katherine.
1965	Orson Welles's *Chimes at Midnight* adapts Act 2, Scene 2 of *Henry V* as part of its retelling of Shakespeare's Henry plays.
1985	Kenneth Branagh plays Henry in the Royal Shakespeare Company production of *Henry V* at the Barbican theatre, London.

1989	Kenneth Branagh's film version of *Henry V* is released.
1999–2000	Jean-Louis Benoit's French production of *Henry V* is performed at the Avignon Festival and then at the Théâtre de l'Aquarium, Paris. This is the first recorded performance of the play in France.
2003	Adrian Lester plays Henry in the National Theatre production of *Henry V* in London.
2007	Peter Babakitis's film of *Henry V* is released.
2012	A film of the play is produced by the BBC as part of their *Hollow Crown* series, starring Tom Hiddleston as Henry.
2015	Maggie Smales directs an all-female cast in a production of *Henry V* at the Upstage Theatre, York, UK.
2016	Robert Hastie puts on *Henry V* at the open air theatre in Regent's Park, London, with Michelle Terry as Henry.
2017	Hayley Rice directs *Henry V* for the all-female Babes With Blades theatre company in Chicago.

Introduction

Karen Britland and Line Cottegnies

King Henry V is not like any other play by Shakespeare. For Anglophone audiences, watching Shakespeare's play – either in isolation or as the final episode of the second tetralogy – often involves an encounter with a medieval past that is, at best, vaguely familiar and, at worst, as distant as the fantasy world of J. R. R. Tolkien's *Lord of the Rings* or George R. R. Martin's *Game of Thrones*.[1] For a foreign viewer or reader who has no stake in this national history, the reception of the play is perhaps even more estranging since the play's representation of the conquest of France cannot help but give rise to thoughts of England's colonial expansion. For a *French* spectator or reader whose own national history is refracted and distorted by the play's endorsement of English perspectives, the situation is even more troubling. In this collection, we recognize these differing responses and, by bringing together essays written by international scholars, including French ones, offer new, fresh perspectives on a play that has become inseparable from the English cultural imagination. We hope that this will allow for the defamiliarization of a play that scholars and students, and, to some extent, audiences, perhaps feel they know too well, even though the historical events that lie behind it have receded into the mists of time and fable.

Facts, fiction, commemoration

King Henry V (1386–1422) remains in the collective English imagination as the victor of Agincourt – a decisive battle against the armies of the French king, Charles VI, which took place outside the northern French village of Azincourt on 25 October 1415. This major battle of the Hundred Years' War marked a high point for the English, who, between 1405 and 1422, conquered a large share of French territories, most particularly under the leadership of their king, Henry V (1413–22). As narrated in Act 1, Scenes 1 and 2, of Shakespeare's play, Henry followed in the footsteps of his great-grandfather, Edward III, who first asserted his right to the French crown in 1337 – as the last (sororal) nephew of Charles IV of France. It is to vindicate this claim that Edward and his heirs fought in France for over a century, the conflict only ending when the French definitively regained their lost territories in the 1450s.

As the English king whose short-lived reign (fewer than ten years) marks the moment of England's greatest expansion across the Channel, Henry V has been remembered as a warrior king, most particularly thanks to Shakespeare's *Henry V*. The play stages his victorious military campaign in France from the siege of Harfleur (1415) to the Treaty of Troyes (1420). By virtue of the latter, it was stipulated that Henry V would inherit the throne of France by reversion on the death of the French king, Charles VI, but as Henry died the same year as Charles, he could not assert his right. After Henry's death, the French questioned the validity of the treaty, and refused to recognize his successor, the young Henry VI, as their legitimate king. Under Charles VII of France, crowned in Reims in 1427, they gradually regained the lost territories, with the notable assistance of Joan of Arc. The English possessions in France were eventually all lost again to the French: this material is covered by what has come to be known as Shakespeare's first tetralogy.

Agincourt clearly marks a high point in the Hundred Years' War, with Henry V as a successful and energetic conqueror, whose reign was almost entirely taken up by his French military campaigns, and it is this vision of the king that has been embraced in British culture. In the twentieth century, two major motion pictures based on Shakespeare's play helped popularize this version of Henry as a glorious conqueror: first, the film made by Laurence Olivier during the Second World War in 1944; and then Kenneth Branagh's 1989 blockbuster. In 2015, the 600th 'anniversary' of the Battle of Agincourt, described by a popular regional website as 'one of the best-known events in British history',[2] was commemorated in Britain by a special service at Westminster Abbey that involved readings from Shakespeare's *Henry V*. A charity, Agincourt 600, was set up for the occasion, with a grant from the British government.[3]

Understandably, given the humiliating nature of the defeat at Agincourt, which saw the French nobility decimated by the outnumbered English, the commemoration was less straightforward on the other side of the Channel. A local celebration was, however, organized by the Azincourt village authorities and local enthusiasts, who set up a collaboration with Agincourt 600 to organize a re-enactment of the battle. There was music, a banquet, recitations from Shakespeare's *Henry V* by Royal Shakespeare Company actor Sam Marks, and a religious service to commemorate Gallois de Fougières, the first French Gendarme allegedly killed in the battle, whose remains were only recently identified.[4] Finally, a monument commemorating the anniversary was inaugurated in the village of Azincourt itself, in the presence of the British ambassador, Sir Peter Ricketts, and soldiers from the Royal Monmouthshire Royal Engineers and the 5th Regiment of the Royal Artillery, accompanied by 'enthusiastic recitals of *La Marseillaise* and *God Save the Queen*'.[5] As these commemorations show, the history of Agincourt has become inseparable from Shakespeare's account of the battle, which is sometimes read as a straightforward historical document. Meanwhile, a diversion was set up in Paris to draw the public's attention away from the humiliating trauma of Agincourt: the commemoration of the battle itself was conflated with a major exhibition about medieval warfare at the national Musée de l'Armée in Paris in the autumn of 2015. The event was entitled 'Knights and Bombards from Agincourt to Marignano, 1415–1515'.[6] Every French schoolchild has heard about the Battle of Marignano, a resounding victory for the armies of Francis I, the French king, against Milanese troops, exactly one century after Agincourt in 1515. This successful battle was therefore cast as the neat, restorative *terminus ad quem* for the Agincourt disaster. The implied narrative was that, within a hundred years and with state-of-the-art war technology, France had sloughed off its coarse medieval shell, synonymous with failure, finally to emerge as a Renaissance centre of power.[7]

This cursory glance at the turn taken by the commemoration of 1415 across the Channel is a wonderful illustration of the fact that military history, even when it is about a fairly remote past, remains a highly politicized discipline, which can be put to use in conflicting national narratives. It also illustrates in a crucial way that Shakespeare's play has become part and parcel of the way these events have been remembered and retold by successive generations.

While, for the French, the play stages a traumatic, if distant historical event, for many English-speaking spectators and readers, *Henry V*, as the climax of the second tetralogy, has acquired over time a peculiar status as a celebration of its heroic king and a paean not just to the English, but to members of the various nations of the British Isles who are shown to unite into a 'band of brothers' on the battlefield. Written in 1599, in the wake of the resounding 1588 victory against the Spanish Armada, at a time when history had become a fashionable subject on the English stage, it is often read as a patriotic text, 'the National Anthem in five acts', as the director

Trevor Nunn called it,[8] in which the English, in unison with Welsh, Scottish and Irish soldiers, cut a dashing figure against the French, who are reduced to parodies and stereotypes of themselves. As a consequence, while the German Romantics admired it as a model of epic theatre,[9] the play has never been popular with the French: in fact, as we learn from Anne-Marie Miller-Blaise and Gisèle Venet's chapter on the play's stage history, *Henry V* was only performed professionally in France for the very first time in July 1999 (at the Avignon Festival), 500 years after it was written.[10] In England, after a moment of eclipse in the neo-classical age, the play has never really disappeared from sight, and it seems to have benefited from a marked revival of interest since the turn of the millennium, with a major performance almost every other year or so, its patriotism – as some of the essays here discuss – alternatively showcased or treated as problematic.

Today, it has become almost a critical commonplace to describe *Henry V* – and its titular character – as polarized, and several of the essays in this collection deal extensively with the critical tradition that has solidified around its complex treatment of the figure and achievements of Henry V, as well as Shakespeare's transformation of his sources. It has been well established that Shakespeare drew on the second edition of Holinshed's *Chronicles of England, Scotland and Ireland* (1587), alongside an anonymous play – *The Famous Victories of Henry the Fifth: Containing the Honourable Battell of Agincourt* – written sometime before 1594 and published in 1598.[11] Although they bear his name, the *Chronicles* were a compilation made after Holinshed's death by about a dozen authors, with the result that they sometimes provide conflicting perspectives on single historical events. This might be one reason for the play's ambiguity,[12] but Shakespeare clearly made a point of emphasizing the ambivalence of Henry V: in 4.6 in particular, the king's blood-curdling order to kill all the French prisoners is offered without even an attempt at an apology or a word of explanation, where the *Chronicles* took great pains to explain it away. Shakespeare thus highlights what can appear as a callous, anti-chivalric streak in Henry, which surfaces at key moments in the play. This complicates the picture of the king as an heroic figure, and calls to mind his harsh treatment of Falstaff, his former friend and drinking companion, particularly at the end of *2 Henry IV* when the newly crowned Henry rejected Falstaff with the words, 'I know thee not, old man. Fall to thy prayers' (5.2.46). This highly charged episode is indirectly recalled in 2.3 of *Henry V*, when Falstaff's tavern companions mournfully recollect their heartbroken friend's sickness and death.

Falstaff is a strangely absent presence in *Henry V*. Mentioned only twice by name (at 2.3.6 and 4.7.50), his influence nevertheless lurks behind all the remarks about Henry's wild and drunken youth and he is the unnamed subject of the emergency in 2.1, when his pageboy calls Bardolph, Pistol and Mistress Quickly back to the Eastcheap tavern with the words, 'you must come home to my master . . . He is very sick and would to bed' (2.1.82–3). Known to London theatre audiences through his virtuoso performances in *Henry IV, Part 1* and *Part 2*, Falstaff would go on to become the chief character in the stand-alone comedy *The Merry Wives of Windsor*, which was reputedly written at the behest of Queen Elizabeth I and performed 'before her Maiestie' in 1602.[13] He was also the subject of Maurice Morgann's influential character study, *An Essay on the Dramatic Character of Sir John Falstaff* (1777), which sought to exculpate the knight from accusations of cowardice and instead proposed that he was courageous at heart.[14] Morgann's study influenced the work of A. C. Bradley, the famous literary critic, and was consulted by composer Edward Elgar, when the latter was preparing his orchestral study, *Falstaff* (1913).[15] In other words, Falstaff's character very quickly took on a stand-alone life beyond the *Henry IV* plays, and it works in *Henry V* as a sign that draws attention to the debts and burdens of Henry's past. In Morgann's words, 'we can scarcely forgive the ingratitude of the Prince in the new-born virtue of the King' (11). The passages that invoke Falstaff, then – among many others – challenge our perception of Henry as the positive hero of both the play and the tetralogy.

Approaching *Henry V* as the final piece of a tetralogy nevertheless produces some very different interpretations from approaching it as a stand-alone play: the experience of watching King Henry V emerge after sowing his wild oats as a wayward young prince allows the spectator sympathetically to follow his education and his gradual metamorphosis into a king in full glory: seen as the last stage of this process, *Henry V* shows the end of a political, existential and spiritual progress for a prince who finally comes into his own and achieves the legitimacy that was denied his father, Henry IV, who wrested the crown of England from the unfortunate Richard II. However, as John Drakakis explores here, *Henry V* offers no simple answer to the question of individual or generational guilt. Critics have also been divided about the degree of ingenuity that must be attributed to the character of the king. While some take as genuine Henry's risking all to earn all as a form of political and spiritual wager, and accept the king's providential reading of his victories at face value, a more critical reading of the play has now emerged, which interprets Henry V as deftly staging his victories – and by the same token stage-managing the confirmation of his election as a Christian king in a cynical way. When read as a stand-alone play, it is more difficult to see a complex, dialectical pattern emerge, and it is tempting to treat Henry as a conqueror whose depths can more easily be ignored.

The early texts and performances of *Henry V*

Henry V's textual situation has been mobilized by editors and critics to help explain the play's complex treatment of Henry. It is discussed in detail in James Mardock's opening chapter for this volume and revisited in Emma Smith's chapter on twenty-first-century developments in criticism. *Henry V* – which was preceded on the early modern stage by the anonymous play *The Famous Victories of Henry the Fifth*, performed by the Queen's Men in the 1590s – is extant in two main publications: a quarto text (Q) published in 1600 and the 1623 folio text (F).[16] Q is shorter and – because in places it is obviously corrupt – was, for a long time, identified as a 'bad quarto', described, variously, as an early rough draft of the play; as a version that was cut to accommodate the smaller cast of a provincial touring company; as the product of memorial reconstruction by one or more of the actors; or as the result of play-house piracy (where a copyist in the audience took down the text during a performance).[17] However, as Mardock notes here, more recent theories about the relationship between the two texts have suggested that Q shows the signs of 'deliberate adaptation of the earlier text that served as the basis for F, rather than corruption of that text' (25). Andrew Gurr posits that F 'certainly precedes the script of the play as staged' because it has 'a number of slips and irregularities that must have been corrected before the play was first performed', while Q's text was 'mediated through what seems to have been a transcript of the performed play'.[18] That is, F is derived from a longer pre-performance version of the manuscript and Q from a shorter post-production version. Lukas Erne similarly sees Q as a theatrical text, identifying F as a more literary work, 'designed for a reception in which the intellect is much involved'.[19] In sum, current thinking about the textual situation leans towards the idea that the text printed in the Folio was taken from an early manuscript of the play that was later abridged for performance, with Q representing a version of the play after it had been performed.[20]

In his chapter for this book, Mardock proposes that both versions of the text make 'a subtly different argument', with Q providing 'a less ambiguous, arguably more positive version of King Henry than does the longer Folio version'. An analysis of Q's omissions of passages in F supports the idea that it presented a much less ambivalent view of Henry. It not only omits F's Choruses, whose approving, nationalistic sentiments are jarringly juxtaposed against events in the scenes which follow them, but as Annabel Patterson has described, it also omits 1.1, 'where the bishops cynically discuss how they are to motivate the war'. In Patterson's words, Q also cuts

> the Hostess's claim in 2.1 that Falstaff is dying because 'The King has killed his heart'; almost all of the Harfleur episode, including the famous 'Once more unto the breach' speech by Henry and most of his threats of violence upon the besieged citizens; much of the material in the scene before the battle of Agincourt, especially Henry's closing soliloquy on the hardships of kingship; several scenes in the French camp; all of Burgundy's speech on the damages suffered by France in the war; and much of the wooing scene between Kate and Henry.[21]

The result is a version of the play that tones down the ambiguities in the character of Henry, presenting a much more straightforwardly complimentary version of the king and his actions. Q's probable connection with early staged versions of the play also raises the question of whether the Choruses were performed or omitted from performances in the 1590s.

The omission of the Choruses from Q importantly removes a crucial piece of internal evidence used by critics to date the composition of the play. *Henry V*'s first performance date of 1599 has been posited from internal allusions in the Act 5 Chorus, which concludes by comparing the victorious Henry, returning to London, with 'the General of our gracious Empress', who 'from Ireland coming', brings 'rebellion broached on his sword' (Chorus, 5.0.30–2). Most critics concur that these lines allude to Robert Devereux, 2nd Earl of Essex, who was sent as Elizabeth I's Lord Lieutenant of Ireland to put down a rebellion led by Hugh O'Neill, 2nd Earl of Tyrone. Essex left London for Ireland in March 1599 with great fanfare, and was expected rapidly to crush Tyrone's forces. However, as time dragged on, and in a manner that gives the lie to the hopes laid out in Shakespeare's Chorus, he found himself unsuccessful, exhausted and 'disillusioned by the tenacity of Irish resistance'.[22] His return to England that autumn was far from glorious: he was immediately arraigned to face charges of insubordination and mismanagement. Although – as Emma Smith delineates in this volume – some critics have suggested that the Chorus's topical allusion is not to Essex, but to Charles Blount, Lord Mountjoy, who led English forces to Ireland in February 1600, a further reference in *Henry V* to a 'beard of the General's cut' (3.6.75–6) is generally thought to substantiate the identification of Essex, since Essex was known for having a broad 'Cadiz beard'.[23] If the Chorus to Act 5 does indeed gesture towards Essex, then the play's first performances can be dated between March 1599 and the late summer of the same year, before hopes of a glorious victory were dashed by the earl's ignominious return.[24]

This date is substantiated by the first Chorus's evocation of the circumstances of the play's staging. Drawing attention to its imminent violation of the classical unities of time and place, the Chorus asks:

> Can this cockpit hold
> The vasty fields of France? Or may we cram
> Within this wooden O the very casques
> That did affright the air at Agincourt?
>
> (Chorus, 1.0.11–14)

In the winter of 1598–9, Shakespeare's acting company, the Lord Chamberlain's Men, vacated their former venue, the Theatre, which they dismantled and rebuilt as the Globe over the river in Southwark. Although it has been suggested that *Henry V*'s first performance took place at the Curtain in Shoreditch while the Globe was under construction, recent archaeological evidence has shown that the Curtain was rectangular, not round.[25] The Folio text's evocation of a 'wooden O' therefore indisputably refers to the Globe, suggesting that the first Chorus was written specifically for this venue and that the play's first performances took place after the new theatre was completed in early 1599.

While the use of a time machine might ultimately be the only way to sort out the textual relationship between F and Q, both versions may well represent different iterations of a performance text. Nevertheless, as we have noted, until 2000, when Gurr produced an edited version of Q for the New Cambridge Shakespeare Quarto series, F has been the source text for modern editions and has consequently stood behind modern theatrical and film productions. This means the questions that have most concerned critics about *Henry V* have tended to focus on the Folio text. It is to these critical preoccupations that we now turn.

Themes and issues of performance

Early theatrical commentators on *Henry V* were most frequently concerned about the play's disregard for the neo-classical unities of time, manner and place. From 1616, when Ben Jonson commented derogatorily on plays that deployed Choruses to waft their audiences 'o'er the seas', to Voltaire's comment in the late eighteenth century about the indecorous nature of *Henry V*'s wooing scene, Shakespeare's history play has provoked controversy because of its neo-classical rule breaking.[26] More recently, though, critics have turned their attention away from the play's structural issues to contradictions in its narrative. In Lukas Erne's words, the preoccupations of contemporary criticism include

> the Chorus and the question of its reliability; the character of the King, especially his harsh treatment of former friends (Falstaff, Bardolph, the traitors) and of the prisoners as well as his night-time argument with Williams; the justification of the war advanced by the bishops; and the portrayal of the French antagonists.[27]

These issues are taken up and explored in the chapters that follow.

From the start, *Henry V* presents its king not only as a text to be read, but as a text that resonates differently with different characters. The play's opening scene with the bishops, centring as it does on the churchmen's attempts to decipher and understand their king, certainly sets the tone for the play's depictions of Henry. Canterbury describes the king as 'full of grace and fair regard' (1.1.22), presenting him as someone who has cast off the wildness of his youth, while Ely similarly notes that Henry 'obscured his contemplation / Under the veil of wildness' (1.1.63–4). Recognizing the king as multilayered and acknowledging his new presentation of himself, the bishops ultimately succeed in persuading him to take up arms. This martial decision is expedited by the French Dauphin's diametrically opposite lack of observation and his outdated assumptions about Henry. In 1.2, the French Ambassador brings the new English king an insulting gift of tennis balls and the patronizing message that Henry savours 'too much of [his] youth' and should be aware that there 'is naught in France / That can be with a nimble galliard won' (1.2.221–3). By reading Henry, not in a new light, but in an outdated one, the French make a resounding tactical error that tips them into war. The king's new persona as an educated and mature monarch is layered over the memory of his youthful excesses, and the play shows him from different – and sometimes clashing – viewpoints. In 1977, Norman Rabkin influentially read *Henry V* in the context of the comic *1 Henry IV* and the darker *2 Henry IV*, suggesting that early audiences were encouraged to participate in the play's sense of conflict by being challenged to choose between opposing interpretations of Henry.[28] More recently, rather than asking readers to choose between different versions of Henry, critics have recognized the king's multiplicity and sought to explore its various significations.

The play's theatrical tradition traces a similar trajectory. Moving on from earlier presentations of Henry as – in George Bernard Shaw's words – an uncomplicated 'Jingo hero', recent theatrical and cinematic versions of *Henry V* have grappled with the ambivalence inherent in the Folio text's portrayal of the king. While in 1944 Laurence Olivier famously turned the play into positive wartime propaganda, Kenneth Branagh's 1989 film version, which was clearly in dialogue with Olivier's earlier movie, presented what Sarah Hatchuel calls here a 'deeply ambivalent picture of war as something that is, at the same time, disgusting and heroic, hellish and glorifying, repulsive and attractive', but nevertheless toned down the clashes between the Chorus's nationalism and the Folio text's subversions of the same. For Hatchuel, 'Henry's actions never contradict the Chorus's version' and any potential subversion in the text 'is diverted in favour of an empathetic discourse aiming to raise feelings of collusion, understanding and pity for the main character in power' (109–10).

Other productions have been less generous. As Miller-Blaise and Venet discuss, Michael Bogdanov's 1986 stage production for the Royal Shakespeare Company invoked both English jingoism in its portrayal of Pistol and his companions as a bunch of drunk football hooligans, at the same time as it made anti-war and anti-Thatcherite allusions to the Falklands conflict. Reworked for television in 1989, the production satirized what Hatchuel has called 'the rhetoric of patriotism that was used by Margaret Thatcher to restore her weakening popularity in the early 1980s', presenting not only 'a disenchanted view of armed conflicts but also a cynical, brutal and insensitive king' (112). In 2000–1, for the New Millennium Season, *Henry V* again seems to have chimed in with fresh topical concerns about the definition of a British identity at the dawn of a new century: the Royal Shakespeare Company inaugurated a theatrical season where all eight of the history plays were shown, beginning with *Richard II* and ending with *Richard III*. *Henry V* was performed to cheering audiences, who were invited to boo the French, which they did so well that it caused some embarrassment to foreign visitors, including the French ones. More recently, productions have sought to allow the text's ambiguity to play itself out: for example, instead of prosecuting a pro-heroic or anti-war agenda, Gregory Doran's 2015 version of the play for the Royal Shakespeare Company was, in Hatchuel's words, a production that avoided 'triumphalism and anti-war postures altogether', allowing the text, 'with all its ambivalent, contradictory passages', to appeal to 'our own imagination and partiality' (120). Since its original appearance on the London stage around 1599, then, *Henry V* has been made and remade by theatre practitioners, musical composers, critics, students and politicians. The essays that follow plot its transformations through the ages and shed light on its possible metamorphoses in the years to come.

James Mardock lays out the play's critical backstory, exploring in detail *Henry V*'s textual situation, before turning to discuss how the play has been edited and delineating the development of the 'binary response' that 'would come to characterize later criticism'. Exploring the ways in which critics have approached the play's apparent contradictions, he explains that they tend either to deny the apparent conflict in the presentation of the king, or attempt 'to reconcile the opposition', seeking to 'find a way in which the play might demonstrate both sides, its ambiguity being the whole point'. None of Shakespeare's other protagonists, Mardock points out, have received such complicated critical responses, and none have 'provoked such firmly polarized interpretations' (21). His chapter provides a welcome guide through what he calls the play's 'curiously polar history'.

Anne-Marie Miller-Blaise and Gisèle Venet then tackle *Henry V*'s rich stage performance history, first exploring Shakespeare's infraction of neo-classical dramatic 'rules', before discussing how various directors have grappled with the contradictions in Shakespeare's text (in 1975, for example, director Terry Hands expressed doubt that the bishops' scene in 1.1 was original since it was omitted from Q). Pointing out that Shakespeare's *Henry V* fell out of favour after 1660, Miller-Blaise and Venet note that it was replaced by a version penned by Roger Boyle, Lord Orrery, in which the 'war heroics' of Shakespeare's version gave way to the 'love heroics so dear to the Restoration' (55). In the years that followed, stage versions of the play shifted with the taste of the times, sometimes – as with Aaron Hill's 1723 reworking of Act 2's conspiracy scenes into a one-act tragedy – attempting to restore a notion of a 'unity of genre' and a 'unity of place' to the play. Miller-Blaise and Venet survey a selection of recent stage productions from around the globe, concluding that '*Henry V*'s commitment to a new sense of history, based on the awareness and acceptance of the contingencies of the present rather than on faith in an eschatological or mythical scheme, is made relevant in a growingly globalized and Westernized world' (74).

Emma Smith's chapter builds on Mardock's review of earlier critical trends to explore advances in *Henry V* criticism since the new millennium, noting that the 'impression of the play in the twenty-first century' is 'one of particular and pressing topicality, where the historicism that structured so much of the critical history prior to 2000 has ceded to more anxious forms of presentism' (76). Noting, with David Coleman, that *Henry V* was, from the first, 'deeply implicated in the strategies of colonial violence undertaken by the Elizabethans in Ireland' (77–8), Smith shows how it was appropriated by various political commentators in the twenty-first century in support of modern wars. Guilt and responsibility is also, then, a resonant theme in recent criticism and builds on the play's implication that Henry must deal with the 'ancestral guilt of Lancastrian usurpation' (79) – his father's deposition of Richard II – as well as his legal culpability for the invasion of France. Looking forward, Smith notes that issues of nationhood, memory, religion and gender 'are all current topics to which an energetically always-current play has much to contribute' (101). Productions with women in the title role will open up new interpretations, complementing critical approaches that 'attempt the recovery of Katherine from the passivity assigned to her by many readings of the play' and providing new ways of understanding the play's preoccupation with genealogy, inheritance, translation and national language (96–7).

Sarah Hatchuel's chapter complements Miller-Blaise and Venet's round-up of stage productions by evaluating film adaptations of *Henry V*. Film adaptations, she claims, have to address the play's various paradoxes and tensions, and this means that the play can signify differently for directors working in diverse political contexts. As evidence of this, Hatchuel pits Olivier's famous 1944 morale-boosting piece of propaganda against Bogdanov's 1989 production, which was used to undermine Thatcher's 'rhetoric of patriotism' (112). She also provides a helpful round-up of moments when *Henry V* has been cited in popular movies or television shows, including *Buffy the Vampire Slayer* and *Star Trek*, concluding that, for the English-speaking world, '*Henry V* appears as a repository of symbolic power and cultural authority about kingship and the cost of war' (125).

In his chapter on 'New Directions', John Drakakis opens up for examination the genre of the history play in the context of what Smith calls the 'religious turn' in early modern studies. His chapter shows 'the various ways in which issues of a "religious" nature are negotiated in relation to the new King Henry V's attempts to reinstate, and reinvigorate, and thereby reauthorize, the discourse of the Divine Right of Kings after the regicide of Richard II' (129). Taking to task a criticism that aims to strip *Henry V* 'of its ideological investments in religion and politics', producing instead what he calls 'cynical' readings of the play, Drakakis instead advances an interpretation that invites us, 'with a real sense of belief', to share in an 'experience of recognition, doubt, fear and "vivification", or as Calvin puts it, "the consolation that arises out of faith"' (144). The play, he concludes, 'balances the king's successes against his inner turmoil, with the result that we are never quite sure of the full extent of his reformation, or indeed, of the incontrovertible efficacy of providential power' (155).

Christopher Ivic takes up the notion of early modern kingship as he explores the idea of nation-building in the play. Arguing that *Henry V* is the product of a moment in the nation's history when 'matters English were giving way to matters British', Ivic situates the play 'within a two-island (Britain and Ireland), three-kingdom (England, Ireland and Scotland) and four-nation (England, Ireland, Scotland and Wales) framework', exploring the play's 'rich complexities and contradictions' and revealing, ultimately, how 'in its openness to national differences' the play is 'less committed to forging or consolidating a sense of Englishness' than Shakespeare's earlier histories, and more eager to participate in 'making and remaking communal identities' (159, 162, 173, 179).

Christine Sukic then explores the ways in which the play juxtaposes notions of heroism and criminality, underlining the fragility of Henry's status as a hero. Arguing that characters such as Captain Fluellen place war 'within a distinct, and ancient, legal system', Sukic shows how the play's comic subplot throws into relief both Henry's riotous past and his current legal infractions. 'The shadowy memory' of Henry's past, she notes, 'frequently undercuts our interpretation of the king's actions', while the subplot 'helps us to understand the human costs of Henry's choices, showing how the law works contingently for the benefit of some and not others' (189, 190).

Elizabeth Pentland brings to the fore documents that are not usually consulted by Shakespeare scholars when she investigates representations of Agincourt and its aftermath in French historiography. Considering poetry by the medieval French writers Charles d'Orléans (who fought at Agincourt and was captured by the English), Christine de Pizan and Alain Chartier, alongside reports of the battle in the French chronicles, she notes that although 'Agincourt goes unnamed' in much of this work, French writers nevertheless acknowledged the devastating loss of life by emphasizing the French nobility's tears and mourning for those who fell in the battle. An evaluation of French responses to Agincourt provides a startlingly different perspective from that familiar to Anglophone audiences of Shakespeare's play and Pentland's chapter opens up many avenues for future work on this under-researched aspect of *Henry V*.

In our final chapter, Gillian Woods and Laura Seymour explore *Henry V*'s continuing presence in our culture by reflecting on the resources available for scholars, teachers and students who wish to study this play. They also suggest pedagogic strategies for teaching Shakespeare's text and for making it relevant for a new generation of students. Drawing our attention to the study topics of 'staging', 'genre', 'character', 'language', 'gender' and 'texts', they point us not only to helpful articles and exercises, but also to a wealth of online materials that can enrich our own and our students' experience and understanding of this fascinating drama.

From its probable inception as the first play to be performed on the Bankside in the new Globe theatre to its recent incarnations as a vehicle of political critique, *Henry V* has proved remarkably adaptable to the tastes of the times. This book takes a long look at the play's past and then considers the futures that might be imagined for Henry V, the 'star of England', who was confined in 'little room' by Shakespeare's pen (Epilogue 3–6).

1

The Critical Backstory

James D. Mardock

In 1986, after nearly four centuries of critical reaction to the play, Edward Berry wrote that 'criticism of *Henry V* stands at an impasse'. The discussion of this most divisive of Shakespeare's histories, the play that more than any other in the canon has tended to produce binary and irreconcilable critical reactions – especially toward its central figure and its portrayal of kingship and war – had, for Berry, 'reached the point of diminishing returns'.[1] Ironically, as we will see, Berry wrote these words just at the crucial moment in the mid-1980s when, among other things, American 'new historicism' and British 'cultural materialism' were breathing new life into the controversy by putting it into the context of French philosophers of ideology. The current book's contents strenuously give the lie to charges of critical enervation; the conversation around *Henry V* is as robust in the twenty-first century as it has ever been. Nevertheless, coming when it did, Berry's observation on the play's critical history was understandable. The dichotomous response to the play has been unique among Shakespeare's plays for reasons having to do with the nature of *Henry V* itself.

The play's subject matter is not a 'life' of Henry V in any strict sense, or even a selection of his life's greatest hits; instead it compresses its representation of history to a greater degree than even Shakespeare's earlier histories, which could collapse years or even decades into hours of playing time. Admittedly, the historical King Henry V's reign and life were short, but even so, Shakespeare's *Henry V* adopts a strikingly narrow chronological focus, depicting a total of some eight months in the year 1415 and a single day in 1420. The 1600 Quarto's published title page misleadingly presents the Battle of Agincourt as a subtitle,[2] but it is the main event; every scene leads up to or follows directly from the climax of England's most one-sided and famous victory.

Moreover, the play concentrates almost exclusively on its central character. It has no true subplots, and even the scenes in which Henry does not appear comment on the king and his choices. The play is, as Alexander Leggatt puts it, an 'anatomy', in whose episodic quality lies its purpose: 'We are not so much following an action as looking all round a subject, often in a discontinuous way.'[3] *Henry V* consists of a set of arguments about kingship, about politics, about power and about English identity, all converging on the character of Henry and the multiple views of him that the play produces. It operates on a strategy of parallax; the play's different viewpoints effectively produce different Henrys, and confronting these conflicting definitions of the king is the play's main business.

The history of the critical reception of *Henry V* is as idiosyncratic as the play is in the Shakespearean canon, in that critics have tended to adopt the play's narrow focus on the peculiarly unresolved portrait of its central character, attempting to explain, accommodate or otherwise deal with the ambiguities of that portrait. As Henry's defining moment is a campaign of conquest, his journey crowned by bloody warfare, criticism has overwhelmingly, perhaps understandably, focused on arms and the man, on the nature of 'the warlike Harry' (Prologue 5) and on the arguments the play has been seen to make about war, patriotism and power.

The most frequently discussed focal points in the play are those scenes that heighten the binary portrait of Henry and his war. The first two scenes, for example, can be read as simply patriotic, or as demonstrating the Machiavellian wranglings of realpolitik. The traitor scene (2.2) seems to undercut claims of national unity, as does the scene with the bickering captains (3.2). Henry's threats to Harfleur have been the focus of much ethical and moral discussion, both justification and condemnation. His conversation with Williams – both an ethical argument over the king's responsibility for his soldiers' lives and a sermon about his responsibility for their souls – has been read as evidence both of Henry's traditional piety and of his rhetorical sleight of hand. Henry's winning gestures toward the democracy of the battlefield – asserting that 'there is none of you so mean and base / That hath not noble luster in your eyes' (3.1.29–30) and joining men of every rank into a 'band of brothers' (4.3.60) – sits awkwardly with his list of English dead, carefully broken into men 'of name' and the other sort (4.8.106). His wooing of Katherine (5.2) either gives the play the resolution of a romantic comedy, or coldly illustrates a political power play tantamount to rape.

Critics have tended to approach the binary portrait of Henry that such elements produce in two main ways, each presuming knowledge of authorial intention: either by denying the apparent conflict – by demonstrating that Shakespeare could have intended only one interpretation and that the other pole of the binary is illusory – or by attempting to reconcile the opposition, to find a way in which the play might demonstrate both sides, its ambiguity being the whole point. The former response tended to dominate earlier criticism, while the latter emerged more strongly in the twentieth century. Both responses suggest that critical fascination with the play seems to lie in its apparent refusal to take a stand, to resolve the binary distinction between the portrait of war as a glorious adventure and war as an unholy mess, between Henry as the mirror of all Christian kings and as a general who threatens infanticide and orders the cutting of prisoners' throats. Other Shakespearean protagonists have received complicated critical responses, of course, but none have provoked such firmly polarized interpretations, and it is this inability to escape dichotomy that provoked Berry's call for new critical approaches in 1986. This critical backstory will trace the curiously polar history of *Henry V* criticism to Berry's impasse and beyond.

Sources and early critical contexts

The earliest surviving response to Shakespeare's *Henry V* came from contemporary playwrights. The prologue to the revised version of Ben Jonson's *Every Man In His Humour*, printed in 1616, ridicules the exigencies required by the chronicle history plays, with particular scorn for how Shakespeare's Chorus 'wafts you o'er the seas'.[4] John Fletcher's *The Noble Gentleman* (1624) includes an apparent parody of Canterbury's Salic Law speech (1.2.33–95).[5] Beyond these two explicit references, Shakespeare's adaptation of the anonymous *Famous Victories of Henry the Fifth* – printed in 1594 but performed in the 1580s – seems to have provoked a minor cottage industry in the dramatic portraiture of Henry V in late-1590s London. As a reaction to Shakespeare's *Henry IV* plays (1596–7), especially their depiction of Sir John Falstaff, originally named 'Oldcastle' after the fifteenth-century Lollard martyr, a group of playwrights led by Anthony Munday collaborated on an Oldcastle play, published in 1600 and sombrely depicting the historical king's relationship with the martyr.[6] Also contemporary with *Henry V* was Thomas Dekker's *Shoemakers' Holiday* (1599), a comedy whose plot is brought to resolution by an unspecified King Henry who strongly resembles Shakespeare's Harry in his madcap humour and his plan to invade France. The Lord Chamberlain's Men's staging of Henry's evolution from prince to king must be considered among the sources of these two contemporary plays.[7]

No other early commentary on Shakespeare's *Henry V* survives and, for whatever reason, the play seems not to have been particularly popular in the years following its first performances. It was performed for the court of King James I in 1605 – most likely, as Andrew Gurr suggests, without the broadly comic Scots Captain Jamy – but no other record of a performance in the seventeenth century survives.[8] Perhaps, as Emma Smith argues, the play's topical references to the summer of 1599 'meant that it was quickly, and seemingly irrevocably, out of fashion'.[9] Or perhaps the foreign policy of King James – whose motto was 'Blessed are the peacemakers' and whose insistence on avoiding involvement in continental wars of religion throughout his reign made him increasingly unpopular among certain of his subjects – made a poor backdrop for a play celebrating English military adventures in a foreign land.

Even with only these early dramatic responses to consider, however, we can begin to trace, and to explain, the binary response to Shakespeare's play that would come to characterize later criticism. Shakespeare's contemporaries and the Protestant historiographers who, in the several editions of chronicles published under the authorship of Raphael Holinshed, provided them the story, remembered King Henry V for two difficult-to-reconcile reasons. He was the king who forsook his madcap youth to become the hero of Agincourt, the greatest military victory in English memory, but he was also the king who persecuted the Lollards, which put him, in the minds of those English Protestants who considered the Lollards their spiritual ancestors, on the wrong side of Reformation history. These dual, duelling legacies of Henry V both appear in the chronicle sources of the Elizabethan Henry V plays: *The Shoemakers' Holiday* and *Famous Victories* focus on the common-touch heroism, while *Sir John Oldcastle* remembers the persecution. Shakespeare's Henry plays, even after the replacement of Oldcastle with Falstaff, suggest that the playwright was attuned to both.

Reading the text(s)

If the ambivalent treatment of Henry in Protestant history provides one suggestive origin point for the tradition of reading ambivalence in *Henry V*, then the examination of the printed texts, and the scholarly controversy over them, provides another. *Henry V* exists in two radically different forms, printed twenty-three years apart, that we might think of as competing witnesses to Shakespeare's play.

The 1600 version of the play was printed in the small, affordable quarto format, so named for the fact that a standard sheet of paper was folded into quarters and thus made into eight leaves of the book. Referred to by modern scholars simply as Q (or Q1, since two more quartos would be produced in 1602 and 1619), the First Quarto was produced by the printer Thomas Creede under the title *The Cronicle History of Henry the fift*. Its text is fairly well printed, but contains apparent errors, as well as many discrepant readings that appear only in comparison with the Folio text. It consists of 1,717 lines, printed entirely as verse.[10] The version of *Henry V* printed in the First Folio of 1623 (F) – published by Isaac Jaggard and Edward Blount with the approval and help of Shakespeare's fellow actors – is nearly twice as long at 3,381 lines and printed as a combination of verse and prose.

Since nearly every edition of the play is based upon the Folio text, readers of the Quarto will find that it omits many of the scenes and speeches with which they are most familiar. Among the most obvious are the omissions of all the Chorus's speeches and Henry's 'Once more unto the breach' speech before Harfleur (3.1). The Quarto version opens not with two bishops plotting in private, but with the public council scene (Scene 1 in Q; 1.2 in the Folio) that culminates in the Dauphin's gift of tennis balls. The squabble between Fluellen and the Irish captain (3.2.57–142) does not appear in Q, nor does the scene of the French preparing on the morning of Agincourt (4.2). The Quarto version's list of speaking roles is also smaller than F's. The bishops are reduced to one, Bedford gets no lines, and the characters of Jamy, Macmorris, Westmorland, Erpingham, the English Herald and the French Queen do not appear at all.

The earliest editors of the play, in the eighteenth and nineteenth centuries, suggested three theories to explain the cuts, omissions and patterns of discrepancies: that the Quarto represents a source text by another author (akin to *The Famous Victories*); that it represents a rough draft by the young Shakespeare; or that it was poorly transcribed and pirated by an unscrupulous audience member in the playhouse at a performance of the longer version of the play that was later printed in the Folio with the authority of the playing company. Later critics dismissed these early theories, pointing out that they proceeded without the benefit of our fuller knowledge of Elizabethan shorthand, the practices of the printing house and playhouse, and a fuller range of dating evidence,[11] but critical derogation of the Quarto text continued well into the twentieth century. In 1909, A. W. Pollard grouped the 1600 Quarto in the category he labelled 'bad quartos', corrupt texts published without the permission of Shakespeare and his company and degraded by the publishers of the First Folio as 'stolne and surreptitious copies'.[12] Quarto *Henry V* was thus, for much of the twentieth century, bound to a narrative of piracy, unauthorized memorial reconstruction[13] and the hatchet surgery supposed to be attendant on and necessary for provincial touring.

Although the stigma of 'badness' dies hard, this narrative was complicated after 1979 when Gary Taylor found in Q the signs of deliberate adaptation of the earlier text that served as the basis for F, rather than corruption of that text. Taylor asserted that 'Q represents an accurate text of a different version of the play' – a 'deliberately adapted version'.[14] As Taylor points out, the Quarto corrects several errors found in the more familiar Folio, and several discrepant readings seem to indicate intelligent revision, rather than mishearing, corruption or introduced error: for instance, the substitution in Q of 'leno', a rarer and more fashionable word for a pimp, for F's 'pander' (4.5.14).[15] The most glaring difference between the Q and F texts is the identity of the boastful French lord who composes a sonnet to his horse and becomes the butt of the constable's mockery (3.7). In the Folio text, this is the Dauphin (who historically did not fight at Agincourt), but in Q he has been replaced by the Duke of Bourbon. These textual differences have been primarily discussed as evidence for the dating, priority, relationship and relative authority of the 1600 and 1623 documents, but taking them as two different authoritative witnesses to the evolution of Shakespeare's play, each making a subtly different argument, further illustrates the multiple, competing interpretations at play in Shakespeare's portrayal of his subject matter.

While not as bluffly jingoistic as *The Famous Victories*, Shakespeare's source play, the Quarto does provide a less ambiguous, arguably more positive version of King Henry than does the longer Folio version. In the Folio, the Chorus's speeches at the beginning of each act contain the most insistent declarations of the nobility of the English military enterprise, but these idealizing representational lines are often at odds with the presentational picture of Henry and his war found in the subsequent scenes. Without the Chorus, the Quarto version of the play avoids these jarring juxtapositions. As Annabel Patterson has argued, although it lacks many of the most stridently pro-Henry lines, the Quarto's version of the play comes across as paradoxically more sympathetic to the king because it lacks the ironizing potential of this mismatch between celebratory remembrance and personated history.[16] Similarly, the fact that the Quarto version begins with the bishop's justification for war without the additional opening scene in the Folio showing that justification in the cynical light of episcopal politics presents a less troublesome version of Henry's actions. The omission of Jamy and Macmorris may have had practical causes, but it also has the effect of omitting the internecine squabbles that plague the Welsh and Irish officers in the Folio. In the Quarto, Henry ends the scene with the soldiers before Agincourt with a joke, rather than with a soliloquized complaint about his subjects' ingratitude. The horrors of war that he promises to visit on Harfleur (3.3.1–43) are substantially lessened by the Quarto's shorter version of the scene; threats of rape and infanticide are notably missing, as are, at the scene's end, Henry's confession of his army's sickness and his plans to retreat. Taylor sees these omissions as 'deliberate and coherent ... in the interests of simplifying the play into patriotism'.[17]

Taylor's study began a movement toward considering Q's independent authority – whether its differences reflect the authority of Shakespeare alone or the collective authority of the playing company in which he worked.[18] Taylor's own edition of 1982 incorporated Quarto readings that he considered authoritative, Andrew Gurr produced a modernized edition of Q for Cambridge in 2000 as an addendum to his Folio-based edition, and my edition for the Internet Shakespeare Editions (2013) presents both texts separately and fully as two authoritative plays.[19] Quarto and Folio *Henry V* make two distinct arguments and produce two versions of Henry. The ambivalence that later critics have consistently found in Shakespeare's dramatic portrait seems to have been built into the play and managed at different points in the play's evolution for different audiences.

Reading character

In their introductions and annotations to the plays, eighteenth-century editors initiated scholarly Shakespeare criticism in earnest. Until Samuel Johnson's 1765 edition of the plays, however, editorial commentary on *Henry V* had mainly focused on the decorum, or perceived lack thereof, of certain scenes. In particular, the English lesson Alice gives to Katherine (3.4), with its bilingual bawdy and bad French, proved embarrassing to editors hoping to establish and clarify the reputation of the great English poet. Thomas Hanmer in 1744 dismissed it as the product of a lesser hand, and demoted the entire 'wretched piece of ribaldry' to a footnote, arguing that it was doubtless 'foisted in by the Players after [Shakespeare's] death, to please the vulgar audiences by which they subsisted'.[20] In 1747, William Warburton followed Hanmer's lead, though he grudgingly admitted that he could find no evidence to reject the scene as a non-authorial interpolation. Johnson's commentary on the scene illustrates both his patriotic bent and his approach to Shakespeare's craft, which was to influence the following century's critical approach. While it is but meanly diverting, Johnson wrote, 'there is in it not only the *French* language, but the *French* spirit . . . Throughout the whole scene there may be found *French* servility, and *French* vanity.'[21] Chauvinism aside, this comment is characteristic of Johnson's approach to Shakespeare, whom he saw as above all a delineator of character, however his dramaturgy might have been lacking in other areas. Polonius-like, Johnson dismisses the 'Crispin's day' speech in 4.3 as 'too long' and regrets the last act as a 'great defect of this play',[22] but he sees the character of Falstaff – with whom he, like many later critics, is virtually obsessed, despite Falstaff's absence from *Henry V* – as bursting the seams of the play and taking on a life beyond Shakespeare's creation. Noting that we were promised Falstaff's inclusion in the Epilogue to *2 Henry IV*, Johnson speculates that Shakespeare 'could contrive of no train of adventures suitable to his character', as though Falstaff, somehow more than a fiction, pre-existed Shakespeare's creation of him.[23]

Johnson's treatment of Henry is similar. The main reason he objects to the wooing scene is that he assumes that when Henry speaks and behaves with a 'military grossness and unskillfulness in all the softer arts' that does not line up with his portrait in the *Henry IV* plays, the disjunction demonstrates Shakespeare failing the character (rather than, say, Henry's ability to strike multiple rhetorical poses).[24] For Johnson, there is an essence to the character of Henry that is not attributable simply to Shakespeare. Moreover, the purpose of characterization seems, for Johnson, to be the expression of the universals of human nature; when Henry soliloquizes his complaint about the pressures of kingship and the emptiness of ceremony – surely a speech with limited potential for audience identification – Johnson responds in a parenthetical note 'Something like this, on less occasions, every soul has felt.'[25]

Johnson's focus on character was to have a profound influence on criticism, especially after Maurice Morgann took it as inspiration for his 1777 *Essay on the Dramatic Character of Sir John Falstaff*, in which he attempted to refute the opinion that Falstaff was a coward, and established a long tradition of describing an emotional connection between Falstaff and the audience. Morgann's essay is innovative in its prolonged treatment of a single character and notable for its defence of Falstaff as a semi-historical figure, distinct from the dramatic contexts that spawned him. This mode of character-based Shakespeare criticism – a tendency to judge the success of a play based on moral judgements of characters' decisions, as though they had an existence outside the confines of the play – was to dominate the nineteenth century, reaching its apogee in A. C. Bradley at the turn of the twentieth. While Romantic and Victorian critics were certainly concerned with issues of nationalism, the morality of war and the qualities of monarchial leadership, they channelled almost all their responses through examination of Henry's character.

The Romantic critic William Hazlitt wrote the first extended critical study of *Henry V* as a whole, in his 1817 *Characters of Shakspeare's Plays*, and while he positioned himself against Johnson – whom he thought had reduced Shakespeare's lovingly-drawn individual characters to mere types[26] – his emphasis on reading character in isolation owes more to Johnson than to his much-admired German contemporary, A. W. Schlegel, whose lectures on Shakespeare's histories downplayed individual character and emphasized the plays' unity as parts of a whole.[27]

Hazlitt's reading of Henry, unlike the more empathetic character studies elsewhere in his book, is the first to take a scathingly negative view of the king. His treatment of the character's moral ambiguity, hardly to be repeated for a century, is informed by his ideological biases, in this case disgust with Napoleonic militarism combined with a streak of anti-monarchical radicalism. Though he appreciated the poetry of the more splendid passages, Hazlitt considered *Henry V* 'but one of Shakspear's second-rate plays'.[28] Hazlitt lamented the play's celebration of might as right and of morality selectively applied according to rank, but '[s]uch', he writes, 'is the history of kingly power, from the beginning to the end of the world'.[29]

Hazlitt assumes that Henry was intended by the playwright to be seen as a hero, but that Shakespeare fails to justify his own admiration for the king. Shakespeare's Henry

> was fond of war and low company: – we know little else of him. He was careless, dissolute, and ambitious: – idle, or doing mischief. In private, he seemed to have no idea of the common decencies of life, which he subjected to a kind of regal licence; in public affairs, he seemed to have no idea of any rule of right or wrong, but brute force, glossed over with a little religious hypocrisy and archiepiscopal advice.[30]

The highest praise that Hazlitt can give Henry is to call him 'a very amiable monster'; we enjoy this pageant of violent patriotism only in the way we enjoy seeing a caged beast – distanced and ratified by history – but 'we . . . feel little love or admiration for him' as a historical king.[31]

Hazlitt's radical attack on the character was met with predictable opposition. His fellow English Romantic Samuel Taylor Coleridge saw Shakespeare's histories as a schoolhouse for national pride, their goal 'to make Englishmen proud of being Englishmen',[32] and there is little doubt that they were put to that purpose. Thomas Carlyle's 1841 study of heroism is a more representative response to the play, which Carlyle saw as Shakespeare's national heroic epic, for its 'noble Patriotism . . . A true English heart breathes, calm and strong, through the whole business.'[33]

In 1846, with *Shakspeare's Dramatic Art*, the German critic Hermann Ulrici reacted against the trend of character-based criticism, especially in the histories, where the approach removed both character and play from their larger contexts. Drawing upon the arguments of Schlegel and anticipating twentieth-century critics like E. M. W. Tillyard in his interest in the workings of order and chaos in the histories, Ulrici argued that apparent weaknesses in the characterization of Henry and the play's 'want of an interesting plot, and of all dramatic substance' come from a misconception about its genre – a history is neither tragedy or comedy – and its specific place in the larger organic cycle of Shakespeare's history plays. If we think about *Henry V* as the conclusion to *Henry IV* or as the prelude to *Henry VI*, we are forced to judge the political situation, the war and the king's choices in a different light.[34] Even as he focuses on the organic whole of the play and the histories, however, and even as he dismisses Hazlitt's characterization, Ulrici is forced to engage with and participate in Hazlitt's approach with regard to *this* history play. He concedes of *Henry V* that,

> even the unreasonable demand, that the unity of interest should be found to centre itself in some one personage, appears in the present piece to be satisfied. Prince Henry may well pass for such a leading character ... His character well deserves the ample development which Shakspeare has bestowed upon it in three dramas, and if Hazlitt has wretchedly misunderstood it, his own political prejudices, and his blind hatred of a monarchy, are to blame.[35]

The broadly aesthetic and structural discussion of Shakespeare's historiography that follows continually leads Ulrici back to character, and he evaluates Henry's choices regarding Falstaff and his dubious claim to France in the light of the king's 'moral power, his manly energy and his true kingly mind'.[36]

Such a positive response to the character typified most Victorian-era criticism, even outside England. Another German scholar, G. G. Gervinus, finds in the play a patriotic argument about idealized kingship and asserts that Shakespeare's histories deal with the public sphere rather than the private, but focuses entirely on the characterization of Henry: 'The whole interest of our play lies in the development of the ethical character of the hero.'[37] Henry is 'a many-sided man' and able to adapt to the situation at hand, but Gervinus sees this adaptation as a praiseworthy diversity rather than anything devious or immoral. Somehow despite his many stances, Henry is without contradiction, loyal to the 'truthfulness of his nature' even in moments of passion, indeed 'incapable of dissimulation'.[38]

In a similar vein, the American H. N. Hudson's 1872 study, *Shakespeare: His Life, Art, and Characters*, seems concerned to protect Shakespeare's king from accusations of insincerity and deceit. Hudson insists that '[t]here is no simulation, no disguise, no study for appearances, about' Henry. This view requires some cherry-picking of evidence: ignoring Hal's own soliloquy in *1 Henry IV*, Hudson argues that his disgust for the deceit of the court, rather than a desire to 'show more goodly' (*1 Henry IV* 1.2.214) by 'glittering o'er [his] fault' (1.2.213) is what kept Henry from participating in his father's reign.[39]

Probably the most representative Victorian character study, and certainly the most influential work of English Shakespeare criticism of the late nineteenth century, was Edward Dowden's often reprinted *Shakspere: A Critical Study of his Mind and Art* (1875). Dowden sought to 'connect the study of Shakspere's works with an inquiry after the personality of the writer'.[40] Perhaps understandably, since he saw the plays as Shakespeare's workshops for building his own morality and 'fortif[ying] himself for the conduct of life', Dowden focuses his discussion of *Henry V* almost entirely on the moral character of the king.[41] While Dowden did not ignore the moral ambiguities presented in the play, he argued that Henry was the playwright's 'ideal of the *practical* heroic character', the ideal, that is, of a king in the real world.[42] The Victorian sense of practicality, however, does not include much complexity for Henry's character, let alone the hypocrisy and Machiavellianism that Hazlitt had discovered. Dowden's Henry has fewer rough edges than in other interpretations, with all the virtues of a bourgeois gentleman, indeed, a didactic exemplar of straightforward virtue: '[h]is courage, his integrity, his unfaltering justice, his hearty English warmth, his modesty, his love of plainness rather than of pageantry, his joyous temper, his business-like English piety'.[43]

The fact that the discussion of character that dominated nineteenth-century Shakespeare criticism concentrates so much on defending Henry's character is itself telling; it would not have been so pronounced did the play and the character not admit of other interpretations. Hazlitt was the first, though not the last, to raise the spectre of Machiavelli in discussing the king's political manoeuvres. In his *A Study of Shakespeare* (1880), A. C. Swinburne remarked in passing that what distinguishes Henry's character is self-interest, 'evidently the mainspring of Henry's enterprise and life'. In contrast with the calculating and effective politician, Swinburne argues that Hotspur, whom he calls 'the last of all Arthurian knights', represents the chivalric ideal. Conversely, Henry 'is the first as certainly he is the noblest of those equally daring and calculating statesmen-warriors whose two most terrible, most perfect, and most famous types are Louis XI. and Cæsar Borgia'.[44]

W. W. Lloyd's *Critical Essays* (1875) presents if anything a more excoriating view of Henry than Hazlitt's, and an even more essentialist mode of character criticism. Lloyd, anticipating many later negative assessments of the king's character, dismisses those aspects of Henry that his contemporary Dowden praised as 'mere vigour of personal character' rather than a true moral fortitude.[45] 'The poet does not permit us to regard the king as duped or directed' by the bishops, argues Lloyd. Rather, his Henry cynically pretends indifference to the bishops' cause, playing upon their greed and anxiety to secure a war that the critic characterizes as a second crime to secure the results of the first: that is, the deposition and murder of Richard II.[46] Lloyd notes the chop-logic of Henry's debate with Williams – the king turning a discussion about political responsibility into an unanswerable theological argument[47] – and accuses the king's soliloquy before Agincourt, in which Lloyd finds 'as much of weakness of mind and superstition as hypocrisy' of 'self-imposing affectation'.[48] Even the apparent humility of the post-battle prayer is 'at best refinement of pride, whether audaciously claiming to be the representative and arm of the divinity, or mounting to the fantastic trick of partnership with or even generosity to God'.[49] Most innovatively, Lloyd's negative reading of Henry turns Hazlitt's radical interpretation into radical authorial intention. Lloyd absolves Shakespeare of Henry's sins; the playwright merely described 'the basenesses that are compatible with glories of this class, and the essential narrowness of the minds to which the glory of simple military achievement is all-sufficient'.[50]

In 1901, A. C. Bradley was elected to the first Oxford Professorship of Poetry, a move that established the model for the institutional study for modern literature. In his lectures and especially in his *Shakespearean Tragedy* (1904), Bradley's work reified character criticism as the standard approach to Shakespeare, at least until L. C. Knights offered an influential corrective in an ironically-titled 1933 lecture 'How Many Children Had Lady Macbeth?' that sought to put an end to the habit of treating Shakespeare's fictions as real people.[51] In a 1902 lecture, 'The Rejection of Falstaff', Bradley emphasized the mixture of good and bad qualities in the character of the king, but with more weight given to the latter: Bradley's Henry had inherited, and been corrupted by, the 'vile politics' of his father. While Henry was clearly right to turn away from his former self, he had 'no right to talk all of a sudden like a clergyman',[52] and he was dishonest and disingenuous not to acknowledge and take responsibility for his deliberate amusement among his former companions. While the king was 'kindly and pleasant' enough, Bradley writes, he proved himself – by his rejection of Falstaff – 'incapable of affection'.[53] In this assessment, Bradley brings character criticism of *Henry V* back to its roots, echoing both Samuel Johnson and Morgann in anchoring an interpretation of the play in the absent figure of Falstaff. And like Johnson, Bradley sees the playwright as failing his character. Shakespeare intended us to approve of Henry's decision to discard Falstaff, but by the time he wrote *Henry V*, the character of Sir John, and his audience's sympathy for him, had moved beyond the author's control: 'We wish

Henry a glorious reign . . . but our hearts go with Falstaff . . . to Arthur's bosom or wheresomever he is.'[54]

Irony and its discontents

While a survey of nineteenth-century character-based criticism can demonstrate the ambiguities within the play by way of comparative critical readings, the limitation of the approach is that it encourages the individual critic to downplay those ambiguities and to take a side. With the exception of Lloyd, both Henry's admirers and his detractors among these critics assume that we are meant to take the Chorus's aggrandizement of the ideal hero-king at face value, that Shakespeare's portrait of Henry was intended as unambiguously positive. The real question that divides such critics is whether such a portrait is successful, whether it should be read as a strength of the play or its fundamental weakness. This response is not confined to the nineteenth century; the denial of the play's ambiguities is a remarkably long-lived critical strategy. As late as 1951, A. P. Rossiter, ironically enough in a lecture celebrating the unrelenting ambivalence that he found to characterize the moral environment of Shakespeare's histories, complained that *Henry V*, alone among those plays, allows for only a 'one-eyed' approach. For Rossiter, it was 'a propaganda-play on national unity, heavily orchestrated for the brass'.[55]

In 1919, however, Gerald Gould's 'New Reading of *Henry V*' suggested an alternative to the critical tradition of emphasizing only one half of the play's insistently binary protagonist. Gould argued that critics who, like Hazlitt, suppose that whatever their own feelings about Henry, Shakespeare must have liked him, miss the point: *Henry V* is unfailingly ironic, a deft satire on monarchy, debased patriotism, imperialism and war.[56] Is Henry's war about his rightful inheritance or is it to 'busy giddy minds' (*2 Henry IV* 4.5.213)? According to Gould, the answer is 'yes': the war is about both, and the contradictory motives for it expose Henry's insincerity. In *1 Henry IV*, the rebel Mortimer's claim to the throne can only be denied by denying female inheritance, an irony that would not have been missed by the audience, and an irony, Gould argues, that forms the only justification for the otherwise extraneous Salic Law scene: 'unless its intention is the obvious cynical one, there is no intention at all'.[57] Against A. C. Bradley, Gould argued that our love for Falstaff was not a dramatic failure on Shakespeare's part, but rather the conscious design of a playwright who hated the 'unscrupulous brutality' that Hal/Henry represented and used Falstaff and his rejection to underscore the king's flaws.[58] The immediate juxtaposition of the traitors' execution with the death of Falstaff is yet another of the ironies that contribute to the play's implicit critique.

Gould's influence on twentieth-century criticism is hard to overemphasize. Postwar criticism of the 1920s and 1930s continued to produce some one-sidedly heroic/patriotic readings of the play, but sophisticated scrutiny of the play's ironies and ambivalences and of Shakespeare's consciously multivalent arguments would gain traction throughout the ensuing decades. In *The Meaning of Shakespeare* (1960), Harold C. Goddard responded to Rossiter's curious reading of *Henry V* as 'one-eyed'. Goddard interrogates the nature of the Chorus and treats him as a character with a point of view rather than as an expression of the author's own perspective. For Goddard, the Chorus represents the voice of agreed-upon history, of popular opinion, and is intentionally at odds with the play's representation of the action: 'Through the Choruses, the playwright gives us the popular idea of his hero. In the play, the poet tells the truth about him. We are free to accept whichever of the two we prefer.'[59]

In nearly every scene, Goddard, employing the intense scrutiny of text characteristic of 1950s New Criticism, finds the immediate action in parallel with and commenting ironically on the larger concerns of the play: Henry's portrait of Scroop's hypocrisy reflects Henry's own, for example, and Bates' displacement of responsibility for the war on to Henry echoes Henry's similar shirking of responsibility on to

Canterbury.⁶⁰ The last act's wooing scene, which Samuel Johnson had deemed a poetic failure, becomes for Goddard a triumph of irony, the scene's promise of an heir intentionally undercut by the Epilogue's reminder of Henry VI's failure and death.⁶¹

One of the most influential late twentieth-century readings of *Henry V* was Norman Rabkin's 1977 essay, 'Rabbits, Ducks, and *Henry V*'. Like many twentieth-century critics, Rabkin discussed the duality of the play and its main character, but rather than asserting, as Gould and Goddard had, that Shakespeare had an ironic, satirical purpose, or that he was forced to split Henry into good king and flawed man as, for example, John Dover Wilson and Una Ellis-Fermor had argued in the 1940s,⁶² Rabkin sees the duality itself as the play's raison d'être. Critics who attempt reductively to paint Henry as either good or bad, or to reconcile the disparate views with irony, he argues, miss the point. Like the famous image from gestalt psychology that can be seen as either a rabbit or a duck, but not both at once, the play resists any attempt to find a compromise position between the binary interpretations, forcing its audiences and readers to make a choice: 'In *Henry V* Shakespeare creates a work whose ultimate power is precisely the fact that it points in two opposite directions, virtually daring us to choose one of the two opposed interpretations it requires of us.'⁶³ Rabkin focuses on the role of the audience, taking as the key to the play the Chorus's assertion that it is our thoughts that must deck our kings. He demonstrates that the original audience would have been trained to expect one play by the comic festivity of *1 Henry IV* and quite another by the Machiavellian politics and darker tone of *2 Henry IV*. Which version of *Henry V* we encounter, the rabbit or the duck, depends on a variety of factors, but the fundamental point is irresolution: 'The terrible fact about *Henry V* is that Shakespeare seems equally tempted by both its rival gestalts. And he forces us, as we experience and re-experience and reflect on the play, as we encounter it in performances which inevitably lean in one direction or the other, to share its conflict.'⁶⁴ Rabkin's conclusion, that the dilemma of interpretation is fundamentally linked to Shakespeare's own ambivalence, was the capstone on Edward Berry's pronouncement of an impasse, but in his stress on the 'intransigently multivalent' nature of interpretation and of representation,⁶⁵ Rabkin laid the groundwork for later critics, notably Larry Champion, Phyllis Rackin and Claire McEachern, who, reading *Henry V* in a similarly dialectical fashion, see Shakespeare calling attention to the problem of contingency and perspective in the making of history.⁶⁶

History and historicisms

The royal, or critical, 'we' frequently employed by William Hazlitt and A. C. Bradley in their discussions of the play is telling: character criticism often rhetorically assumes or asserts the unity, if not the universality, of critical response. But more often than not, response to the play has been determined by a critic's own historical contexts, especially in times of war. Thus when John Stuart MacKenzie approached the play in 1920, his argument that Henry seemed a troublesome hero had much to do with his exercise in postwar moral stock-taking. While Shakespeare intended us to regard Henry with sympathy and admiration, the horrors of the First World War rendered such a view no longer possible. The best MacKenzie can say of Henry is that his deep flaws, his lack of scruples, his shifting series of manipulative poses are unintentional; he is an 'unconscious poseur' who simply 'does not really understand himself'.⁶⁷ Similarly, John C. McCloskey's 1944 reading of the character as 'a savage barbarian unrestrained by Christian ethics' was informed by McCloskey's revulsion at the twentieth-century notion of 'total war'.⁶⁸

There has always, however, been a strain of criticism, now often going under the name of 'historicism', that seeks, with varying degrees of success, to replace the limited historical perspective of the critic with the contexts of the play's production and the assumptions of its original audience. Gervinus, in 1875, was one of the first critics to attempt to read the play in the political and national contexts of the 1590s: he finds in it unashamed post-Armada patriotism and a commentary on Henri IV of France (1553–1610).[69] If his readings are more suggestive than rooted in specific historical examination, Gervinus was nevertheless innovative in trying to find a picture of Elizabethan society in the play.

Richard Simpson's 1874 essay, 'The Politics of Shakspere's Historical Plays', was far more systematic in its analysis of the early modern political conversation of which *Henry V* was an active part, to a degree unique for its time; indeed, his approach – and his suggestion, familiar today, that the play could be politically subversive – would not be taken up again with any seriousness until the mid-twentieth century. He reads the play as advocating the ideas of the Earl of Essex, as participating in specific contemporary discussions about the justice of war, and as satirizing the practices of the English Church. In its historical specificity, Simpson's essay was by far the most forward-looking piece of criticism of its time.

The 1940s, unsurprisingly, saw a resurgence in conservative arguments for a heroic Henry, as the Second World War became the overwhelming interpretative context: G. Wilson Knight's *The Olive and the Sword* sought to muster *Henry V* as a source for 'refuelling [the] national confidence' at the same time as Laurence Olivier's film version of the play was pressed into the service of the War Office.[70] On the surface, such occasionally motivated and conservative readings of the play would seem utterly bound to their moment, but they appeared contemporaneous to and in harmony with a renewed interest in Shakespeare's historical contexts. John Dover Wilson, who sought in his 1947 edition to recuperate Henry's heroism in the face of the anti-Henry legacy of Hazlitt, concedes that the play is more complex than reductively patriotic readings, both before and after Gould, would suggest. Perhaps Henry is not Shakespeare's ideal man, Dover Wilson argues, hearkening back to Dowden's picture of virtuous practicality, but he is a successful king in a flawed world. Dover Wilson's conception of war is informed by his moment, but by arguing that Shakespeare's was similarly influenced by his, he finds a way to counter Hazlitt's attack:

> [Henry's] war against France is a righteous war, and seemed as much so to Shakespeare's public as the war against the Nazis seems to us. Once this is realized, a fog of suspicion and detraction is lifted from the play; the mirror held up in 1599 shines bright once more; and we are at liberty to find a hero's face reflected within it.[71]

This move, anchoring a critical interpretation in the beliefs and habits of mind that can be claimed for Shakespeare and his original audience, is characteristic of the brand of historicism pioneered by Dover Wilson's contemporaries, E. M. W. Tillyard and Lily B. Campbell.

Tillyard, one of the mid-century's most influential critics of Shakespeare's history plays, saw Shakespeare as participating in the propagation of the so-called Tudor myth, a 'universally held and still comprehensible scheme of history: a scheme fundamentally religious, by which events evolve under a law of justice and under the ruling of God's Providence, and of which Elizabeth's England was the acknowledged outcome'.[72] This teleological reading of Shakespeare's use of history was dismissed by later critics, particularly the new historicists and cultural materialists of the 1980s, but even Tillyard's detractors agree that *Henry V* is involved in the ideologically inflected production of history.

As its subtitle indicates, Campbell's 1947 *Shakespeare's 'Histories': Mirrors of Elizabethan Policy*, like Dover Wilson and Tillyard, took it as read that Shakespeare's plays reflected the playwright's age, indeed that for his contemporaries 'the chief function of history was considered to be that of acting as a political mirror'.[73] 'Each of the Shakespeare histories,' Campbell writes, 'serves a special purpose in elucidating a political problem of Elizabeth's day and in bringing to bear upon this problem the accepted political philosophy of the Tudors.'[74] Like Tillyard's, Campbell's understanding of Shakespeare's political arguments is that they are basically conservative and grounded in contemporary orthodoxy, though her exhaustive examination of non-literary, non-philosophical texts and the contexts of the 'problems' she identifies in the plays is more specifically focused than the more essentialist 'Elizabethan world picture' that Tillyard constructed. Campbell reads Fluellen's insistence on 'Roman disciplines', for example, as a parody of contemporary disputes about classical and modern (gunpowder-based) warfare and tactics as seen in late sixteenth-century military treatises; and she discusses the morality of Henry's Agincourt campaign in the contexts of Elizabethan tracts and sermons about just war, finding a parallel between Henry's deliberations with his bishops and Robert Dudley's 1585 correspondence with his own Archbishop of Canterbury, John Whitgift, about the justice of military action in the Low Countries.[75] The brand of scholarship that Campbell and Tillyard initiated has often been disparaged in the past seven decades as reductive and reactionary, but with the exception of Simpson's essay, their attempt to read *Henry V* in the political contexts of its time – today such an ingrained approach that ignoring such contexts is virtually unthinkable – was an innovation. By placing Shakespeare's plays into a discourse with the ideas of his times, however conservative they assumed the playwright's voice to be, they built upon Gerald Gould's assertion that the play contains ironic complexities by giving concrete textual support to the polyphonic Elizabethan conversation in which Shakespeare participated.

In the 1980s, two similar critical approaches began to dominate Shakespeare studies, both of which sought to explore the cultural work done by such multivalent, paradoxical texts as *Henry V*, and both of which used the play to describe early modern English culture in terms of complicated binary oppositions. The criticism that would come to be called the 'new historicism' – to distinguish it from that of Tillyard and

Campbell – was inaugurated in large part by Stephen Greenblatt's 1981 essay, 'Invisible Bullets'. Greenblatt's approach – heavily influenced by French philosopher of history Michel Foucault and his theory that state power works to suppress the potentially subversive, transgressive agency of the individual – advocated the pursuit of a 'cultural poetics', reading literary texts alongside other non-literary products of the culture that produced them. His essay thus uses cartographer and reputed atheist Thomas Harriot's 1588 description of North American natives and Thomas Harman's sensationalist catalogue of the London underground, *A Caveat for Common Cursitors* (1566), to build a theory of how social order was constructed and sustained in the Elizabethan period by incorporating the subversion that threatened it, in order to contain that subversion. Greenblatt then turns to the character of Prince Hal, whom he sees as a 'conniving hypocrite' shoring up the power that he will one day exercise as King Henry, a power that amounts to 'glorified usurpation and theft'.[76] But moral judgment is not really Greenblatt's aim: he sees Henry's career with Falstaff and the Eastcheap contingent as a concerted effort to obtain the language and theatrical skills of his future subjects, the ability to mimic their voices in order to repress the threats they represent. *Henry V* is, for Greenblatt, the ultimate illustration of the Foucauldian model of power. Potentially subversive elements in the play – the Cambridge treason, the bickering captains, the argument with Williams, and the accusations of Henry having killed Falstaff – are repeatedly voiced only to be disarmed, their 'potential dissonance being absorbed into charismatic celebration'.[77] 'In this play,' writes Greenblatt, 'moral values – justice, order, civility – are secured through the apparent generation of their subversive contraries.'[78]

The rather cynical moral that readers took from Greenblatt's essay (including the many critics who would embrace and emulate his approach over the ensuing decade) was that true resistance to power was and is impossible, that subversion is always already contained, already part of the workings of power. '[I]t is not at all clear,' Greenblatt writes, stepping briefly into stage criticism, 'that *Henry V* can be performed as subversive.'[79] He acknowledges that Shakespeare's theatre, even subject to Elizabethan state censorship, could potentially demonstrate 'containment subverted' rather than 'subversion contained' – even if it did not do so in the histories[80] – but, for the most part, the new historicist model would stress, as Foucault did, that institutional power has the upper hand in the binary arrangement.

As new historicism took hold in America, Jonathan Dollimore and Alan Sinfield laid the foundations – especially with the publication of their *Political Shakespeare* (1985), a volume that reprinted Greenblatt's essay – for a similarly politicized, historicized approach in England that came to be known as 'cultural materialism'. Where the new historicist master narrative was supplied by Foucault and posited 'power' as a sort of abstract agent, Dollimore and Sinfield were more influenced by the theories of Marxist Louis Althusser, and more interested in the specific material conditions that enabled the Elizabethan practices of ideology, which they define as 'those beliefs, practices, and institutions that work to legitimate the social order – especially by the process of representing sectional or class interests as universal ones ... Ideology is not just a set of ideas, it is a material practice, woven into the fabric of everyday life.'[81] Where Greenblatt stressed power's use of representation to contain subversion, they would argue that ideology, even in the Elizabethan state, is never entirely successful, precisely because 'to silence dissent one must first give it a voice, to misrepresent it one must first present it'.[82] Dollimore and Sinfield read *Henry V* as an ideological text presenting a fantasy of national unity written in Elizabethan contexts – Essex's failure in Ireland and subsequent rebellion, religious nonconformity both Catholic and Protestant, and enclosure riots – that threatened English stability. As it constructs its celebratory fantasy, however, the play exposes the workings of its own ideological function, 'reveal[ing] not only the strategies of power but also the anxieties informing both them and their ideological representation'.[83] So, for example, Henry's pre-Agincourt soliloquy is not a pious meditation on kingship, but a declaration of 'his awareness of the ideological role of "ceremony"' and, more to the point, an awareness of its failure in the face of opposition from the likes of Williams: 'What really torments Henry is the inability to ensure obedience.'[84]

The twin methodologies of new historicism and cultural materialism held such a sway over Shakespeare studies, and indeed literary criticism generally, that thirty years later their influence continues to be felt. Indeed, the past three decades of criticism have been largely characterized by emulation of, and reaction against, the historicist/materialist mode. In the realm of *Henry V* criticism, Graham Bradshaw's 1993 *Misrepresentations* voices several complaints against the materialists: the approach relies narrowly on a few contexts while claiming knowledge of Elizabethan patterns of thought; it can be as reductive as the Tillyardian approach – 'old historicism with a Foucauldian facelift'[85] – and it downplays the author's own conscious choices, presuming that the critic, in outlining the containment–subversion binary, can unearth Shakespeare's subconscious anxieties about the workings of power. Bradshaw reads the traditional sites of contradiction and irresolution in the play as Shakespeare's intentional critique of historiography: the playwright is 'demonstrably more "interrogative," more "radical" and above all, far more intelligent than [the materialists] allow'.[86] More recently, the 'presentist' school of criticism has taken a more fundamental issue with historicism of all kinds, arguing for the mere impossibility of recovering the past in the ways that historicists have claimed to do, and advocating instead an exploration of what and how we – readers, critics and audiences in our own contemporary contexts – use Shakespeare to mean.[87]

Looking forward

This critical backstory has focused, as most criticism of the play has itself done, on the interpretation of Henry and his war, the seemingly intractable binaries that emerged from the competing perspectives on Henry, his politics and his war. Edward Berry may not have seen a way out of his impasse in 1986, but the end of the twentieth century produced several promising ways forward. Perhaps understandably, given the play's relative paucity of female characters, feminism, psychoanalysis and gender studies have tended not to figure as largely in *Henry V* criticism as other approaches, but the 1990s saw Dollimore and Sinfield extend their study of ideological anxieties in the play to include threats posed to the social order by representations of gender,[88] and Jean Howard and Phyllis Rackin's excellent feminist study of Shakespeare's histories, *Engendering a Nation* (1997), read the play as a comparative study in forms of performed masculinity: chivalry, violent sexual conquest and battlefield camaraderie. Expanding and nuancing Lance Wilcox's 1985 arguments about the motif of sexual violence in the play with early modern conceptions of gender, Howard and Rackin put *Henry V* into conversation with feminist arguments about 'the nascent bourgeois ideal of heterosexual marriage and the savage fantasies of rape that attend it'.[89]

Three other aspects of the play and its historical contexts garnered more sustained attention in the 1990s and early twenty-first century, and they offer promising directions for future study. The first is the role of *Henry V* in fostering a sense of nationhood. Studies that have focused particularly on the play's participation in contemporary debates about Irish identity and Elizabethan colonization of Ireland have included David J. Baker's postcolonial exploration of otherness and national identity, Michael Neill's reading of Henry's conquest as a coded commentary on the Elizabethan settlement of Ireland, and Andrew Murphy's comparison of the unruly Macmorris to the Irish rebel leader Tyrone.[90] The role of Welsh identity in the play saw increased interest after the turn of the century, in light of Fluellen's prominence relative to the other captains and Henry's explicit identification of himself as Welsh. See, for example, Lisa Hopkins's study of the role of Welshness as a pseudo-historical symbol, and Philip Schwyzer's discussion of the Tudor dynasty's use of Welsh identity as a propaganda tool.[91]

It is also only in the 1990s that critics began to consider the play in the contexts of its original London audience's experience of war with Spain, both the memory of the 1588 Armada and the fear of a new invasion in 1599, the year of the play's first performances. James Shapiro has written about *Henry V* as Shakespeare's 'Belated Armada Play'. Joel Altman explains the ambiguity in Henry's character as Shakespeare's response to an anti-war atmosphere in 1599, and Nick de Somogyi considers the play's urging its audience to renew the military feats of their ancestors in the context of a London filled with defensive musters and on edge after a decade of constant war.[92]

A third fertile direction in recent *Henry V* criticism examines the tension inherent in presenting a glorious Catholic hero for a nominally Protestant audience, and considers the play's role in Elizabethan religious discourse. Critics who have put the famously 'reformed' king (see 1.1.33) into Shakespeare's Reformation context include Camille Slights, who reads the play as a meditation on the Protestant concept of the workings of conscience; Michael Davies, who argues that Falstaff fits John Calvin's description of the reprobate and that Henry demonstrates his election by casting off the fat knight; Phebe Jensen, who finds in Falstaff Shakespearean arguments about both Puritan anticlericalism and pre-Reformation festivity; and most notably David Womersley, whose *Divinity and State* considers the chronicle history plays of Shakespeare and others in the light of competing post-Reformation historiographies.[93] These are by no means an exhaustive list of current and ongoing critical conversations around *Henry V*, but they do presage the new directions in twenty-first-century criticism to be discussed in Chapter 3 and illustrated by the essays in this book.

2

Performance History

Anne-Marie Miller-Blaise and Gisèle Venet

The 1997 production of Shakespeare's *Henry V* at the new Globe Theatre in London's Southwark was expected to be a milestone in the play's performance history. *Henry V* was chosen as the inaugural play for the new playhouse not least because the Elizabethan Globe itself is thought to have opened with *Henry V* in May or June 1599. After thirty years of archaeological research instigated by the American director and actor Sam Wanamaker, who was the driving force behind the construction of the new Globe, the 1997 production of *Henry V* gave extra significance to the venue and to the play as a theatrical event. Although the effort to restore the conditions of Elizabethan acting was not entirely new – William Poel had promoted research on the cultural and material conditions of the theatre in the age of Shakespeare and staged an Elizabethan *Henry V* as early as 1901 – the experience of the Globe as an exact replica, with its apron stage strewn with rushes, its standing spectators and its two Corinthian pillars sustaining the roof, was expected to be more complete. What Wanamaker had perhaps not foreseen, however, was that his cultural ambitions would soon have to compete, in spite of academic and scholarly attempts to maintain the original project, with commercial drives and mass tourism.[1]

The 1997 *Henry V* was directed by Richard Olivier, whose famous father, Laurence Olivier, was responsible for the lavish 1944 movie version of the play. This family connection served to link the new Globe's production to a longer history of performances of *Henry V*, a link that was also mirrored in the theatre's mission to recover 'original' theatrical practices. The new Globe production was archaeological in its attempt to replicate the playing conditions at Shakespeare's original theatre in a manner that coincided with an insistent critical concern with gender and the question of all-male casts.[2] The cast of the 1997 production was all-male, with Mark Rylance, the director of the new Globe, recruited to take the part of Henry.[3]

Reviewing the first performance for the *Independent* (Sunday, 8 June 1997), Paul Taylor stressed the historically minimalist option of the Globe and underscored 'Mark Rylance's excellent performance as Henry V', although he found the direction disappointing. It demonstrates, he added, 'that subtlety of psychological shading can be communicated at this theatre. This actor's total, beautifully unforced rapport with an audience is a wonder to behold (whether he's letting us into Henry's pained sense of kingly burden or extracting exquisite comedy in the wooing scene with Toby Cockerell's delectably coy Katherine) and the Globe provides the ideal arena for it.'[4] In a similar fashion, the audiences of the 1997 production applauded its radical experimentation, in spite of the rain or the disappointing Corinthian pillars (which turned out, as in the time of Shakespeare, to block the view). The carefully researched Elizabethan costumes were praised, but it is clear that some members of the audience were bewildered by the play's diction, as well as the actors' gestures and postures, which were choreographed to reflect early stage practices. Reactions were not all quite as expected: according to Paul Taylor, 'Listening to the crowd hiss at and boo the dastardly French ... you may wonder if Olivier's handsome but dull production does enough to put such atavistic jingoism into perspective.'[5]

In 1999, this anti-French play was selected for another Shakespeare celebration performance, this time on an eminent French stage in Avignon.[6] Jean-Louis Benoit, the director, did not retain the English tradition of the all-male cast, since, even in the sixteenth century, the French never banned women from the stage. However, the bawdy French words that Shakespeare made Katherine use under cover of the English lesson in 3.4 made the French audience roar with laughter.[7]

These two celebration performances came as a welcome change after the highly politicized productions of the three previous decades. Although inventive as new versions of heroism and leadership, these earlier twentieth-century productions had been intent on reappropriating the play to make sense of contemporary events or crises alien to the original *Henry V*. In the 1980s, for example, the play became a rallying cry, first in the anti-Thatcher fight against budget cuts, and then again when Britain became embroiled with Argentina in the war over the Falkland Islands. Indeed, as we shall see, *Henry V*'s production history is largely one of political reappropriation, often closely connected to moments of contemporary conflict.

'O for a muse of fire': Shakespeare's irreverent poetics

Henry V did not wait until the twentieth century to be staged as a mirror for political events. Contemporary political events at the time of the play's composition have helped critics to date it and to decide which text was originally performed. As James Mardock notes in Chapter 1, the two versions are different, with the Quarto providing 'a less ambiguous, arguably more positive version of King Henry than does the longer Folio version' (26). While ultimately it may be impossible to ascertain which version gives us the closest analogy to an early performance text, Andrew Gurr has suggested that this was a version of the text that included the Chorus to Act 5 with its topical allusion to 'the General of our gracious Empress' and his arrival 'from Ireland' (5.0.30–1). Gurr argues that this was probably a reference to the Earl of Essex, before defeat in Ireland led to his fall from favour with the queen. In other words, the original play text was less like the 1600 Quarto text, which omitted the Choruses and Prologue, and more like the text of the 1623 Folio, which included them.[8] Like the more contentious *Richard II*, which – with its famous deposition scene – was staged on the night of Essex's 1601 uprising against the queen, *Henry V* therefore seems to bear witness to Shakespeare's connections with Essex and the latter's adventurous political life.

At the same time as Shakespeare was embroiled in the political crisis of Essex's rebellion, he was also involved in another quarrel, of lesser importance in terms of the political future of the nation, but vital to the development of stage poetics at the end of the sixteenth century. In his *Defence of Poesie*, published in 1595 but written before his death in 1586, Sir Philip Sidney observed that English plays had been 'cryed out against' because they were deemed to be 'faultie both in place and time, the two necessarie Companions of all corporall actions'.[9] Ben Jonson soon rallied to Sidney's cause and described the ideal playwright as one who, as 'best critics [had] designed', observed the 'laws of time, place, [and] persons' and who never swerved from any 'needful rule'.[10] Shakespeare's Prologue in *Henry V* mounts a significant challenge to these neo-classical precepts.

Addressing his audience through his Prologue's penitent voice, Shakespeare feigns to apprehend verisimilitude as meaning literal similarity, which would require no less than 'A kingdom for a stage, princes to act, / And monarchs to behold the swelling scene' (Prologue 3–4). He ironically pairs this sheer impossibility with emphatic self-disparagement: 'But pardon, gentles all, / The flat unraised spirits that have dared / On this unworthy scaffold to bring forth / So great an object' (8–11). Thus, through his Prologue, Shakespeare seems eager to share with his audience an anti-classical fondness for the rough side of things. In doing so, he grants his audience a real creative capability, that of an imagination on the move. With lines such as, 'Think, when we talk of horses, that you see them / Printing their proud hoofs i'th' receiving earth. / For 'tis your thoughts that now must deck our kings' (26–8), the audience is invited to make up for the obvious dearth of realistic effects on the stage.

This was the basis of a whole dramaturgy, which gives us clues about the way the play was first staged. For example, the play makes no effort to mask the limits of its staging, most particularly in the Chorus's self-deprecating remark before the famous Battle of Agincourt: 'Where – oh for pity! – we shall much disgrace / With four or five most vile and ragged foils / Right ill-disposed in brawl ridiculous / The name of Agincourt' (4.0.49–52). Shakespeare's caustic rival, Ben Jonson, criticized this kind of diminished stage effect when he remarked ironically upon indecorous stage battles waged 'with three rusty swords'.[11] Here, though, Shakespeare not only draws attention to the limited ability of stage props to represent anything but fakery, but encourages his audience to 'sit and see, / Minding true things by what their mockeries be' (4.0.52–3).

Through his Prologue and Chorus, Shakespeare proves ever more determined to infringe the new 'rules' prescribed by theorists of the classical stage, such as Sidney, who mocked plays which staged 'Asia of the one side, and Affricke of the other'.[12] *Henry V*'s Prologue, for example, allows the impertinent playwright to destroy the unity of time, explicitly recommending 'jumping o'er times, / Turning th'accomplishment of many years / Into an hour-glass' (Prologue 29–31). The Chorus to Act 2 goes on to infringe the unity of place by drawing attention to the fact that 'the scene / Is now transported, gentles, to Southampton' (2.0.34–5), before mentioning the most indecorous effect of a sea voyage and pleading not guilty: 'We'll not offend one stomach with our play' (2.0.40). Jonson must have been once again on the watch to comment on his rival's trespasses. In the 1599 text of *Every Man Out Of His Humour* (published 1600), Mitis, a character in the Induction, wonders,

'How comes it, then, that in some one play we see so many seas, countries, and kingdoms, passed over with such admirable dexterity?', while the Prologue to the 1616 text of *Every Man In His Humour* makes a point of mentioning better-made plays, '[w]here neither Chorus wafts you o'er the seas'.[13]

Shakespeare's Prologue and Chorus are a humorous invitation to directors and actors to infringe all the rules of the 'page' and the 'stage'. Meanwhile, the audience, the best ally or worst enemy of both playwright and director, are courteously invited to share in the creative process and to '[p]iece out our imperfections with your thoughts' (Prologue 23). The text of the play itself challenges 'stage' interpretation, intended as it is to 'jar' between unreconciled opposites: it juxtaposes political cynicism and deliberate wartime cruelty with the poetics of unpredictable heroism and comic modesty. The cynicism of the two bishops, who, in 1.1, encourage Henry to declare war on France for their own selfish ends, is unambiguous enough, but Henry's manipulation of them to further his plans is not so clear, allowing for different stage interpretations of the leading character. In 1975, the director Terry Hands, moved by his desire to restore a 'real Shakespeare', expressed doubt that the bishops' scene was original (since it appears only in the 1623 Folio and not in the 1600 Quarto) and deliberately cut their 'saintly' report of the king's amazing reformation from his production, the better to enhance 'the doubts and uncertainties inherent in the role of Henry'.[14] In 1988, on the contrary, Michael Pennington relied on Henry's sudden change to interpret the character: 'What is strong in Henry V, and very actable,' he noted, 'is that his sense of mission has cost him youth, ease, and spontaneity.'[15] Directors also seem unsure about the scene immediately preceding Henry's departure for France and the king's fierce handling of the conspirators whose treason he reveals he had known about all along. This scene is often omitted altogether, with directors failing to adjust technically to the unwelcome mood or judging it psychologically discordant with their one-sided vision of an idealized Henry. The upsetting episode appeared so distinctly different from the rest of the play to the eighteenth-century playwright Aaron Hill that, as we will discuss, he turned it into a stand-alone melodrama.

Jarring undertones also lurk behind scenes of deceptively clear-cut comicality. Pistol's straightforward bragging, reminiscent of the swaggerers of the *commedia dell'arte* and mentioned as an asset in the 1600 Quarto title,[16] becomes awkward when he encounters Master Fer and threatens to 'cut his throat', a threat that is then humorously rendered into cod French as 'cuppele gorge' (4.4.32–7). This aggressively comic moment was excised in performances as different as Macready's, Kemble's and Kean's in the nineteenth century and by Olivier's and Branagh's in the twentieth.[17] The other comic moment frequently omitted from performance is Fluellen's comparison of an idealized Henry with Alexander the Great. Fluellen's repeated confusion of the Welsh Monmouth with remote Macedon, and his mispronunciation of 'Alexander the Great' or 'big' as 'Alexander the pig', takes us beyond the laughable confusion of words into an uncomfortable world of dubious allusions. It is as if Shakespeare was playing a double game with both his hero and his audience, for this Alexander who 'killed his friend' while 'in his ales and his cups' (4.7.44, 45) recalls 'Harry Monmouth' who, 'being in his right wits and his good judgements, turned away the fat knight with the great-belly doublet' (4.7.45–7). In other words, Shakespeare brings back the cruellest memory from *2 Henry IV*, that of a cold-hearted Henry on his coronation day, parting from Falstaff with the fatal words, 'I know thee not, old man' (*2 Henry IV* 5.5.46).

Fluellen's reminder of Falstaff's dismissal hints at one of the blind spots of *Henry V*: the fat knight's offstage death is reported in Act 2 and he is denied a return to the stage, betraying the promise of the Epilogue in *2 Henry IV*.[18] It also points at a specific difficulty when it comes to staging *Henry V* as an independent unit, when the play is also obviously part of a series. Producers tend more and more to stage it as the final episode in a 'Wars of the Roses' cycle, but performances of more limited scope are content with adding a tavern scene to remind or inform the audience of the time when Henry was the unruly Prince Hal – as was the case in the French Avignon performance in 1999. The play is often made to open on the last scene of the previous play with Henry's coronation and the remorseless dismissal of Falstaff. Topicality has sometimes interfered with the stage logic, though, as in 1761, when the coronation scene came as a *conclusion* to the play, to celebrate the newly-crowned sovereign George III.[19]

Henry V in the Restoration: 'not of an age, but for all time'?

After the English Civil Wars, which saw the public theatres closed from 1642 to 1660, there seems to have been a declining interest in staging Shakespeare's history plays. This declining interest is all the more surprising as Jonson himself, in his poem prefixed to the 1623 Folio edition of Shakespeare's dramatic works, had published his famous prognostication that Shakespeare 'was not of an age, but for all time'.[20] As late as 1668, John Dryden showed his vibrant admiration for Shakespeare in his essay *Of Dramatick Poesie*, describing the playwright as 'incomparable', above all his contemporaries, even Jonson. Dryden seemed here to favour the 'irregularities' of the English stage and the habit of mixing dirge and mirth, discarding uniformity of feelings: 'Why imagine the soul of man more heavy than his Sences? Does not the eye pass from an unpleasant object to a pleasant in a much shorter time then is requir'd to this? and does not the unpleasantness of the first commend the beauty of the latter?'[21] And yet the same Dryden vetoed Shakespeare's *Histories*: his 'Chronicles of Kings' were the unhappy business of 'thirty or forty years, crampt into a representation of two hours and a half, which is not to imitate or paint Nature'.[22] No further mention is made of any of these historical plays by name, but obviously Shakespeare's amused awareness in *Henry V* that he was 'Turning th'accomplishment of many years / Into an hour glass' (Prologue 30–1) must have sounded transgressive to the ears of Dryden, who was definitely the neo-classical master of his age.

Yet a neo-classical adaptation of Shakespeare's *Henry V* did make it to the stage. Samuel Pepys reported in his *Diary* on 13 August 1664 that he was to see '"Henry the Fifth"; a most noble play, writ by my Lord Orrery' (i.e. Roger Boyle). Pepys enthusiastically sums up the plot, 'full of height and raptures of wit and sense'.[23] In this *Henry V*, the war heroics give way to the love heroics so dear to the Restoration.[24] Prominence is given to the love rivalry between the king and Owen Tudor, who historically became Katherine's second husband after Henry's early death. Agincourt, in this context, becomes a battle waged for love, and Boyle duly provided a parallel rival love plot between the Duke of Bedford, brother to Henry, who was in love with Anne of Burgundy, the daughter of the arch-enemy of France and dubious ally of England.[25] The interest in the king remained, and possibly reverence for the name of Shakespeare, but his play was rewritten as a neo-classical romance – a form of rewriting that affected all of Shakespeare's plays in the seventeenth century.

The eighteenth century; a new era

No full production of Shakespeare's *Henry V* seems to have been staged between the last-known performance at court in 1604 and the belated revival of the original play in 1738. When *Henry V* was staged at Drury Lane in 1723, it was a new adaptation of one single episode from Shakespeare's play: the conspiracy against Henry in Act 2. The author, Aaron Hill, wished 'that a Taste for *Tragedy* may be restor'd',[26] and cleansed the play of all comic traces with a new title, *King Henry the Fifth; Or, The Conquest of France, By The English, A Tragedy*. In the wake of Boyle's play and the seventeenth century's taste for romance, an unexpected 'tragedy' was thus given prominence against the background of the conspiracy: a fictional Harriet, niece to Lord Scroop, having been seduced by

Henry, is shown planning her revenge and getting involved in her uncle's conspiracy, when suddenly her hatred of Henry turns to love. She then discloses to the king all she knows, before stabbing herself. However sentimental this rewriting might be, the final Chorus is most unsentimental in its conclusion: Henry VI's poor health and its consequence – the Wars of the Roses – find their flattest explanation in Hill, who draws attention to Henry V's near impotency with the line, 'Tho' bold in war, his feats, in love, were faint!'[27]

Around twenty years later, in 1746, the topical again overcame the fictional when Hill's version of *Henry V* was tailored into a one-act play and given a new title: *The Conspiracy Discovered*. The even more explicit subtitle, *French Policy Defeated*, gave the play a political twist in the context of the contemporary crisis of the previous year's defeated Jacobite conspiracy, which was followed by the resounding trial and execution in London of three Scottish lords for collusion with France and Scotland.[28] In both versions, Hill asserts a 'unity of genre' and a 'unity of place' – the plays start at Harfleur with no Chorus offering to 'waft you o'er the seas' – and the time frame is restricted to the time it takes Harriet to make a quick decision to seek revenge, then to yield to love and die. However, as James Loehlin claims about Hill's *Henry V*, 'the play on the whole stands as a fascinating instance of the way Shakespeare is refashioned in performance in response to changing cultural values'.[29]

The return of *Henry V* and the rise of patriotic reverence

Shakespeare's war play had no love plot to charm the Restoration audiences, nor any female parts likely to appeal to the new actresses, more intent on playing Desdemona, Juliet or Cleopatra than Katherine, who is forced to respond to a man's immodest proposal to '*baiser en* Anglish' even 'before they are married' (5.2.260–4).[30] Yet, paradoxically, the play's first revival in 1738 was due to 'the Desire of Several Ladies of Quality' to see it performed, when the Shakespeare Ladies' Club obtained its staging, with its Prologue and Choruses restored, at Covent Garden. The next year, the resurrection was confirmed with a performance 'By His Majesty's command', King George II being present. This official and glorious return of *Henry V* on stage would trigger a succession of performances in the context of the Seven Years' War against France (1756–63), which underlined the play's topicality and its inspiringly jingoistic power since Britain was fighting the French abroad. Nevertheless, the play suffered remarkable amputations during this period, largely because Katherine was now performed by an actress: the indecorous language scenes were cut and the irreverently anti-classical Chorus was often dropped as irrelevant.[31] Major additions, like the inclusion in 1761 of the coronation scene from *2 Henry IV*, were continued late into the nineteenth century, in keeping with the new antiquarian interest in historical accuracy, solemn pageants and crowded stages, but also out of an increasing cultural reverence for the soon-to-be 'Bard' of the Romantic age.

The play had little to offer lead actresses, but neither did it attract major male actors to play Henry. Garrick acted the part of the Chorus three or four times between 1747 and 1759, but never attempted Henry V. Edmund Kean, who took the risk, was 'booed off the stage'.[32] The play, as it was rendered in the prompt-book for productions at Covent Garden, was finally printed in 1773. Comparing this version with the 1600 Quarto of the play, Emma Smith suggests that it 'adds a retrospective endorsement to the dramatic qualities of this often disparaged early text'.[33] This publication inspired a renewal of interest in the play, with John Kemble performing as Henry V at Covent Garden between 1789 and 1792. The play was stripped of whatever jarring effects or disconcerting metatheatrical biases were left, instead emphasizing the jingoistic celebration of Englishness, with the French as a favourite target as the Seven Years' War was followed by the tumultuous years of the French Revolution, and Napoleonic rule raised new fears of invasion.

The nineteenth century and the return of history

In the lull that followed Napoleon's defeat, the play almost faded out of view again until William Macready gave it a new visibility, with a striking illustration of the new nineteenth-century taste for historical realism and antiquarian minutiae. If the play had meant romance to the seventeenth and tragedy to the eighteenth, it would mean history to the nineteenth century. Between 1819 and 1839, Macready turned the play into a gigantic historical tableau while restoring the text to its original length, in the wake of the eighteenth-century editions and their new philological approaches. For his last 1839 performance, huge scenic dioramas by the painter Clarkson Stanfield gave each act a realistic historical background against which the Chorus duly represented Time passing with scythe and hourglass.[34] Macready played Henry himself with a speed and energy that contrasted with Kemble's slow delivery.[35]

Charles Kean's production at the Princess's Theatre in 1859 was also historical in outlook, again with a Chorus (performed by Kean's wife) who represented Clio, the muse of History. Kean was a Fellow of the Royal Society of Antiquaries, and his archaeological approach entailed bringing hundreds of extras onstage for the siege of Harfleur, and compelled him to bring even larger crowds onstage for the return of Henry from Agincourt to fit Shakespeare's own relation of this triumphant entrance into London. Kean's biographer praised his subject for 'carefully following the account of an eye-witness whose MS had been preserved'.[36] However spectacular the result, Kean himself insisted that '*Accuracy*, not *show*, has been my object.'[37] Even the *Te Deum* that was given after the battle was assigned its accurate date.

The historical context occasionally gave the play a new topicality: Charles Calvert, producing the play in 1872,[38] still in a highly spectacular style, initiated a new approach to the anti-war aspects of the play, highlighting, for once, the sufferings of the French in the context of France's war with the Prussians.

From jingo hero to anti-hero

The succession of realistic productions continued, and so did the textual reduction that they involved, in the service of a by-now-engrained 'Jingo hero',[39] as George Bernard Shaw called Henry V. The play was still meant to chime with contemporary political events at the beginning of the twentieth century, such as the patriotic effervescence during the Boer War. The exception, in 1901, was William Poel's experimental production of the play, on a bare stage, which restored the full text and underscored the anti-illusionistic stance of the Chorus. The devastating experience of the First World War, however, shook idealists out of their illusions about the heroics of war and gave a future to the play by reminding viewers that Shakespeare's text was more ambivalent about war than had generally been assumed.[40]

For his 1937 stage production, in the context of a dominant pre-Munich pacifism, Laurence Olivier played a subdued Henry more reminiscent of his own Hamlet, removed from the jingoism that he was himself to promote in his later 1944 film. More unexpected is the first postwar *Henry V*, directed by Dorothy Green in 1946, which, although Green was praised by critics for having 'done a man's job', contrasted with the triumphalism of Olivier's film in a manner that emphasized the darker undertones of the play.[41]

Henry V after the Second World War: staging scepticism

The wave of scepticism which settled over Europe after the Second World War put an end to the one-sided heroics that had for so long prevailed in the staging of *Henry V*, as once again the historical context interfered with the poetics of the play. It meant that some episodes of *Henry V*, which had been altered or removed for centuries as unpalatable, were reinstated, together with the original scene order from the 1623 Folio. The execution of Bardolph in the presence of Henry and the conspiracy scene before the latter's departure for France were no longer either edited or excised. The murder of the luggage boys by the French and Henry's subsequent execution of his French prisoners were staged more often, emphasizing the horrors of war as the price to pay for victory. In 1964, Peter Hall staged *Henry V* for the Royal Shakespeare Company (RSC) as part of his cycle entitled 'The War of the Two Roses', commemorating the 400th anniversary of Shakespeare's birth. In Hall's interpretation, the reordering of the plays was everything, giving precedence to the chronology of historical facts over the order of publication of the Histories: that is, Hall staged the second tetralogy before the first tetralogy. The glory surrounding the victory at Agincourt was therefore not simply checked by the prediction of the short reign of Henry VI in the Epilogue to *Henry V*, but was cancelled by the cycle of civil wars and murders in the three parts of *Henry VI* and *Richard III*. The point was further emphasized by the casting of Ian Holm as both Richard III and Henry V, whom the actor portrayed as a pugnacious but cynical politician, breaking with the tradition of the 'epic' Henrys.

Terry Hands' 1975 production dismissed the subject of the war altogether by giving a different meaning to the epics of the young king and his haggard army. The challenge for Hands consisted in keeping the rallying strength of the play without making it a 'play about war'. He used it as a weapon in the 'war of the theatres' against the political funding cuts that threatened them. More importantly, he made it a play about theatre itself – an aspect long lost – with the power to rally a company of actors. According to Hands, *Henry V* deals with 'improvisation, interdependence, unity', not war.[42] No place was left for the trappings of illusion as the play unfolded on a bare stage, with the actors already present in plain clothes, while the audience entered, and donned their military costumes as the Chorus of Act 2 was still speaking. The costumes, not historically accurate, contrasted a medieval style for the French, stuck in the past, with the timeless dress of the English. In Act 1, Henry was obviously uncomfortable in his royal robes when, as an inexperienced king, he responded to the Dauphin's challenge; but, as a military ruler at Agincourt, all responsibilities accepted, he wore his armour with aplomb. Alan Howard as Henry centred his performance on the role-playing forced on Prince Hal; that is, the masks the prince was constrained to wear until he could eventually be himself, having found his own persona through action. The death of Bardolph was staged to underline the fragile unity between the king and his army, with the soldiers refusing to join in the singing following the execution despite Henry's exhortations. Faithful to the spirit of the text, Hands was careful not to push any restrictive political agenda, but to dig out instead the deeper meaning of the play, which is the work achieved by a company of actors. To him, the war metaphor was only there to help discriminate between fake unity – the medieval discipline imposed in the French camp – and true unity as that generated through interdependence. Henry was shown to understand the meaning of personal responsibility during his meditation the night before the battle, and his St Crispin's Day speech was played more as an accompaniment to the men's morning preparations than as a hectoring rally cry. When, after the battle, Henry asked them to sing the *Te Deum*, his army broke into a marching song, finally accepting the order they had refused after Bardolph's execution. In sum, they had become 'a band of brothers'.

Adrian Noble's 1984 production at Stratford made room for the ambiguities at the heart of the play and could be seen as both apolitical and reminiscent of the contradictory responses to Britain's post-Falklands crisis, the staging pointing to a vision of victory over chaos and the paradoxical recovery of harmony. A distinctive feature was the importance given to the Chorus, played by Iain McDiarmid, who, from the start, adopted a sarcastic and mocking voice. He stayed onstage throughout the play, his tone turning particularly biting as he described the war preparations, pausing only as Pistol, Bardolph, Quickly and Nym walked onstage. Noble's production revolved around antitheses: the sardonic Chorus was opposed to a very young and sensitive Henry, played by Kenneth Branagh (then aged twenty-three), who was himself contrasted with the stocky Brian Blessed as Exeter. In Act 3, Exeter ignored Bardolph's pleading eyes and executed him with his bare hands, as Henry, on whose order Exeter was acting, struggled not to cry. Upstage, hidden under blankets or wood logs and drenched by torrential water falling on the stage, the army were watching, until Henry joined them. Noble also restored Henry's order to execute the prisoners to its rightful place, before the king learned about the killing of the luggage boys (see 4.6.37 and 4.7.1–10). The Chorus eventually raised a curtain revealing butchered children, as if to suggest that the responsibility was Henry's. The spirit of Noble's interpretation went into Kenneth Branagh's film, made after the production in 1989.

In 1986, between the two versions starring Branagh, Michael Bogdanov returned to a highly political and anti-militarist, anti-Thatcherite interpretation of the play, with the Falkland Islands conflict as background. The play was to mirror the blatant social inequalities of Margaret Thatcher's years as Britain's prime minister, given as the fateful conclusion to a Wars of the Roses cycle, staged for the newly founded English Shakespeare Company. Michael Pennington impersonated an 'ideal' Henry for the purpose, efficient and blasé as a military leader, brave but merciless, entirely unappealing, and determined to win at all costs. Bogdanov's *Henry V* struck a contemporary note with its brutal staging, which echoed the recent Heysel football stadium disaster in Belgium – when a group of English football fans attacked the opposing team's supporters, leading to the deaths of thirty-nine people. Bogdanov staged the English landing in France by flying banners carrying the message 'Fuck the Frogs'. He also drew comparisons between Henry's war and the war over the Falklands, noting that '[n]othing had changed in six-hundred years, except the means'. Loehlin, describing this production, noted that Bogdanov's 'populist approach' was uneven, but 'egalitarian and brisk', 'with an absence of subtlety'.[43] In her account of the production, Emma Smith adds a welcome quotation from a reviewer in the *Guardian* (23 March 1987), who observed that this was 'the first version I've ever seen where you wanted the French to win!'[44]

In 1994, Matthew Warchus's production for the RSC commemorated the anniversary of the outbreak of the First World War with an entrenched Henry (played by Iain Glen) appearing on a stage strewn with poppies as reminders of Remembrance Day.[45] In 1997, the year of Rylance's Henry at the Globe, Ron Daniels, again for the RSC, similarly evoked the First World War, opening his play with Henry 'studying a flickering old film of a First World War trench battle, his own shadow cast ominously across the screen as he did so'.[46] Clearly, late twentieth-century directors of Shakespeare's play turned to *Henry V* as a lens through which to contemplate their century's devastating familiarity with global war.

The twenty-first century: a multiracial and feminist appeal

By 2000, the doleful twentieth century and its war commemorations seemed over. Directing *Henry V* at the RSC, Edward Hall (the son of Peter Hall) opted to set the play in a near-present that was again epitomized by soccer pennants strung across the stage and with France invaded by football supporters. Suzannah Clapp shrewdly pins down the discrepancy of 'such extravagant visualisation' in the context of a play that 'appeals to the audience to be indulgent with the lack of resources on the stage'. However, she praised the subtle William Houston as a Henry who was 'neither an Olivier-style aristo nor a bloodthirsty anti-hero', but who had 'the hungry, foxy look of Boris Becker at Wimbledon' and who delivered his 'Once more unto the breach' speech like 'a desperate coach at half-time'.[47]

It seems that *Henry V* had returned with stimulating performances in the early twenty-first century. While retaining the scepticism of productions from the later part of the twentieth, they fully belonged to a new age, reflecting the cultural imperatives of our multicultural societies, even as they retained their ability to comment upon contemporary conflicts. At the RSC, in 2003, Nicholas Hytner, satiric throughout, set the play in an emblematically bleak Iraq. His decision 'to undercut the rhetorical glamour surrounding war' meant that Henry, played by Adrian Lester, was portrayed as having hardly any humanity left.[48] According to veteran theatre critic Michael Billington, this was '[a] *Henry V* for our age', yet without 'the moral ambivalence' that Billington suspected was 'part of Shakespeare's intention'.[49] This contrasts with the critic's later appreciation of Michael Boyd's *Henry V*, performed as part of the RSC's 2007 History Cycle, which, in his opinion, was a production that articulated the play's tensions 'between celebration and subversion'.[50] Boyd's Henry, Geoffrey Streatfeild, was made to woo Katherine while standing over coffins, and his performance never settled the question of whether Henry was a '[w]arrior-hero or war criminal'.[51]

In June 2016, at the Open Air Theatre in London's Regent's Park, *Henry V* continued to reflect the preoccupations of the new millennium when a woman was cast in the title role.[52] Billington observed of the production, '[I]t seems appropriate that, at a time of heightened awareness of gender equality, the title role should be played by a woman in the shape of the astonishing Michelle Terry.'[53] Terry's performance was described variously as 'no girl-man act. No shoulder-rolling. No big-boot work'[54] and 'no five-act national anthem or cynical dissection of war' either.[55] Robert Hastie's remarkably clever production staged the selection of Terry as Henry as largely unplanned: among actors in everyday clothes, Charlotte Cornwell as the Chorus was portrayed as looking for someone to play the king, discarding male actors to finally hand the crown to Terry. Monarchy, in this rendition of the play, had become 'a performance', and Henry had 'to assume a variety of conflicting roles ... between military necessity and natural instinct', which Terry assumed beautifully.[56]

Crossing the Channel: *Henry V* in Europe

Shakespeare's most jingoistically English play is hardly ripe for cultural exportation, especially to the other side of the Channel. As noted earlier, it was not produced in a major venue in France until 1999 – although a French production was performed in Belgium at the Rideau de Bruxelles in 1953.[57] Claude Etienne's staging of François-Victor Hugo's translation was less indebted to Belgium's resistance to French cultural annexation than it was a tribute, in the wake of the Second World War, to Olivier's highly influential film, which was carefully imitated in the design of the actors' costumes.[58] While the French, ever since Voltaire, have been suspicious not only of *Henry V* but also of Shakespeare's offences against good taste more generally, the Germans and Austrians have had political and aesthetic reasons to welcome Shakespeare's historical play with more enthusiasm.

The first serial staging of Shakespeare's histories, including *Henry V*, interestingly took place in Germany in 1864.[59] Schiller and Goethe had exchanged enthusiastic letters about the histories and expressed their desire to see them adapted for the German stage. In an 1808 lecture, Schlegel had also described the two tetralogies as forming one long 'historical epic poem in dramatic form'.[60] Their wishes for German adaptations would be fulfilled only later in the century, when Franz Dingelstedt, then the director of the Weimar Theatre, decided to add a staging of *Henry V* to complete his 1863 performances of *Richard II* and *Henry IV* as a celebration of Shakespeare's tercentenary year (1864). Dingelstedt revised both tetralogies extensively with the intention of giving them a neo-classical, five-act structure, playing them back to back. For Dingelstedt, *Henry V* was the 'third act' of this long 'epic' drama, while the demise of the anti-heroic Richard III was the fifth and final act of this grand narrative. The staging of Shakespeare's history cycle must have taken on a particularly topical meaning in the context of the gradual unification of Germany.[61] After the First World War, some critics continued to praise Dingelstedt's production of the play for its sensitivity in the depiction of ethnic and cultural differences between the English and the French.[62]

Henry V was, however, seldom produced again in the German-speaking world until the 1960s. Loehlin notes how Leopold Lindtberg's 1961 production at the Burgtheater in Vienna yielded a much 'subdued' approach to the play and its 'military heroism',[63] prefiguring the Western cultural revolution and the rise of pacifist ideals. One of the most noteworthy German-language productions was Peter Zadek's *Held Henry* (Henry, the Hero), premiered in Bremen in 1964 and turned into a movie in 1965. It was described as a 'pacifist collage, an historical multimedia show against heroism and militarism'[64] that conflated the figure of Henry V with Hitler. Zadek had the lead role, making a salute against a backstage screen showing German troops marching into Paris.

Like Bogdanov two decades later, Zadek explicitly adopted a Brechtian approach, appealing to a popular audience. He refused an intellectual theatre, opting for sharp contrasts to shock his audience.[65] *Henry V* was no longer about the British and the French, but a mirror allowing Germany to look at itself, to examine its own collective conscience and, as Emma Smith conjectures, to address its own 'uneasy fascination with and terror of military heroes'.[66] The stage featured the portraits of fifty kings and queens whose faces merged with those of twentieth-century dictators, football stars, rock singers, Nazi scientists and early television evangelists. *Der Spiegel*'s theatre critic sternly suggested that Zadek himself was the 'Falscher Held' ('false hero') or a literary 'Gag-Mann' ('gagman'), proficient in the already long-standing art of Shakespeare experimentalism, perfected here by the use of microphones, screens, musical recordings and cigarette smoking onstage.

Ivo van Hove's very recent *Kings of War* (performed in Dutch by the Toneelgroep Amsterdam company and premiered in June 2015 at the Vienna Festival) restored, against the order of Shakespeare's composition of the plays, the historical chronology of England's rulers. The production took the audience from Henry V's rational and strategic exercise of power and (illusory) moral governance, to Henry VI's ineffectual rule and the crumbling of the nation, to, finally, Richard III's egocentric and destructive madness. As in Zadek's earlier production, great use was made of screens. The stage was laden with them; one, for example, showing a magnified, front view of a coronation that was simultaneously taking place, laterally, before the audience's eyes. The very graphic effect produced by the wealth of monitors was much sleeker than Zadek's experimental 'collage'. The monarchs' modern military outfits, elegant suits and ties, fashionable eye-gear and headsets, bespoke a sense of businessman-like control that was belied by more decadent scenes of intimacy, testifying to the underlying corruption of the royal leaders. The hard and clinical nature of the bunker and corridors, which composed the other sets, only highlighted the horror and violence beneath neat surfaces. The dramatic aesthetics of this excised version of Shakespeare's historical cycle inserted the Shakespearean drama of power within the cultural framework of a television series even while denouncing the modes of communication deployed by modern political leaders. The enthusiastic *New York Times* reviewer of van Hove's production in Brooklyn pointed out the cross-over with the aesthetics of TV, noting that '*Kings of War* takes the home-viewing pleasures associated with serial television portraits of cutthroat schemers, like those in *House of Cards* and *The Sopranos*, and magnifies them to the proportions of grand opera'.[67]

Ivo van Hove's production illustrates at once the general discomfort of European directors with *Henry V* as a single play and their need to insert it in a more general historical narrative in order to erase or work out its ambiguities. Alongside this is a tendency to stage the play as a topical reflection on political communication and viciousness, or the legitimacy or illegitimacy of war, rather than to focus on the dramatic art of embodying the play's own representations of history and historical time onstage. Like Zadek's earlier performance, van Hove's *Kings of War* gestures towards, while denouncing, the hegemony of North American television culture in the Western world, itself instrumental in the more-or-less willing confusion, tacitly endorsed by our leaders themselves, between their political images and public functions. The creative collage of disturbing sounds – a sudden, dissonant brass fanfare, the ticking of a clock, an amplified heartbeat – during the play's performances spurred the viewers to harken to an inner voice and reminded them that the stage has a depth unknown to plasma screens.

Taking the field in the United States

Henry V seems to have enjoyed unprecedented popularity in America in the 1950s, 1960s and 1970s. The history of its performances over these years underlines the special status of Shakespeare within the American educational curriculum, as well as the playwright's gradual appropriation by a country bent on making Shakespeare resonate more directly with its heroic and democratic national narrative.

Among the earlier recorded American productions of *Henry V* was a performance at St Bernard's School in New York by schoolboys all under the age of thirteen. Boys from the school performed the play in 1932, 1941, 1952, 1958, 1999 and 2012.[68] Indeed, *Henry V* is described as a school favourite by

V. E. C. Manders, who notes that it is 'full of the warlike pageantry dear to the heart of the boy'. Manders commends it as 'giving invaluable education and producing whole-hearted team work'.[69]

In 1952, *Henry V* was performed as part of the entire cycle of histories at Antioch College in Yellow Springs, Ohio. It was the first production since Frank Benson's at Stratford-upon-Avon in 1906 to present the full cycle of history plays, and spoke to American college theatre's willingness to use Shakespeare for educational purposes. In his review of the college production, Louis Marder sees this project as giving 'great impetus' to 'the movement toward Elizabethan staging' in America. There was no scenery whatsoever on the outdoor stage constructed on the steps of the century-old main college building, but the 'appreciative audience did not refuse to piece out the imperfections with their thoughts'.[70] Many other college productions, most often in the open air, were to follow in the United States.

In their very recent production, The Babes With Blades, an all-female company dedicated to promoting women trained in stage combat,[71] staged *Henry V* as a play performed at an all-girls' school, with 'an enthusiastic teacher armed with an overhead projector' as the Chorus.[72] This production both legitimized the exclusively female cast and satisfied the public's taste for a type of combat spectacle popularized by video games. It also revealed once more the intimate link, in the American collective mind, between Shakespeare and his play's educational uses. *Henry V* was made to support the claims of a cultural and educational system in which everyone, especially minorities and women, is encouraged to learn social ease and self-assertiveness through gaining new skills, whether physical or intellectual. Each individual is taught to be a leader, or driven to become one, like Prince Hal. Hayley Rice's production was praised less for its 'signature realistic violence' and its swordplay stunts than for its clever pedagogical framing.[73]

The New York Classical Theater's production for the 2011 River to River Festival was less educationally bent, but just as recreational: the audience was invited to follow the actors around Battery Park for a selection of early scenes, then, when Henry V (Justin Blanchard) decided to invade France, they were herded onto a ferry to Governors Island (a former military base) and roused by the actors to become part of the troops. A reviewer noted that 'the French lose the battle, but the real casualty here is the play', which was 'noticeably abridged' to allow for the time-consuming crowd movement.[74] Nevertheless, he commended the great Agincourt battle scene, the participatory mode of the production and Blanchard's moving performance of Henry's famous St Crispin's Day speech (see 4.3.18–67). This chimed nicely with the pervasive democratic aspirations that are commonly read into the play. Indeed, this motivated director Stephen Burdman's choice: with this free performance, he hoped to make Shakespeare 'accessible to anybody'.[75]

Henry V had already literally taken the field in New York parks in 1960 and 1984 when Joseph Papp and then Wilfred Leach staged it in Central Park's Delacrote Theater for the annual New York Shakespeare Festival. Kevin Kline as Henry is said to have epitomized the 'tradition of the noble American Henrys', 'at once humane and heroic' and 'earnest in soliloquy'.[76] As has often been the case, the lead part overshadowed other aspects of the play, notably the comic scenes of the 'surviving tavern rowdies'. However, in the wooing scene, Kline was commended for restoring 'comic panache' to the play, letting loose both his 'charm' and 'devilishness':

> he plays the scene allegro, never hitting a wrong note. Whether he is mangling the French language or putting on false airs of towheaded boyish modesty ... Mr Kline walks the line between vanity and chivalry as if it were a high wire. By the time he kicks away the train of his intended's gown to steal a kiss, the courtship is as tender and sexually hot-blooded as it is hilarious.[77]

The American involvement in Vietnam ultimately provided the most fertile soil for the translation, appropriation and cultural rootedness of the play in the United States. Michael Kahn's daring anti-war update of the play, first performed at the Shakespeare Festival in Stratford, Connecticut, in 1969, and then transferred to New York, best illustrates this trend. Although accused of 'depos[ing] Britain's most religious and heroic king' on account of his 'sardonic antiwar tract', Kahn appeared 'extraordinarily ingenious'.[78] His production was part of a much broader cultural revolution that involved both artistic experimentalism and a turn to violence in activist movements in response to discrimination and political conservatism. Before the play per se actually began, Kahn had members of the company, white and black, gradually come onstage, throw frisbees at each other, dribble basket balls, hula-hoop and wrestle, demonstrating that the stage, whether political or theatrical, was analogous to a battleground. In the production's programme, Kahn noted:

> The play is set on a stage which is a playground which is an arena which is a battlefield. The games of this play are the games of war, of conquest, of territory, of power, of betrayal, and of love – games played every day in the playground – and the space is transformed, as the playground is, into whatever or whatever the players want it to be.[79]

The Battle of Agincourt took on the appearance of a savage hockey match, but Kahn did not shy away from representing the execution scenes directly onstage. Critic Caldwell Titcomb, though, considered the production a failure because of its attempts to 'depose' Henry from his perceived status as 'a national hero-conqueror' and because of its apparent trivialization of war through its association of the battlefield with the playing field.

The association of games with war and politics is, however, suggested in Shakespeare's original text by the Dauphin's gift to Henry of a 'tun' of tennis balls (1.2.255–6),[80] and, as early as 1936, Robert Atkins used the Ring boxing stadium in Blackfriars as an apt theatrical space for his production of the play. This sporting device has contributed greatly to the shaping of a distinctively American approach to *Henry V*, with Ben Shaktman using it again in 1977 at the Pittsburgh Public Theater.[81] The longevity of the device hints perhaps at the self-affirmative quality of American individuals and of American culture at large, one that is best articulated in terms of games and sports. For better or for worse, 'life is a ballgame' and all the world's a playground.

Henry V takes the world

Thanks in great part to the successive RSC worldwide tours, *Henry V* has moved from the cramped 'wooden O' of the Globe Theatre (Prologue 13) to expand its influence across the globe. For example, a 1953 performance of *Henry V* at the Singapore Arts Theatre by the local Arts Theatre Group, 'composed of people of all racial communities living in the peninsula', bore witness, according to Sir Gerald Templer, Representative of the British Council, not so much to the memory of the British East India Company as to 'a sense of nationhood in a plural community'.[82] Henry's influence, then, does not always have to carry with it the threat of invasion.

To this day, popular undertakings throughout the world testify to a common commitment to Shakespearean culture, if not to chauvinistic Bardology. A full-scale temporary working replica of the Globe Theatre, the Pop-Up Globe, mounted in 2016 in Auckland, is now established in Melbourne. It promises its audience 'cannons, flaming arrows, hundreds of litres of fake blood, hand-forged armory and over 450 beautiful bespoke period costumes pieces'.[83] Director Miles Gregory and his actors certainly succeed in getting the crowd to cheer for war and 'fxxk the frogs', a motto, as we have seen, that was used earlier in 1986 by Bogdanov in England. However historically informed, the Australian project relishes its ability to provide pure, and sometimes rowdy, entertainment, alongside relatively authentic early modern dramaturgy.[84]

One of the most politically alert appropriations of *Henry V* in the Anglophone world was probably Michael Langham's memorable 1956 production at the Stratford Shakespeare Festival in Ontario. It was committed, like performances in England in the same decade, to the restoration of Elizabethan staging, performed on the beautiful half-Elizabethan, half-classical thrust-stage designed by Tanya Moiseiwitsch for Tyrone Guthrie, Langham's predecessor as director of the festival. English-born, and a former prisoner of war, Langham's genius was to seize on the topical implications of the play's English–French bilingualism for a bilingual, Canadian audience. Langham pulled off a 'diplomatic move' by transporting the play to Canada and a 'theatrical coup' by casting Québécois actors from the Théâtre du Nouveau Monde in the French-speaking roles.[85] The production was such a success that, for once, the play travelled the other way around across the Atlantic to be performed at the Edinburgh Festival in September 1956. In sum, while the 1950s, 1960s and 1970s saw *Henry V* gradually exported and transplanted throughout Western and Eastern Europe and the Anglophone world, particularly through RSC performances, this most English of Shakespeare's histories is now going fully global in the hands of directors with consciously cultural agendas such as Tyrone Guthrie, who oversaw the creation of the Ontario Theatre Festival and also the opening of the Metropolitan Theatre in Sydney.

In Japan and China – where audiences showed an early taste for Shakespeare's great tragedies – *Macbeth*, *Hamlet*, *King Lear* – interest has recently turned to *Henry V*. After staging the *Henry VI* trilogy in 2009 and *Richard III* in 2012, the New National Theatre in Tokyo produced *Henry V* in the spring of 2018. The theatre's website describes the play as a 'hidden gem', yet a 'very popular work in its native United Kingdom'.[86] Similarly, after bringing an English production of *Henry V* to China in 2015, the RSC and the Shanghai Dramatic Art Center worked closely together to produce *Henry V* in

Mandarin. Directed by Owen Horsley, this version was premiered in Shanghai in November 2016. The play, previously unfamiliar to the Chinese public, spoke to their new interest in the history of Shakespeare's birthplace and in Anglophone culture. Unlike Chinese historic classics, Shakespeare – known in China predominantly for his comedies and tragedies – has the advantage of not raising suspicious eyebrows from the Chinese authorities. Horsley was intent on downplaying the political aspects of the play, but also recognized that one of the reasons for the great success of the Mandarin production was the play's juxtaposition of the rhetoric of the glory of battle against the gruesome reality of war. Speaking of this tension in Harry's incognito visit among the soldiers, Horsley declared, 'You don't need to do anything to it to make it land.'[87] Yet, perhaps what this growing global popularity of *Henry V* truly illustrates is the embedded presence in the play of a worldview that, despite imperial tendencies, is ultimately democratic in its broad appeal.

The world's his stage

If Shakespeare's original anti-classical aesthetic has never been fully recovered despite the archeological endeavours of the twentieth and twenty-first centuries, *Henry V*'s commitment to a new sense of history, based on the awareness and acceptance of the contingencies of the present rather than on faith in an eschatological or mythical scheme, is made relevant in a growingly globalized and Westernized world. *Henry V*'s mingled poetics, whether well treated or mistreated onstage, speak, despite all chauvinistic appearances, to a world that is empty of myths and tuned to a growing common interest in history.

3

The State of the Art

Emma Smith

Ever topical, *Henry V* has taken on new resonances with the new century. 'We can never, finally, evade the present,' Hugh Grady and Terence Hawkes write in their introduction to *Presentist Shakespeares* (2007):

> And if it's always and only the present that makes the past speak, it speaks always and only to – and about – ourselves. It follows that the first duty of a credible presentist criticism must be to acknowledge that the questions we ask of any literary text will inevitably be shaped by our own concerns, even when these include what we call 'the past'.[1]

The concerns of a new world order epitomized in the attacks of 9/11 have affected every aspect of Western culture, including Shakespeare, and perhaps most especially this play. Attitudes to its text, its depiction of character and to ideas of history as discussed by James D. Mardock in Chapter 1 of this book have all recently been inflected through a broadly presentist lens, and even more obviously historicist readings – of early modern religion, for instance – have particular resonances when considered in the context of religious wars in our own time. This account of twenty-first-century criticism moves from explicitly presentist accounts of the play that are directly implicated in the politics and warfare of the modern period, to recapitulating the rabbit/duck dichotomy that so structured late twentieth-century accounts, and thence to themes of religion, metatheatre and the role of the self-conscious Chorus, and the place of *Henry V* amid Shakespeare's other plays on English history. Recent criticism on nationalities and on gender will also be surveyed here. The impression of the play in the twenty-first century is thus one of particular and pressing topicality, where the historicism that structured so much of the critical history prior to 2000 has ceded to more anxious forms of presentism.

Presentism

'No one bored by war will be interested in *Henry V*,' wrote Gary Taylor in the introduction to his Oxford Shakespeare edition in 1982: among Shakespeare's plays, only this one 'wholly dedicates itself to dramatizing this brutal, exhilarating, and depressingly persistent human activity'.[2] The history of *Henry V* has indeed always been shaped by contemporary conflicts, from the Elizabethan war in Ireland that was the backdrop to its first performances, to Crimea and the trenches of the Somme. This association has continued in the twenty-first century. Writing in the tense months preceding the 2003 American invasion of Iraq, a defence strategist at the Naval War College in Newport, Rhode Island, suggested a new tactic of psychological warfare against Iraqi civilians. The strategist quoted selectively from Henry's threats to the people of the besieged city of Harfleur (with the worst of the rape warnings silently omitted):

> What is it then to me if impious war,
> Arrayed in flames like to the prince of fiends,
> Do with his smirched complexion all fell feats
> Enlinked to waste and desolation?

(3.3.15–18)

No doubt recalling that Harfleur surrendered after this rhetorical barrage, he concluded that 'this speech should be printed in Arabic on leaflets and dropped on Baghdad, Basra, and especially Tikrit'.[3] Once the long-awaited war began, *Henry V* was indeed quickly mustered. Press coverage of Lieutenant-Colonel Tim Collins's 2003 eve-of-battle speech to the Royal Irish Regiment in Kuwait compared it to Henry's speech before Agincourt, describing the military commander as a 'Henry V in Raybans'. Less positively, writing for a British newspaper in 2003, Gary Taylor quoted Henry's claim that the English victory belonged to God (4.7.86), and observed, 'If our illegal invasion of Iraq appals you, blame Shakespeare.'[4]

As the new century dawned, John Sutherland and Cedric Watts's collection of literary detective essays (2000) took as its title *Henry V, War Criminal?*. The eponymous essay explored the implications of the play's double demand for the execution of the French prisoners, concluding that 'there are prisoners and prisoners': what Henry calls 'prisoners of good sort' are not killed, but ordinary soldiers, as Williams sombrely predicts, are 'merely a logistical burden'.[5] This ethical murkiness did not prevent (or perhaps it subliminally influenced) commentators in reaching for *Henry V* after the terrorist attacks of 9/11, one describing how, when American President George W. Bush 'stood atop part of the rubble of the World Trade Center, he came as close as he ever will to delivering a St Crispin's Day speech' and another seeing him as 'an easy-going Prince Hal transformed by instinct and circumstance into a warrior King Henry'.[6] David Coleman's 2008 essay, 'Ireland and Islam: *Henry V* and the "War on Terror"', identified the parallels between twenty-first-century geopolitics and the play as 'common and unpleasant: questionable interpretations of Salic Law and of United Nations Constitutions; the portrayal of military commanders as masters of Henrician eloquence, urging their troops unto the breach like the mirror of all Christian kings; Guantanamo, Abu Ghraib, and the execution of the French prisoners'.[7] Coleman builds on important work from the 1990s on the play as 'deeply implicated in the strategies of colonial violence undertaken by the Elizabethans in Ireland', connecting this historicist reading with the presentism of appropriations of the play in contemporary politics. He reads Tim Collins's own Irishness as part of the play's ongoing 'colonial gaze' which conflated 'Irish and Islamic alterity [in] an apparently conservative political manoeuvre'.[8]

Mary Polito also offers a presentist analysis of the cultural work done by the play in discourses of self-help and corporate training. Suggesting that, in seeking professional advice from literary texts, 'executives are the new humanists', Polito argues that 'King Henry V is himself a liberal subject and pastoral governor who is learning to perform his profession as he works to teach others to do so as well'.[9] Comparing Thomas Elyot's *Book of the Governor* with modern business manuals employing an exemplary Shakespeare, she finds that both discourses share the mantra 'know thyself'.[10]

Rabbit and duck

Few plays, perhaps, have such a prominent critical touchstone as *Henry V*. Almost all the works discussed here take their coordinates from Norman Rabkin's 1977 article 'Rabbits, Ducks, and *Henry V*': Rabkin, as Mardock explains earlier in this volume, suggested that the play's power is that – like the gestalt image that looked at one way is a rabbit and another a duck – 'it points in two opposite directions, virtually daring us to choose one of the two opposed interpretations it requires of us'.[11] Henry is thus *both* a Machiavellian prince and the 'mirror of all Christian kings' (2.0.6), but not at the same time.

Rabkin's defining image of the rabbit-duck continues to structure twenty-first-century understandings of the play's radical and irreconcilable ambivalence. Tom McAlindon's essay, 'Natural Closure in *Henry V*', seeks to counter this orthodoxy, arguing that Henry's 'heroic distinction lies precisely in his capacity to unite opposites'. McAlindon retrieves a world of 'natural order as a system of discordant concord or concordant discord driven by and combining antipathetic and sympathetic forces', and through close analysis of the play's imagery, stresses the play's 'resolved opposites'.[12] Nevertheless, McAlindon concedes that the play 'does not represent Shakespeare at his best', since the central figure is seen 'too much from the outside; there is insufficient recognition of the inner stress which should accompany or precede some of his most decisive actions': this is presented as an aesthetic failing rather than an intentional scepticism.[13] Malcolm Pittock's conclusion is rather different, although argued over similar ground. For him, 'The Problem of *Henry V*' is 'that Shakespeare the man intended to write a simple patriotic play celebrating a warrior hero, but Shakespeare, the universal artist, could not allow him to do so'.[14] Reviewing the history of critical approaches to this problem, Pittock revisits the familiar loci – the speech before Harfleur, the claim to France, the killing of the French prisoners – and concludes that it is 'a play which has taken over three hundred years to come into its own, but having done so, it can no longer sustain the old heroic view of Henry'.[15]

Bradley Greenburg identifies Henry's trait of displacing responsibility onto others in his '"O For A Muse of Fire": Henry V and Plotted Self-Exculpation'. He argues that 'the success of the play as a presentation of the paragon of kingship ... rides on Henry's ability to deflect and thereby control or manage all conflicts and challenges', such as when he shifts responsibility for his wars onto French aggression via the ambassador in 1.2. Greenburg suggests that Henry deals with the ancestral guilt of Lancastrian usurpation – his father's deposition of his predecessor as depicted in *Richard II* – by 'enacting a version of the saint's discourse and then by using it to initiate the hero's discourse'.[16] Guilt is a key term in Dennis Kezar's 'Shakespeare's Guilt Trip in *Henry V*': analysing forms of legal culpability in the play, Kezar, following Foucault in 'What is an Author?', implicates 'our bending author' (Epilogue 2) in this self-reflexive analysis. Arguing that 'responsibility and the possibility of guilt represent for Shakespeare an important and disappearing conception of artistic creation, ownership and existence in this play', Kezar connects the play's own ethical dilemmas with its ambiguous 'fusion of authorship and history'.[17]

Rabkin's powerful concept dominates questions of Henry's character and the ethical charge of his behaviour, but the modern critical mistrust of binaries has resulted in a change of emphasis towards 'both/and' instead of 'either/or'. Rabkin's stress on irreconcilable polarities has been modified into an exemplary model of ambiguity or into a carefully manipulated self-image made by Henry himself.

Religion

New approaches have also intervened. The so-called 'religious turn' in early modern studies has had its impact on approaches to *Henry V* – as John Drakakis explores in this book – and has begun to modify the terms of the debate about Henry's character. John S. Mebane notes that 'a formalist analysis is a necessary prerequisite for a discussion of a play's ideology', arguing that across the sweep of his history plays, Shakespeare is concerned to dramatize 'the discrepancy between the pacifism grounded upon key elements of the New Testament, on the one hand, and the devotion of the aristocratic warrior classes to an ideology of warfare, on the other'.[18] This ideology of warfare, Mebane suggests, 'is a compound of codes of chivalry, traditional Judeo-Christian "just war" doctrine, and pagan heroic tradition', and he reads *Henry V* as undercutting the theory of the just war through 'persistent and aesthetically sophisticated' devices including hyperbole and anticlimax, irony, juxtaposition and parody, with a particular focus on the self-interested politics of the episcopal discussion which opens the play in 1.1.[19] For Mebane, Henry's prayer before Agincourt (4.1.286–302) suggests that 'the king knows that his public justifications for the invasion of France are Machiavellian fraud and that he fears not only that he will lose the battle, but that he may be damned' for his father's usurpation of Richard II.[20] Mebane emphasizes as a kind of 'Freudian slip' Henry's use of the charged word 'vile':

> he today that sheds his blood with me
> Shall be my brother, be he ne'er so vile
> This day shall gentle his condition.
>
> (4.3.61–3)

This, Mebane argues, is Henry's true opinion of his soldiers – as the *Oxford English Dictionary*'s definition has it, the word 'vile' means 'despicable on moral grounds; deserving to be regarded with abhorrence or disgust'.[21]

Arguing over similar passages, David Womersley in his *Divinity and State* (2010) takes a consciously different view and helpfully reviews the critical history, observing:

> In suggesting that Shakespeare re-modelled the material he inherited with a view to presenting Henry V as an ideal monarch, in whom military, political, and spiritual authority were combined, I am clearly departing from the common view that Shakespeare's Henry V is at best an ambiguous, at worst a negative character. This interpretation of Henry as anti-hero seems to have begun with Hazlitt, writing in the wake of the Napoleonic Wars, and it revived immediately after the First World War: the aftermath of titanic conflicts was obviously an encouraging climate for such views. So too were the 1950s, when Hazlitt's originally revisionist view strengthened into an orthodoxy under the twin stimulants of Cold War fears and suspicion of warlike leaders. Helpful, as well, to the thriving of such interpretations was the New Critical creed that ambiguity was the natural state of great literature.[22]

For Womersley, *Henry V* shows how 'questions of monarchical legitimacy and religious orthodoxy became intertwined as a consequence of that vigorous re-imagining of the national past':[23] the so-called 'religious turn' leads him to stress the play's parallels with popular Protestant theology. Henry's dissatisfaction with the 'idol ceremony' (4.1.237) 'foreshadows his explicit condemnation of Catholic doctrine and practice, as well as all other acts of the will, as "nothing worth"'.[24] When Williams and the frightened soldiers imagine Judgement Day, the scene is less about the costs or justifications for war, but rather 'dramatizes the movement from a state of spiritual reprobation to a state of grace . . . And it puts on stage an act of reformation in which Henry shows himself to be a pattern of Protestant monarchy.'[25] Thus, for Womersley, what is at stake in the play is a particularly Protestant understanding of judgement and personal responsibility, making Henry into an anachronistically reformed model of spirituality, educating his people about how to prepare themselves for death.

For Camille Wells Slights, 'conscience', another contemporary religious term, is key to the play's religious and spiritual heart. Conscience 'is the nexus where internal self-awareness and external political action, the obligations of obedience and the authority of personal judgement, converge' in Shakespeare's history plays.[26] *Henry V* 'scrutinises the conscience of a king who would also be his country's conscience', exploring the role of an emergent Protestant conscience in early modern England.[27] In this light, the discussion between Bates and Henry about moral and political responsibility cannot ultimately be resolved, but for Slights, the effect of this irresolution is 'not to render the figure of Henry ambiguous but to engage the consciences of the audience with these doubtful cases'.[28] Rabkin's rabbit/duck has here become a tool to stimulate active ethical discrimination by the audience: a moment of ambiguity passing moral responsibility from the fictional agents within the play to their witnesses in the theatre.

Maurice Hunt, building on work by Patricia Parker in the late 1990s, begins his religious and ethical analysis from a linguistic point – that *Henry V* contains Shakespeare's most frequent use of the word 'breach', suggesting that it is part of the rhetoric of dilation by which a heroic king is represented and, partially, qualified: 'the presence of breaches in a dilated entity provides a way of understanding how the notoriously discordant elements in Henry's character – his capacities for Machiavellian intrigue, heroic valor, and Christian piety – can coexist without a denial of or preference for any one of them'.[29] Hunt analyses the Chorus's introductory work of 'swelling' the scene (Prologue 3), and argues that other speeches also serve to dilate Henry's character. The famous 'breach' at Harfleur unto which the soldiers must return comes to figure the damaging gap between the anti-heroic conduct of Pistol, Nym and Bardolph, and Henry's heroic rhetoric: 'all of the breaches in *Henry the Fifth* call attention to and give place to the primary breach of this play: that between idealized portraits of the king and his flawed, human behaviour'.[30] Revisiting Rabkin, Hunt suggests that the interpretative choice can be made too stark: 'while [Henry] is not an exemplary mirror of a Christian king, he is nevertheless a Christian king whose faults do not finally eclipse his Christian humility'.[31]

Hunt uses a similar method – again putting pressure on a repeated word to open up larger thematic questions – in an essay on 'Brothers and "Gentles"' in the play. Here fraternal rhetoric and the social mark of gentry are interwoven: Hunt reminds us of Cain's guilty abdication of responsibility, 'Am I my brother's keeper', and suggests that in *Henry V* the 'larger, Christian sense [of brotherhood] involving humanity' is at play. Hunt explores associations between the work of the philosopher, Montaigne – particularly Montaigne's essay, 'Of Friendship' – and contemporary ideas of empathy (we know that Shakespeare was reading John Florio's translation of Montaigne in manuscript around this time and was drawing extensively on it for *Hamlet*). Hunt finds the deferred duel between Henry and Williams to be a nexus for the issues of horizontal versus vertical relationships that the play dramatizes, offering brotherhood as a genuine alternative to feudal subservience. Hunt is certain that 'King Henry in his St Crispin Day speech honestly intends to regard his courageous soldiers as brothers, and he well might like to "gentle" their "condition."

He is not self-consciously Machiavellian in this regard.'[32] Ultimately, Hunt's version of *Henry V* is as an authentically inclusive drama, and the Chorus's opening address to 'gentles all' is – perhaps somewhat sentimentally – cast as 'the preface to a redefinition of a humane viewer of the spectacle of history – of life'.[33]

In 'Polysemic Brotherhoods in *Henry V*', Christopher Dowd's view of the function of brotherhood in the play draws on a different, more complicated and less idealizing methodology. Dowd reads the play's overlay of fraternal and national discourse, suggesting that Shakespeare encodes ideological ambivalences in polysemic language, and tracing the occurrence of fraternal rivalry across his histories, comedies and tragedies. He argues that 'brotherhood is defined as biological, national and spiritual', three categories that 'highlight three areas of English identity when dealing with others – race, nationality, and religion'.[34] Groups of brothers – the conspirators Cambridge, Scroop and Grey, the national captains Jamy, Fluellen, Gower and Macmorris, and the Eastcheap contingent Pistol, Nym and Bardolph – embody the contradictions inherent in the relationship: 'by describing a subject's relationship with a king as brotherly, Shakespeare allows for victory and failure, love and hate, in the same moment'.[35] Dowd concludes that Rabkin's foundational dichotomy is unnecessary because the rich connotations of Shakespeare's language provide a vocabulary for the nuance and ambiguity of internal conflict.

Also using a religious heuristic, albeit a more sharply theorized one, Jeffrey Knapp discusses the paradoxical work of history plays to 'recurrently uncover a kind of internationality within the "English" isle'.[36] Knapp suggests that throughout *Henry V*, 'Shakespeare silently contrasts a violent "fellowship" of warriors financed by a corrupt Catholic church to the peaceful communion of an audience in active remembrance of blood spilt'.[37] His argument that the theatre becomes 'sacramental' and that the experience of audiences 'has strong affinities with orthodox English Protestant conceptions of the eucharist' replaces the play's internal logic of military comradeship – 'a communion liberated from the confines of the church to the open battlefield' – with the more imaginative and humane work of theatre-going.[38] Theatre presents itself as the alternative institution to the fractured Church. Henry's claims to be fighting a holy war are demystified when he executes Bardolph for the theft of a pax (a holy tablet marked with a crucifix). Given that the play opens with the bishops discussing Henry's own plans to sequester 'the better half of [their] possession' (1.1.8), perhaps it could be said that both Bardolph and the king have stolen from the Church. Henry's wartime egalitarianism is part of the play's – and, for Knapp, the histories' – opposition to bishops as self-interested hypocrites (Knapp's term is 'anti-prelaticalism'). 'Just as Harry demystifies the bishops' privileged relation to spirituality, so the theatre demystifies the seemingly esoteric scholarship of the king,' opening up arcane knowledge in ways that resonate with a particularly Protestant theology. The Prologue's famous injunction to 'piece out our imperfections with your thoughts' (Prologue 23) here invokes a 'reformed hermeneutics' of imagination over Catholic materialism.[39] Rather than *showing* (a 'Catholic' aesthetic), the play *discusses* and *imagines* (more 'Protestant' modes): Knapp's interest in the form of the play overlaps with critical approaches that I have grouped under the term 'metatheatre' below.

One common interpretation of the cultural role of theatre in the early modern period is that it forms part of a process of secularization. Knapp's book explicitly tries to challenge this narrative and to reintroduce an ongoing religious dimension to the theatre, arguing that playwrights nevertheless maintained a distance from doctrinal disputes. Discussing 'the turn to religion' in early modern studies more generally, Ken Jackson and Arthur F. Marotti argue that it arises from the need, identified by new historicists, to engage with 'the other' – the radical alterity of the divine, as well as the specifically historical alterity of a culture shaped by belief. They also suggest that 'the turn to religion – in critical theory and in the hyper-historicizing of early modern literary studies – suggests that we may still be more "religious" than we wish to be – even in our most secular of critical methodologies'.[40] Jackson and Marotti were writing in 2004: world events have continued to challenge modernity's claims for increasing secularization and instead locate religion as a major agent in human culture. It is unsurprising that the ever-topical *Henry V* has been part of this critical movement.

Metatheatre

An increasing interest in the effects of Shakespeare's plays in performance has focused attention on its particular formal qualities. What Mardock calls in this book '[i]rony and its discontents' has fed particularly on the role of the Chorus in introducing, narrativizing and interpreting the play's actions. One way to think about these effects is through the term 'metatheatre': the ways in which the play engages with its own theatricality and its status as a play.

Many readings of the play, like Knapp's, turn on its Prologue's famously stirring and complicated opening speech. In his work on 'The Experience of Ceremony in *Henry V*', Matthew J. Smith takes the phrase 'ciphers to this great account' (Prologue 17) to unpack the play's – and its hero's – 'struggle with ceremony'. His phenomenological approach understands 'the play as a historical gerund, as an event being experienced', an entertainment dependent upon and suspicious of the paradox of ceremony.[41] In place of the Protestant reading that sees Henry's disillusionment with the 'idol ceremony' as a conversion narrative away from Catholicism (as exemplified by Womersley above), Smith reads the play's own formal and representational self-consciousness alongside scepticism about monarchical ceremony. In attending to the theatrical alongside the theological, his essay combines different approaches to the play – including speculative performance ideas about stagecraft and in particular the hermeneutic weight of the cloak Henry borrows from Erpingham to go among his frightened men – with work on the senses and the role of feeling in phenomenological interpretations of drama. His Henry does not turn his back on ceremony in his eve-of-battle soliloquy, but rather reinvigorates it, creating in his St Crispin's Day speech 'a remarkable instance of ceremony making'.[42] Shakespeare 'brings his audience ... through the unresolved journey of Henry's struggle with ceremony': 'like the iconoclast who, in destroying sacred objects, unintentionally acknowledges their spiritual power'. Smith positions Henry as a 'bearing point', somewhere between the historical king and the historiographical Chorus, for the audiences' felt experience of theatre.[43]

'The ironic self-referentiality of its dramatic form' is also crucial to Alison Thorne's account of the play in her essay 'Awake Remembrance of These Valiant Dead'.[44] The play's ideologically ambivalent effects are located in its rhetorical form: '[it] insistently foregrounds the interpellative techniques used with fearsome efficiency by various characters, laying open its own ideological stratagems in the process'.[45] For Anja Müller-Wood in 'No Ideology without Psychology', the play's emotional effects are to be understood from an evolutionary perspective. Drawing on cognitive science and reader reception, she traces 'how Shakespeare choreographs human emotions to make ideological propositions meaningful and acceptable (both onstage and off)' while grounding 'the emotions thus patterned in a concrete cognitive-emotional reality: that of the evolved human psychology'.[46] Arguing that the play's ideological investments are enabled and sustained by the emotional expectations on which it is predicated, she shows that ideology and emotion are interconnected, speculating about how early audiences might have responded:

> Shakespeare *expected* viewers of *Henry V* to react just like the soldiers at Agincourt, namely, in tune with the reactions of the king ... Just as Henry urges his loyal subjects to share his political goals – and justify the means by which he seeks to achieve them – so Shakespeare urges his audiences to affirm and participate in the play's ideological intentions.[47]

As one of the few Shakespearean plays with a sustained choric structure (*Pericles* is the other play built in this way), *Henry V* directs attention to the gap between narrative showing and telling, and to the processes of 'spin' that shape the historical record. Its final chorus speech, the Epilogue, alludes specifically to the play's position amid other history plays, directing attention to those 'which oft our stage hath shown' (Epilogue 13). The question of how far the play is part of the sequence has continued to exercise modern critics.

Histories

The extent to which *Henry V* is a stand-alone play, or the culmination of what earlier scholarship called the 'second tetralogy' (*Richard II*, *1 Henry IV*, *2 Henry IV* and *Henry V*), is a continuing question for criticism and for performance. In his essay 'Henry V's Claim to France: Valid or Invalid', Cedric Watts suggests that the English claim to the French throne is invalidated by its illegitimacy and by the bleakness of the Epilogue, which links the play back to the earlier histories 'like a snake swallowing its tail', or like the 'repeat play' stage direction that ends/continues Samuel Beckett's 1964 *Play*: 'there are few modern experimentalists whom Shakespeare has not anticipated'.[48] Other historicist investigations establish different intertexts. Richard Hillman's analysis of the imaginative relations between England and France during the early modern period suggests that Shakespeare 'partially modelled Henry V on Henri IV' of France and that the play's final *entente* between the two nations shadows the 1598 Treaty of Vervins between France and Spain and the Edict of Nantes which ended the French wars of religion by extending civil rights to Protestants.[49] Vimala C. Pasupathi's materialist account of clothing, 'Coats and Conduct', places *Henry V* in the context of costume and its social and hierarchical connotations in *Henry IV*: soldiers' coats are explored alongside contemporary documents about army provisioning and the obligation of subjects to fight on behalf of the Crown. The 'war-worn coats' (4.0.26) of the English forces before Agincourt meet Henry's own disguise in Erpingham's cloak to stage 'the vexed relationship between the loyalty subjects can wear and how they actually feel about their service debt'.[50]

For Eric Pudney, *Richard III* is the comparator: while these two rhetorically powerful monarchs may look like ethical opposites, 'the similarities between them are perhaps even more striking than the differences', particularly their use of deceit ('Mendacity and Kingship in Shakespeare's *Henry V* and *Richard III*').[51] Pudney argues that both plays 'draw attention to their own rhetorical distortions' in keeping with contemporary humanist scepticism about political persuasion.[52] Carrie Pestritto compares the 'balanced description' of Henry to *Julius Caesar* in which Brutus 'is portrayed as an entirely moral and upright citizen' ('Outlooks on Honor').[53] Identifying the play's own comparison of Henry with Caesar, another Roman play – this time *Coriolanus* – provides Rita Banerjee's comparison text ('The Common Good and the Necessity of War'). Banerjee notes that the writing of *Henry V* immediately predates Shakespeare's shift into Roman history and suggests that it anticipates the republican ideals of the classical plays. 'The common people' are identified as the most articulate critics of war in *Henry V*, as a republican version of history 'breaks through the façade of the official ideology and historiography to which *Henry V* ... only nominally subscribes'.[54] Banerjee argues that the suffering of the ordinary soldiers – in the play and in Elizabethan society – demonstrates that war is not in the common interest and that the play critiques 'the Machiavellian notion of the perennial necessity of warfare for the well-being of a state'.[55]

Cyndia Clegg explores that oft-used epithet 'Machiavellian' in more specific textual and historical detail in her essay 'Feared and Loved: *Henry V* and Machiavelli's Use of History'.[56] Covering similar ground, Hugh Grady suggests that *Henry V* is Shakespeare's 'most Machiavellian' play, 'celebrating a Prince who succeeded in astonishing feats of conquest and national unification while coolly depicting how that Prince's heroic achievements were accomplished by political manipulation, image manufacture, violence, and the threat of violence'.[57] Grady suggests that Shakespeare is drawing specifically on the troubling Machiavellianism of the court faction around the Earl of Essex, and sees in its simultaneous depiction and undermining of heroism a response to the tensions of this political moment.

For Alison Chapman, asking 'Whose St Crispin's Day Is It?', the play's intertexts are accounts of shoemaking by Thomas Dekker, Thomas Deloney and others: St Crispin turns out to be the patron saint of shoemakers. Uncovering associations between shoemakers, community and calendar, she suggests that 'Henry V invokes the shoemakers' ability to remake the ritual calendar and then displaces this ability onto the king himself', using the traditional holiday to 'celebrate monarchical instead of artisanal power'.[58] Reading the play alongside these shoemaker stories, Chapman reveals its strategies of authoritarian containment and the ways in which Henry invokes horizontal relationships in order to enforce vertical ones. Elsewhere there are other contrasts. For example, Adrian Poole explores David Jones's 1937 poem on the First World War, *In Parenthesis*, as an attempt to decentre Henry and with him traditional readings of literary history. Jones's poem is more interested in Fluellen than in the king ('The Disciplines of War, Memory and Writing').[59]

Nationalities

If, as Mardock mentions earlier in this book in his comments on the work of David J. Baker, Michael Neill and Andrew Murphy, late twentieth-century work on the play was concerned with *Henry V*'s depiction of English and Irish identities, the twenty-first century has opened new avenues. Exploring 'the absent presence of the Turk in Shakespeare's histories', Jerry Brotton argues that the spectral figure of the Turk generates some of the pleasurable ambivalences of *Henry V*. Brotton is attentive to the force of allusions such as the promise to Katherine that their son will 'go to Constantinople and take the Turk by the beard' (5.2.206–7), suggesting that Shakespeare did not engage directly with these popular theatrical fictions because of 'dramatic Turkish fatigue' brought about by the success of Marlowe's *Tamburlaine* and its subsequent imitators.[60] Brotton elucidates both the ambiguities of Henry's character and the mixed ethnic identity of his apparently nationalistic avatars such as St George, 'a figure contested between Christianity and Islam'. If the 'spectre of turning Turk haunts Henry and the play he inhabits', Brotton argues, then *Henry V* has its dramatic continuation and fulfilment not in the next episode of the historical saga in *Henry VI*, but in the story of Othello, 'an apparent Christian convert who ultimately turns Turk in a tragic fulfilment of what Henry threatens to do'.[61]

Benedict S. Robinson's 'Harry and Amurath' begins with the same moment in the scene between Henry and Katherine as a 'door to some serious questions about the political theology of the nation'.[62] Noting that 'post-Reformation religious politics generated notions of identity and affiliation that went well beyond the narrow space of the nation', Robinson sees 'a wider struggle between Christendom and the nation as theo-political spaces, a struggle that took place in significant measure over the figure of Muslim difference'.[63] As with Brotton, the points of comparison are thus not the other English histories but the more explicitly exotic identity politics of *Tamburlaine* and *The Battle of Alcazar*. Robinson reads the play's inscription of brotherhood in the context of Ottoman politics as well as Christian theology, bringing the suppressed family violence of his own historical narrative back unbidden into Henry's triumph: 'Against the specter of a sultanate established by fratricide, Henry projects the image of a band of brothers united in the pursuit of a heroic and godly war.'[64] Thus the traces of Islam in *Henry V* open up questions of political theology and religious identity, reflecting implicitly on 'an international politics of Christian or European identity that sits strangely alongside Henry's rhetoric of Englishness'.[65]

Alison Walls takes a different approach to issues of nationality and identity in her linguistic study, 'French Speech As Dramatic Action in Shakespeare's *Henry V*', noting that the play's use of French is non-naturalistic, restricted to specific characters and scenes, and that 'somewhat paradoxically, a more profound comprehension of the text can be contained within linguistic incomprehension' in performance before a monolingual audience.[66] Also using a linguistic lens, Philip Searjeant's 'Ideologies of English in Shakespeare's *Henry V*' offers 'a reading of the play that draws upon the methodological apparatus that has been developed within linguistic anthropology, and which views language usage as cultural'.[67] Drawing on the historical development of English in the period of Henry V and of Shakespeare, Searjeant is interested in the way linguists use 'the *indexical* layer of language, whereby certain aspects of language usage point towards embedded beliefs about the social, political, or epistemic nature of the situated act of speech' (emphasis in original).[68] Focusing particularly on the play's use of French and the accented speech of the national captains, he shows that the play disrupts easy equivalences between national identity and language, concluding that 'language use in the play is provided always with a symbolic function, but this is never dogmatically asserted, nor does it fully correspond to the strands of ideological belief which constitute a modern ideology of linguistic nationalism'.[69]

Ireland is still present, however. John Kerrigan's 'Oaths, Threats and *Henry V*' investigates instances of the binding language of swearing, particularly as they cluster around the angry Irishman Macmorris (prominent in late twentieth-century criticism). In part, this is explained historically as 'the contextual pressure from Ireland':[70] contemporary accounts of the Irish wars by Sir Henry Sidney and others were full of oaths given, taken and broken. But it is also structural and linguistic. Interlacing the oaths of the conspirators and the 'three sworn brothers' of Eastcheap with other instances of verbal bonds including wagers and troth-plighting, the article rereads Henry's quarrel with Williams as an exploration of the power of oaths: 'swearing may incline to formal, ritual encapsulation, as though divinely or self-empowering, but its potency turns out to depend on the interpretative slant of the agents involved, their witnesses, their status and intentions'.[71]

Jonathan Baldo's essay, 'Into a Thousand Parts', arrestingly describes the play's opening Chorus as a 'metaphorical conscription-scene', and goes on to unpick the play's particular interest in arithmetic and numbers 'in the light of homologies and frictions between theatrical and Parliamentary representation'.[72] Baldo reveals similarities between Shakespeare's Chorus and a parliamentary speech of 1593 by Sir Edward Coke, the Speaker of the House of Commons, showing how both parliamentary and theatrical representations require the arithmetic of the cipher. The play's counting and recounting – of men, of war-dead, of foils, of widows – offers 'a creative accountancy underlying this imaginative historical account', by which the play 'slyly reminds audiences of what Henry and his official historian, the Chorus, would have us forget'.[73]

Memory

Questions of cultural memory and the construction of history have brought provocative new methodologies into the study of Shakespeare. Asking 'Where Are the Archers In Shakespeare?', Evelyn Tribble draws attention to the complete suppression of the English longbowmen in Shakespeare's version of Agincourt, and uses this absence deftly to explore 'the ecology of skill and memory in early modern England'. Tribble traces parallels between the two embodied disciplines of archery and theatre, arguing that archery is an 'embodied skill' transmitted across generations and, as such, a kind of metonym for historical memory: 'the case of archery in early modern England precisely shows the intergenerational tensions and discords that arise from attempts to graft a traditional bodily practice honed in the late medieval period into the very different "mental universe" of the late Elizabethan period'.[74] Tribble's method combines historical investigation into the human and mechanical technologies involved in longbow archery, the social functions of these skills in elite humanist texts by Sir Thomas Elyot and Roger Ascham, military discourse of the period, and the anthropology of skill acquisition, curation and transmission. Considering archery in other history plays, she shows the development of the trope of shooting either on- or offstage, or of a character entering impaled with an arrow, to depict archery in the theatre, using the Shakespearean counter-example of Act 4 from *Titus Andronicus*. Staging pragmatics are 'only a partial answer to the question of the absence of the archers at [Shakespeare's] Agincourt', given that other contemporaneous accounts in plays, chronicles and ballads emphasized the tactical importance of the archers' role at the battle.[75] 'Shakespeare's forgetting of the archers does seem deliberate and is certainly conspicuous':[76] archery is associated with the past and there is no place for these nostalgic physical feats in a modern stage which values a different embodied skillset: 'the early modern theater afforded "prestigious imitation" [Tribble takes the phrase from the cultural anthropologist Marcel Mauss] of a range of embodied skills, including gesture and the command of the body, swordplay, and dance, but equally erased others from the stage, participating in the creation of an ecology of skill and prestige that had little place for archery'.[77]

Also concerned with memory and nostalgia is Lucy Munro, in her 'Speaking History: Linguistic Memory and the Usable Past in the Early Modern History Play'. Munro is interested in the ways that 'plays share with nondramatic histories the capacity to bring the past to life through archaism; unlike nondramatic texts, they can also actively rematerialize and re-embody the past through the act of staging itself'.[78] Discussing self-consciously archaic language in historical texts including those by Marlowe, Spenser and Greene, Munro settles on the character of 'Ancient Pistol' and his curious idiolect, identifying him as a 'contemporary Vice' with 'temporally unstable language'. He exemplifies the process of historical writing: 'As Pistol's example shows, to "speak history" in the 1590s history play is not merely to revive the past but to reanimate it and to question it.'[79]

Material memory is the focus of H. Austin Whitver's 'Materiality of Memory in Shakespeare's Second Tetralogy': the function of tombs as monuments to Shakespeare's kings is self-consciously deployed by Henry, who incorporates Richard II's ceremonial reburial 'into his permanent, personal, legacy-building project'.[80] Shakespeare's first audiences could still see in Westminster Abbey 'a damaged but enduring physical manifestation of a glorious past' in Henry's own battered tomb, towering over the monuments of previous kings.[81] For Isabel Karremann, discussing *The Drama of Memory in Shakespeare's History Plays*, *Henry V* is marked by 'a strategy of distraction' she calls 'nationalist oblivion'.[82] Karremann studies the play's iconic moments – St Crispin's Day, the Chorus, Salic Law – as scenes of self-conscious remembrance that actually perform forgetting or oblivion. Drawing on theories of nationhood, she identifies erasure as a key dynamic: for her, the play's metatheatricality ironizes the work of spectacle and memory in creating national unity. Karremann argues that juxtaposed scenes in the play place theatrical memory and nationalist oblivion in tension, concluding that 'the play's meaning cannot be determined in terms of ideology alone. Redirecting our focus on its formal features allows us instead to describe the interplay of attention and distraction generated by a pattern of contrapuntally arranged scenes.'[83]

Gender

Following seminal work by Phyllis Rackin and Jean Howard at the end of the twentieth century, feminism and gender criticism have made some new inroads into this apparently most masculinist of plays. Meghan C. Andrews uses a seminal article by Louis Montrose on *A Midsummer Night's Dream* to discuss the methodology and historiography of allusions to, and identifications of, Queen Elizabeth I in readings of early modern literature:

> If we have learned to read *A Midsummer Night's Dream* as Simon Forman's dream, we might be tempted to read the Henriad as Essex's: a fantasy, a cultural wish fulfilment in which England is a masculine, warlike state, unencumbered by feminine caution or sensibilities, with a strong male heir waiting to inherit the realm and restore a patriarchal gender hierarchy.[84]

Andrews suggests that Hal continues to 'acquire feminine characteristics' across the *Henry IV* plays and into *Henry V*, highlighting his copious, potentially effeminizing rhetoric, and his ongoing commitment to an alternative world of 'holiday and lady terms' as particular sites of this gender uncertainty.[85] Andrews reads the Oedipal struggle between the Henrys, father and son, as versions of Elizabeth herself and of 'the repressed feminine', noting, 'I would suggest that [Elizabeth's] image is bifurcated in these kings. Henry [IV] encapsulates all the disabling aspects of Elizabeth's 1597 persona – her age, infirmity, loss of control – while Hal embodies her strength, vitality, and effective ruling strategies.' Far from banishing women's authority and presence, Andrews sees the history play sequence as confirming Elizabeth's power by attempting to appropriate and master it: 'Women thus do not have a small role in the second tetralogy solely because it offers the (impossible) fantasy of history as a masculine preserve; they do not appear because they are too threatening and because, more importantly, femininity is always already there.'[86] As Andrews points out, her argument disrupts conventional ideas about gender and genre, suggesting that it is in the history plays that female agency is most irrepressibly foregrounded.

Corinne Abate's approach, in an article entitled 'Once More Unto the Breach', is to attempt the recovery of Katherine from the passivity assigned to her by many readings of the play, arguing that she 'is the only person, and more importantly the only woman, who is resistant to all of Henry's shifting roles'.[87] Abate's close analysis of 5.2 suggests that, just as early modern theories of conception stressed mutual pleasure, so too Henry needs 'Katharine's willingness to help him produce heirs'.[88] The scene thus provides 'an unexpected opportunity for a fictional wife to fashion herself into an equal marriage partner'.[89] Judith Haber's take on the play discusses its apparent elision of women and its oft-noted preoccupations with patrilinear identities as, in fact, 'an attempt at what one might call "filial parthenogenesis": we are presented, that is, with the spectacle of a son trying to adopt a father, in a backward-looking effort to secure a legitimate line'.[90] Through a close linguistic analysis of paradoxes such as 'the war-like Harry, like himself' or 'but by loving likelihood', Haber comes to a reading of the 'wooing scene', arguing that Katherine's silence at Henry's demand for a kiss denotes neither submission nor assertion: 'it clearly doesn't mean at all'. Using Derrida and Deleuze to understand such gaps within the uneasy translations of this part-French, part-English scene, Haber finds this miscommunication a defining example of the play's 'constellation of inadequate, failed comparisons and similes'.[91] Sarah Werner's essay 'Firk and Foot' materializes questions of gender by focusing on the work of the male body in stage representations by young male actors.[92] Drew Daniel recovers a queer narrative to Henry's 'capacity for cloaking, mimicry, and imitation' and uses modern audio sampling practices as a way to reframe Henry's rhetorical skills as 'the reproduction of a soldierly identity that is neither fully organic nor fully artificial'.[93]

Texts

New editorial work re-examining early texts of Shakespeare's plays, aided by digital copies of the Quarto and Folio editions online and combined with an emphasis on materiality, has been an important critical strand in the twenty-first century. Textual studies of the two versions of the play – the Quarto printed in 1600 as *The True Chronicle History of Henry the Fift* and the 1623 Folio's *The Life of Henry the Fifth* – have continued to generate new questions about the transmission of Shakespeare's plays on page and stage. Duncan Salkeld reviews some of these arguments in 'The Texts of *Henry V*', concluding that 'recent scepticism regarding such matters as memorial reconstruction, piracy and the "badness" of some of the early imprints has yet to prove persuasive', and 'that evidence of memorial error, misreading and mishearing suggest that the Quarto was produced via a combination of memorial reconstruction and dictation, probably in that order'.[94] In his influential study *Shakespeare as Literary Dramatist* (2003), Lukas Erne takes the two texts of *Henry V*, alongside *Romeo and Juliet* and *Hamlet*, as exemplary of 'the trajectory from a predominantly oral to a heavily literate culture', where the shorter texts 'record in admittedly problematic fashion the plays as they were orally delivered on stage'.[95] The Folio-only passages, Erne argues, 'share certain characteristics. They are not necessary for the understanding of the plot. Most of them are not particularly stage-worthy. They are good reading material', 'purple patches' written into the plays 'in the knowledge that they might well be omitted on stage'.[96] Cyrus Mulready's article on the Quarto text ('Making History in Q *Henry V*') argues that, like other print products including abbreviated chronicles and ballads on historical material, 'Q *Henry V* presented a simplified, entertaining, and easily-digestible version of history'.[97] Mulready's careful argument about history as a developing print genre qualifies Erne's argument, suggesting that, rather than being closely allied with theatrical scripts, the short Quarto should be read alongside other historical products of the print marketplace, where epitomes and abbreviations of longer works were a staple. 'Q inherently emphasizes the compatibility of "chronicle history" and drama,' Mulready argues, pointing out its particular use of appositive stage directions to 'render a theatrical text manageable for the reader'.[98]

Richard Dutton recontextualizes *Henry V* in the moment of Essex's downfall, describing the play as 'a succession work, grounded in the anxieties of a country whose queen in 1599 had reigned for over forty years'.[99] Excavating the play's concerns with genealogy and succession, the Salic Law speech becomes an important locus, and the play's inscription of Scottishness as important as the more-noticed references to Ireland: 'the simple fact is that a 1599 audience could hardly fail to identify a Jamy with a broad Scots burr ... with James VI of Scotland'.[100] Dutton finds references to other claimants to the English throne in the play's references to France and particularly Burgundy, and in its shadowing of Elizabeth's Irish campaign. He suggests that the absence of much of this vital and topical material from the Quarto texts implies some form of censorship, perhaps preemptive by the Lord Chamberlain's Men, rather than enforced by the Master of the Revels. Looking anew at the near-consensus that the play dates from 1599 (largely based on the assumption that the allusion in the Chorus to Act 5 is to the Earl of Essex), he proposes instead that Shakespeare revised the play in 1602 to take account of the changing English fortunes in Ireland under the new general, Charles Blount, Baron Mountjoy.

The reported death of Falstaff in 2.3 and his mysterious 'Table of greene fields' (Folio reading) is one of Shakespeare's most notorious cruxes, emended by Lewis Theobald in the eighteenth century to 'a babbled of green fields' (2.3.16). In her essay 'Anticipating Nostalgia', Linda Charnes investigates the legacy of this textual intervention to understand the invention of nostalgia, an eighteenth-century medical term that has cast its shadow across the play and across current critical debates between 'presentism' and 'historicism'. Thus the article toggles between the micro-example – Falstaff's green fields – and the macro-discourse of history and hermeneutics, drawing on philosophies of temporality and periodization as well as on the medical history of nostalgia.

Theobald's persuasive emendation sticks in part because it sentimentalizes Falstaff's character: 'we see Harold Bloom's Falstaff – midwived by Theobald' (the reference is to Bloom's 1998 *Shakespeare: The Invention of the Human*).[101]

Performance

Finally, studies of performance on stage and screen have flourished. Both James N. Loehlin for the Shakespeare in Performance series and Emma Smith for the Shakespeare in Production series approach stage history via Rabkin's interpretative dichotomy. Loehlin traces Henry's shift from Edwardian hero across the twentieth century; Smith takes a longer view, annotating a text of the play with performance choices from the eighteenth to the twentieth centuries.[102] Film productions are discussed as part of Sarah Hatchuel and Nathalie Vienne-Guerrin's volume, *Shakespeare on Screen: The Henriad*. More detailed work on particular productions includes Anita Helmbold's account of Kenneth Branagh's 1989 film ('Take a Soldier, Take a King'), which discusses its ambiguous attitude to war and to Henry, arguing that critics who interpret the film as pro-war do so because they like Henry's character: 'in reading criticism of the film, the unavoidable conclusion would seem to be: it is axiomatic that to like the king is to condone his war'.[103] Deborah Vukovitz focuses on the effects of Patrick Doyle's score for Branagh's film in '*Henry V* Rendered in Music', while José Ramón Díaz-Fernández has provided 'The Henriad On Screen: An Annotated Filmo-Bibliography' for Hatchuel and Vienne-Guerrin's collection.[104]

Where next?

This survey has sketched the ways in which broadly presentist critical concerns have impressed themselves on the scholarly reception of *Henry V* in the twenty-first century. Religion, nation, gender and memory are all current topics to which an energetically always-current play has much to contribute. Textual and performance studies are enjoying a new currency across Shakespeare studies, and *Henry V*, with its two early editions and a strong and sustained stage history, is no exception. But predicting where interest will go next is riskier. Current – 2018 – critical trends interrogate time and space in new ways that account for theatricality and narrative in an exciting manner: perhaps there is work to do on the specific imaginative dimensions of a play that pushes temporal and spatial dimensions. Work on sexuality may have more to say about the implications of brotherhood. New productions – for example, the first major production with a woman in the title role, directed by Rob Hastie in Regent's Park Theatre, London, in summer 2016 – will open up new interpretations. So there is more of *Henry V* to come: in any case, it is surely too much to hope that its 400-year association with war and violence might come to an end any time soon.

4

Henry V on Screen

Sarah Hatchuel

The case of *Henry V* on screen is a complex one since the source material is historical, dramatic and cinematic. In their attempt to revive a play by focusing on accurate historical details, or to supersede previous films by updating the story with new aesthetics or bolder textual and directorial choices, the *Henry V* films oscillate between readaptation and remake, continually foregrounding ongoing cultural debates about war and authority. As they choose to emphasize specific aspects of *Henry V* through the adaptation process, filmmakers necessarily suggest political and ethical worldviews – the films speak through Shakespeare, co-opting the play into a certain worldview. The aim of this chapter is to give a contextual, aesthetic and ideological overview of the screen productions by Laurence Olivier (1944), Michael Hayes (*An Age of Kings*, 1960), David Giles (BBC, 1979), Kenneth Branagh (1989), Michael Bogdanov (The Wars of the Roses cycle, 1989), Peter Babakitis (2007), Thea Sharrock (*Hollow Crown*, 2012) and Gregory Doran (RSC Live, 2016). This chapter explores particularly the films' representation of war, their depiction of the royal figure of the king and their handling of potential ironies created by the diverging discourses embedded in the play. A coda examines how *Henry V* has been cited and appropriated in other films and television shows.

As others in this book have observed, Norman Rabkin posits that *Henry V* engenders two opposed, almost incompatible, interpretations.[1] Productions on stage and screen reflect this critical dichotomy as they have tended either to celebrate the military triumph of England over France or to destabilize ideas of heroism and patriotism. For a play which, according to Alexander Leggatt, presents an anatomy of war, with its political and financial causes, its consequences, military hierarchy, heroism and horrors, Shakespeare's *Henry V*, surprisingly, does not feature any war scenes.[2] The play shows what takes place before and after a battle, but does not dramatize what happens in the midst of it. The representation of the battle at Agincourt is reduced to a quarrel between a greedy English soldier (Pistol) and a cowardly French one (Monsieur Le Fer) in a farcical parody of chivalric combat. While Holinshed's *Chronicles* contained historical information that could have been used by Shakespeare, the play does not reveal any details of the actual battles. However, as I will discuss through a chronological exploration of the various adaptations from cinema to television, the possibilities offered by the medium of film have encouraged directors to go beyond the simple altercation between Pistol and Le Fer to show the Battle of Agincourt in a literal, 'realistic' way, influenced by the politics and representations of contemporary conflicts.

The film adaptations also need to address the issue of the various paradoxes and tensions in the play. Ironies can generally be stressed in performance, either by creating a discrepancy between the Chorus's laudatory, nationalistic lines and the more complex, down-to-earth actions that question the official version; or by playing the Chorus as a sarcastic character, reflecting wryly on the English and their war. In both cases, the handling of ironies is strongly related to the Chorus's part and the way it is interpreted. According to some critics, the play owes its idealistic quality to the Chorus only,[3] while its subversive quality comes from the gap between the choric discourse and the unfolding action. While the drama shows one version of the facts, the Chorus frames each act by telling another version of the story. It is through this particular construction, with its oscillation between conflicting stories and modes of showing and telling, that irony arises. For instance, the laudatory speech delivered by the Act 4 Chorus to introduce the night scenes before the Battle of Agincourt is contradicted by succeeding events: far from cheering his men up, King Henry, disguised as a common soldier, only hears curses and challenges from his subjects.[4] By telling us the official story of Henry, the Chorus narrates a contrapuntal version which competes with the performed action.

However, another trend of performance asserts the exact opposite: the dramatic action can be portrayed as patriotic while the Chorus conveys subversion by presenting a cynical view of the situation. Director Adrian Noble followed this line in his stage production for the Royal Shakespeare Company in 1984, which is also discussed in Chapter 2 of this volume. Henry, played by a young Kenneth Branagh, was presented as a juvenile, inexperienced and earnest king, while the Chorus, played by Ian McDiarmid, was a blasé and cynical observer. McDiarmid's Chorus added a derisive touch to 'Now all the youth of England are on fire' (Chorus 2.0.1) and insisted on the cupidity of the English soldiers by cynically pronouncing 'crowns imperial, crowns *and* coronets, / Promised to Harry and his followers' (Chorus 2.0.10–11).[5] Adrian Noble also cut the end of this speech to place it after the pitiful discord in the tavern scene, so that the Chorus's claim that 'The French, advised by good intelligence / Of this most *dreadful* preparation' (Chorus 2.0.12–13)[6] could legitimately be uttered ironically; that is, the French would have nothing to fear if the English army was indeed composed of such clowns.

In Laurence Olivier's 1944 sumptuous Technicolor film of *Henry V*, the Chorus (Leslie Banks) delivers his lines with nationalistic admiration for the king. The dramatized action is cut drastically and adapted to remain in line with the epic statements. In accord with the narrative nature of the film medium, the Chorus is presented as an objective, omniscient and reliable character.[7] Olivier's film was shot during the Second World War as a homage to the British soldiers who were engaged in fighting the Nazis, and who, at the time of the film's release, had just landed in Normandy with their Allies. It is common knowledge that the film was partly funded by the British government and that Winston Churchill instructed Olivier to direct it as morale-boosting propaganda for British troops. The opening sequence even dedicates the film to Britain's forces, the 'spirit of whose ancestors', a caption tells us, the film attempts 'to capture'. Olivier's film presents the war as a righteous enterprise, the English as the 'good guys' and the French as their effete and silly sidekicks. Some of the English king's harsher traits are deliberately left out – such as his threat to unleash his troops to kill old men, rape young girls and pillage the town of Harfleur, as well as the reference to the hanging of his former friend, Bardolph. No traitors come to threaten the unity of the army or question the legitimacy of war. The nostalgic mention at the end of the play about how England eventually 'lost France' (Epilogue 12) is also omitted. Harry's stirring speeches are filmed with the camera gradually drawing backwards, creating a long shot where the king becomes one with his soldiers, implicitly including the cinematic audience and inviting them to feel that Henry's words are addressed to them at a time of national crisis.

During the night before the battle, Olivier allocates Williams's graphic lines about 'legs and arms and heads chopped off' (4.1.135–6) to another soldier, Court, performed very innocently by a teenage boy. According to Stephen Buhler, 'Court's apparent youth suggests that his fears stem from inexperience, a lack of battle-seasoning; his immediate somnolence suggests that fatigue contributes to such jitters.'[8] The subversion of Williams's description is therefore not only toned down, but also recalls the massive enrolment of younger and younger men during the Second World War.

Renowned for its emphasis on stylized metafiction, Olivier's film starts with a framing device, opening in the Globe, set in a

London that is presented as a dreamlike fairyland. The experience of cinema begins only when the Chorus mentions the departure of the English army and allows us to escape the confines of the theatre, but the distorted perspectives, inspired by medieval illuminated manuscripts, continue to reveal the artificiality of the sets. When the film reaches the moment of the Battle of Agincourt, it eventually drives the viewers into a real, exterior setting. This alternation between a theatrical, a stylized and a realistic direction produces a commentary upon the theatrical medium for which the play was written and the cinematic medium to which it has been adapted. Olivier's battle is shot in saturated colours and under a bright sun, and evokes Michael Curtiz's 1938 *Robin Hood*, starring Errol Flynn. As the soldiers fight almost painlessly in a bright green meadow, the tone is exhilarating and heroic: blood is never shown on screen and the different captains are performed to provide comic relief. While, in Shakespeare's play, Henry and the Dauphin never confront each other directly, but always speak though a messenger, Olivier's film interpolates a sequence where the two men settle their differences in a duel. With alternating cuts of the two charging armies, the editing directly calls to mind battle scenes from Hollywood westerns, a genre that fitted well with the patriotic response the director wanted to evoke.

Contrary to cinema, television has presented *Henry V* in the context of the historical tetralogies. *An Age of Kings* – a monumental production directed by Michael Hayes and broadcast by the BBC from April to November 1960 – was a high-budget, serialized saga in fifteen parts covering *Richard II*, both parts of *Henry IV*, *Henry V*, the three parts of *Henry VI* and *Richard III*. It dramatized Acts 1–3 of *Henry V* as episode 7 ('Signs of War') and Acts 4 and 5 as episode 8 ('The Band of Brothers'). The repertory cast included Robert Hardy (as a brisk, hearty and capable Henry), Judi Dench (as the French princess) and William Squire (as the Chorus). The series was generally filmed in intimate medium shots and close-ups, and many episodes ended with teasers announcing the next ones. For example, 'Signs of War' concluded with a shot of a signpost that read 'Agincourt', standing as a kind of cliff-hanger for the battle to come. The serialized presentation also gave actor Robert Hardy the opportunity to evolve from Prince Hal to King Henry. Both a critical and popular success (it garnered three million viewers in the United Kingdom), the show emphasized the country's literary and historical heritage at a time when the British Empire was actually in decline.

Almost two decades later, the BBC *Henry V* – part of the Corporation's mission to dramatize all of the Shakespeare corpus – was shot in a television studio, which placed limitations on the battle scenes. It used most of Shakespeare's text, yet tellingly omitted Henry's graphic invective to the citizens of Harfleur. The production was broadcast on 23 December 1979 at the end of a four-week series dramatizing the second history cycle, all the parts of which were directed by David Giles. David Gwillim's performance as Henry V was an explicit development of the king's younger self as Hal: the first scenes of *Henry V* betray his inexperience as well as his yearning for advice before going to war, and even the scar on his cheek is a reminder of a wound he suffered during the battle at the end of *1 Henry IV*. Although Gwillim orders the killing of the French prisoners, his delivery emphasizes the shame he feels at saying the line. With the BBC endeavouring to 'can' the canon, or 'box the Bard',[9] in as unabridged a manner as possible, television asserted itself as a memorial vessel. For Graham Holderness, the series was 'produced in the image of the Corporation itself: a classical monument of national culture, an oppressive agency of cultural hegemony'.[10]

After these televised 'heritage' renditions, Kenneth Branagh's 1989 *Henry V* marked the beginning of a new wave of Shakespearean adaptations on the big screen and made the play accessible to a broad audience. Branagh viewed his adaptation process less in terms of the suppression of parts of Shakespeare's text and more as an addition to Olivier's film. As he stated in his introduction to the published script, 'I decided on including some significant scenes that Olivier's film, for obvious reasons, had left out: in particular, the conspirators' scene ... The violence and extremism of Henry's behaviour and its effect on a volatile war cabinet were elements that the Olivier version was not likely to spotlight.'[11]

Branagh resorts to techniques appropriate to a war documentary to represent medieval battles. During the retreat at Harfleur, the soldiers, running to escape the horrors of the battlefield, are filmed with their backs towards the audience, as if followed by a camera in the trembling hands of a reporter. The idea of the war correspondent is evoked again when we join the Chorus, played by veteran Shakespearean actor Derek Jacobi, just before the Battle of Agincourt. He walks rapidly towards us along a palisade of wooden stakes, earnestly describing the enormous event about to take place. At the end of the battle, the corpses of the slaughtered boys are shown in one continuous shot, once more filmed frenziedly as if by the hand-held camera of a journalist, suggesting both distress and disbelief. Eventually, the film replaces the comic altercation between Le Fer and Pistol with a brutal and bloody battle.

From the scene that Shakespeare chose to leave in the shadows, Branagh creates the longest and most outstanding sequence in the film. When he was preparing for his role as Henry V on stage in the 1984 RSC production, he was already relying less on Shakespeare's text and more on history, and observed in his autobiography, 'The first [elusive area] was war, and I tried to do something about this by reading ... historical documents about the combat detail at Agincourt. I was very slowly beginning to picture the horrors of a hand-to-hand medieval combat.'[12] Branagh's film stresses the atrocities of war by showing blood, mud, wounds, impaled bodies and looting. Time seems to stretch infinitely while damp, foggy weather intensifies hardships. The use of slow motion turns the Battle of Agincourt into a chaotic and dreamlike sequence verging on nightmare. Slow motion adds power to the combatants' blows and, by dilating time, underlines the soldiers' heroism and physical effort. The battle becomes a timeless and ceaseless fight, a never-ending tumult that symbolizes every other armed conflict: Mera J. Flaumenhaft, for example, has compared Branagh's battle scene with 'an animated Guernica, with falling horses, a human head bleeding at the mouth, and "all those legs and arms, and heads chopped off in battle"'.[13]

Branagh's *Henry V* was shot in England at a time when films expressing the disillusion of warfare were inevitably influenced by the conflict in the Falklands and the memory of the destructive consequences of the First World War, which had ended seventy years previously. In 1986, Branagh had played the part of a young First World War soldier, suffering from deep emotional trauma, in the film *A Month in the Country*, whose director of photography, Kenneth McMillan, also worked on *Henry V*. The first scene of *A Month in the Country*, in which an exhausted soldier crawls through muddy trenches, anticipates the scene of the Battle of Agincourt, shot two years later. Branagh acknowledges this, noting that – as he had hoped – 'the whole [Agincourt] sequence at times resembled other kinds of conflict, most notably the First World War and its trenches'.[14] Through scenes that show the solidarity between men, united in their fighting, Branagh's film gives a deeply ambivalent picture of war as something that is, at the same time, disgusting and heroic, hellish and glorifying, repulsive and attractive. Chris Fitter notices that 'the structure ... owes much ... to Vietnam movies of the 1980s, particularly its moral ambiguity: war is hell but it heroizes'.[15]

In the first version of the screenplay, the Chorus was intended to appear 'gently ironic', with, for example, his '[h]umorous eyes and his whole tone shot through with irony'.[16] Branagh's first intention seems, then, to have been directed towards a contrapuntal version of the Chorus, who was to comment wryly on the action. However, in the finished movie, Jacobi, as the Chorus, never mocks the action. By reducing the length of the Chorus's speeches and disseminating them in many places throughout the film, Branagh weakened the clash between the Chorus's lines and the king's actual actions, while creating consistent narrative links between the key scenes of the film. Contrary to the start of Olivier's film, Branagh's Chorus does not welcome us to the Globe theatre but, 'with the clarity and warmth of the great story-teller',[17] invites us into a movie studio filled with props that we will notice throughout the film, thus adapting the *mise-en-abyme* effect to the medium of film.[18] The subversive effects are suppressed in favour of a narrative immersion in the fiction. The Chorus is Henry's ally, his voice remaining soft and admiring. Moreover, Henry's actions never contradict the Chorus's version. During the Chorus's speech introducing the night scenes, for instance, the camera shows us the king actually touring the camp and reassuring his soldiers. Branagh has thus moved away from Noble's 1984 direction. The Chorus adds rhythm and consistency; he does not disturb the action or hurt the image of the king. With this interpretation of the Chorus, potential subversion is diverted in favour of an empathetic discourse aiming to raise feelings of collusion, understanding and pity for the main character in power.

While Olivier builds his film on long, epic shots, Branagh bases his on more intimate reaction shots. He even uses flashbacks to delve into the king's mental space and establish the friendship that Henry shared with Falstaff, Pistol and Bardolph. During the execution of the latter, Branagh's film shows close-ups of the king who vainly tries to conceal his tears, paradoxically creating empathy towards the executioner rather than the victim. The king is constructed as a young, earnest and conflicted man. A Hamlet-like figure filled with doubts regarding the legitimacy of war and of his power, he becomes the tragic victim of the prelates' conspiracy to go to France as a diversion to protect the Church's financial interests.

The corpses of the English boys mercilessly killed by the French against the 'law of arms' are discovered by Gower, Fluellen and Henry in 4.7. This tragic moment is kept in the script, but the king's two orders leading to the vengeful execution of the French prisoners are removed, thus mitigating the king's calculating nature.[19] Henry's reaction in front of the boys' corpses creates a pathos yet unequalled in other performances of *Henry V*. Branagh clearly wanted to protect this pathos and therefore cut Henry's controversial orders to kill the French prisoners in 4.6 and 4.7, noting that 'to have him do that at that point was utterly inconsistent with the rest of what we were presenting as a troubled and ambiguous character'.[20] Branagh thus tends to go back to a tradition that attempts not to tarnish Henry's image in order to present him as a redeemed figure before Princess Katherine in the last Act.

Branagh ends the battle with the now famous *Non nobis* sequence in which the king, followed by his soldiers, crosses the battlefield in one uninterrupted four-minute tracking shot with a score composed by Patrick Doyle that soon builds into a crescendo of orchestra and voices. As soldiers start to sing the *Non nobis*, Henry picks up a boy's corpse and makes his way among the ruins of the battlefield. Carrying the dead boy like a cross on his back, he is turned into a Christ-like figure, bearing his soldiers' sins and miseries. At the end of the travelling shot, the camera cuts to a close-up of Henry's bloodstained face and the king's head drops as if in shame. The end of the sequence is cathartic, liberating both the emotions of the king and those of the spectators. But, again, it is through Henry's eyes, the eyes representing royal power, that all the wasteful carnage is finally observed.[21] By focusing on the king's personal suffering and redemptive march, the end of the sequence seems to minimize the huge human cost. Indeed, after watching the movie at a special conference screening, Michael Hattaway noted that conference delegates 'from both "Eastern" and "Western" Europe' were reminded 'of the fascist movies of their youth' by the film's 'swooning melody accompanying a heroic leader who was glamorized by artful camera work'.[22]

Branagh's *Henry V* has in fact often been criticized for its reactionary nature: while Ian Aitkin commented on its 'royalist ideology', Curtis Breight has deemed the film 'conducive to Thatcherism'.[23] However, one needs also to recognize the impressive balance that this *Henry V* achieves. While Shakespeare's play creates ambivalence by oscillating between parodic subversion and epic speeches, Branagh's film never fluctuates in tone, but both denounces and glorifies conflicts *at the same time* through a clash between terrible images of slaughter and swelling triumphal music. If Olivier stresses the impressive number of charging French warriors in a travelling sequence shot across the sunny battlefield and accompanied by William Walton's rousing score, Branagh insists on the daunting number of the dead.[24] For Warren Chernaik, 'Branagh allows for a reconciliation of the heroic and the anti-heroic, King Harry as existentialist hero, a warrior with conscience'.[25] The operatic *Non nobis* sequence underlines the sharing of pain while stressing the hero's initiatory journey and isolated masculinity.[26] Branagh's screen version thus appears more in line with Jonathan Hart's view, which posits that '*Henry V* is a both/and play rather than an either/or play'.[27] The film's specificity resides in a tension between two poles that we apprehend simultaneously rather than in turn, the history play verging on the problem play.

Michael Bogdanov, on the contrary, turns his production of the same year into a powerful charge against war politics. His *Henry V*, recorded for television in 1989 and released on video in 1990, was part of The Wars of the Roses cycle of history plays staged by the English Shakespeare Company, and discussed in this book in Chapter 2. In the wake of the Falklands War, the production denounces the rhetoric of patriotism that was used by Margaret Thatcher to restore her weakening popularity in the early 1980s. The production not only presents a disenchanted view of armed conflicts but also a cynical, brutal and insensitive king (played by Michael Pennington), a Henry more like Richard III than Hamlet. Bogdanov does not hesitate to include the two orders of execution, without any attempt to protect Henry's honour. As the king delivers the St Crispin's Day speech, his exhausted soldiers are not roused by his hollow jingoistic rhetoric. Any positive idea of authority is thus expunged, but the soldiers are also depicted as mad hooligans who unfurl a banner reading 'fuck the frogs', while the Chorus brandishes a poster saying 'Gotcha!', recalling the *Sun* newspaper's notorious headline in

May 1982 after the controversial sinking of the Argentinian warship *General Belgrano* by the Royal Navy during the Falklands War. The chauvinistic men behaving in inhuman ways drive us to question military acts and the point of war in general.

Kenneth Branagh's 1989 cinematic production had such a huge impact on the world of Shakespeare-on-film that it triggered a whole new wave of Shakespearean adaptations, including Branagh's own *Much Ado About Nothing* (1993) and *Love's Labour's Lost* (2000). However, audiences had to wait nearly fifteen years before another director dared to make a movie of *Henry V*. Peter Babakitis's version of the play (filmed in 2004 and released on DVD in 2007) appears as a kind of synthesis of earlier cinematic versions, conflating Olivier's metafictional artifice and Branagh's drive towards brutal authenticity. Babakitis's adaptation is primarily distinctive in its use of digital effects: images are sometimes given the look of Penny Arcade video games in a style reminiscent of the digitally composed shots in Julie Taymor's *Titus* (2000), where surreal, nightmarish images of fire and body parts were superimposed between characters, creating shared memories of violence and murder. In Babakitis's *Henry V*, however, the digital shots serve less to delve into the landscapes of the characters' minds than to underline the heterogeneity of the filmic material. The Chorus's first speech is accompanied by graphic images successively displaying a skull, a medieval illuminated book, the agitated hoofs of horses viewed through red filters, and two castles (standing for the kingdoms of France and England) separated by a digitally shortened English Channel and standing out against an artificial-looking, cloudy sky. In other words, the first sequence sets the tone of a film resolutely constructed around the notions of collage and heterogeneity. The sequences presenting the siege of Harfleur and the Battle of Agincourt both include digitally processed shots in which splashes of saturated colours contrast with a predominantly greyish background. The combat sequences are often shown in slow motion, through filters which keep changing from warm to cool colours or through the dazzling glitter created by the interaction between sunlight and the camera lens.

With the aid of special effects, unusual viewpoints are adopted, allowing for such exotic subjective shots as those following the course of arrows throughout the air. Reality is mingled with the occult, as black-hooded figures of death are seen hovering over the battlefield, recalling the powerful, *memento-mori* image of the skull at the start of the film. Through computer-assisted techniques, the film fragments space, supernaturally juxtaposing dimensions and working on visual associations.

In such a context, Henry is dehumanized and 'digitalized'. He is often filmed in exaggerated close-ups and low-angle shots, through colour filters, in stylized slow motion or in front of digitally composed sets. Since Henry often stands out against an alien setting, he seems to belong to a different dimension and to embody an autonomous and self-governing figure from another place and time zone. These effects convey the king's independent spirit, and also provide him with powerful immunity against the hazards of life. As Henry passes through the battlefield, hails of arrows fall around him; yet, magically, none touch him. In fact, this 2004 Henry is hardly interacting with the outside world at all. He is generally located in a frame of his own, without any other character invading his space. Henry may not interact much with the other characters, but he is the only one in the film to build a relationship with the audience. This king regularly delivers his lines directly to the camera, displaying histrionic and Machiavellian qualities.

If Babakitis revels in new technologies and avant-garde cinema, he also aims at providing a feeling of authenticity, stating that the Battle of Agincourt 'ought to look like CNN coverage of all the wars that go on today, with all the chaotic, unplanned shocks that appear in real documentary footage of the so-called "embedded" video journalists'.[28] Babakitis's cinematography was indeed influenced by the media footage of the 2003 British and American invasion of Iraq. The final battle is turned into a chaos of soldiers, bowmen and horses through a *mise-en-scène* that uses a crowd of extras (apparently digitally magnified), but also through deliberately confusing editing and disorganized framing. The horrors of the battlefield are displayed in the form of bloody stabbing and ruthless beheading. By adopting the specific style of jump-cut editing and amateurish, raw footage, Babakitis's fiction film plays with one of the most popular forms of television at the start of the twenty-first century: the 'docu-drama' – that is to say, a TV drama based on actual occurrences and real people. Although it is based on historical research, documentation and evidence like a documentary, it uses the dramatic and narrative codes of fiction film to mediate and appropriate the real world, whether present, past or anticipated.[29]

The appropriation of the docu-drama style appears in the director's emphasis on accurate reproduction: 'I turned to ... the Medieval Reenactment Society [whose members] are experts at staging sieges at historical castles and the like, with hundreds of participants in full 15th century gear.'[30] The concept of fiction seems to have been abandoned in favour of an effort to *re-enact* medieval battles in every detail. It is actually revealing that Babakitis chose to open the first scene of the film with a date written at the bottom of the screen – 1415. The film presents itself as a documented reconstruction of the past, attempting to offer a faithful experience of bygone events. Nevertheless, the absence of logical links between the shots gives rise to a series of alienating effects, distancing the spectators from events and presenting the film as a constructed, sutured piece. No music can be heard to soothe the artificial, jump-cut effects, but only atonal music (sometimes eerie vocals) and the rattling noise of the military operations.

As Babakitis states, he was 'attracted by this play because [he] thought it would be fascinating to get into the mind of this rather cold-blooded killer who believes he's doing God's work'.[31] This aspect is notably brought out in the film as Henry announces that Bardolph is to be hanged for stealing from a church. Contrary to Branagh's film, Babakitis's version does not focus on the king's pain and emotional distress at ordering the hanging, instead concentrating on Henry's cruelty and unperturbed conscience. More importantly, the cold-blooded facet of Babakitis's Henry V is revealed in the decision to keep one of the king's orders to execute the French prisoners during the battle, while cutting the scene in which Henry discovers the slaughtered boys. Babakitis's adaptation thus emphasizes calculation over pathos. As the order is only given in cold-blood, the film endeavours to wipe out any sign of emotional, revengeful motivation for the execution.

The Chorus, performed in the Prologue scene by a young woman (Sabaa Rehmani), is later sometimes turned into an impersonal voice-over, recalling the kind of narrative voice usually found in documentaries. Beyond the originality of a minority-ethnic, female Chorus, the voice-over suggests the existence of a superior authority, which embodies knowledge and know-how, exposing facts, contextualizing images, creating an ideological frame through which to perceive events, and perpetuating a hierarchical relationship between the show and the spectator. The heroic, official version delivered by the Chorus thus becomes more difficult to criticize. As the Chorus admiringly delivers the speech, 'Now all the youth of England are on fire' (Chorus 2.0.1), the audience is actually shown soldiers preparing for their military campaign, trying out their bows, practising fighting and checking their armour and helmets. Even when the voice-over mentions that 'crowns and coronets' are promised 'to Harry and his followers' (Chorus 2.0.10–11), a shot focuses on hands exchanging money. As the voice-over epically and poetically evokes the embarkation of the king and his followers at Southampton, the screen images offer to our sight a digital forest of masts and sails highly reminiscent of the stylized, colourful flotilla in Olivier's 1944 film. In Babakitis's film, the boarding sequence produces a lyrical and passionate pause just before the battle, presenting all the future fighters in high spirits. The flag that waves in slow motion at recurrent moments in the film is arguably the most powerful symbol of a screen adaptation that attempts to demythologize nationalism and royalty, but eventually tends to create epic contemplation and imperial legitimacy, celebrating the nation and the conquest of foreign lands.

In July 2012, English heritage was once again celebrated when the BBC aired a new version of the second tetralogy in the first season of the TV series *The Hollow Crown*. The fourth instalment – after versions of *Richard II* and the two parts of *Henry IV* – was *Henry V*, directed by Thea Sharrock. While the context of the wars in Afghanistan and in Iraq and the global 'war on terror' could have spurred a disillusioned anti-war episode, Sharrock's version generally streamlines the subversive passages, rejects most of the progressive views on the play and provides a very patriotic message just before the 2012 Olympics that took place in London. Its most original move, however, is to open with Henry's funeral, attended by the grieving population, his former companions in arms and his widow queen cradling the infant Henry VI. By showing a dead Henry from the start, the film encourages a retrospective and analytical view of what follows – since the play's events become flashbacks with added suspense as spectators unfamiliar with the action may well expect Henry to die during the different sieges and battles in France. The cathedral in which the king's body is displayed at the beginning and conclusion of the film becomes the 'wooden O' from which the story will be told. The Chorus, performed by John Hurt, is at first a disembodied, anonymous voice-over that sends us back to a time when Henry (Tom Hiddleston) was still a dashing king, riding horses and practising archery. The production centres on Henry and his good looks (which is, according to David Livingston, a 'stark contradiction to his own less than flattering description of himself when wooing Catherine'),[32] evading the issue of the king's legitimacy, minimizing the clergymen's cynical plotting and suppressing the three traitors' scene entirely. Even the killing of the luggage boys is left out. Henry's authority, the country's unity and the military conquest of France are left unquestioned and untarnished.

As in serial productions of the whole set of Henriad plays, the king's past is extensively documented and his relationships with Falstaff, Pistol and Bardolph are emotionally charged. However, these past connections are not built upon to stress Henry's rejection of Falstaff or to engender parodic mirroring between the Chorus's statements and Henry's rhetoric on the one hand, and the common soldiers' actual experience of war and what they feel about it on the other. Hiddleston's Henry tries to become a soldier like any other as he voices his stirring speeches conversationally, addressing each line to small groups of men, sometimes even to singled-out individuals. In fact, his speeches betray a lack of confidence in the power of words. The real blows given during the gruesome, hand-to-hand combats seem more crucial to him. Even Henry's terrible threat to the governor of Harfleur is delivered while the governor is already on his knees and the town already taken.

The king's Machiavellian side is revealed in two ways. First, Hiddleston imports spectral echoes of the role that made him internationally famous: in 2011, he played the villainous Loki, Thor's adoptive brother and arch-enemy, first in Kenneth Branagh's blockbuster, *Thor*, and then in Joss Whedon's *The Avengers* – a film that premiered in the same month that *The Hollow Crown* aired. Second, Henry mercilessly orders the execution of the prisoners, who are soon gathered and killed by arrows. However, as this angry order is given in a field covered by bloody corpses, it appears more as a military necessity to try to win a battle that seems a lost cause. If the slaughter of the boys has been excised from the story, the threat of such slaughter remains. Falstaff's Boy is the target of a French soldier who is about to shoot his arrow – just before being killed by York. This Boy also becomes the camera's target as he is often filmed watching the events unfolding, from the preparation of war to the horrors of the battlefield. The Boy becomes a seasoned eyewitness, filtering the play through a new point of view and recalling the *mise-en-abyme* achieved through a child's vision in both Adrian Noble's *A Midsummer Night's Dream* (1996) and Julie Taymor's *Titus* (1999). As the film reaches the Epilogue, the Boy is seen attending Henry's funeral, while flashback images and elegiac music rekindle the glorious moments of this 'star of England' (Epilogue 6). In an original twist, the Boy is revealed to have grown into John Hurt's Chorus: an old man now, he has been telling his story all along. At this final touching moment, *Henry V* becomes less a play about a king's war than a boy's survival and attempt to make sense of it.

The latest screen *Henry V* – Gregory Doran's 2015 Royal Shakespeare Company stage endeavour, filmed for RSC Live in 2016 – is aesthetically hybrid and ideologically balanced. The RSC Live productions generate stimulating reflections on the evolving relations between the media of stage and screen since they are theatre productions that are simultaneously broadcast in cinemas. Located between stage and screen, live and recorded shows, theatre archive and films in their own right, they have become an attractive way to capture some aspects of the sociability that theatre-going represents. The two audiences – that in the theatre and that in the movie house – are carefully addressed as the performance is specifically tweaked for the different cameras in place, allowing for various shots and rhythmic editing. The RSC Live productions, first broadcast live and then released on DVD, differ dramatically from the archive videos formerly used by the RSC for its stage productions, which were made with a single fixed camera, recording the action from afar, and then stored in the Shakespeare Centre in Stratford-upon-Avon for the sole benefit of scholars or theatre practitioners.

The recording of Doran's *Henry V* makes no attempt to erase the limits of stage space or to make us forget that we are watching a theatrical event on a particular night. Although the film does not cut to show reactions in the audience, it does not avoid shots in which the public can be seen. As the stage is largely bare, spectators become actual participants, being asked by the Chorus to work on their thoughts and to stand as the soldiers harangued by Henry (otherwise alone on stage) during the siege of Harfleur. Since this production completed the tetralogy Doran started to direct two years before, actor Alex Hassell could bring to the king a little touch of Hal, a role he had played to critical acclaim in the *Henry IV* plays (opposite Antony Sher's Falstaff). Hassell's Henry appears as neither war hero nor war criminal, but as a guilt-ridden, religious Action-Man, a young king possessed by his mission who delivers his rallying speeches panting for breath. Oliver Ford Davies's kind, white-haired Chorus, in casual cardigan and red scarf, oscillates between admiring anchorman and comic observer, reflecting a production that avoids triumphalism and anti-war postures altogether, and lets the text, with all its ambivalent, contradictory passages, appeal to our own imagination and partiality.

Henry V citations

If the screen adaptations of Shakespeare's play have positioned themselves on a large ideological spectrum – from Olivier's unrepentant pro-war agenda to Bogdanov's brazen denunciation of jingoism – the references to *Henry V* in other films and television series replicate the same gulf. As Mariangela Tempera has shown, the play is often cited and appropriated either to convey 'feelings of unabashed nationalism and self-righteous patriotism or, alternatively, to expose them to ridicule'.[33] The representation of military conflicts, be they 'real' or fictional, can be given an aura of nobility with lines from *Henry V*.

In Penny Marshall's 1994 *Renaissance Man*, for example, Danny DeVito plays a reluctant instructor who takes a group of aspiring marines to see a production of *Henry V* in Stratford, Ontario. The actors give a lively performance of the siege of Harfleur and catch the enthusiastic attention of the young, multi-ethnic soldiers; the noisy reactions irritate the white middle-class spectators who remain oblivious to the fact that the trainees are the only ones in the theatre who may, because of their age and social class, find themselves fighting to defend the country. Later in the film, one of the privates recites the St Crispin's Day speech during a drilling exercise, importing Shakespeare into the US army with a straight face.

Henry V is also appropriated by a group of Scottish soldiers in David L. Cunningham's *To End All Wars* (2001). In a very harsh Japanese prison camp during the Second World War, prisoners attempt to regain dignity and prove implicitly the superiority of British culture by rehearsing and staging the St Crispin's Day speech under the direction of a Shakespearean actor. The speech is performed before the Japanese guards during an attempt to escape and is recited again when the Japanese surrender is announced.

Irony is much more prevalent in Carrie Preston's *29th and Gay* of 2005. An out-of-job gay actor is offered the part of the Chorus in a very low-budget production of *Henry V* which, as the director explains, uses 'all of Shakespeare's text' but is 'sung to modern day original music and set in the Gulf War'. The setting is supposed to be the first Gulf War but, at the end of the performance, a huge American flag is drawn aside to disclose a life-size cut-out of George W. Bush, thus conflating the two Iraq wars fought by the Bush father and son. The performance, attended by a sparse (but fervent) audience, is meant to scorn the way George W. Bush was presented in the media as a new Henry V and to denounce the annexation of Shakespeare to celebrate US belligerence. Similarly, Kevin Costner's post-apocalyptic film *The Postman* (1997) makes use of Henry's speeches after a nuclear war has precipitated the USA into chaos. As ruthless General Bethlehem and his army attempt to control the country by terrorizing the few survivors, an ex-actor (Costner) is challenged to a match of Shakespearean quotations. Henry V's lines come to mirror the situation of hopelessly outnumbered men who refuse to accept Bethlehem's orders.

The Postman is part of a trend of quoting Shakespeare in western movies to symbolize the advance of 'civilization' through the Wild West, the clash of 'high' and 'low' cultures and the American longing to claim a part of the Shakespearean tradition. In John Ford's 1962 western, *The Man Who Shot Liberty Valance*, civilization finds a representative in Dutton Peabody, who owns the local newspaper. Aware that his fellow citizens have chosen not to fight the outlaws led by Valance, he quotes imperfectly remembered versions of the St Crispin's Day and Harfleur speeches before being beaten up by Valance's men. Notably, the legendary Wild West celebrated by Hollywood often tells the story of towns defended by a band of a 'happy few' who win against all odds and become heroes.

At the beginning of Richard Brooks's *Blackboard Jungle* (1955), Richard Dadier (Glenn Ford), a shy veteran, is being interviewed for a teaching job in an inner-city high school with violent pupils. Asked to project his voice more, he recites the beginning of the 'Once more unto the breach' speech (3.1.1–34), which mesmerizes the headmaster, who eventually asks, '*Henry IV*, is it?' A newly poised Richard replies, 'It was *Henry V*, I believe.' Citing Shakespeare's play lands him the job and shows that he has the literary knowledge and leadership skills to teach tough teenagers English.

Henry V can even be quoted in animated films aimed at very young audiences. In David Grossman's *George of the Jungle 2* (2003), produced by Disney, jungle king George tries to convince the wild animals to fight against the bulldozers of developers who are about to destroy their environment. Henry's famous lines are adapted by George in an attempt at a rousing speech: 'We few, we happy few, we band of brothers, for he today that sheds his fur with George shall be George's brother, and other animals in the jungle shall think themselves accursed they were not here.' As no one is inspired, George continues with his more usual style: 'Land all we have. George King. And King ask animals to join him and save homeland.' This time, the animals are convinced and band together to win against the developers. The non-Shakespearean speech is comically revealed to be far more efficient and, as Mariangela Tempera argues, the scene 'crisply encapsulates the difference between George's predicament and Henry's. The King of the Jungle is fighting for his own territory, while the King of

England, with his dubious claim to the French throne, was not.'[34]

Although *Henry V* is obviously not a popular play in France, Jean-Luc Godard cited it in a positive light in his 2001 film, *Éloge de l'amour*, in which a young intellectual interviews journalist and historian Jean Lacouture (who plays himself) about Christianity, the spirit of resistance and Anglo-French families. Lacouture asserts that one of the greatest love scenes ever written is to be found in *Henry V* when the French princess learns a few erotic words in English. Lacouture attempts to strengthen his optimistic view of Anglo-French relations by presenting the marriage of Katherine and Henry as a genuine love story rather than part of a political and financial settlement.

Television series, either from the UK or the US, have cited *Henry V*, generally for laughs. In its first episode, broadcast in 1983, Rowan Atkinson's comic sitcom *Black Adder* includes a parody of both the Harfleur speech and the St Crispin's Day speech before an alternative version of the Battle of Bosworth, thus merging a rewriting of *Henry V* with that of *Richard III*. Episode 5.22 of Joss Whedon's *Buffy the Vampire Slayer* (1997–2003) includes a joking reference to the Agincourt speech. As Buffy has just tried to galvanize her friends before they leave to fight Glory, the hellish goddess, Spike (a made-good vampire who originally came from England) comments that her speech was 'not exactly the St Crispin's Day speech, was it'. Giles (Buffy's mentor and father figure) follows this by quoting, 'We few, we happy few', before Spike finishes the line with his personal interpretation, 'We band of buggered.'

Shakespearean quotes can often be found in the *Star Trek* science-fiction franchise. In *Star Trek*, not only does Shakespeare make it into the future, but he remains a poetic icon and cultural authority for all civilizations, even extra-terrestrial ones.[35] In 'The Defector', a 1990 episode of *Star Trek: The Next Generation*, one man in medieval attire, standing near a tent, quotes from *Henry V*'s night-scene before the battle, asking another, 'Brother John Bates, is not that the morning which breaks yonder?' (4.1.86–7). A clever android then stiffly speaks Henry's lines in a shortened version of the king's disguised visit among his soldiers. The set is soon revealed to be a computer-generated hologram, with Captain Jean-Luc Picard (Patrick Stewart) playing soldier Williams. Picard interrupts the play's rehearsal, but this Shakespearean play-within-the-episode announces that the whole instalment is to be seen as a 'microadaptation' of *Henry V*.[36] Picard is presented as a leader who, like Henry, needs to make difficult choices. He must decide whether to strike first after receiving unverified intelligence about a pending attack and thus risk starting a catastrophic war. He asks the android about the mood of the *Enterprise* crew, because, as he says, 'Unlike King Henry, it is not easy for me to disguise myself and walk among my troops.' After having been reassured, the captain cites one of Williams's lines: 'Now if these men do not die well it will be a black matter for the King, that led them to it' (4.1.143–5). In the end, the enemy backs off and combat is avoided, as if voicing Shakespeare's *Henry V* could spread peace instead of war.

In episode 2.10 of Ronald D. Moore's *Outlander* (aired in 2016), dashing Highlander Jamie Fraser leads the Jacobite army against the British army in the 1745 Battle of Prestonpans. The whole episode is interspersed with moments inspired by *Henry V*, including Jamie's speech before the battle assuring the soldiers they can leave with money if they are not motivated enough; the moral pangs and doubts during the night vigil; the terror at the thought of being outnumbered by a much more powerful army; and the eventual relief (and disbelief) of learning that the day has been won. This serves as a reminder that it is not necessary to hear a single word from the play to recognize its influence on a story, but also that Shakespeare's *Henry V* seems to encompass all war narratives, be they glorifying or not.

If one film cannot render all the ambiguities of Shakespeare's play, the confrontation of different versions conveys the multiplicity of conflicting viewpoints contained in the text and produces a kaleidoscope of meaning. As films of *Henry V* have a life of their own, they also reveal the multifarious facets of the play whose ambivalent nature is bound to feed interpretations of all sorts. *Henry V* appears as a repository of symbolic power and cultural authority about kingship and the cost of war, but its adaptations, appropriations, spin-offs, quotations and misquotations have very rarely gone beyond the confines of British and American cultures, as if the play's screen circulation was still profoundly linked to the English-speaking culture.

5

New Directions

Shakespeare's *Henry V* and Religion

John Drakakis

From religion to ideology and beyond

In his *Characters of Shakespeare's Plays* (1817), William Hazlitt wrote of the figure of Henry V that 'in public affairs, he seemed to have no idea of any rule of right or wrong, but brute force, glossed over with a little religious hypocrisy and archiepiscopal advice'.[1] He went on to call *Henry V* 'but one of Shakespeare's second-rate plays'.[2] T. W. Craik, the Arden 3 editor of the play, observes that a chink in Hazlitt's critical armour can be detected when he 'begins quoting fine passages from this "second-rate" play' and then 'presently commends the hero's "patient and modest" behaviour in adversity'.[3] Craik goes on to suggest that Hazlitt's reason for his dislike of Henry V reaches its apotheosis in the ambivalence of A. C. Bradley's judgement, whereby the 'national hero'[4] is thought to embody, with his 'many fine traits', 'a few less pleasing'.[5] But this is what Bradley also has to say about 'Henry's religion': 'Henry's religion, for example, is genuine, it is rooted in his modesty; but it is also superstitious – an attempt to buy off supernatural vengeance for Richard [II]'s blood; and it is also in part political, like his father's projected crusade.'[6] At the end of the second tetralogy (*Richard II*, *1 Henry IV*, *2 Henry IV* and *Henry V*), Henry's relationship with religion is inevitably complicated by the actions of his forebears.

Bradley's critical discourse, focused as it is on what he takes to be Hal's revealing rejection of Falstaff, contains an outmoded vocabulary, but the ambivalence that he detected in *Henry V* has fuelled much subsequent criticism of the play. At one end of the spectrum we have the heroic king, emphasized in Laurence Olivier's wartime depiction, and reinforced by the Arden 2 editor J. H. Walter's description of him as 'a true Christian monarch'.[7] Indeed, Walter goes on to suggest, in quasi-Bradleyan vein, that,

> If Henry has proved less interesting a man than Richard [II], it is because his problems are mainly external. The virtuous man has no obvious strife within the soul, his faith is simple and direct. He has no frailties to suffer in exposure. It is just this rectitude and uprightness, this stoicism, this unswerving obedience to the Divine Will that links both Aeneas and Henry, and has laid them both open to charges of priggishness and inhumanity. Both are complete in soul.[8]

At the other end of the spectrum are those critics who systematically expose the political investment that the play makes in 'religion'. For example, in their groundbreaking essay, 'History and Ideology: the Instance of *Henry V*' (1985), Jonathan Dollimore and Alan Sinfield undertake a radical rewriting of the metaphysical assumption that lay behind the Tillyardian concept of 'the Elizabethan World Picture' in their observation that 'This metaphysical vision has its political uses, especially when aiding the process of subjection by encouraging renunciation of the material world and a disregard of its social aspects such that oppression is experienced as a fate rather than an alterable condition.'[9] Underpinning their reading of *Henry V* is the important observation that 'the more ideology (necessarily) engages with the conflict and contradiction which it is its *raison d'être* to occlude, the more it becomes susceptible to incorporating them within itself'. This leads, not to a *containment* of subversion, but rather to an exacerbation of contradiction, 'whereby to silence dissent one must first give it a voice, to misrepresent it one must first present it'.[10] This, perhaps, needs to be taken a stage further whereby, in addition to an acknowledgement of the text's inclusivity, it is also necessary to recognize both the investment of the critic and what it is in the text that foregrounds its contemporary relevance.

In an essay that offers a variation on this process in relation to the *Henry IV* plays and *Henry V* and that has come to define the project of new historicism in its formative stages, Stephen Greenblatt addresses what he takes to be 'a sceptical critique of the function of Christian morality in the New World'.[11] The comments on religion in Thomas Harriot's *A Brief and True Report of the New Found Land of Virginia* (1586) are crystallized in his analysis of an anecdote concerning what looks to a modern observer like a fraudulent theological explanation for the occurrence of disease in the colony. The issue revolves around the simultaneous acceptance of religion *and* a 'sceptical critique' of its functioning in 'the New World'. Greenblatt draws from this a general conclusion:

> We may feel at this point that subversion scarcely exists and may legitimately ask ourselves how our perception of the subversive and orthodox is generated. The answer, I think, is that 'subversive' is for us a term used to designate those elements in Renaissance culture that contemporary authorities tried to contain or, when containment seemed impossible, to destroy and that now conform to our own sense of truth and reality. That is, we locate as 'subversive'

in the past precisely those things that are *not* subversive to ourselves, that pose a threat to the order by which we live and allocate resources.[12]

At a later stage in the evolution of new historicism, Greenblatt went on to repeat this perception, but within a revised context.[13] The question is not so much 'how our perception of the subversive and orthodox is generated' as how we make texts from the past contemporary with our own concerns; in short, how we value the relationship between past and present, how we disentangle 'our' voices from those that come to us from history. To this extent 'religion' is an important test case, because it allows us to make structural comparisons between our own and different epochs, comparisons that are sharpened when, as in our own time, cultures, dogmas and ideologies confront each other.

This chapter seeks to chart a pathway through these different interpretations and to show the various ways in which issues of a 'religious' nature are negotiated in relation to the new king Henry V's attempts to reinstate, and reinvigorate, and thereby reauthorize, the discourse of the Divine Right of Kings after the regicide of Richard II. As the second tetralogy develops from *Richard II*, through the *Henry IV* plays, to *Henry V*, a gap looms up between the tawdry political *reality* of monarchical practice and the *myth* of Divine Right that, in theory, protects and sustains monarchical power. *Henry V* discloses, whether intentionally or not, the contradiction between the culturally received myth of the perfect king, in all his heroic glory, and the Machiavellian machinations that gradually expose the link between the figure of the king as an expression of divine purpose and the discursive mechanisms that sustain his role, thereby offering a glimpse of religion itself as an ideological instrument that in hegemonic terms softens the otherwise authoritarian reality of rule and subjection, privileged freedom and 'responsibility' and obligation. Throughout the play the king's vaunted political maturity and the heroism with which he is accredited are systematically undermined by both a practical questioning *and* a recurrent fear of divine retribution. Indeed, although that retribution is, in the event, postponed (a matter already represented graphically in Shakespeare's first tetralogy), it hangs like a Damoclean sword over the entire action of *Henry V*. Indeed, the play's exposure of the sophisticated ruses of power points towards a modern suspicion of hierarchies and the ways in which they are politically sustained and, at times, open to challenge.

Henry V and the tribulations of political theology

Shakespeare's second tetralogy of history plays has, for a considerable time, been embedded in a particular kind of religious debate, centred at one level on the bibliographical instability of specific textual details in the *Henry IV* plays, and on the question of censorship with particular regard to the 'Oldcastle/Falstaff' controversy.[14] Gary Taylor carefully resurrects the documented history of this controversy and draws attention to the ways in which generations of editors, who have opted for the designation 'Falstaff' instead of 'Oldcastle', have effectively obscured 'the much more important fact that he [Shakespeare] portrayed a Protestant martyr as a jolly hypocrite'.[15] The Epilogue in *2 Henry IV* explicitly rejects the association of Falstaff with Oldcastle and, as Taylor points out, both *The Merry Wives of Windsor* and *Henry V* specifically resurrect Falstaff's already extant theatrical identity.[16] The debate has also, more recently, touched on biographical speculation concerning Shakespeare's own Catholic leanings.[17] Another strand concerns itself with the case for and against the figure of Henry V as 'the mirror of all Christian kings' (Chorus 2.0.6).[18] In this two-pronged debate, the 'political theology' of *Henry V* has, until recently, been relegated to a secondary consideration,[19] or has, as we have seen, been focused on a consideration of 'ideology' as the material basis of the operations of political power. The question remains about how, in an age of growing religious and philosophical controversy, where scepticism about the realities of politics could coexist alongside serious revisions of religious emphasis and perspective, a play such as *Henry V*, that advertises its own theatricality in the Globe theatre, a new venue, both presents and represents issues of moment, *including* the relation between ideology and religion. A secondary consideration is how we might read, and indeed appropriate, Shakespeare's play as a means of reflecting our own religious and cultural concerns at a time when religions and ideologies combine and are in open conflict with each other, and where the concerns of radically different configurations of 'church' and 'state' are interrelated in new and ever more disturbing conflicts.

In order to do this we need to retrace our steps, while remaining conscious of the likelihood that the four plays in this tetralogy retain a relative independence from each other. The Shakespearean *Henry V*'s precursor – the anonymous play *The Famous Victories of Henry V*, performed by the Queen's Men – was entered in the Stationers' Register in 1594, but not printed by Thomas Creede until 1598, a year before the first performances of Shakespeare's play.[20] Henslowe records some thirteen performances of 'harey the v' between 28 November 1595 and 15 July 1596,[21] before the rise to prominence of the 2nd Earl of Essex who was appointed Earl Marshal in 1597 and whose failed exploits in Ireland are referred to briefly in the Chorus's comments at the beginning of Act 5 in the 1623 Folio version of Shakespeare's play, but not in the 1600 Quarto version. That early audiences and readers were capable of sophisticated, although to us implausible, allegorical reading is evidenced by the fortunes of Dr John Hayward's *Life and Raigne of Henrie IIII* (1599). Hayward was hauled before the Privy Council to explain an alleged allegorical connection between, on the one hand, Bolingbroke (Henry IV) and Richard II, and on the other, Elizabeth I and the Earl of Essex. Clearly, in historical reading of this kind, context is everything, and Haywood's influential contemporaries (and those who represented the law itself) discerned both a connection *and* a motive behind his biography of Henry IV.[22] It was therefore not necessarily dangerous or contentious to write about Henry V, but the exploits of the play's monarch might resonate in different ways in changing political climates.

What came down to Shakespeare via the chronicles of Hall and Holinshed was a curious amalgam of historical material and contemporary reflection upon which the playwright further elaborated. For example, Hall's *Chronicle* (1548) notes the way in which the new king, Henry V, began his reign:

> Remembryng that all goodness cometh of God, and that al worldly thyngs and humain Actes bee more weaker and poorer then the celestiall powers & heauenly rewardes, determined to begin with some thing pleasant and acceptable to God. Wherefore he first commaunded the clergie sincerely and truly to preache the worde of God and lieu after the same, so that thei to the temporaltee might be the Lanternes of light and mirrors of virtue.[23]

Hall identifies the reasons for the division within Catholicism as being caused by the 'most ambicious desire and avaricious appetite of certain persones calling themselues spirituall fathers, but in deede carnall coueteours and gredy gluttōs aspiring for honor and not for virtue to the proud see of Rome, desiring more to pille then to profite Christes flocke or Christian religion'.[24] Of the Battle of Agincourt, Hall also asserts that the English have God on their side, assisting them in wrongs committed by the French: 'God of his iustice wyll scourge and afflicte them of their manifest inuries and open wronges to us and our realme dayly committed and done.'[25] It is within this context of an assertion of 'right' that the success in the battle is attributed to God: 'And first to geue thankes to almightie God geuer & tributor of this glorious victorie, he caused his prelates & chapelaines first to sing this psalme *In exitue Israel de Egipto etc.* commanding euery man to knele downe on the ground at this verse *Non nobis domine, non nobis, sed nomine tuo da gloriam.*'[26] At no point in the crucial moments of this narrative is there any serious reflection upon the prospect of God delivering justice upon Henry's army for the regicide of Richard II.

The Famous Victories adopts a similar approach, with minimal reference to divine assistance for the English cause. Aside from occasional oaths, such as 'God forbid' (sig. B1^v), 'Gog's wounds' (C1^r, C2^r), 'God's name' (C2^v) and 'God is my witness' (C4^v), the religious implications of the transfer of power from Henry IV to his son are only very lightly touched upon, and even then the emphasis is upon the practical business of securing and maintaining military power:

Hen. 4. God giue thee joy my sonne,
   God blesse thee his seruant,
   And send thee a prosperous raigne.
   For God knows my sonne, how hardly I came by it,
   And how hardly I haue maintained it.
Hen. 5. Howsoeuer you came by it, I know not,
   But now I haue it from you, and from you I will keepe it:
   And he that seekes to take the Crowne from my head,
   Let him looke that his armour be thicker then mine,
   Or I will pearce him to the heart,
   Were it harder then brasse or bollion.

(C4^V–D1^R)

It is the case that in *The Famous Victories* the ambassador from the French king Charles VII is the 'Archbishop of Burges [Bruges]', whereas in the first Quarto of *Henry V* the embassy is comprised of the less explicitly ecclesiastical '*ambassadors from France*', and Henry himself is left to assert his religious affiliation: 'We are no tyrant, but a Christian King, / To whom our spirit is as subject, / As our wretches fettered in our prisons.'[27] Indeed, both in Q1 and F, Henry IV's *political* advice to his son is practical, although it hints at a regicidal past: 'be it thy course to busy giddy minds / With foreign quarrels, that action hence borne out / May waste the memory of my former days' (*2 Henry IV*, 4.5.213–15). That 'memory' is couched in *Henry V* in a much more sustained and explicitly religious discourse within which both the ecclesiastical and monarchical establishments articulate their shared political concerns. For example, the initial politicking of the Archbishop of Canterbury and Bishop of Ely is as much about concern for the retention of their lands as it is the result of their general uncertainties about the behaviour of the new king, hence their interest in fostering a war with France. In exactly the same way, the new king is shown to be following his dead father's political advice, and seeks to 'sanctify' his political strategy by having it authorized by representatives of the Church.

Canterbury's opening address sets the tone for what follows: 'God and his angels guard your sacred throne / And make you long become it!' (1.2.7–8). Henry's response reinforces the link between Divine Right and practical policy:

> My learned lord, we pray you to proceed,
> And *justly* and *religiously* unfold
> Why the law Salic that they have in France
> Or should, or should not bar us in our claim.
>
> (1.2.9–12; italics added)

Henry wishes 'with right and conscience' (1.2.96) to make his claim, and Canterbury responds with an appropriate biblical reference. A war with France will create political problems at home, as Ely acknowledges, but it is Exeter and Canterbury who, between them, provide an analogy between divine harmony and the practical demands of successful government. Exeter's account of 'government' has a long pedigree and is important in this connection:

> For government, though high and low and lower
> Put into parts, doth keep in one concent,
> Congreeing in a full and natural close,
> Like music.
>
> (1.2.180–3)

And it is underscored by Canterbury's extension of the religious discourse into the realm of a politically theological example (augmented by a fable about honeybees) that legitimizes it:

> Therefore doth heaven divide
> The state of man in diverse functions,
> Setting endeavour in continual motion,
> To which is fixed, as aim or butt,
> Obedience. For so work the honey-bees,
> Creatures that by a rule in nature teach
> The act of order to a peopled kingdom.
>
> (1.2.183–9)

In his essay '*Henry V* and the Bees' Commonwealth', Andrew Gurr questions the pertinency of Canterbury's reference to the fable of the bees, and constructs a much more critical view of the king than those who insist upon his consistently 'heroic' demeanour. His conclusion is worth quoting in full:

> The play studies kingship under pressure, utilizing a collection of self-interested wills in a war whose cause is doubtful only in the moral sense. Societies work contrariously. As Mandeville put it much later, all bees are out for themselves. Foreign war has the advantage of drawing all interests into one consent, and of strengthening lenity to friends through harshness to enemies. Henry is in his more secretive and complex way following his father's advice to busy giddy minds with foreign quarrels. That is the way he chooses to release his title from the pressure put on it by his father's doubtful purchase.[28]

Of course, since Gurr, the 'doubtful purchase' to which he refers has become the lever with which to prise open the *ideological* investment in religion that Shakespeare's play makes persistently.

The tension that informs *Henry V*, and that the play carefully diverts into a domestic comedy of marriage, has its origin in *Richard II*. At the point of his accession to the throne as King Henry IV, Bolingbroke (who is also known by the title of the Duke of Hereford) asserts, 'In God's name I'll ascend the regal throne' (*Richard II*, 4.1.114). The ambiguity of Bolingbroke's usurpation is countered directly and forcefully by the Bishop of Carlisle's apocalyptic vision of the consequences of the violation of 'a Christian climate':

> O, forfend it, God,
> That in a Christian climate souls refined
> Should show so heinous, black, obscene a deed.
> I speak to subjects, and a subject speaks,
> Stirred up by God thus boldly for his king.
> My Lord of Hereford here, whom you call king,
> Is a foul traitor to proud Hereford's king.
> And if you crown him, let me prophesy
> The blood of English shall manure the ground,
> And future ages groan for this foul act.
> Peace shall go sleep with Turks and infidels,
> And in this seat of peace tumultuous wars
> Shall kin with kin and kind with kind confound.
> Disorder, horror, fear and mutiny
> Shall here inhabit, and this land be called
> The field of Golgotha and dead men's skulls.
>
> (4.1.130–45)

Henry IV, Parts 1 and *2* act out this vision of chaos alternating between pious intention, a Machiavellian politics and a carnivalesque undermining of political and domestic propriety.

That this is an issue of a divinely sanctioned sovereignty is, perhaps, reinforced by Jean Bodin's comments in the *Six Books of the Commonwealth* (1576, but translated by Richard Knollys in 1606) on the issue of 'the prerogatives of sovereignty':

> ... dukes, counts and all of those who hold of another or receive laws or commands from another, whether by force or legal obligation, are not sovereign. And we will say the

same of the highest magistrates, lieutenant-generals of kings, governors, regents, dictators. No matter how much power they have, if they are bound to the laws, jurisdiction and command of someone else, they are not sovereign. For the prerogatives of sovereignty have to be of such a sort that they apply only to a sovereign prince. If, on the contrary they can be shared with subjects, one cannot say that they are marks of sovereignty. For just as a crown no longer has that name if it is breached, or if its rosettes are torn away, so sovereign majesty loses its greatness if someone makes a breach in it and encroaches on a part of its domain.[29]

We will need to return to this when considering the definition of 'kingship' that Henry formulates on the eve of the Battle of Agincourt. But it is Carlyle's apocalyptic vision of chaos, articulated in and through various episodes in an archetypal Christian narrative, that hovers over the action of *Henry V* in the form of an ever-present threat. To this extent, and whatever the shifts of emphasis, all of the plays in this tetralogy share a common philosophy in that they either depict the direct consequences of regicide or, in the case of *Henry V*, disclose a pathological fear of the contradiction between a ruthless practical Machiavellian politics that responds pragmatically to political challenges, and the necessity of a hegemonic force charged with uniting disparate interests into one unity of consent and 'obedience' to a cause. The war with France can be justified – indeed, *legitimized* – by the ecclesiastical narrative that partakes in exactly the same strategic ploy that Henry himself adopts, and this trumps the claim that this is a 'just' war. But – and this has been generally underplayed in examinations of the play's manifest ideological investments – what gets exposed is a cynical undercurrent that both sustains and provides a critique of that ideology.

That cynical undercurrent is derived from a political truth, an empirical description of historical reality that contemporaries associated with the figure of Machiavelli. Machiavelli reached the popular Elizabethan consciousness through, among other representations, the figure of Machevil, who speaks the Prologue to Marlowe's *The Jew of Malta* (c. 1591). Marlowe's play retained its power in metropolitan England throughout the final decade of the sixteenth century, and Machevil was a combination of charismatic iconoclasm, subversive power and autocratic government and ambition:

> To some perhaps my name is odious,
> But such as love me guard me from their tongues;
> And let them know that I am Machevil,
> And weigh not men, and therefore not men's words.
> Admired I am of those that hate me most:
> Though some speak openly against my books,
> Yet will they read me, and thereby attain
> To Peter's chair; and when they cast me off
> Are poisoned by my climbing followers.
>
> (*Jew of Malta*, Prologue, lines 5–13)[30]

It was Machiavelli who was among the first to be aware of the division at the heart of charismatic leadership *and* of the volatility of all who were subjected to its control. In his citation of 'ancient writers' in *The Prince*, he anticipates the behaviour of Shakespeare's Hal:

> Who says that *Achilles* and many other of those ancient Princes were intrusted to *Chiron* the Centaure, to be brought up under his discipline; the morall of this, having for their teacher one that was halfe a beaste and halfe a man, was nothing else, but that it was needful for a Prince, to understand how to make his advantage of the one and the other nature *because neither could subsist without the other*.[31]

Here, in the 1640 English translation of his text, Machiavelli invokes what Jacques Derrida calls 'a zoophilic perversion' that comes close to affirming that 'bestiality could well be the proper of man'.[32] But Machiavelli also notes the essential *relational* nature that inheres in the concept of 'virtue'. Machiavelli's London publisher drew attention to this in his 'Epistle to the Reader' when he invoked what, by 1640, had become an aphoristic commonplace: 'From the same flower the Bee sucks honey, from whence the Spider hath his poyson.'[33] Dicing with Machiavelli on the English stage exposed to view, and brought into question, the efficacy of a political theology now challenged by a new political realism. Shakespeare's second tetralogy explores the nature of that threat via the mobile figure of the prince (Hal) and the questioning of the links between 'heroism', power and religion that sustained monarchical authority.

In *Henry V*, the conflict with France is clearly *not*, as it would have been historically, between two kings who shared the same allegiance to a Catholic authority. The threat of Henry's seizure of ecclesiastical property is, according to this revealing dramatic representation, one that would deprive the Church of its wealth, and recalls the dissolution of the monasteries during the Henrician Reformation. Canterbury's strategy, therefore, is to pre-empt the seizure of Church lands by offering generous financial assistance to the new king, along with a theologically underwritten authorization of his political intention:

> For I have made an offer to his majesty,
> Upon our spiritual convocation,
> And in regard of causes now in hand
> Which I have opened to his grace at large,
> As touching France, to give a greater sum
> Than ever at one time the clergy yet
> Did to his predecessors part withal.
>
> (1.1.75–81)

What is not quite clear here is whether Canterbury has himself initiated the strategy to invade France as a pre-emptive manoeuvre that is folded into a Christian narrative of 'fall' and 'redemption'. If so, then it is the obverse side of Carlisle's apocalyptic vision of the kingdom, even though it is generated *not* by Henry himself, but by ecclesiastical authority. The historical record available to Shakespeare through Hall and Holinshed points towards the reign of a successful Christian king, but it is the Church that gives that narrative a miraculous and mythological, one might even suggest an illusory, colouring. And yet, against this picture of the perfect king we are continually invited to juxtapose the doubts and anxieties that remain despite his miraculous transformation.

Religion or ideology

We have become familiar with an approach to *Henry V* that aims to strip it of its ideological investments in religion and politics. This has produced various 'cynical' readings of the play, and has occasionally led to the conclusion that whatever its subversive content, our modern perspective insulates us, in the interests of a quietist politics, against the possibility of contamination. This is substantially the view propounded by Stephen Greenblatt in his essay 'Invisible Bullets', a modified version of which appeared in his book, *Shakespearean Negotiations: The Circulation of Social Energy* (1988).[34] Leaning heavily on some aspects of the theory of Michel Foucault, Greenblatt argues that within the boundaries of sixteenth-century religious scepticism, a distinction was made between 'interpretations of experience' that were 'sanctioned' by political and ecclesiastical authority and others that were 'excluded'.[35] On the one hand, Greenblatt drew attention to 'the very core of the Machiavellian anthropology that posited the origin of religion in an imposition of socially coercive doctrines by an educated and sophisticated lawgiver on a simple people'.[36] On the other hand, what allowed commentators such as Machiavelli to retain their faith without hypocrisy was that they could sustain a clear distinction between the origins of religion and its pragmatic usage as an ideological support in acts of conquest and colonization, choosing to emphasize its political efficacy in actual situations. The Hal that emerges from Greenblatt's account into the king of *Henry V* is possessed of a 'charismatic authority' that, 'like that of the stage, depends upon falsification'.[37] What, for Greenblatt, negates the radically political force of this observation is what he takes to be the fact that the theatre – itself 'subject to state censorship' – operated to contain its own 'relentlessly subversive' potential, indeed neutralized its potential effects. In a gesture of comparable neutralization, Greenblatt concludes that '*we* are free to locate and pay homage to the plays' doubts' (emphasis added), but we can only do so 'because they no longer threaten us. There is subversion, no end of subversion, only not for us.'[38]

Given the way that *Henry V* approaches the 'myth' of the Christian king, and given Shakespeare's sophisticated theatricalization of the issue, we need to look more closely at the ways in which ideological critique emerges in the play alongside the effort to re-establish a theologically authenticated monarchy whose own claim to legitimacy remains morally questionable, but politically and practically strong. Indeed, as Graham Holderness has suggested, the play points up 'the artificiality of the dramatic medium' at the same time as it refuses to sanction an acceptance 'of certain dramatic conventions' that permit the unproblematic substitution of 'kingdoms and princes ... in the minds of the audience for the stage and actors'.[39]

In his book *The Sublime Object of Ideology* (1989), Slavoj Žižek argues that Marx's definition of ideology 'implies a kind of basic, constitutive *naïveté*: the misrecognition of its own presuppositions, of its own effective conditions, a distance, a divergence between so-called social reality and our distorted representation, our false consciousness of it'.[40] *Henry V* cannot be accused of *naïveté*, since the 'knowing' prince, and now the 'knowing' king, is fully aware of both his situation and his responsibilities, just as the play itself is fully conscious of its own theatricality. Canterbury's prefatory account of Hal's transformation describes a monarch who combines 'theory' and 'practice':

> Turn him to any cause of policy,
> The Gordian knot of it he will unloose,
> Familiar as his garter, that when he speaks,
> The air, a chartered libertine, is still,
> And the mute wonder lurketh in men's ears
> To steal his sweet and honeyed sentences.
> So that the art and practic part of life
> Must be the mistress to this theoric:
> Which is a wonder how his grace should glean it.
>
> (1.1.45–53)

A sceptical reading of this passage might conclude that the politic Canterbury is himself now duped by a transformation that only *appears* miraculous to the unknowing. On the other hand, Canterbury may be simply *affecting* incredulity while, at the same time, participating in an illusion that, in Žižek's words, fulfils the role of 'structuring their reality, their real social activity'. Canterbury and Ely are perfectly well aware of 'how things really are' but they behave in such a way 'as if they did not know',[41] choosing to align reality with the Christian narrative of redemption while at the same time repressing the implications of the larger scheme of a providential history in the interests of preserving their own politically circumscribed power.

For Žižek, a revisionary reading of the Marxist theory of ideology involves two stages: 'The illusion is therefore double: it consists in overlooking the illusion which is structuring our real, effective relationship to reality. And this overlooked, unconscious illusion is what may be called the *ideological fantasy*' (emphasis in original).[42] Shakespeare gives us too much for us to be satisfied with the claim that the 'illusion' to which the bishops subscribe is simply located in what Žižek calls 'knowledge'. However, their implied cynicism cannot be read as a refusal to believe in 'ideological truth' even though they perceive 'the real state of things'. It is, to use Žižek's words, to occupy a 'cynical distance' that is '[j]ust one way – one of many ways – to blind ourselves to the structuring power of ideological fantasy: even if we do not take things seriously, even if we keep an ironic distance, *we are still doing them*' (emphasis in original).[43] Both the bishops are acutely aware of the capacity of – indeed the *value* of – their religion to legitimize – indeed authorize – power, at the same time as they are prepared to acknowledge the psychological transformation of the new monarch. And yet both, along with the Machiavellian king, are able to sustain the 'ideological fantasy' of the monarch's *essential* divinity as they reconstitute him as a practical ruler capable of plumbing the depths of all knowledge. At no point do they question their own subjection, just as King Henry persists in invoking 'God' as the origin of his own monarchical power. The point is that, at the level of belief, both parties share a fundamental religious allegiance to a providential interpretation of history whose outcome they cannot know. Indeed, Canterbury's claim of Hal's transformation that 'Consideration like an angel came / And whipped th' offending Adam out of him, / Leaving his body as a paradise / T'envelop and contain celestial spirits' (1.1.28–31) reverses the Fall and returns the kingdom to a paradisal garden governed by a king whose person is the distillation and proxy of supernatural authority.

To this extent, Hal's putting aside of his past profligacy resembles a process outlined by Calvin in his *Institutes* where he says that:

> [W]e are very often enjoined to put off the old man, to renounce the world and the flesh, to bid our evil desires farewell, to be renewed in the spirit of our mind [Eph. 4.22–23]. Indeed, the very word 'mortification' warns us how difficult it is to forget our previous nature. For from 'mortification' we infer that we are not conformed to the fear of God and do not learn the rudiments of piety, unless we are violently slain by the sword of the Spirit and brought to nought. As if God had declared that for us to be reckoned among his children our common nature must die![44]

From one perspective, the quasi-Calvinistic path that Hal takes combines a complex knot of fear and renewal of faith as elements that support the elevation of a Machiavellian strategy to the status of 'miracle'. A little earlier, Calvin speaks of the path of 'penance' that 'consists of two parts: mortification and vivification'. Mortification is explained as 'sorrow of soul and dread conceived from the recognition of sin and the awareness of divine judgment', but Calvin then goes on to describe the path of repentance:

> That is when a man is laid low by the consciousness of sin and stricken by the fear of God, and afterwards looks to the goodness of God – to his mercy, grace, salvation, which is through Christ – he raises himself up, he takes heart, he recovers courage, and as it were, returns from death to life.[45]

At one level, the process of heroic myth-making exposes to view what Peter Sloterdijk – in an Althusserian gesture whereby it is claimed that 'God' is invented by 'Man' – has termed 'the religious eye [that] projects earthly images into heaven'.[46] To this extent, the whole play smacks of an early modern cynicism, in which what we might call the 'artfulness' of deceivers is the means by which, in Sloterdijk's terms, '[h]egemonic powers, once they have been induced to start talking, cannot stop themselves from letting out all their secrets'.[47] But while from a modern, post-Enlightenment perspective we might be encouraged to view the matter from a more secular, quasi-scientific perspective, the play invites us to share in – to augment with a real sense of belief – the experience of recognition, doubt, fear and 'vivification', or as Calvin puts it, 'the consolation that arises out of faith'.[48] The bond that the play forges with its audience creates a community that combines nationalism and faith, heroic image and doubt, both of which are put to the test in the suspense of battle and, in its aftermath, require a domestic, sacramental solution for the sins of the flesh.

Notwithstanding Hal's progress, the paradise that Canterbury invokes is less secure than it would seem at first for two reasons: firstly the recurrence of the carnivalesque anarchy of Bardolph, Nym and Pistol, and the heralding in 2.1 of Falstaff's final demise; and then, more dangerously, the treason of Cambridge, Grey and Scroop that immediately follows it. Here demotic anarchy and sinfulness expand their remits to include treasonous deception, and it is Bedford who sets the scene with his remark, "Fore God, his grace is bold to trust these traitors' (2.2.1). Indeed, the traitors are made to rehearse the very judicial process to which they will themselves be subject as their combined duplicity is unmasked. As the three are invited to dissuade the knowing king from showing mercy to a convicted felon, so he responds with a telling quasi-religious allusion to their hypocrisy, in which he imitates the process of divine judgment:

> Alas, your too much love and care of me
> Are heavy orisons 'gainst this poor wretch.
> If little faults proceeding on distemper
> Shall not be winked at, how shall we stretch our eye
> When capital crimes, chewed, swallowed, and digested,
> Appear before us?
>
> (2.2.52–7)

The traitors seek to temper the earthly God's 'mercy' with their 'orisons', but the all-seeing eye of authority turns their logic against them. Indeed, their treason is viewed by the very instigator of its reversal as a repetition of the Fall of Man, when Henry asserts:

> Such and so finely boulted did'st thou seem:
> And thus thy fall hath left a kind of blot
> To mark the full-fraught man and best endued
> With some suspicion. I will weep for thee,
> For this revolt of thine, methinks, is like
> Another fall of man.
>
> (2.2.137–42)

But there is more to the traitors' confessions. Scroop's admission that 'Our purposes God justly hath discovered' (2.2.151) is a displacement that makes of Henry a Christian deity, and himself an exponent of a free will deprived of the constancy to persevere in subjection.[49] Cambridge's confession fudges the issue by admitting one motive while at the same time hinting obliquely at something more substantive in excess of an archetypal Christian narrative, that may be the beam in his judge's eye: 'For me, the gold of France did not seduce, / Although I did admit it as a motive / The sooner to effect what I intended' (2.2.155–7). Grey's confession is the most telling of all in that it divides the subject radically against himself in such a way that it exposes to view the precarious nature of the 'fortunate' Fall:

> Never did faithful subject more rejoice
> At the discovery of most dangerous treason
> Than I do at this hour joy o'er myself,
> Prevented from a damned enterprise.
> My fault, but not my body, pardon, sovereign.
>
> (2.2.161–5)[50]

Each condemns himself by his own understanding of judicial process, thereby allowing the king to justify and to claim capital punishment as part of the larger Christian narrative of Fall, death and repentance as the prerogative of God:

> Get ye therefore hence,
> Poor miserable wretches, to your death,
> The taste whereof God of his mercy give
> You patience to endure, and true repentance
> Of all your dear offences!
>
> (2.2.178–82)

These deflections that occur throughout the play are an important part of a discursive strategy designed to reclaim monarchy for the political theology of 'Divine Right'. Indeed, the projection of a terrestrial politics into the realm of a Christian metaphysics sustains an ideological fantasy, while at the same time acknowledging and relocating a quotidian reality in a post-lapsarian world. This quotidian reality that can both sentimentalize the passing of Falstaff while at the same time acknowledging the far more dangerous political excesses of Pistol and his companions is something that the play never manages to contain. Indeed, the 'offending Adam' and his accompanying deceptions remain, and the crimes that he and his fellow post-lapsarians commit (Bardolph's robbery of a church 'pax', the treason of Cambridge, Grey and Scroop, and Pistol's inventive capitalization on the predations of war) remain as excesses, sins of the flesh, that, as Christine Sukic observes elsewhere in this volume, no appeals to a Christian deity can ameliorate or expunge. Indeed, the final comedy of the marriage between Henry and Katherine appears to be an attempt to legitimize and harness these excesses of 'the flesh', to transform them into a political alliance and to displace blame for man's incessant 'falling' onto a feminine cause. The play's form therefore oscillates between the claims of ideology and the claims of religion in the full confidence that 'divine' retribution for regicide will be exacted at some stage in a future that the theatre audience has already been allowed to glimpse.

Internalizing monarchical anxiety

And yet, for all the play's manifest gesturing in the direction of the exemplary Christian warrior prince, there remains an anxiety and a self-consciousness that persistently undermines the myth's efficacy. In the 'history' of *Henry V* this anxiety comes from the *longue durée* of a secret providential design that, as the play's Epilogue reminds us, will impose itself on Henry's successor. This essentially Protestant reading of history can only acknowledge the secret workings of providence from the evidence of its *effects*. Following the regicide of Richard II, the 'weaknesses' that bedevilled the reign of Henry IV – and that manifested themselves in the struggle for power within what we might call a particular class fraction – remain and threaten in *Henry V*. What in *Richard II* emerges as an emptying out of the theatrical power of the sovereign image, resurfaces in *Henry V* in its renovated form, arriving as it does with the new venture of the Globe theatre. The question is: does the image regain its veracity as a representation of the 'truth' of sovereignty, or is this an attempt by Shakespeare and his company to harness for themselves the power of an image that continues to be necessary but that is now exposed as an early manifestation of 'the seeds of the crystallisation of modern, self-reflexive cynicism'?[51] This might go some way to explaining the anxiety of the protagonist and, in particular, his propensity for self-reflection at a crucial moment in the play.

The first four acts of *Henry V* are mediated in the Folio text by the Chorus, who, after having elicited the complicity of audience members in the spectacle and having stimulated their emotions, steers them through various parts of the action. The first Chorus doubts the theatre's capacity to represent the epic scope of Henry's history: 'But pardon, gentles all, / The flat unraised spirits that hath dared / On this unworthy scaffold to bring forth / So great an object' (Chorus 1.0.8–11). The Act 2 Chorus exposes the fissure between the aspirations to 'honour' and the material, potentially delusional, pressures of war:

> Now thrive the armourers, and honour's thought
> Reigns solely in the breast of every man.
> They sell the pasture now to buy the horse,
> Following the mirror of all Christian kings
> With winged heels, as English Mercuries.
> For now sits expectation in the air
> And hides a sword from hilts unto the point
> With crowns imperial, crowns and coronets,
> Promised to Harry and his followers.
>
> (Chorus 2.0.3–11)

The gap between representation and reality here is stark, exposing as it does the contradiction between the materiality of war and the rhetoric of its representation. What resides 'in the breast of every man' (including that of Henry, 'the mirror of all Christian kings') is the prospect of wealth and power. But more than that, 'honour's thought' is *not* the preoccupation of 'every man'. Within the realm, aspirations to 'honour' are undermined by the activities of an 'unnatural' progeny:

> What mightst thou do, that honour would thee do
> Were all thy children kind and natural!
> But see thy fault France hath in thee found out,
> A nest of hollow bosoms, which he fills
> With treacherous crowns.
>
> (Chorus 2.0.18–22)

Although, as we have seen, this unnatural force is exposed and overcome, the mere *fact* of its existence adds fuel to an anxiety that finally surfaces on the eve of the Battle of Agincourt.

The Chorus in Act 3 returns to the business of expanding, half apologetically, the heroic fantasy and concludes by imploring the audience, 'Still be kind, / And eke out our performance with your mind' (Chorus 3.0.34–5). By this point in the play, the audience is assumed to be of one 'mind', having now been persuaded to enter fully into the theatricalized ideological fantasy that has now been created. But it is the Chorus of Act 4, like that of Act 2, that offers a more extended version of anxiety as it explores the contrasting emotions of heroic longing, foolhardy arrogance, fear and the necessary deception that is designed to persuade. Compared to the confident French,

> The poor condemned English,
> Like sacrifices, by their watchful fires
> Sit patiently and inly ruminate
> The morning's danger; and their gesture sad,
> Investing lank-lean cheeks and war-worn coats,

> Presenteth them unto the gazing moon
> So many horrid ghosts.
>
> (Chorus 4.0.22–8)

We are never told by the Chorus what the inward ruminations of this 'ruined band' are, and it is not clear whether they are themselves 'ghosts' or whether it is the moon that presents to them the ghosts of the past. By this time, what has now become a nervous tic in the play between heroic discourse and a seriously conflicted reality is now internalized, inviting discriminating interpretation. The 'royal captain' visits his troops and displays a demeanour in which 'there is no note / How dread an army hath enrounded him' (Chorus 4.0.35–6). Later in the scene the audience is treated to the variegated substance of these royal visitations, and to an important consequence.

Just before the dawn of the Battle of Agincourt, the disguised King Henry visits his troops. In the dialogue that ensues between Henry and Bates and Williams, the king reveals something about his role as sovereign that implicitly challenges the definition of sovereignty laid out by Bodin in the *Six Books of the Commonwealth*. Williams asks of the king's alleged commander, 'what thinks he of our estate?' (4.1.97). The disguised king responds with a negative evaluation. What follows is a curious piece of indirect discourse in which Henry in disguise offers a speculative account of his own thoughts:

> I think the King is but a man, as I am: the violet smells to him as it doth to me; the element shows to him as it doth to me; all his senses have but human conditions; his ceremonies laid by, in his nakedness he appears but a man; and though his affections are higher mounted than ours, yet when they stoop they stoop with the like wing. Therefore when he sees reason of fears as we do, his fears, out of doubt, be of the same relish as ours are. Yet, in reason, no man should possess him with any appearance of fear, lest he, by showing it, should dishearten his army.
>
> (4.1.102–12)

Bates's response is to reinforce the very distinction between sovereign and subject that the disguised king has attempted to obscure: 'we know enough if we know we are the King's subjects. If his cause be wrong, our obedience to the King wipes the crime of it out of us' (4.1.130–3). Williams proceeds to expand upon the responsibility of the king should his 'cause be not good', and to emphasize the level of consequent personal anxiety: 'the King himself hath a heavy reckoning to make when all those legs and arms and heads chopped off in a battle shall join together at the latter day' (4.1.134–7). Henry's response to Williams's nice juridical distinction is a distinctly Protestant one:

> Every subject's duty is the King's, but every subject's soul is his own. Therefore should every soldier in the wars do as every sick man in his bed, wash every mote out of his conscience; and dying so, death is to him advantage; or not dying, the time was blessedly lost wherein such preparation was gained; and in him that escapes, it were not sin to think that, making God so free an offer, he let him outlive that day to see his greatness and to teach others how they should prepare.
>
> (4.1.175–84)

For Henry, 'war' is God's 'beadle', but all the 'sick' soldier can do is to take responsibility for cleansing his own conscience *in the event* of death on the battlefield. The act of cleansing here is, however, personal and it eschews the public ritual of ecclesiastical mediation: the soldier makes his own preparation and if he is fortunate to survive, then he passes on to others 'how they should prepare'. This does not expunge the psychological or ethical difficulties that Alan Sinfield identified in his account of Protestant thought,[52] mainly because doubt and uncertainty remain, and these anxieties filter down into the practical details of 'ransom'. The effects of this uncertainty emerge in the soliloquy that follows this telling encounter, spoken by a Henry, who, at the start of the speech at least, is still in disguise. The soliloquy begins with what some very recent editors assume to be a quotation:[53]

> Upon the King! 'Let us our lives, our souls,
> Our debts, our careful wives,
> Our children and our sins lay on the King!'
>
> (4.1.227–9)

In the light of what was said in the exchange with Williams and Bates, this is not a quotation but an *interpretation*, and a crude one at that. We may argue that Henry offers here a glimpse of his own inner thoughts in which he *feels* himself to be the victim of his role: 'O hard condition, / Twin-born with greatness, subject to the breath / Of every fool whose sense no more can feel / But his own wringing!' (4.1.230–3). This complaint evolves immediately into a distinction between the 'infinite heart's ease' denied to kings but 'that private men enjoy' (4.1.233–4) and to a reluctant admission that the distinction between the 'private' man and the monarch is nothing more than 'thou idol ceremony' (4.1.237). Here the king is caught on the horns of a dilemma: on the one hand, he wants to be a 'private' man, but on the other hand, he is forced to acknowledge what it is that gives expressive form to his claim to the throne and what he resents as an 'idol'. His anxiety derives from both the uncertainty of his claim *and* the doubt about the true veracity of the 'idolatrous' rituals upon which he is forced to rely. But even more, there is also greater uncertainty that in the forthcoming battle he may die, and that death may not be the 'advantage' that he earlier claimed it could be. Evidently, although Henry can shake off his past, and although thus far his campaign has been successful, there still remains a clear sense of a residual unworthiness and uncertainty that the frank and trenchant utterances of Williams and Bates have ignited.

As Henry convinces himself, reluctantly, of the ritualistic trappings of sovereignty, so he romanticizes the carefree life of his 'subject' whose identity alternates between a free agent and a 'wretched slave':

> No, not all these, thrice-gorgeous ceremony,
> Not all these, laid in bed majestical,
> Can sleep so soundly as the wretched slave,
> Who with a body filled and vacant mind
> Gets him to rest, crammed with distressful bread:
> Never sees horrid night, the child of hell,
> But like a lackey from the rise to set
> Sweats in the eye of Phoebus, and all night
> Sleeps in Elysium; next day after dawn
> Doth rise and help Hyperion to his horse,
> And follows so the ever-running year
> With profitable labour to his grave.
>
> (4.1.263–74)

It is not until his prayer that ends the scene that we are made fully aware of what lies behind this generalized monarchical anxiety: 'O Lord, / O not today, think not upon the fault / My father made in compassing the crown' (4.1.289–91). This is both an acknowledgement of divine presence *and* – something that seriously undermines the myth of the 'heroic' king – an admission of terrestrial unworthiness that produces an anxiety. It is also an acknowledgement that God intrudes, albeit mysteriously, into human history and, by implication – since this is a 'play', a representation – into the art of the theatre. Even though the theatre audience is endowed with a foresight denied to the player king, there is no absolute guarantee that divine justice will always be withheld. Even though the practical politics of the play gesture towards the competence of the sovereign, and even though the play opens up a space for ideology critique, it continues to reinforce the *existence* of God as the ultimate source of the authorization (and withdrawal) of sovereign power. While we may, from a modern perspective, recognize this as an ideological fantasy, we are forced to acknowledge the reality and the expressive power of the model as having some structural relevance for us, despite the *difference* that inheres in its detail. Indeed, in a sense, the introspective king 'blabs indiscreetly', to use Peter Sloterdijk's phrase, and in doing so reveals the state of his own individual 'soul' and his very precarious relation with God in whose hands, it is now claimed, rests the success or failure at Agincourt.

We see very little of the heroics at Agincourt, with the strategy parodied in the exploits of Pistol and exaggerated in the commentary of Fluellen, while Salisbury invokes divine assistance with his 'God's arm strike with us!' (4.3.5). Exeter's report of the deaths of Suffolk and York, especially York's insistence that Suffolk 'tarry' so that '[m]y soul shall thine keep company to heaven' (4.6.16), followed by Henry's '[p]raised be God, and not our strength, for it!' (4.7.86) when he hears of victory, all link their success to divine power. When the list of dead has been completed, Henry is quick to acknowledge the source of victory:

> O God, thy arm was here;
> And not to us but to thy arm alone
> Ascribe we all. When, without stratagem,
> But in plain shock and even play of battle,
> Was ever known so great and little loss
> On one part and on th' other? Take it, God,
> For it is none but thine.
>
> (4.8.107–13)

Here providence and nationalism are brought into alignment with each other, while at the same time Henry, the exponent of the 'stratagem' *par excellence*, is eager to invoke divine responsibility for his remarkable victory. The payment for the price of usurpation is postponed and, temporarily at any rate, the rhetoric of Divine Right and the political theology that sustains it is refurbished, albeit in self-consciously theatrical form. Only then can the play shift genre and register and move into the domestic comedy of the marriage between Katherine and Henry that sows the seed for future dynastic unrest.

The tone of the final Chorus is apologetic, seeking the audience's indulgence for an author who has 'pursued the story, / In little room confining mighty men, / Mangling by starts the full course of their glory' (Epilogue 2–4). We have already seen what that mangling involves: a partisan account that traverses the anxieties and the successes of an angst-ridden sovereign. *Henry V* was one of the first, if not *the* first, play to be performed in the new Globe playhouse, hence its theatrical self-consciousness. The narrative was already endowed with a heroic ethos that has clearly outlived its historical context, but the claim of the new theatre to be able to represent that which, by its own initial admission, was beyond its capacity to represent, is one that we should, perhaps, take with a pinch of salt. We should remember that a 'Henry V [who] is as full of valour as of kindness' and 'Princely in both', as Shakespeare describes him, is not quite the 'hero' that Michael Davies suggests he is.[54] Rather, he is a king racked with anxiety, torn between the 'role' of the sovereign and the personal responsibilities that it demands, fearful lest the crime of his father be visited upon him, and relieved that, albeit temporarily, the rhetoric of Divine Right is reinstated in and through its effects. The rituals are now those of the theatre, and it is the king's 'soul', alternating between confidence and uncertainty in the face of a divine providence, that is both 'known' (since the content of the play is already 'history') and *not* known (in the sense that the theatrical *experience* of the event invites the audience to share in the suspense of the moment). To conclude, the play itself balances the king's successes against his inner turmoil, with the result that we are never quite sure of the full extent of his reformation, or indeed of the incontrovertible efficacy of providential power.

6

New Directions

Making and Remaking the British Kingdoms – *Henry V*, Then and Now

Christopher Ivic

Given its frequent voicing of the words 'England', 'English', 'Englishman' and 'Englishmen', it is hardly surprising that Shakespeare's *The Life of Henry the Fift* – as the play is titled in the 1623 Folio – has been labelled (and appropriated as) the playwright's most patriotic work.[1] However, one would be hard pressed to find many contemporary readers of the play willing to label it unproblematically as such. As recent criticism attests, *Henry V* registers an acute awareness of and, at times, anxiety about the complex geopolitical situation facing England at the turn of the seventeenth century. At the time of the printing of the 1600 Quarto, England's political stability was threatened not only by the unresolved issue of who would succeed the kingdom's aging and childless monarch, but also by a nasty, brutish and lengthy war (now referred to as the Nine Years' War, 1594–1603) raging in Ireland, Queen Elizabeth I's other kingdom. James Shapiro's description of *Henry V* as not 'a pro-war play or an anti-war play' but rather 'a going-to-war play' nicely captures Shakespeare's subtle and nuanced use of the novel genre of the history play.[2] *Henry V* reflects critically on the impact that England's wars, past and present, have had and are having on a real and imagined English polity, one paradoxically represented as besieged by hostile neighbours but also incorporating neighbouring nations. Far from merely celebrating England and Englishness, the Folio version of this play is alert to England's shared past, present and future with Ireland, Scotland and Wales, the nations with which it makes up an archipelago. Shakespeare's final engagement with the genre of the history play during Elizabeth's reign supplies a sustained reflection on nation-building and national identity. It does so, moreover, by drawing upon, as well as interrogating, the myths of English nationhood.

'This imperial throne'

Accompanying the play's frequent voicing of the words 'England', 'English', 'Englishman' and 'Englishmen' is another key word, 'imperial', whose six occurrences in *Henry V* amount to more than in any other of Shakespeare's dramatic works. A variety of definitions apply to the play's various inscriptions of the adjective 'imperial', one of them being 'majestic'. To suggest that 'imperial' is a synonym for 'majestic', however, forecloses reflection on why this particular word surfaces as often as it does in this particular play. When the Archbishop of Canterbury attempts to persuade King Henry to pursue his claim to the French crown, he opens his lengthy speech on Salic Law with a reference to 'this imperial throne' (1.2.35).[3] Again, 'imperial' could be glossed here, as it is in T. W. Craik's Arden edition, as 'majestic', but such a gloss seriously underestimates the play's preoccupation with England's imperial status, not only in relation to the past (Henry's conquest of France) but also, and especially, in relation to the present.[4] In this particular instance, given the early fifteenth-century context in which the play is set, a specific and arguably anachronistic meaning is intended: 'Of or relating to a sovereign state which in its independence and importance ranks with an empire' (*OED* adj. 2a). 'Said chiefly of England, in the 16th cent.,' the *Oxford English Dictionary* adds, 'in assertion of its independence of and sovereign equality with the Holy Roman Empire.' In other words, there is an ideological and patriotic investment in the concept of empire in *Henry V* – that is, empire as understood in relation to nation-building rather than expansion.[5] 'In medieval and particularly sixteenth-century political thought,' Roger Mason reminds us, 'the idea of empire had less to do with territorial aggrandizement than with assertions of national autonomy.'[6] The central action of the play – Henry's claim to the French throne – is, of course, a personal, dynastic claim rather than an assertion of national autonomy, as is exemplified in Henry's assertion, 'May *I* with right and conscience make this claim?' (1.2.96; italics added). Motivating and underpinning Henry's personal decision to invade France, however, is a rhetoric of empire or nationhood – the stuff of post-Armada Elizabethan chronicle history.

The play's use of the word 'imperial' owes much to a signal moment (a moment that Shakespeare and Fletcher would return to in a later and final history play) in the history of English national self-determination and self-definition: King Henry VIII's break from Catholic Rome. The Act in Restraint of Appeals (1533) famously declared that 'This realme of Englond is an Impire'.[7] According to the *Oxford English Dictionary*, 'Impire' is used here to mean 'A country that is not subject to any foreign authority; an independent nation' (*OED* n. 3). Just how much England's nation-formation owed to Henry VIII's break from Rome cannot be overemphasized. However, as Richard Helgerson remarks, although Henry VIII declared England an empire, it took a generation of Elizabethan writers to make sense of that claim: that is, to *write* England.[8] More so than any other of Shakespeare's English histories, *Henry V* marks a valuable contribution to such writing on the nation because, unlike earlier histories, the plot is not dominated by civil broils and competition for the crown. The play is also a product of a moment (or moments) in Shakespeare's career when matters English were giving way to matters British.[9]

At the play's opening, Henry's claim to the French throne as well as a host of French territories is presented as a privilege and right of his royal lineage. Canterbury speaks of

> The severals and unhidden passages
> Of his true titles to some certain dukedoms,
> And generally to the crown and seat of France,
> Derived from Edward, his great-grandfather.
>
> (1.1.86–9)

Canterbury's 'Edward' is King Edward III, whose mother, Isabella, was the daughter of the French King Philip IV, and it is this matrilineal link that in Canterbury's eyes sanctions Henry's claim to the French throne. Given this claim, the play seems representative of what Benedict Anderson terms 'older imaginings' of the pre-national 'hierarchical dynastic realm': in other words, a time before the advent of modern conceptions of the nation.[10] Henry *is* England, and England *is* Henry. In fact, at times in the Folio version of the play, Henry's speech prefix is given precisely as '*England*'.[11] The Prologue's anticipation of the ensuing action is thoroughly monarchical: 'A kingdom for a stage, princes to act, / And monarchs to behold the swelling scene' (Prologue 3–4). The 'peopled kingdom' (1.2.189) that Canterbury imagines is by no means a 'deep, horizontal comradeship'.[12] Even Henry's St Crispin's Day speech (4.3.19–67), which is often read as voicing such comradeship, is representative of early modern England's 'never quite complete passage from dynasty to nation'.[13] Thus, *Henry V* could be cited in support of Helgerson's claim that '[i]n Shakespeare's English history plays . . . England seems often to be identified exclusively with its kings and nobles'.[14] England's social elites, to be sure, constitute the play's central characters: among the 'band of brothers' to whom Henry speaks are his actual brothers and cousins – 'We few', indeed (4.3.60). But, as a host of critics have shown, this manifestly elitist and exclusive play paradoxically abounds in the language of nationhood, if not nationalism.[15]

Consider, for example, the rhetoric that Henry's peers employ to incite their monarch to pursue his claim to the French crown and therefore to prepare an English invasion of France. It begins with Canterbury's stirring invocation of King Edward III as well as his eldest son, Edward the Black Prince:

> Look back into your mighty ancestors.
> Go, my dread lord, to your great-grandsire's tomb,
> From whom you claim; invoke his warlike spirit,
> And your great-uncle's, Edward the Black Prince,
> Who on the French ground played a tragedy,
> Making defeat on the full power of France,
> Whiles his most mighty father on a hill
> Stood smiling to behold his lion's whelp
> Forage in blood of French nobility.
>
> (1.2.102–10)

These powerful lines are seconded initially by the Bishop of Ely – 'Awake remembrance of these valiant dead, / And with your puissant arm renew their feats' (1.2.115–16) – and then by Exeter: 'Your brother kings and monarchs of the earth / Do all expect that you should rouse yourself / As did the former lions of your blood' (1.2.122–4).

These lines are laden with the language of dynasty (the association of lions with English monarchy, for example), but they also draw upon a key component of discourse on the nation: namely, cultural memory. If Henry's social peers expect him to re-enact the military exploits of his exemplary forefathers – Edward III and his eldest son, Edward, the Black Prince – then they do so by drawing upon the constitutive and interpellative power of cultural memory. These lines, moreover, manifest the psychosocial dynamics of the stage, for they serve to rouse not only those on stage but also the theatre's socially heterogeneous audience. Even the play's French King reiterates the play's dominant discourse on Edward, the Black Prince, and he does so – in a voice appropriated by an English actor – that would have been music to the ears of London's theatre-goers:

> The kindred of him hath been fleshed upon us,
> And he is bred out of that bloody strain
> That haunted us in our familiar paths.
> Witness our too much memorable shame
> When Cressy battle fatally was struck,
> And all our princes captived, by the hand
> Of that black name, Edward, Black Prince of Wales.
>
> (2.4.50–6)

By foregrounding French shame at the loss of the Battle of Crécy, these lines could be read as an instance of the play's assertion of English nationhood, as well as an anticipation of English victory at Agincourt. Certainly, Thomas Nashe – whose reflections on the theatre are often cited as an example of the ideological and cultural work performed on the early modern stage – interpreted a stage version of the history of Henry V (probably the anonymous *The Famous Victories of Henry the Fifth*) in such a manner, noting, 'what a glorious thing it is to haue *Henrie* the fifth represented on the Stage leading the French King prisoner, and forcing both him and the Dolphin to sweare fealty'.[16] As much as Shakespeare's version of Henry's reign celebrates the English victory at Agincourt, it is, ultimately, a less glorious, less jingoistic account than its source play(s).

Significantly, the play refuses to allow its audience to forget the loss of England's continental holdings. This is most evident in the Chorus's closing lines:

> This star of England. Fortune made his sword
> By which the world's best garden he achieved,
> And of it left his son imperial lord.
> Henry the Sixth, in infant bands crowned King
> Of France and England, did this king succeed,

Whose state so many had the managing
That they lost France and made his England bleed.

(Epilogue 6–12)

Here is another instance where 'imperial' could mean majestic. However, given that King Henry VI was a dual monarch of England and France, the term 'imperial lord' carries political significance.[17] The inclusion of 'imperial' is also ironic, for during Henry VI's reign England 'lost France' and in the fifteenth century England's continental empire rapidly receded. The play's closing lines, it could be argued, offer its audience a sober reminder of England's loss of Calais, its last hold on the Continent, in 1558.[18] As Jonathan Baldo notes, the loss of Calais marked 'the only period in English history since 1066 when the country had no overseas possessions (except Ireland)'.[19] *Henry V* re-enacts a moment in English history wherein an English army defeats France and the English monarch lays claim to the French throne. The play, however, was produced at a time when the English monarch's hold over continental territories was nil.

Of Wales and Ireland, however, the same could not be said. Shortly after King Henry VIII declared 'This realme of Englond is an Impire', the principality of Wales was politically incorporated into England (1536–43), and the English monarch's title changed from Lord to King of Ireland (1541). Shakespeare's Queen Elizabeth, then, was ruler of England and Ireland, and in 1603, with the accession of King James VI of Scotland to the English throne, Shakespeare and his fellow English subjects – indeed, English, Irish, Scottish and Welsh subjects – became subject to a composite monarchy of England, Scotland and Ireland.[20]

To broaden the concept of empire while still retaining the emphasis on nationhood, I wish to situate the play within a two-island (Britain and Ireland), three-kingdom (England, Ireland and Scotland) and four-nation (England, Ireland, Scotland and Wales) framework. Why? Because *Henry V* – the play itself and the cultural moment(s) of its production – invites, if not demands, such an archipelagic approach. An archipelagic approach to the play entails a rejection of Whig history, which takes for granted the early modern English nation and its national territory since its 'strategy is to focus on the modern nation and its national territory, the realm of England, and to project it backwards into the past'.[21] To approach this play from such an uncritical and ahistorical perspective runs the risk of overlooking the play's rich complexities and contradictions. The 'kingdom of England,' Steven Ellis reminds us, 'had ceased to exist as an autonomous entity in 1066.'[22] 'Since 1066,' he adds, 'England has always been a part of a wider polity, whether a Norman empire or a United Kingdom.'[23] Before James I's accession in 1603, England's dynastic and imperial involvement with the continent and other Atlantic archipelago nations, Ellis argues, must be regarded as a form of English, not British, imperialism: 'the thrust of state-building initiatives by successive English kings in the British Isles down to 1603 was firmly English, not British. The aim was to create "little Englands" in "the Celtic Fringe", not as later to subsume the constituent parts and peoples of the British Isles in a supranational British state.'[24]

In support of Ellis's claim we could point, on the one hand, to the English populations (often referred to in the period as Englishries) in Tudor Wales and the English Pale in Tudor Ireland as instances of English imperialism and, on the other hand, to proposals for a union of the kingdoms of England and Scotland under King James VI and I as an example of British imperialism. For Ellis, therefore, 'state formation was English rather than British before 1603 . . . because successive English kings were traditionally far less interested in developments elsewhere in the archipelago than in their ties with continental Europe'.[25] To a certain extent, Shakespeare's English histories buttress this point: unlike France, the realms of Ireland and Scotland and (to a lesser extent) Wales do not figure repeatedly as sustained settings in the history plays.[26] Still, Ireland, Scotland and Wales (and characters from these nations) figure prominently in Shakespeare's histories, and the foregrounding of archipelagic geopolitics in these plays reflects a historical reality: that is, a politically incorporated Wales; an Irish kingdom/colony; and an independent Scottish kingdom ruled by a monarch potentially in line to the English throne. The 'loss of the French territories in 1449–53', Ellis notes, 'marks a watershed' for the English nation precisely because this loss led to 'the refocussing of English policy from Europe to the British Isles'.[27] Although mostly set in France and dramatizing an English victory over the French, *Henry V* can be read as a play that mirrors this refocusing of English policy.

'Th'ill neighbourhood'

Although France is England's enemy in *Henry V*, the play also represents England as a kingdom or nation under serious threat from its proximate neighbours. The belief in England's inviolable elect-nation status so often voiced in Shakespeare's earlier English histories is less evident – perhaps absent – in this play. The Prologue makes reference to England and France, or more specifically Dover and Calais, as 'abutting fronts' separated by the 'perilous narrow ocean' (Prologue 21, 22). Whereas other history plays invoke the English Channel and the cliffs of Dover to signify an England favoured by both nature and providence, this play, with its numerous references to breaches (more than any other Shakespeare play), presents a porous, vulnerable England. The Chorus's 'O England, model to thy inward greatness, / Like little body with a mighty heart' (2.0.16–17) can and has been read as a nod to England's insularity, if not John of Gaunt's 'sceptred isle' speech (*Richard II* 2.1.40). But do these lines boast of an island kingdom or nation? It is possible to read 'inward' and 'little' as reflecting the fact that England shares a land mass with Scotland and Wales. For a play that traces an English army's voyage across the Channel and, furthermore, recounts a miraculous English victory over the French, the emphasis on inwardness and littleness seems out of place, for it goes against the grain of the play's presentation of an aggressive England on the march.

The play's uneven movement, oscillating between aggression and defensiveness, manifests itself from the start. The scene in which Henry's peers rouse him to pursue his claim to the French throne is troubled by the fear that England's northern border may be breached when the English army is conducting war in France. King Henry is the play's first character to invoke the northern threat:

> We must not only arm t'invade the French,
> But lay down our proportions to defend
> Against the Scot, who will make road upon us
> With all advantages.
>
> (1.2.136–9)

Here Shakespeare follows his source material, which includes the anonymous play *The Famous Victories of Henry the Fifth*, although in this earlier version Canterbury advises Henry to conquer Scotland before conquering France:

> Then my good Lord, as it hath bene alwaies knowne,
> That Scotland hath bene in league with France,
> By a sort of pensions which yearly come from thence,
> I thinke it therefore best to conquere Scotland,
> And *then* I think that you may go more easily to France.[28]

A similar English invasion of Scotland is proposed in *Henry V* by Westmorland:

> But there's a saying very old and true,
>   If that you will France win,
>   Then with Scotland first begin.
> For once the eagle England being in prey,
> To her unguarded nest the weasel Scot
> Comes sneaking and so sucks her princely eggs.
>
> (1.2.166–71)[29]

But any plan to march north is rejected in favour of an invasion of France. Just as he persuades Henry to pursue his French claims, Shakespeare's Canterbury attempts to reassure his monarch of England's ability to defend its borders:

> They of those marches, gracious sovereign,
> Shall be a wall sufficient to defend
> Our inland from the pilfering borderers.
>
> (1.2.140–3)

Canterbury's 'Our inland', acoustically close to 'our England', gives ample voice to the play's concern with England's inter-island relations; indeed, these lines serve as a reminder that the English nation is bordered by Scotland and Wales ('those marches').[30] The Frenchman, Rambures, refers anglocentrically to 'That island of England' (3.7.140), which may be the only instance in the play when England is imagined as an island unto itself.[31] If John of Gaunt's 'sceptered isle' speech presents the nation as coinciding 'with a certain bounded geographic space', such nation-defining boundaries are less distinct, even porous, in *Henry V*.[32]

England's monarch is not initially convinced by Canterbury's claim that 'They of those marches' stand to guard England against 'the pilfering borderers'. In response to his archbishop, Henry is still harping on Scotland:

> We do not mean the coursing snatchers only,
> But fear the main intendment of the Scot,
> Who hath been still a giddy neighbour to us.
> For you shall read that my great-grandfather
> Never went with his forces into France
> But that the Scot, on his unfurnished kingdom
> Came pouring like the tide into a breach,
> With ample and brim fullness of his force,
> Galling the gleaned land with hot assays,
> Girding with grievous siege castles and towns,
> That England, being empty of defence,
> Hath shook and trembled at th'ill neighbourhood.
>
> (1.2.143–54)

The words 'neighbour' and 'neighbourhood' invoke Anglo-Scottish proximity, but such proximity undermines rather than consolidates any sense of neighbourliness. Shakespeare uses the word neighbourhood just three times in his plays and two of those instances occur in *Henry V*, highlighting the Folio text's attention to 'th'ill neighbourhood'.

Although the Quarto version of this speech does not actually employ the words 'neighbour' or 'neighbourhood', it, too, reflects on the concept of 'th'ill neighbourhood':

> We do not meane the coursing sneakers onely,
> But feare the mayne entendement of the Scot,
> For you shall read, neuer my great grandfather
> Vnmaskt his power for *France*,
> But that the Scot on his vnfurnisht Kingdome,
> Came pouring like the Tide into a breach,
> That *England* being empty of defences,
> Hath shooke and trembled at the brute hereof.[33]

Instead of the Folio's 'at th'ill neighbourhood', the Quarto reads 'at the brute hereof'. The primary meaning of 'brute' or 'bruit' here is noise. Given Shakespeare's love of puns, what other possible meanings of 'brute' or 'Brute' are at play? Early modern writers often punned on 'bruit' to signify Brutus or Brute, the legendary Trojan founder and first king of Britain. The *OED* also lists 'A Briton, a Welshman' (*OED* n². 1) as an early modern denotation of Brute. When Pistol twice terms the Welsh captain Fluellen a 'base Trojan' (5.1.19, 32), he is drawing upon the association between the Trojan Brutus and the Britons/Welsh. In the Folio version of the play 'the Scot' poses the main threat to English sovereignty. The Quarto version hints at an England besieged from the north ('the Scot') and the west ('the brute').

The Scottish/Welsh problem is addressed by a wily Canterbury, who proposes that the king divide England's military forces into four, leaving three-quarters of England's defence 'at home':

> Divide your happy England into four,
> Whereof take you one quarter into France
> And you withal shall make all Gallia shake.
> If we with thrice such powers left at home
> Cannot defend our own doors from the dog,
> Let us be worried and our nation lose
> The name of hardiness and policy.
>
> (1.2.215–21)

Why this division into four? With one quarter of the army in France, are the remaining three-quarters or parts in place to guard against the potential threat of not just Scotland and Wales, but also Ireland? This is one way of interpreting Canterbury's division. Interestingly, these lines mark the play's first use of the word 'nation'. In the play's early scenes, English nationhood is measured by the assertion of English sovereignty and military might. A sense of Englishness also emerges in relation (or opposition) to 'th'ill neighbourhood' circumscribing England. As the play progresses, however, Englishness, especially as manifested in its king, becomes a rather fluid identity.

'Made in England'

Who exactly makes up Henry's 'peopled kingdom' (1.2.189)? An obvious answer to this question is his English subjects, represented in the play mostly by an English army. Again and again, the play makes reference to England and the English: 'noble English' (1.2.111); 'the youth of England' (2.0.1); 'English Mercuries' (2.0.7); 'those men in England' (4.3.17). Henry's speech at Harfleur certainly assumes an English army: 'you noble English' (3.1.17); 'made in England' (3.1.26). And in the wake of the Battle of Agincourt, Henry refers to 'our English dead' (4.8.103). Bates, an English soldier, speaks of 'English fools' (4.1.219) and the French speak at various points in the play of an English enemy.

Henry's army, however, is not solely English. The English soldier Williams has a Welsh name, and among the 'English dead' is a Welshman, 'Davy Gam, esquire' (4.8.105).³⁴ Alongside the English captain Gower (another Welsh name) is the Welsh captain Fluellen. In fact, Fluellen's first appearance in the play is followed by the introduction of Gower, as well as an Irish and a Scottish captain, to whom modern editors give the speech prefixes 'Macmorris' and 'Jamy'.³⁵ What are these four captains doing in this play, for they were not 'made in England'? Or, more accurately, what is this *scene* of the four captains doing in this play? (Macmorris and Jamy's appearance is restricted to this one scene.) For some critics, the play's rhetoric of brotherhood extends to the four captains' scene: for example, Jean Howard and Phyllis Rackin note that the 'play is premised on the consolidation of national identity through violence against foreign enemies. In war, Henry's men – whether Irish or English, Scottish or Welsh, yeoman or earl – temporarily become a band of brothers.'³⁶ If a singular 'national identity' is being consolidated in this play, then what exactly is that national identity? Under what inclusive term could an English, Irish, Scottish and Welsh captain be placed? The obvious answer is British, and some critics do speak of Henry's 'British army'.³⁷ Although the word 'British' does not appear in the text, this has not stopped critics from detecting an emergent British identity in the play.³⁸ Claire McEachern notes, for example:

> Perhaps the most evident personification of the coincidence of hegemony and collectivity is that of 'Britain' constructed in the four persons of Captains Fluellen, Gower, Jamy, and Macmorris. Despite Holinshed's report that Welsh and Irish soldiers were to be found fighting on the side of the French at Agincourt proper, and the long-standing alliance of Scotland and France against England, here the four parts of Britain unify, however improbably, in a fight against a common enemy. Individual wills and Britain's traditional regional feuding are subsumed to greater purpose in a fantasy of national (male) bondedness.³⁹

Many critics would take issue with the reference to 'the four parts of Britain', not only on the basis that Ireland is a separate island from Britain, but also because, after James's accession to the English throne, there was considerably less push to include the Irish among a potential sense of Britishness: that is, a British cultural identity inclusive of all of Britain's inhabitants. Many critics would, however, agree with the argument that the play's commitment to an inclusive British identity is both improbable and a fantasy. But is such a commitment that improbable?

Part of the difficulty of answering this question is determining the date of the play's composition – not an easy task. Many editors, as discussed in the Introduction to this book, determine the date of the play's composition by pointing to a topical allusion in the Folio version of the text. This reads:

> How London doth pour out her citizens.
> The Mayor and all his brethren in best sort,
> Like to the senators of th'antique Rome
> With the plebeians swarming at their heels,
> Go forth and fetch their conquering Caesar in;
> As, by a lower but by loving likelihood,
> Were now the General of our gracious Empress,
> As in good time he may, from Ireland coming,
> Bringing rebellion broached on his sword,
> How many would the peaceful city quit
> To welcome him! Much more, and much more cause,
> Did they this Harry.
>
> (5.0.24–35)

Critical consensus maintains that 'the General' refers to Robert Devereux, Earl of Essex, who, on 25 March 1599, was appointed Lieutenant-General and Lord Lieutenant of Ireland, departing for Ireland two days later. An unsuccessful Essex returned to London on 28 September 1599, which is why many editors fix the date of the play's composition to the summer of 1599.[40] But, as T. K. Craik notes in his Arden edition of *King Henry V*, another contender for 'the General' exists: Charles Blount, Lord Mountjoy, who, succeeding the disgraced Essex, departed for Ireland in February of 1600 and was recalled to England on 26 May 1603, having successfully subdued the Irish. Given the reference to 'our gracious Empress' (Queen Elizabeth), these lines were clearly written before Elizabeth's death on 24 March 1603. If we accept that 'the General' is Mountjoy and not Essex, as some critics have, then the play, or parts of it, were written later than 1599.[41] There is also the issue of the four captains' scene. According to Andrew Gurr, 'Macmorris and Jamy do seem to be late inserts in the manuscript which was used to print the First Folio text.'[42] Was the four captains' scene, then, 'added after James came to the throne in 1603, possibly for the performance of the play at court in the 1604–5 Christmas revels'?[43] If the four captains' scene was a Jacobean addition, then this scene adds, to rephrase Shapiro, a having-won-the-war element to the play. Given the play's unevenness and contradictions – that is, a reference to 'the weasel Scot' (1.2.170) and the inclusion of (and Fluellen's praise for) a Scottish captain – perhaps we should treat the Folio version of *Henry V* as a palimpsest: the product of not just a single and fixed cultural moment but a variety of cultural moments, Elizabethan and Jacobean, English and British.

It is tempting to accept that Shakespeare wrote the four captains' scene after James's accession to the English throne, but there is no evidence that he did so. The scene could easily have been written in anticipation of James's succession; one critic, in fact, labels the play 'a premature welcome to the Scottish king'.[44] That the Scottish captain is named Jamy – at one point in F, he is called 'Captain Iames' (TLN 1202–3) – is no coincidence. Fluellen's praise for Captain Jamy could easily be read as pre- or post-1603 praise for King James, who, of course, became Shakespeare's theatre company's patron:

> Captain Jamy is a marvellous falorous gentleman, that is certain, and of great expedition and knowledge in th'anchient wars, upon my particular knowledge of his

directions. By Cheshu, he will maintain his argument as well as any military man in the world, in the disciplines of the pristine wars of the Romans.

(3.2.77–83)

But the four captains' scene is not as harmonious as some critics represent it. One finds little or nothing along the lines of a consolidation of national identity. In fact, the scene erupts into an argument between the Welsh Captain Fluellen and the Irish Captain Macmorris upon the invocation of the word 'nation':[45]

> FLUELLEN Captain Macmorris, I think, look you, under your correction, there is not many of your nation –
> MACMORRIS Of my nation? What ish my nation? Ish a villain, and a bastard, and a knave, and a rascal? What ish my nation? Who talks of my nation?

(3.2.121–6)

What, indeed, is Macmorris's nation? His speech prefix fixes him as '*Irish*' in the Folio, marking Fluellen as '*Welsh*', but his 'hybrid surname' suggests Anglo-Norman descent since, as Michael Neill points out, it is 'a Gallicized [*sic*] version of Fitzmaurice'.[46] Macmorris, therefore, might descend from the Anglo-Norman invaders of Ireland, who mingled with Ireland's native population and, in the eyes of Elizabethans, became Irish. Is '*Irish*', then, an apt speech prefix for this captain? Is Macmorris's 'What ish my nation?' a claim to an (Old) English identity? The word frequently used in the early modern period to describe the ethnic alteration that Macmorris has perhaps undergone is 'degeneracy'.

Although the *word* 'degeneracy' is not used in this play, the *concept* is certainly present. Canterbury's lengthy speech on Salic Law hints at degeneracy: 'Where Charles the Great, having subdued the Saxons, / There left behind and settled certain French' (1.2.46–7). We never learn what comes of this French settlement, but the spectre of degeneracy is a possibility.

The concept of degeneracy, itself underpinned by a rhetoric of civility, occupies a central place in early modern English discourse on the nation. The use of the term 'mere', meaning pure, when delineating Ireland's various inhabitants – that is, mere Irish, mere English – is a prime example of the ideological and cultural work underpinning the concept of degeneracy.[47] Macmorris is by no means the play's only 'degenerate' character or 'bastard'. A wider and all-encompassing degeneracy or bastardy is exposed in *Henry V*, and the attitude towards such alteration and intermingling in the play is surprisingly relaxed.

'Bastard Normans, Norman bastards'

As much as *Henry V* invokes 'England', 'English', 'Englishman' and 'Englishmen', it also bastardizes Englishness. This process of bastardization is particularly evident in the comments made by the play's French nobles, including the Duke of 'Britain' (or Brittany),[48] in relation to their English enemies:

CONSTABLE
    An if he be not fought withal, my lord,
    Let us not live in France; let us quit all,
    And give our vineyards to a barbarous people.
DAUPHIN
    O Dieu vivant! Shall a few sprays of us,
    The emptying of our fathers' luxury,
    Our scions, put in wild and savage stock,
    Spirt up so suddenly into the clouds
    And overlook their grafters?
BRITAIN
    Normans, but bastard Normans, Norman bastards!
    Mort de ma vie, if they march along
    Unfought withal, but I will sell my dukedom
    To buy a slobbery and a dirty farm
    In that nook-shotten isle of Albion.

(3.5.2–14)

The references to Henry's English army as the mixed offspring of Norman invaders and barbarous Saxons displays a sense of cultural superiority, if not arrogance, on the part of the French. But to dissociate these lines from the play's other instances of bastardy and hybridity does the play an injustice. By reimagining the enemy of the French as 'bastard Normans, Norman bastards', they eschew any sense of 'mere' Englishness. There are moments in this play – and these lines constitute one of those moments – where any sense of pure Englishness is deflated.

Also intriguing here is the reference to 'Albion', a term often used in the early modern period to designate the island of Britain. In the 1600 Quarto, the lines delivered by the French Duke of 'Britain' are instead given by Burgundy, who states:

> Normanes, basterd Normanes, mor du
> And if they passe unfoughtwithall,
> Ile sell my Dukedome for a foggy farme
> In that short nooke Ile of England.[49]

Why does the Folio use 'Albion' instead of England? What did Albion signify to Shakespeare and his contemporaries at the time these lines were written (whenever that was)?

'Albion' is frequently invoked in the succession literature that greeted King James upon his arrival in England. Consider, for example, the following lines from John Savile's *King Iames his entertainment at Theobalds*:

> Besides your sacred selfe, doth bring with you,
> A Kingdome never knit to these till now,
> As *Camdens Brittaine* tells, since *Brutus* daies,
> Than let us thank our God, sing Roundelaies,
> England rejoyce, Saint *George* for England shout,
> For joy Saint *Denis* crie, all Fraunce throughout.
> Double thy joys o *Albion*, harke *Cambrian* banks,
> God hath enrich'd thee with a Prince, give hartie thanks.[50]

For Savile, as for many other panegyrists in 1603, James's reign marked a reunification of Britain, and Albion was one of the names used to signify a united England and Scotland. But not all of James's English subjects were so accommodating. In an unpublished anti-union tract, Henry Spelman, a parliamentarian and a founding member of the Society of Antiquaries, writes:

> [I]f the honorable name of England be buried in the resurrection of Albion or Britannia, we shall change the goulden beames of the sonne for a cloudy day, and drownde the glory of a nation triumphant through all the worlde to restore the memory of an obscure and barberous people.[51]

If *Henry V* is anything to go by, Shakespeare seems less troubled than Spelman with the resurrection of 'Albion' and its supposedly 'barberous people'.

'An Englishman?'

In the wake of the Battle of Agincourt, King Henry resumes a dispute with the common English soldier Williams, who wears a glove as a gage in his cap. The glove is Henry's, but Williams is unaware of this because his initial dispute with Henry occurred while the king was in disguise as 'a gentleman of a company' (4.1.39). No longer in disguise, Henry asks Williams why the glove is in his cap. Williams explains that the glove is a gage, and Henry then asks whether Williams's quarrel was with 'An Englishman?' (4.7.122). Williams responds in the affirmative, but the audience already knows the answer: of course the king is an Englishman. This, though, is slightly disingenuous: Henry may be positioned as an Englishman, but he nevertheless has other national identities mapped on to him, and also lays claims himself to non-English identities. For example, at the close of the play, Henry hails the French king as 'our brother France' and the queen as 'our Sister' (5.2.2); the

French king responds with 'brother England' (5.2.10); and, if modern editors are to be believed, the queen with 'So happy be the issue, brother England / Of this good day and of this gracious meeting' (5.2.12–13). However, the queen's appellation, 'brother England', is only to be found in the 1632 Second Folio: the 1623 First Folio text reads 'Brother Ireland' (TLN 2999), and the 1600 Quarto does not contain the passage at all. Macmorris, it seems, is not just Henry's subject but also his countryman.

There is also the issue of Henry's claim to Welshness. The historical King Henry V might have been 'porn at *Monmouth*' (4.7.11), but he had 'no Welsh ancestry whatsoever'.[52] Shakespeare's stage version of Henry is another story, not least when, informing Pistol that he is not 'of Cornish crew' (4.1.51), Henry states, 'I am a Welshman' (4.1.52). As I discussed earlier, King Edward III and Edward, the Black Prince, are invoked early in the play in the service of English nationhood. However, after England's victory over the French at Agincourt, the subject of the two Edwards re-emerges to a different purpose:

FLUELLEN Your grandfather of famous memory, an't please your majesty, and your great-uncle Edward the Plack Prince of Wales, as I have read in the chronicles, fought a most prave pattle here in France.

KING They did, Fluellen.

FLUELLEN Your Majesty says very true. If your majesty is remembered of it, the Welshmen did good service in a garden where leeks did grow, wearing leeks in their Monmouth caps, which your majesty know to this hour is an honourable badge of the service; and I do believe your majesty takes no scorn to wear the leek upon Saint Tavy's day.

KING I wear it for a memorable honour,
For I am Welsh, you know, good countryman.

FLUELLEN All the water in Wye cannot wash your majesty's Welsh plood out of your pody, I can tell you that. God pless it and preserve it, as long as it pleases his grace, and his majesty too!

KING Thanks, good my countryman.
FLUELLEN By Jeshu, I am your majesty's countryman.
(4.7.91–110)

In this instance, the invocation of cultural memory produces, if not a British Henry, then an English monarch who aligns himself with more than a single national identity.

This scene is by no means the play's sole instance of an attitude to nationality that is marked by accommodation. The French princess, Katherine, despite her 'broken English' (5.2.243), is termed an 'Englishwoman' (5.2.122) – marking the only use of this word in all of Shakespeare's work. Moreover, when Henry speaks prophetically to Katherine of his future male heir, that child is imagined as hybrid: 'Shall not thou and I, between Saint Denis and Saint George, compound a boy, half French, half English' (5.2.204–5). If the historical marriage of Henry V to Katherine of Valois resulted in a son, the 'half French, half English' Henry VI, then – importantly – Katherine's second marriage, to the Welsh Owen Tudor, produced (via Edmund Tudor and Margaret Beaufort) King Henry VII, England's first Tudor king, the grandfather of Queen Elizabeth I and an English monarch who was most certainly of Welsh and French descent.

'These kingdomes'

Henry V is particularly striking in its use of language that anticipates discourses about an Anglo-Scottish union that emerged shortly after King James's accession to the English throne. The suggestion that Shakespeare 'was writing to a royal, unionist commission' may be an overstatement.[53] But the language that surfaces at the play's conclusion – a language notably absent from the 1600 Quarto version – either anticipates or reflects much of the pro-union discourse. The French king and queen's addresses to Henry emphasize concord and union (although the word 'union' never surfaces in the play). Consider, for example, the French King's lines on Henry's impending marriage to Katherine:

> Take her, fair son, and from her blood raise up
> Issue to me, that the contending kingdoms
> Of France and England, whose very shores look pale
> With envy of each other's happiness,
> May cease their hatred, and this dear conjunction
> Plant neighbourhood and Christian-like accord
> In their sweet bosoms, that never war advance
> His bleeding sword 'twixt England and fair France.
>
> (5.2.342–9)

Although this speech clearly concerns England and France, the reference to 'neighbourhood' echoes the play's earlier use of this word (in the phrase, 'th'ill neighbourhood') in reference to the contending kingdoms of England and Scotland. Given the Folio's inclusion of a Scottish captain, these lines can be read as evincing a reassessment of Anglo-Scottish neighbourliness.

The French queen's lines to Henry about his marriage also, unsurprisingly, smack of the language of union:

> God, the best maker of all marriages,
> Combine your hearts in one, your realms in one!
> As man and wife, being two, are one in love,
> So be there 'twixt your kingdoms such a spousal
> That never may ill office or fell jealousy,
> Which troubles oft the bed of blessed marriage,
> Thrust in between the paction of these kingdoms
> To make divorce of their incorporate league;
> That English may as French, French Englishmen,
> Receive each other. God speak this amen.
>
> (5.2.353–62)

The key words in these lines – spousal, paction (covenant), league – all invoke a sense of union by interweaving marital and political metaphors, ones favoured by authors of pro-union tracts as well as King James himself.[54] Although the play cannot be said to inscribe a sense of Britishness – no character, for example, claims to be British, and none of the characters declare themselves a subject born in Britain, as Sir Francis Bacon did to King James – it does, though, reject rigid, monolithic identities in favour of fluid, collective identities. Put another way, 'What ish my nation?' is offered up to the play's audience, not in a declarative but rather an interrogative mode. In Shakespeare's final engagement with the history play, his co-authored *King Henry the Eighth* (1613), Archbishop Cranmer's prophecy of England's future monarchs hails James as a sovereign who will 'make new nations' (*King Henry VIII*, 5.4.52). In its exploration of England's shared past, present and future with its Irish, Scottish and Welsh neighbours, Shakespeare's final English history play is less committed to forging or consolidating a sense of Englishness than his earlier histories. Indeed, in its openness to national differences, *Henry V* participates in making and remaking communal identities.

7

New Directions

'His Bruised Helmet and his Bended Sword' – The Politics of Criminality and Heroism in *Henry V*

Christine Sukic

There is no doubt that the historical Henry V was part of the heroic imagination in early modern England. When, in 1606, the poet Robert Fletcher dedicated his 'lives' of the *Nine English Worthies* to Henry, Prince of Wales, he described Henry V as follows:

> This Henry was a king whose life was immaculate, and his living without spot, this king was a prince whom all men loved, and was of none envied, this prince was a Captaine against whom fortune never frowned, nor mischance once

spurned: this Captaine was a Shepheard, whom his flocke both loved and obeyed. This Shepheard was such a Justitiary, that he left no offence unpunished, nor good desert unrecompenced & fully rewarded. This Justitiary was so feared, that all rebellion was banished, and Sedition suppressed.[1]

While it might be argued that Fletcher's depiction of Henry V's immaculate life was politically motivated, helping to affirm the bright future of Prince Henry, whose biography concluded the volume,[2] many other portraits of the medieval king from the same period provide evidence of Henry's exemplary heroism, locating him, for example, as 'the mirror of Christendome & the glory of his country ... the floure of kynges passed, and a glasse to them that should succeede'.[3] In contrast, and therefore surprisingly, Shakespeare's *Henry V*, even though it evinces an awareness of a concept of kingship and heroism inherited from ancient and medieval textual cultures, compels its audiences to reconsider King Henry's position as a stable, political, legal and moral centre in the play.

In 1817, William Hazlitt pertinently suggested that theatrical audiences might struggle to love or admire Henry, whom he described as a hero 'ready to sacrifice his own life for the pleasure of destroying thousands of other lives'. Asking his famous question, 'How then do we like him?', he answered by pointing to the intrinsically oxymoronic quality of the king:

We like him in the play. There is he a very amiable monster, a very splendid pageant. As we like to gaze at a panther or a young lion in their cages in the Tower, and catch a pleasing horror from their glistening eyes, their velvet paws, and dreadless roar, so we take a very romantic, heroic, patriotic, and poetical delight in the boasts and feats of our younger Harry, as they appear on the stage and are confined to lines of ten syllables; where no blood follows the stroke that wounds our ears, where no harvest bends beneath horses' hoofs, no city flames, no little child is butchered, no dead men's bodies found piled on heaps and festering the next morning – in the orchestra!⁴

Nowadays, we mainly remember the famous paradox of Henry as a 'very amiable monster', but Hazlitt also importantly remarked on Henry's inherent dramatic quality when he called the king a 'splendid pageant' upon which 'we like to gaze'. Stressing the notion of spectacle, Hazlitt's remarks can serve as a starting point from which to question and try to define the nature of spectacle and power in Shakespeare's play, and they can be related to Lorna Hutson's analysis of the sacredness of the monarch's body in sixteenth-century historical drama, and her reassessment of readings of Ernst Kantorowicz's work.⁵

Kantorowicz, in *The King's Two Bodies*, developed a theory of medieval political theology based on two ideas of the body: the 'body politic' (the king's ineffable ability to rule and unite the nation) and the 'body natural' (a king's mortal, human body).⁶ Pushing back against critics who adopted Kantorowicz's ideas, Hutson contests the assumption that monarchs in Elizabethan history plays personified 'the early modern body politic or the sacred "justice" on which it [was] founded'.⁷ Instead, she argues, it was the audience that took precedence and who were asked by the playwrights and acting companies to participate in a collective construction of justice, 'to infer and imagine characters' intentions and motives, as well as their unstaged "facts" or deeds'.⁸ Following Hutson, and invoking this close relationship between drama and penal practice, I argue that Henry V's oxymoronic quality (Hazlitt's 'very amiable monster') can be envisaged as an aesthetic, as well as an ideological, issue. Shakespeare deliberately constructs a changing, ungraspable monarch, refusing to take sides on the question of the king's heroism. This could be seen as a political necessity – a Tudor playwright's refusal to be seen to legitimize the Lancastrian Henry IV's son – but it is also an aesthetic choice – one that invokes the multiplicity and instability of reality. The king's heroism is thus difficult to perceive because it is aesthetically fraught with dramatic interferences that prevent spectators from getting a fully developed image of Henry's character, instead presenting them with a fragmentary portrait. Dramatically, the play seems to construct a rigid legal frame that forces the king to act with a sense of equity, since he is supposed to represent legal power. However, at the same time, the constant intrusion onto the stage of representations of criminality – as well as of moral and legal faults that are either part of the plot or echo what is presented as Henry's wayward youth – tend to blur our perception of the king.

The play, then, points to an aesthetic and political decentring of the monarch. As Kevin Sharpe has shown, the performance of monarchical power in the early modern playhouses perhaps helped to change popular perceptions of authority and rule, deflating the king's sacredness.[9] As an early modern depiction of a medieval king, Shakespeare's Henry is displaced from the legal centre of the play and his body is not overtly endowed with any kind of mystical Divine Right. His anti-heroic aspects could therefore be interpreted as a political comment on Shakespeare's part, underlining that, in the early modern period, political legitimacy was moving from a reliance on a sacred, moral order towards a pragmatic programme of statecraft that, as in *Richard III*, reveals the king's modernity.[10]

Legal discourse in *Henry V*: 'the answer of the law'

Henry V's opening scenes establish a legal atmosphere that sets the tone of the play. After the epic tone of the Prologue with its promises of 'puissance' and 'mighty monarchies' (Prologue 20–5), the play's first scene – which turns out to be a discussion between two churchmen over legal matters concerning Church possessions – has a bathetic quality. This impression is compounded in 1.2, where the audience is confronted by a long speech in which the Archbishop of Canterbury attempts to convince the king, once and for all, that the latter's claim to France is legitimate and grounded within a legal framework. Canterbury's refutation of the Salic Law is an impressive sixty-three lines long (1.2.33–95). Its style is copious, with an accumulation of proper nouns and lists, as well as long sentences amplified by run-on lines. The archbishop begins by insisting that the Salic Law – defined as '*In terram Salicam mulieres ne succedant*' or 'No woman shall succeed in Salic land' – does not pertain to 'the realm of France', asserting instead that 'the land Salic is in Germany' (1.2.38–44). He then observes that 'the Salic land' (1.2.56) became a French possession many centuries after the death of King Pharamond, the originator of the Salic Law, following this up with a long, genealogical list of French kings who set a precedent for Henry's claim because they held their royal status 'in right and title of the female' (1.2.89). The legal tone of these highly rhetorical passages confirms the link between classical rhetoric and the law.[11] The cataloguing technique here is related both to an epic style supposed to announce the martial action to come – as heroes were typically named in epics as a sign of their valour – but also to the judicial style, which required a list of details when evidence was brought forward and which grounded claims to inheritance on genealogical precedence.[12]

Canterbury's highly rhetorical passage, with its repetitive style and its enumerative form, creates a dramatic impression of legal authority, underpinned by the dignity of the Church. The presence of the two churchmen on stage, presumably decked out in robes and mitres so that the audience could immediately identify them, generates a hegemonic vision of the law akin to that at stake in Holbein's famous painting, the *Ambassadors*. Like the audience of Shakespeare's play, viewers of Holbein's painting are confronted with a representation of power embodied in two ambassadors. Moreover, again like Shakespeare's audience, the painting's viewers soon discover signs within the art work that contradict its vision of worldly power and influence – such as, for example, the famous anamorphic skull in the foreground that invokes ideas of the transitory nature of human life.[13] In sum, Shakespeare's *Henry V* is set within the framework of a rigid legal discourse, but that framework is gradually complicated and qualified, so that by the end of the play it is difficult to perceive it as a stable point from which to interpret and react to the characters and action.

The dialogue between the Archbishop of Canterbury and the Bishop of Ely also mobilizes a series of quasi-proverbial assertions, which point to the king's twofold character: the mad youth and the solid king. Ely, for example, invokes a natural metaphor when he observes that the 'strawberry grows underneath the nettle', while 'wholesome berries thrive and ripen best / Neighboured by fruit of baser quality' (1.1.60–2). He continues:

> And so the Prince obscured his contemplation
> Under the veil of wildness, which, no doubt,
> Grew like the summer grass, fastest by night,
> Unseen, yet crescive in his faculty.
>
> (1.1.63–6)

Although it suggests a dialectic of legitimacy/illegitimacy, this language also underlines the instability of meaning. Ely's metaphors draw on organic images of fruit and grass to suggest that the binarisms they encode are natural and inevitable (wholesome/base; contemplation/wildness), but their repetition – the fact that Ely has to use more than one metaphor to express his idea – points to a fragmented order of things made up of irreconcilable elements. The dialogue between Ely and Canterbury also serves as a mnemonic prompter for the audience, who get a vivid reminder of Henry's 'wildness' and madcap youth. In other words, the heroic discourse surrounding the king is undercut, from the first, by reminders of his youthful excesses, as is emphasized by Canterbury and Ely's stichomythic exchange of one-liners:

CANTERBURY The King is full of grace and fair regard.
ELY And a true lover of the holy Church.
CANTERBURY
　The courses of his youth promised it not.

(1.1.22–4)

Furthermore, in the midst of his speech on the Salic Law, which is supposed to give Henry free rein in his French enterprise, the Archbishop of Canterbury, in Patricia Parker's words, 'repeatedly foregrounds usurpation and illegitimacy'.[14] This is most notable in Canterbury's evocation of Hugh Capet, the French 'usurper' who '[c]onveyed himself as heir to th' Lady Lingard, / Daughter to Charlemagne' (1.2.74–5). Canterbury thus provides the spectators with counter-exempla of kingship, and reminds them of Henry's imperfection. At this point, we cannot help but be reminded of the image of Henry's father as, in the words of Hotspur, 'this vile politician Bolingbroke' (*1 Henry IV*, 1.3.239), or, in the words of Richard II, 'this thief, this traitor, Bolingbroke' (*Richard II*, 3.2.47).

The disjunction between the heroic and non-heroic views of Henry is nowhere more evident than at the start of the Folio text's Act 2. As John Drakakis has explored in this book, Act 2's Chorus 'exposes the fissure between the aspirations to "honour" and the material, potentially delusional, pressures of war'. Although the Chorus gives us an epic evocation of war and the image of passionate young men filled with a desire to fight, the first scene of Act 2 provides a complete change of atmosphere. Meeting in a London street, the characters, Nym and Bardolph – who speak in prose – do not embody the martial spirit evoked by the Chorus. On the contrary, a legal question immediately arises concerning the relationship between Nym and Nell Quickly. As Bardolph puts it, Nym was 'troth-plight' – or betrothed – to Quickly (2.1.20), but 'Ancient Pistol' (2.1.3) has married her. In his edition of the play, J. H. Walter describes troth-plighting as a 'more binding contract than the modern engagement',[15] so it is clear that the relation between Pistol and Quickly is based on a breach of contract and, when Pistol appears on stage, the dialogue soon turns to an exchange of invective and abusive language, undercutting the glorious, martial promise of the earlier Chorus.

The presence of the comic episodes in the play should not surprise us since this dramatic fragmentation is in keeping with a Shakespearean aesthetics of mixing comedy and tragedy, alongside the presentation of different social classes. Here, this dramatic freedom is stressed by the introduction of the character of Captain Fluellen, described by T. W. Craik as 'both comic and respectable'.[16] Fluellen is at once versed in the disciplines of war and involved in a comic plot. However, the comic dimension of the play constitutes more than just a structural element, since it is related to King Henry's wild youth, itself often treated as a comic subject – as it is in *1 Henry IV*. Through its comic subplot, *Henry V* constantly reminds us of the 'courses of [Henry's] youth' (1.1.24) and these linger as a kind of original sin that identifies Henry as an outlaw.

The memory of Henry's wild past also serves as a check to a straightforward reading of the play's motifs of oath-making and oath-breaking, bearing witness – as does the breach of Nym's plighted troth to Mistress Quickly – to the ways in which the passage of time complicates and sometimes overturns the possibility of keeping an oath. The play might bear witness to several rigid legal frameworks, but it also shows how promises and oaths can come into conflict with each other, how time negates outdated systems, and how, therefore, prescriptive language is always inevitably contingent. In *1 Henry IV*, the young Henry was associated with Falstaff, that embodiment of unstable language, whose famous speech on 'that word "honour"' revealed his rhetoric to be based on the impalpable instability of air (5.1.131–40). In *Henry V*, Shakespeare seems to be striving to stress the moral and linguistic difference between King Henry and his earlier, youthful incarnation, but the insubstantiality of language remains to trouble this presentation.

'Keep thy word!': a rhetoric of obligation

Henry V is obsessed with legal oaths that invoke the binding ties of religion. As Joseph M. Lenz has remarked, '*Henry V* begins with the king's resolve to invade France, "by God's helpe", and it closes with his prospective marriage to Katherine, consummating the success of the initial oath.'[17] The play is therefore framed by language that is endowed with binding lawfulness and with the certainty – on Henry's part – of being right. This 'language of right'[18] is particularly obvious at the end of Act 1 when Henry answers the ambassadors of France and evokes his 'rightful hand in a well-hallowed cause' (1.2.294). After his triumph in the wars, and as he looks forward to his marriage, Henry ends the play with a final insistence on oaths, observing to Katherine, his future wife, 'may our oaths well kept and prosperous be!' (5.2.368). As a play that dramatizes the successful accomplishment of the oath with which it began, *Henry V* seems to validate its king as one who keeps his promises. However, it also dramatizes the cost involved in keeping oaths, showing them sometimes to be prescriptive and disciplinarian.

Captain Fluellen is the main proponent of the strict and necessary adherence to laws, rules and oaths. In 4.1, the soldier Williams challenges Henry, his disguised king, to a duel, throwing down a glove to him with the prescriptive imperative, 'Keep thy word' (4.1.218). Meeting Williams later and seeing that he is wearing the glove in his cap, Henry (now undisguised) asks Fluellen his opinion about whether Williams should, by necessity, keep his oath. Fluellen replies:

> Though he be as good a gentleman as the devil is, as Lucifer and Belzebub himself, it is necessary, look your grace, that he keep his vow and his oath. If he be perjured, see you now, his reputation is as arrant a villain and a jack-sauce as ever

his black shoe trod upon God's ground and his earth, in my conscience, la!

(4.7.135–41)

Fluellen is the main proponent of this rhetoric of obligation and oath-keeping in the play. He provides the audience with a constant discourse on the binding laws of war, offering a slightly obsolete and comical vision of heroism, even while he views perjury as a crime.

Fluellen's knowledge of 'the disciplines of the wars' (3.2.59) also becomes a leitmotif. 'Discipline' is a word that can be applied both to instruction and punishment, and Fluellen invokes its more severe meaning at 3.6.55 when he tells Pistol that 'discipline ought to be used' for Henry's erstwhile companion, Bardolph, who must be punished with death for his crime of stealing.[19] Throughout the play, Fluellen demonstrates not only his own rigid vision of the art of war, but also his legal brain – for him, wars should be conducted according to 'the true and anchient prerogatifs and laws of the wars' (4.1.68–9). This places war within a distinct, and ancient, legal system, according to which anybody not abiding by the 'laws of arms' (4.7.2) can be hanged or beaten, as Pistol is in 5.1. Notably, in 3.2, Fluellen lauds the Scottish Captain Jamy's 'knowledge in th'anchient wars' (3.2.79), denigrating Captain Macmorris as an 'ass' who has 'no more directions in the true disciplines of the wars, look you, of the Roman disciplines, than is a puppy-dog' (3.2.70–3). Suggesting to Macmorris that they should undertake 'a few disputations ... as partly touching or concerning the disciplines of the wars, the Roman wars' (3.2.96–8), Fluellen insists on the importance of theoretical and judicial knowledge as a precedent to action. Macmorris, on the other hand, responds that there 'is no time to discourse', since 'the town is besieched, and the trumpet call us to the breach, and we talk, and, be Chrish, do nothing' (3.2.106–10). In *Discipline and Punish*, Michel Foucault draws our attention to the relation between punishment and war, writing that the 'right to punish ... is an aspect of the sovereign's right to make war on his enemies', justifying this assertion by adding that 'the physico-political force of the sovereign is in a sense present in the law'.[20] In the case of *Henry V*, it is not merely Henry who represents the disciplines of war (in all senses of the word), but also Fluellen who upholds them, and whose preoccupations, in the comic subplot, help to draw attention to the interconnections and contradictions between legal theory and pragmatic action.

Although Lenz is right to see *Henry V* as a space in which Henry's opening oath is brought to fruition, the play dramatizes a moment in which Henry appears to violate military law. In 4.7, Fluellen is profoundly distressed to learn that the French have killed the English army's luggage boys, lamenting, "Tis expressly against the law of arms' (4.7.1–2). In revenge, we learn, Henry has ordered 'every soldier to cut his prisoner's throat' (4.7.9–10). Although Conal Condren excuses this as 'Henry's prudent action to safeguard [his troops'] lives where possible', Theodor Meron notes it is 'most likely in violation of the contemporary laws of war'.[21] Whatever its motives, this action reveals Henry as a king who reacts to circumstance, even if this means breaking the rules. While he endorses the execution of Bardolph, his former friend and drinking companion, with the impersonal statement, 'We would have all such offenders so cut off' (3.6.106), he does not necessarily hold himself to the same standards as he holds his subjects when it comes to keeping oaths and laws. The episode with Bardolph provides us with a twofold understanding of Henry, since, on the one hand, the king endorses his former friend's sentence and therefore acts as a keeper of the law, but, on the other hand – precisely because he used to be one of Bardolph's drinking companions – we are reminded of Henry's boisterous youth and his association with seedy characters in *1 Henry IV*. The shadowy memory of his past frequently undercuts our interpretation of the king's actions in *Henry V*, coming close to the surface in moments such as his apparently comic hoodwinking of Williams and Fluellen. Here, Henry again breaks an oath for he does not follow through on his promise to fight a duel with Williams, instead palming Williams's glove off on to Fluellen and binding the latter to a promise to fight in his stead (4.7.151–6). This play is filled with criminal acts and characters, as I will discuss, and the subplot helps us to understand the human costs of Henry's choices, showing how the law works contingently for the benefit of some and not others. The prescriptive nature of law and language, in the play, is at once asserted and called into question: although Shakespeare has the king assert his capacity to keep his oaths, he also introduces contradictory images that stress the insubstantial quality of language and its reversibility.

'He longs to eat the English': staging crime, digesting heroism

As Hazlitt noted and as Christopher Warren has more recently shown, there was no unanimity about Henry V's greatness either in Shakespeare's time or afterwards. Drawing on the work of Alberico Gentili, an Italian lawyer and Protestant refugee in England, Warren states that Shakespeare's Henry 'quite possibly *was* a war criminal for some early modern elites, to say nothing of the moral intuitions of early audiences more generally'.[22] While Henry certainly achieves heroic status in some scenes of Shakespeare's play, not least because he is successful in his French campaign, he is far from completely heroic, appearing to us as a modern king made of flesh and blood. This notion of flesh and blood is deeply embedded in the play, coming to the fore through a persistent imagery of food, consumption and digestion that, while most strongly felt in the comic subplot, also spills over into the main plot and our interpretation of the play's king.

In what follows, I will compare the imagery in the comic subplot involving Bardolph, Pistol, Nym and the Hostess in 2.1 – when Nym discovers that the Hostess has gone back on her word to marry him – with the scene of the aristocratic conspirators, Cambridge, Scroop and Grey, in 2.2, since the latter scene is also based on the idea of a breach of contract and on the incapacity to keep one's word, although the two cases have different implications. Food metaphors are used in both scenes. In 2.1 Nym immediately deflates any notions of heroism that might accrue to owning a sword, when he insists that he 'dare not fight' (2.1.7) even though Pistol has done him wrong. His sword, he says, is 'a simple one', an 'iron' that will 'toast cheese' (2.1.8–9). By associating his sword with cookery and food, Nym divorces himself from the asceticism usually associated with heroism, such as that evoked in Octavius Caesar's speech to Mark Antony in Shakespeare's *Antony and Cleopatra*.

Apostrophizing Antony with a recollection of the commander's former valour in the Roman wars, which Octavius believes has given way to the luxury of an Egyptian retirement, the latter observes:

> It is reported, thou didst eat strange flesh,
> Which some did die to look on. And all this –
> It wounds thine honour that I speak it now –
> Was borne so like a soldier, that thy cheek
> So much as lanked not.
>
> (*AC*, 1.4.68–72)

While Antony's present feasting in Egypt is perceived as a diminution of his heroic valour, his past capacity to maintain an ascetic diet without flinching or losing weight is part of his former heroic identity, based on the inalterability of his heroic body. Nym's toasted cheese, in contrast, marks the subplot character as non-heroic and is in keeping with the comic genre with which he is associated, especially as cheese was marked as a lower-class food and 'generally considered unwholesome except when eaten as an aid to digestion'.[23] Cheese might even be termed the definitive anti-heroic food: in *Troilus and Cressida*, for example, Thersites – an anti-heroic character who is called 'my cheese, my digestion' by Achilles (*TC*, 2.3.39) –

refers, in his turn, to the ancient Nestor as 'that stale old mouse-eaten dry cheese' (*TC*, 5.4.9–10).[24] Toasted cheese and martial heroism, in other words, are inimical.

In 2.1 of *Henry V*, Nym's reluctance to use his sword for anything other than toasting cheese, quickly opens out into other bodily images. Bardolph promises to bestow a breakfast on Pistol and Nym as a way of reconciling them, and Nym, still eschewing a fight, resignedly draws attention to his own mortality when he asserts that he will 'live so long as [he] may' and, 'when [he] cannot live any longer', he will 'do as [he] may' (2.1.11–16). Bodily images proliferate as Pistol arrives and insultingly suggests that, instead of trying to reclaim Mistress Quickly from him, Nym take himself off 'to the spital' and 'from the powdering-tub of infamy / Fetch forth the lazar kite of Cressid's kind' (2.1.75–7). Invoking the heated tubs used to treat venereal disease, alongside the notion of a prostitute affected with leprosy, Pistol distracts from his own involvement in oath breaking by suggesting that Nym take up with a woman similar to the unfaithful Cressida, who deserted Troilus for Diomede during the siege of Troy and who was punished by contracting leprosy.[25] In other words, the scene's frequent recourse to food metaphors and allusions, as well as the images of disease associated with the hospital, make the body of prime importance here, drawing attention to it, not as a sacred body, but as a body of flesh and blood.

At the end of the scene, when Falstaff's Boy enters and announces that his master is sick, this invasion of fleshy excess and disease is confirmed. Prince Hal's former alter ego still appears as an anti-heroic body, but the bon vivant is now afflicted with a disease that spreads out onto the stage, and when the Hostess suggests that Falstaff will 'yield the crow a pudding one of these days', we realize that his end is near (2.1.87–8). The bodily corruption and human finitude of these anti-heroic characters is later confirmed, first by the hanging of Bardolph and Nym, and then by the news that the Hostess 'is dead i'th' spital / Of malady of France' (5.1.82–3). At once recalling the faithlessness of Cressida in its evocation of venereal disease, the line also evokes a sense of heartbreak: the 'malady of France' that has overcome the Hostess is not just syphilis, but also Henry's French war, which has killed her friends. While we might see the disappearance of these characters from *1 Henry IV* as a sign that a new age is dawning for England under the rule of the newly heroic Henry V, Pistol's bitter closing words belie this interpretation. 'Honour is cudgelled' (5.1.86), he asserts, resolving to return to England as a bawd and cutpurse, and concluding: 'patches will I get unto these cudgelled scars, / And swear I got them in the Gallia wars' (5.1.89–90). The criminality that lurks under the surface of *Henry V* is constantly associated with disease and decay – like his wife's, Pistol's scars are potentially those of syphilis not combat – but the poverty that accompanies it is shown to be a systemic problem brought on by the very discourse of heroic action that criminality is positioned against.

Juxtaposed against this scene's deflation of its Chorus's promises, the next scene (2.2) moves the political and moral associations of food into the main plot when the Duke of Exeter explains how the conspirator Lord Scroop has been 'dulled and cloyed with gracious favours' (2.2.9). Later in the scene, Henry himself says he is grieved that Scroop has 'with jealousy infected / The sweetness of affiance' (2.2.126–7). 'Sweetness' here is a polysemic word, whose main senses are related to food, and which echoes the idea of cloying found at line 9. Although Henry will later assert that 'when lenity and cruelty play for a kingdom, the gentler gamester is the soonest winner' (3.6.110–12), he has already, with these conspirators, experienced the dangerous ramifications of a policy of friendly sweetness in contrast to martial asceticism. The use of food imagery in the play creates a metaphoric network evoking the corruption of the flesh and the erosion of morals that undercuts the vision of the body as the main seat of heroism. This is in keeping with the decline of heroic values in the early modern period and in Shakespeare's plays in particular.

The ideal vision of the Greek warrior's body, valued, as Tonio Hölscher has demonstrated, 'both as a real and as a symbolic factor in military fighting',[26] and endowed with a beauty that Jean-Pierre Vernant has described at length,[27] is no longer relevant to the idea of the Shakespearean military hero, be it Hector in *Troilus and Cressida* – whose body loses its beauty after he is killed in anti-heroic fashion by Achilles – or Antony, whose body 'cannot hold this visible shape' (*AC*, 4.14.14). In *Henry V*, in a similar vein, Shakespeare comically and facetiously has Fluellen turn a reference to Alexander the Great into a grotesque picture of a half-man, half-animal creature, 'Alexander the Pig' (4.7.12). Fluellen's remarks about Alexander deflate the idea of the monarch's greatness, shifting its signification from honourable virtue to physical mass: 'Why, I pray you, is not pig great?' he asks in response to Gower's correction that Alexander's title was not 'the Pig' but 'the Great' (4.7.14). 'The pig, or the great, or the mighty, or the huge, or the magnanimous, are all one reckonings,' he says, 'save the phrase is a little variations' (4.7.15–18). By association, King Henry becomes mere flesh, and his greatness is viewed only in terms of size. This is reinforced by the subsequent reference to Alexander's action of killing his friend Clytus, while in his 'ales' and 'cups' (4.7.37–8), in a manner that unmistakably reminds the spectators of the king's earlier career as Prince Hal, associating him with base excess rather than heroism.

Most studies of Alexander in medieval and early modern English literature evoke the ambiguous image of a ruler who was at once a tyrant and an exemplum of heroic courage. Henry Peacham, for instance, compares James VI and I's son, Prince Henry, to Alexander, in one of his dedicatory emblems from *Minerva Britanna* (1612).[28] Charles Russell Stone remarks that this was a common association for the Stuart prince, observing that 'No English prince or king had inspired such frequent or hopeful comparisons with Alexander the Great as did Henry Frederick, Prince of Wales.'[29] On the other hand, Samuel Daniel, in his *Philotas* (1605), drew on classical sources to create in Alexander a tyrannical monarch who thought himself a god. It is therefore not surprising that

Shakespeare should have chosen such an ambiguously heroic figure with whom to compare Henry. He often treated Alexander derisively: in *Hamlet*, for example, Alexander's body is turned, after death, into a stopper for a beer-barrel (*Ham*, 5.1.194), and, in *Love's Labour's Lost*, during the play of the Nine Worthies, the role of Alexander is taken by the curate, Nathaniel, and is thus associated with a ridiculous and pompous character (*LLL*, 5.2.560). The mention of 'Alexander the Pig' in *Henry V* can therefore be understood as another moment in which classical references to traditional heroism are undermined.

Noting that Plutarch 'hymns Alexander's heroical, epical qualities, but also takes the opportunity to portray the king's darker side', Judith Mossman suggests that Plutarch's *Life of Alexander* influenced Shakespeare's play.[30] Even if the extent of that influence is not far-reaching, it is interesting to look at Shakespeare's choice of direct references to Alexander, most of which are not particularly flattering for Henry. These associations do not imply, as Mossman rightly concludes, that Shakespeare deliberately wanted to denigrate the character of Henry through negative associations with Alexander, but rather that the playwright was trying to create a composite being, whose truth was made up of several layers of meanings. Shakespeare, for example, indirectly refers to Alexander's heroic dimension when Henry, in his speech at Harfleur, asks his men to emulate their fathers, who fought like 'so many Alexanders':

> On, on, you noblest English,
> Whose blood is fet from fathers of war-proof,
> Fathers that like so many Alexanders
> Have in these parts from morn till even fought.
>
> (3.1.17–20)

By turning the unique quality of the traditional hero into a multitude of 'Alexanders', Henry disperses heroic substance instead of stressing its distinctive quality.[31] In other

Shakespearean plays, we have seen the singular importance of the heroic name.[32] In *1 Henry IV*, for example, Hotspur asserts, 'My name is Harry Percy', before his final single combat with Hal (*1H4*, 5.4.60), and when Hamlet is trying to adopt a heroic vein, he exclaims, 'This is I, / Hamlet the Dane' (*Ham*, 5.1.246–7). In *Henry V*, in contrast, everyone – and no one – is an Alexander; everyone – and no one – is a hero.

Most of the heroic *topoi* of the play deflate the idea of a stable heroism based on traditional values, and Henry himself points to the disappearance and illusory nature of heroism. In war, he says tellingly, we should '*imitate* the action of the tiger' (3.1.6; my italics). The hero is not necessarily heroic by nature, but he should be able to look like a hero. Henry, then, could be compared to the comical characters of the play, especially Pistol, who is, according to Gower, 'an arrant counterfeit rascal' (3.6.60) with only the 'form of a soldier' (3.6.68), who 'con[s] perfectly in the phrase of war' (3.6.74). The king is no longer a traditional hero, but a modern, Machiavellian one. In *The Prince*, Machiavelli states that appearing to be virtuous is more important than actually being virtuous: 'A ruler, then,' he notes, 'need not actually possess all the above-mentioned qualities, but he must certainly seem so.'[33] The king's heroism is not essential, but it partakes of a kind of modern civility of heroism that Baltasar Gracian would later define, in a maxim of his 1647 *Oráculo Manual y Arte de Prudencia* – or 'Art of Worldly Wisdom' – as 'to do, and make it appear'.[34] Henry, then, as the play's food and disease imagery help us to understand, is a fallible human being before he is an heroic king.

'This frail and worthless trunk': the king's anti-heroic body

As Gisèle Venet has noted, while Shakespeare, in *1 Henry IV*, opposed Hotspur's obsolete heroism to Hal the modern Prince, in *Henry V* he recreated a similar opposition between King

Henry and the French Dauphin.[35] The French prince's values stress the aesthetic aspect of the body – heroic therefore beautiful – but this beauty proves to be unsuccessful in battle and has no efficacy. Henry's body, in contrast, is not endowed with any magic or sacred character, but is subject to the vicissitudes of time and humanity. It is, as he defines it himself, a 'frail and worthless trunk' (3.6.153).[36] As the play's final Chorus notes, the king ultimately refuses to bear his 'bruised helmet and his bended sword' in triumph through London, because he is 'free from vainness and self-glorious pride' (Chorus 5.0.18–20). By refusing to march in triumph, Henry – like Coriolanus – refuses to give in to traditional *topoi* of wounds as heroic signs.

As Sarah Covington has pointed out, wounds received in martial conflict have long been considered to be badges of honour, what she calls 'an expression or signature of war'.[37] There was definitely a change in this perception of soldiers' bodies in the early modern period, when wounds lost some of their symbolic meaning and came to be considered as medical rather than heroic signs.[38] Michel Foucault contends that the 'discipline' of war that was imposed on those bodies changed traditional heroic values, observing that the 'soldier is above all a fragment of mobile space, before he is courage or honour'.[39] It is, of course, not violence itself that is new in this conception of war, since violence was part of an aristocratic ethos that may be seen as part of the culture of honour.[40] It is, rather, a new conception of the body that is at stake. Henry's heroism and his capacity to render justice are separated from the nature of his body. When Henry renders justice, he does not do so within the fiction of a 'royal mysticism', as Hutson calls it,[41] but, rather, within multiple perspectives that prevent the spectators from getting a uniform vision of the king.

Henry's heroic body, we realize, is a social construction submitted to conflicting representations of heroism, including in its Christian dimension, which is deeply ambivalent in the play. To give just one example, while Henry claims to be 'no tyrant but a Christian king' (1.2.242), he also represents himself as Herod against the Innocents (3.3.40–1), a 'reversal of Henry's special claim to Christian imagery'.[42] What is more, Henry's identity is constructed within the framework of a society in which the body is no longer the seat of heroism. As the representative of the English state, Henry's body is subjected to the defects and the moral disabilities of his people, all the more so as, in his younger days, he used to associate with some of them. Even if, as E. F. J. Tucker has pointed out, Canterbury's speech at the beginning of the play (1.1.24–31) can be read as an allusion to 'the King's Two Bodies and especially to the concept of the monarch as a *character angelicus*',[43] the play's conflicting values prevent any sense of monarchical legitimation. The Chorus's 'exaggerated glorification' of Henry V is balanced, as Peter B. Erickson notes, by 'a burlesque undercutting of the king'.[44]

In *Henry V*, heroism is thus subjected to various forms of representation. It is first staged as the traditional, nationalistic, patriotic image of a young king, but this image is questioned both by the presence of anti-heroic and sometimes criminal characters, and by the play itself, since the practice of power, seen through the prism of the theatre, is deflated as an illusory representation. The use of characters from the lower classes anchors the play in the reality of England, with criminality, heroism's apparent opposite, appearing as something to which heroism nevertheless is inevitably bound. Heroism in the play is treated as a 'real' issue, rather than as a heroic *topos* – that is, it is not removed from people's realities, but is readily available to, and spread out among, a 'band of brothers' (4.3.60), its failures leading to poverty, disillusionment and crime. Moreover, the scenes involving Henry's former companions point to the unheroic presence of the body in the play, a body that is not symbolically enhanced by a sacred dimension.

It is ultimately the nature of Henry's heroism to be shaped by the instability of the play's meanings, as made evident by the contradiction between a strong legal discourse and the representation of crime and moral corruption. In 1.2, having been convinced of the legitimacy of his claim over France, he ponders his own heroic destiny:

> Either our history shall with full mouth
> Speak freely of our acts, or else our grave
> Like Turkish mute, shall have a tongueless mouth,
> Not worshipped with a waxen epitaph.
>
> (1.2.231–4)

Here Henry opposes the silence of being unknown to the copious style associated with fame.[45] In doing so, he points towards the vulnerability and the instability of his status as a hero. His heroism is not innate, but depends on circumstances: either he will succeed and will be part of the heroic chronicle of his country, or he will fail and fall into oblivion. Heroism, he realizes, has to be written and cannot be 'tongueless'. Shakespeare's play, rather than endorsing Henry as an unquestionably valiant and heroic king, draws attention to the cross-overs between concepts of heroism and criminality, in the process providing us, as Hazlitt noted, with a complex picture of this 'very amiable monster'.

8

New Directions

Agincourt and After – The Adversary's Perspective

Elizabeth Pentland

Shakespeare's *Henry V* has exerted an outsized influence on popular and scholarly perceptions of the Battle of Agincourt (or rather Azincourt, as it is known in France), particularly among readers and playgoers in the English-speaking world.[1] The contemporary French perspective on Agincourt, however, has received little attention. Philippe Contamine gathered a large array of material in French about Agincourt, mostly from the French chronicles, in his 1964 classic study *Azincourt*.[2] Anne Curry's collection, *The Battle of Agincourt: Sources and Interpretations* (2000), brings together, for the first time in English, excerpts from the major English and French accounts of Agincourt.[3] Yet to this day the perspectives offered by fifteenth-century French poets and chroniclers – who 'sing a rather different song' about Agincourt from their English counterparts – remain virtually unknown to readers of

Shakespeare.[4] Although several French historians have studied some of these sources, there is to date no systematic consideration of the French material about the reception of Agincourt by contemporary French witnesses available to the English-speaking reader.[5] As this chapter will argue, though, even a cursory glance at contemporary French writing about Agincourt yields valuable new insights into the representational politics of Shakespeare's play. My purpose, then, is to bring leading fifteenth-century French poets – writers like Charles d'Orléans, Christine de Pizan and Alain Chartier – into conversation around the topic of Agincourt in order to foreground the range of opinions and the shared concerns that characterize this neglected body of writing. What we find there necessarily complicates our view of Henry's 'famous victory' by revealing a France beset by internal divisions, more vulnerable than Shakespeare lets on, and, in the end, wholly unprepared for the losses it incurred on that terrible day.

The catastrophic loss at Agincourt was cause for considerable soul searching among those in France who survived the battle and witnessed its aftermath. In the fifteenth century, it was the subject of much commentary by French chroniclers and poets, who generated a literature of consolation and of blame as the nation sought to come to terms with the defeat. French sources suggest that somewhere between 4,000 and 10,000 French soldiers were killed at Agincourt, among them the 'flower' of the French nobility.[6] The battle lasted just a few hours. This meant, in effect, that high-ranking families, including those closest to the French crown, suffered sudden and devastating losses, sometimes across generations. In many cases, too, the writers who responded to the battle witnessed the grief of those families – their noble or royal patrons – at first hand. For example, Christine de Pizan's patron, Marie de Berry (c. 1375–1434), the Duchess of Auvergne and later of Berry, lost her husband, her son and her son-in-law at Agincourt.[7] At least two of her cousins were also killed, while another, Jean VII d'Harcourt, was captured.[8] Indeed, inconsistencies among the chronicle accounts about the fate of some of the nobility reflect the debilitating confusion that must have reigned among relatives as they sought information about their loved ones after the battle.⁹

The trauma associated with Agincourt may account for the fact that it goes unnamed in the works of several writers discussed in this chapter.¹⁰ For example, the Religieux of Saint-Denis, a fifteenth-century chronicler, fails to name the field of battle, but writes at considerable length about 'la cause première de ce malheur' [the principal cause of this misfortune].¹¹ Christine de Pizan's *Epistle of the Prison of Human Life* – a 'major work' on the subject – clearly has Agincourt in mind when it alludes to this 'present time of affliction' and to the 'great number of very noble and worthy royal princes of France' who were 'dead or captive' as a result of fighting the English. However, it does not mention the battle. Christine's contemporary, Alain Chartier, also refers to Agincourt without naming it: the speakers in his *Book of the Four Ladies* simply refer to the battle as 'la malheureuse journée' (the woeful day).¹² Similarly, the poet Charles d'Orléans, nephew to the French king Charles VI, only obliquely refers to it. In his 'Ballad LXXXIV', discussed below, he writes of the 'great evils and destruction which war has brought about throughout the whole country' without ever mentioning Agincourt by name.¹³ He did not need to: the context for his writing would have been obvious to his addressee (fellow captive Jean de Bourbon) and other readers. However, not all chroniclers avoided the name: the anonymous *Journal d'un bourgeois de Paris* (*c.* 1449) mentions Agincourt four times in entries written between 1415 and 1419; and Jean de Bueil's *Le Jouvencel* (1461–6) refers explicitly to 'a battle in France called Agincourt, which King Henry of England won because he kept up the spirit of his men . . . whilst the French did the opposite'.¹⁴ So, while some writers seem consciously to have avoided the specifics of the battle, there exists, all the same, a considerable body of work devoted to making sense of the Agincourt catastrophe.

Agincourt was just one in a series of traumas for France at the start of the fifteenth century. Part of the problem was leadership: from 1392 until his death in 1422, the French king, Charles VI, was regularly incapacitated by mental illness. His periods of madness, characterized by delusions, paranoia and violence, led to intense struggles between the two most powerful factions at the French court, with the followers of the Duke of Orléans on one side (the Orléanist or Armagnac faction), and those of the Duke of Burgundy on the other (the Burgundian faction). Queen Isabeau, Charles VI's wife, attempted to mediate between the two sides, while her eldest son, the Dauphin, Louis, Duke of Guienne, stepped in to govern during the king's periods of incapacity.[15] In 1407, after the assassination of Louis I, Duke of Orléans (brother of the French king and father of Charles d'Orléans, the poet) by the Duke of Burgundy's supporters, France descended into civil war.[16] Several of Christine de Pizan's works, including *An Epistle to the Queen of France* (1405) and her *Lament on the Evils of Civil War* (1410), document the effects of this conflict in French politics.[17] Later, the Religieux of Saint-Denis linked the defeat at Agincourt to divisions within the French nobility, noting that it was 'common knowledge that it was the obstinate divisions between the princes which inspired in the enemy the boldness to dare to invade the kingdom'.[18] Henry V embarked for France in August 1415 and captured Harfleur on 22 September. There can be no doubt that the French king's fragile health during this period contributed to Henry's success. As the Religieux remarked afterward, 'That dishonor, it would seem, must reflect on the king, who is nevertheless quite excusable; for it is certain that his courage would have prevented this disaster, had the state of his health allowed'.[19] The Battle of Agincourt took place on 25 October. Then, on 18 December, the Dauphin – who (*pace* Shakespeare) had not fought at Agincourt – died, probably of dysentery, an event that was 'almost as great a blow as the battle itself to a kingdom whose king was incapable of ruling due to insanity'.[20] Notably, the English invasion did not forestall the civil war. Indeed, in 1418, both Christine de Pizan and Alain Chartier were forced to flee Paris because of their political affiliations after the

Burgundian faction gained control of the city. During this time, the Armagnac party was decimated by violence and disease: in May and June 1418, supporters of the Duke of Burgundy killed more than 2,000 Armagnacs, including Bernard d'Armagnac himself; yet another massacre in August was soon followed by an epidemic that killed 'tens of thousands'.[21] A year later, in September 1519, the Duke of Burgundy was murdered by his opponents. Finally, in May 1420, five years after Agincourt, the Treaty of Troyes was signed – which the English chronicler Raphael Holinshed called 'a truce tripartite ... accorded between the two kings and the duke, and their countries' – disinheriting the Dauphin and recognizing the English King Henry V as heir to the French crown.[22] Shakespeare ignores or downplays the internecine conflict and disarray that characterized French politics during this period. In *Henry V*, this serves to heighten the drama of Henry's unlikely victory at Agincourt and his subsequent conquest of France, while also reinforcing English stereotypes about French 'lightness' and 'inconstancy' on the battlefield.

While the French accounts of Agincourt tend to focus on the failures of their own side, they also offer details about Henry V's character and reputation that are relevant to Shakespeare's play.[23] Charles d'Orléans, Christine de Pizan and Alain Chartier have little to say about Henry V, but chroniclers like the Religieux of Saint-Denis, Enguerran de Monstrelet, Jean de Waurin and Jean Le Fèvre expressed respect and even admiration for his leadership. However, in journal entries for 1419 and 1420, the anonymous writer known as the 'bourgeois de Paris' is scathing in his treatment of Henry and his occupying forces, repeatedly calling them 'cruel tyrants', reminding his readers of England's 'great hatred' and ancient enmity toward France, and claiming the invading English had done 'as much harm as the Saracens'.[24] At one point, he appears to claim that the English are committing sacrilege 'a hundred times a day', profaning churches, eating meat on Fridays, raping women, and 'roasting men and children'.[25] 'In short', he writes, 'I believe that the tyrants of Rome, like Nero, Diocletian,

Dacian [i.e. Trajan Decius] and the others, were never as tyrannous as they are and have been' (129).

More typically – and in contrast to the 'bourgeois de Paris' – the Religieux made a 'comparison between the indisciplined conduct of the French soldiers of the period and the good order of the English'.[26] Several chroniclers, including the Religieux and, later, Jean de Bueil, claimed that Henry had won the battle because he had 'kept up the morale of his men'.[27] The French, by contrast, had been 'forced to sleep in a muddy field and then to march to meet their enemy, which exhausted them'.[28] Shakespeare ignores these tactical errors on the French side, and emphasizes, instead, Henry's efforts to inspire patriotic fervour in spite of the overwhelming odds against an English victory (4.3). Le Fèvre's eyewitness account of Henry's famous St Crispin's Day speech clearly helped to lay the groundwork for later versions, including (indirectly) Shakespeare's.[29] The main controversy that French chroniclers had to address with respect to Henry's conduct was his infamous order to kill the prisoners (4.6.37): as Curry notes, 'In French narratives there is never opprobrium against Henry for this act but only against those who caused it to happen'.[30] Although some writers link Henry's decision to the attack on the baggage (which Shakespeare reports only afterward, in 4.7), most accounts suggest that Henry gave the order out of fear that the French forces were regrouping.[31]

In several respects, contemporary French sources bear out the representations in Shakespeare's play. The Religieux, for example, paints a picture of youthful arrogance and inexperience in the French camp that we find embodied in Shakespeare's Dauphin. But since Shakespeare strips away much of the larger political context, we are left with the impression of a proud and foolish French prince who fatally underestimates the political acumen of the recently crowned Henry V. The play offers no explanation as to why the Dauphin, who so clearly misreads his opponent, is in charge. The discussions in 1.1 and 1.2 of Henry's motives for invasion (and the merits of his claim to the French throne) make no mention of the nation's internal divisions or the strategic opportunity they afford. Shakespeare instead suggests that the strategic opportunity for Henry (and his advisors) lay in directing England's attention outward during its own 'unquiet time' (1.1.4) – in using a military campaign to unify the nation against a common enemy. And so, upon receiving the mocking gift of the tennis balls from the Dauphin in 1.2, Henry responds to this 'pleasant' prince (1.2.260) by assuring the French ambassador that 'we understand him well, / How he comes o'er us with our wilder days, / Not measuring what use we made of them' (1.2.267–9). He then promises, in a speech laden with dramatic irony, that:

> many a thousand widows
> Shall this his mock mock out of their dear husbands,
> Mock mothers from their sons, mock castles down,
> And some are yet ungotten and unborn
> That shall have cause to curse the Dauphin's scorn.
>
> (1.2.285–9)

Further presaging what French chroniclers and poets would say, looking back on Agincourt, Henry remarks that 'this lies all within the will of God' (1.2.290), before sending the ambassador away with the promise that when the English invade, 'thousands [will] weep more than did laugh' at the Dauphin's ill-considered jest (1.2.297).

The Religieux of Saint-Denis produced one of the 'fullest statements' on the causes of the defeat at Agincourt, emphasizing the poor leadership of the French, 'as well as . . . the sinful ways of the nation which provoked divine judgment'.[32] His work offers a useful introduction to themes that recur in the French responses. Not all of these pertain directly to the figure of Henry V, but together they present a picture of France at the time of Agincourt that differs from that depicted by Shakespeare. In at least one respect, however, Shakespeare's Henry is right: after Agincourt, France came to be identified with bereaved widows and mothers. As I will discuss, many of the works responding to Agincourt belong to the literature of consolation, and each in its own way takes up the image, literal or allegorical, of the bereaved woman.

Describing how news of the defeat at Agincourt was received at the French court, the Religieux reports that 'the king and the dukes of Guienne and Berry were struck with a great sadness and fell into deep lamentation'.[33] Noting that everyone at court and 'all the inhabitants of the kingdom' reflected on the shame 'this cruel twist of fate' would confer upon their 'century', he then continues:

> Everywhere the lords and ladies of rank changed out of their garments of gold and silk into the clothes of mourning. It was a sight to bring tears to the eyes to see some of the women crying bitterly at the loss of their husbands, others inconsolable at the death of their children and their closest relatives, but especially those who had fallen without glory having taken with them to the tomb those famous names of ancestors which had featured so prominently in the annals of war.[34]

The losses, as this passage suggests, were sudden and devastating. Many of the fallen were the cousins, nephews, and close kin of the French king, the Duke of Guienne (his son) and the Duke of Berry; many were young, and too many were perceived to have died 'without glory' – bringing shame upon the 'famous names' of their ancestors.

Interestingly, this notion of shame is passed over in the English lords' assessment of the battle. Following the account in Holinshed, the playwright has Exeter list the prisoners taken at Agincourt in pragmatic, not emotive, terms: 'Charles, Duke of Orleans, nephew to the King; / John, Duke of Bourbon, and Lord Boucicaut. / Of other lords and barons, knights and squires, / Full fifteen hundred, besides common men' (4.8.77–80). Among some 'ten thousand' dead, as Henry reports in the play, only 'sixteen hundred' were mercenaries: the rest were 'gentlemen of blood and quality' (4.8.88–91). This information is presented here as factual, not judgmental, in a manner that nevertheless reflects well on the English victory. Henry underlines this when he notes:

> O God, thy arm was here;
> And not to us but to thy arm alone
> Ascribe we all. When, without stratagem,
> But in plain shock and even play of battle,
> Was ever known so great and little loss
> On one part and on th'other? Take it, God,
> For it is none but thine.
>
> (4.8.107–13)

Attributing the English victory to divine providence, Henry draws attention to his nation's favoured status as a European power. The shame of French cowardice has no part to play in this: it is more beneficial for the English national project if the French are portrayed here as nobly and honestly defeated.

French commentators, though – as the Religieux's chronicle demonstrates – were less generous to their countrymen. The most notable of these commentators – Charles, Duke of Orléans, the nephew of the French king, Charles VI – was, as Shakespeare notes, captured at the battle and spent nearly twenty-five years as a prisoner of war in England, before being ransomed back to France in 1440. He cuts a valiant figure in Shakespeare's play, but, more than this, during his time in England he wrote a substantial body of verse in both English and French that responded to his experience of war, captivity and exile from his beloved France.[35] Although, as I have noted, Agincourt is never mentioned by name in any of Charles's poems, the duke clearly used his work to reflect on his nation's defeat, wondering how the French overthrow could have happened and what it meant. Sometimes his poems directly address the claims that others had made about the English victory in a manner that shows him deliberating upon, and working through, the various explanations for the disaster. Anne Coldiron has shown, for example, that his 'Complainte I' echoes Henry V's famous claim, reported in the French chronicles, that the English had triumphed 'by God's grace'.[36] This is particularly apparent in the poem's second stanza where the poet addresses his beloved France, asking why she is sad and whether she knows the origin of her misfortune.[37] The wisdom the poet offers by way of an answer is that France's great pride, gluttony, laziness, greed and wantonness have led God to punish her.[38] This spiritual explanation became a commonplace on both sides of the Channel: as we have already seen, the Religieux arrived at a similar conclusion, attributing the defeat to the 'sinful ways of the nation'.

Charles's 'Ballad LXXXIV', addressed to his fellow captive, the Duke of Bourbon, is also concerned with explaining the French defeat. Its second stanza again suggests that the defeat at Agincourt was divinely ordained, but this time allies it more generally with the state of all God's Christian subjects. Positing a future time of peace when both Charles and the Duke of Bourbon will again experience comfort and pleasure, the poet acknowledges the destructive evils of war, comparing them to the punishments that God inflicts on Christians. Nevertheless, he notes, after administering punishment, God always desires to comfort and aid his people by sending them peace. The poem implicitly posits an end to the two dukes' imprisonment, and locates them as suffering Christians, rather than as representatives of a discredited nation.[39] Even in this brief example from the pen of one poet, then, we can see that responses to Agincourt were both agonized and complex as French writers tried to come to terms with their nation's shameful defeat in a manner that would allow them to build a new and better future.

Three years after the battle, the famous French writer, Christine de Pizan, opens her *Epistle of the Prison of Human Life* (*c.* 1418) with a description of her search for a remedy,

> ... which might restrain and dry up a flood of tears ... that has run and runs still – which is a pity – even among the queens, princesses, baronesses, ladies and young girls of the noble royal blood of France, and in general among most of

the ladies-in-waiting ... because of so many various deaths and abductions of kin – husbands, sons, brothers, uncles, cousins, relatives and friends, some killed in battles, others passing away naturally in their beds – and of so many losses and other various misfortunes and adventures which have occurred unexpectedly for some time.[40]

In addition to those 'killed in battle' or taken prisoner, Christine is referring here to the deaths of the Dauphin in December 1415 and of her patron Marie de Berry's own father, the Duke of Berry, in June 1416. Marie, as we have seen, had lost no fewer than eight family members at or shortly after Agincourt. Christine herself was closely connected to the court and shared in its grief: the opening paragraph of *The Prison of Human Life* alludes to 'friends' of her own who 'are missing'.[41] Louise d'Arcens has argued, furthermore, that Christine's own status as a widow was 'crucial to the development of her literary persona'.[42] Many of her works open with what d'Arcens calls a '*topos* of tearfulness' that works to authorize her voice as a woman writer by invoking the *mater dolorosa*, or sorrowing Virgin mother.[43] In an important way, then, grief opened up a space for women's voices in early fifteenth-century France, and it authorized, in Christine's case, writing that was political, philosophical and deeply personal – concerned to bring an end to the nation's suffering after more than a decade of war and civil strife. Although Christine addressed the *Prison* specifically to Marie de Berry, as advice from an older widow to a younger one (she was 54 and Marie was 43), she also intended it to be 'of value to all who have fallen in the aforementioned sufferings'.[44] She tells her patron that she completed the work, begun 'a long time ago', because the deaths of so many friends had caused a sorrow which 'grieved the hearts of loyal and loving ladies' – something 'from which one cannot recover and which is hard to forget' (5). In contrast to the masculine heroism of Shakespeare's play, then, Christine's poetry of consolation provides a fascinating, and specifically woman-centred, perspective on Agincourt and its devastating aftermath.

This finds an echo in *Henry V* only in the French princess Katherine's extremely pertinent question to the triumphant Henry: 'Is it possible dat I sould love de enemy of France?' (5.2.169–70).[45] In a play that relentlessly objectifies women and marginalizes their perspectives, Katherine's question nevertheless stands as a brief acknowledgement of the battle's cost for French women.

Christine's *Prison of Human Life* is a work of Christian neo-Stoicism intended to comfort the Duchess of Berry in her time of grief. The central argument is fairly conventional: 'The day of birth is the entrance into misery and tribulation; the day of death, if one dies well, is the end of all afflictions and miseries' (49). Death releases our souls, which are imprisoned in our bodies, from their mortal suffering and promises 'incomprehensible joy' and eternal blessings to those who die in God's grace. Christine announces to her reader that, 'since my own words may be of little consequence with respect to your great sorrow', her epistle will draw upon the Holy Scriptures and 'what the glorious doctors and many wise authors have written' (7). Her main sources are Boethius's *Consolation of Philosophy*, the Bible and *De Remediis Fortuitorum* (*The Remedies Against Fortune*), a work attributed, at the time, to Seneca. She also draws heavily, for her descriptions of Paradise, on Saint Augustine's *City of God*. She follows Boethius in claiming that we are all, in this life, subject to the 'dangers of false Fortune', and Augustine in assuring her reader that God is just and will punish the wicked – those 'persecutors and destroyers of humankind, avid to shed blood and do any evil' (11). Citing numerous examples from the Scriptures, she argues that, 'whoever doubts God's vengeance is a fool!' (15). While these statements are couched in very general terms, it is easy to imagine that a bereaved reader like Marie de Berry might wish 'vengeance' upon the enemy that had invaded France and taken so many of her family members. In fact, Christine anticipates such a reading by describing how those who died 'attacking the English enemies on one side, and resisting on the other as just defenders, were elected with God's martyrs through battle' (5). Having died for their country, and suffered 'for justice', she assures her reader that they are blessed in God's eyes. This French reaction to Agincourt is seemingly suppressed in Shakespeare's play, only to emerge in the Epilogue's final acknowledgement that the regents of the infant Henry VI 'lost France and made his England bleed' (Epilogue 12).

Despite this reminder of God's justice, Christine soon returns to the question of Marie's grief, offering 'five principal reasons' to take comfort in the loss of her 'good friends'. The first, briefly, is that these men died 'in the manner of good and honorable men' (17) and can therefore be assured of God's favour. The second is that, in death, they have been set free from the misery of human life. The third reason, developed at somewhat greater length, is that – as Seneca reminds us – all living things must die sooner or later; there is no use in fearing something that 'cannot be avoided'. In a passage that strikingly anticipates Shakespeare's *Hamlet*, she then asks, 'Oh, what is man?', concluding, 'He is ... nothing but the vessel of death, the restless pilgrim, the guest of the earth and the food of worms.'[46] Turning once again to Seneca and quoting directly from *The Remedies Against Fortune*, she then argues that 'it is a great folly to pity your friends ... because they died in battle, since their deaths were not worse than in any other place, since death, wherever it occurs, can be received only once, just as the man stricken by many wounds can only die once' (21). Those who die young, she adds, avoid the dangers of old age and the misfortunes that can accrue in the course of a long life. These, however, are bitter comforts, and it is not hard to see how her arguments respond specifically to the loss of young lives and the 'many wounds' inflicted at Agincourt.

At this point in the epistle, Christine turns aside for a moment to consider whether there are any 'cures' that might 'soften the pain' of her patron's loss, proposing that grief might be alleviated by both 'hope in God and doing good' and 'suffering patiently for the love of Our Lord'.[47] On the value of patience (as *praxis*), she cites a passage from one of Saint Basil's

Letters that seems especially poignant in the light of Agincourt: 'you who wish to succeed in this, have patience as your shield and go bravely to the battle of tribulations, and if you defend yourself well against them, nothing will defeat you, and you will come out of it a conqueror and a victor' (25).[48] This inner discipline is available to men and women alike, and enables one not only to endure the suffering caused by war, but to transcend it. Having thus elaborated her arguments in favour of patience, she then returns to the five reasons for taking comfort in the loss of loved ones. Reason number four is that, despite what she has lost, Marie still has much to be thankful for. Indeed, no one is so deprived in this life that they do not have some source of consolation or reason for gratitude. God, Christine says, gives us gifts of grace, nature and fortune, and those gifts and graces 'are sufficient, if there is in you something that wants to go to Heaven after this life'. Nevertheless, she cautions, in a truly Senecan manner, one must use those gifts wisely to 'live well in this world' (42). Although Christine acknowledges that Marie might still feel bereft because her spouse and eldest son had 'fallen into the hands of our enemies while they were doing well in offering their bodies in a chivalrous manner for their sovereign lord', she answers this objection by reminding Marie that 'hope in God, doing good for them, and being patient, can obtain grace for you with Our Lord, so that He may soon bring them back to you' (43).

The fifth and final source of comfort is the promise of 'the heavenly glory that those who die well receive at the end' (51). The last part of Christine's epistle is concerned, therefore, to describe 'the joys of Paradise' in an extended vision of the afterlife that is heavily indebted to Saint Augustine's *City of God*. Reunion with 'fathers and mothers, husband, wife, and children, and all kin and friends' is just one of the many consolations offered to the blessed. Paradise is a place of exquisite beauty and perfect happiness; Christine's argument is, ultimately, that the joys of Paradise far outweigh our suffering in this life. Therefore, she concludes, 'you do not have reason to mourn nor to pity the death of your aforementioned friends', since they have clearly received salvation and will profit more 'from alms, prayers, and good deeds' than from your tears (67). The epistle thus moves from the inward discipline of patience to outward actions that are both socially and spiritually beneficial. The move echoes Christine's own trajectory from tearful widow to courtly poet, turning from her own grief to a form of action (writing) that will help others. These actions become inherently political when we acknowledge what is behind them – the self-disciplined mourning for those who died nobly and blessedly in defence of their crown and country. In sum, then, Christine's work of consolation for the Duchess of Berry is a powerfully woman-centred response to the Battle of Agincourt that offers a new perspective on *Henry V*'s presentation of events. Further investigations of this unique text may well provide fascinating comparative opportunities for scholars, particularly those interested in excavating Shakespeare's representation of Katherine – the French princess who is Henry's trophy bride.

Alain Chartier, Christine's contemporary, also wrote several works responding to the tragedy at Agincourt, which again take up the figure of the bereaved widow in some fascinating ways. The first of these, *The Book of the Four Ladies* (1416–18), presents readers with a fictionalized verse dialogue among four noblewomen whose husbands (or lovers) each suffered different fates on the battlefield. The poet, who is himself suffering the pains of love, encounters the unnamed ladies while walking in the countryside and is asked to determine which of them is 'most worthy of pity'.[49] The stories then told by the ladies reflect the lived experiences of Chartier's contemporaries as each woman attempts to justify why she has the 'greatest cause for grief'.[50] Explaining that her beloved was killed on that 'accursed day', the first lady emphasizes that he nevertheless acted 'with valour' and 'gave great honour to France', fighting in the first ranks where the risk to his life was greatest.[51] Echoing criticism also found in the Religieux's account, she blames the French defeat on those who fled the battle and who thus 'abused and brought low their lineages'

(346–7). The second lady's lover has been captured by the English – 'taken whilst defending himself from his adversaries, who were acting against his prince' – and prays that God 'will bring him back to [her] by means of His kind pity' (347). J. C. Laidlaw, Chartier's modern editor, argues that the information given here about this prisoner 'points to Charles d'Orléans', who was 'not quite twenty-one at the time of Agincourt'.[52] Laidlaw bases his claim on the lady's allusions to the murder of Charles's father, Louis d'Orléans, and to the ten years of civil war that ensued (37). The third lady does not know whether her betrothed is dead or has been taken prisoner, lamenting, 'Between hope and desperation I hover full of doubts, as someone who has a sadness and does not know why' (347), while the fourth is overwhelmed by grief and shame because her lover 'fled as a coward and ran away, so abandoning his honour' (348). The poet, unable to decide among them, suggests that the lady he loves should be asked to arbitrate, since, in Laidlaw's paraphrase, a worthy lady would be 'a more fitting judge of a dispute involving members of her own sex' (34); the poem is addressed, ultimately, to this woman and we are never privy to what she says. Curry, noting Chartier's insistence that 'the French lost the battle because of the behaviour of those who fled', and suggesting that he was 'thinking particularly of those "traitors" of the Burgundian persuasion', calls the *Book of the Four Ladies* a 'significant political poem as well as an unusually pointed discussion of the effects of war on the womenfolk of France'.[53]

Chartier's *Quadrilogue invectif* (1422), written just a few years later, takes the image of the grief-stricken woman one step further.[54] At the beginning of the work, in a conceit that poignantly recalls the figure of Lady Philosophy in Boethius's *Consolation of Philosophy*, Chartier portrays France as 'a distressed lady of noble birth whose once beautiful robe, embroidered in part with the *fleur de lis*, is all dirty and torn' – a reference, Anne Curry argues, 'to the divisions and destruction of France in the face of civil war and English invasion'.[55] The opening of Chartier's dream vision is patterned far more closely on the *Consolation of Philosophy* than Christine's *Prison of Human Life*, borrowing not just the work's arguments, but also, as we see here, adapting its central image to the context of post-Agincourt France. Written he says '*ad morum Gallicorum correctionum*' (i.e. for the correction of French morals), the piece opens with the author awakening to thoughts of the calamities suffered by France: 'There came into my imagination the painful misfortune and piteous estate of the great lords and the glorious house of France.'[56] More specifically, he finds himself thinking about 'the enemies' power and diligence, the disloyalty of several subjects, and the loss of princes and knights, that God has taken from this kingdom by means of that unfortunate battle'.[57] As he oscillates between hope and despair for the nation, believing that France's suffering must be divine punishment 'for our sins', he falls asleep once more, only to find himself in the presence of a lady whose bearing signifies her excellent lineage, but who is so sad, tearful and dishevelled that she seemed to have fallen from an even higher place (6). The parallels with Boethius are remarkable and powerfully adapt the structure and the details of his paradigmatic *consolatio* to this new French context.

Chartier describes in great detail the robe or mantle his lady wears, noting that it is enriched with precious stones and richly embroidered with fleurs-de-lis and the 'banners, heraldic standards, and ensigns of the ancient kings and princes of France' (7). The middle section of the garment is ornamented with figures denoting the sciences that have enlightened the kingdom, while the lower portion is decorated by images of beasts and plants, fruits and crops, that symbolize the realm's fertility. However, Fortune, 'envious of [her] long prosperity', has jealously turned her back on France, allowing this rich garment to be ravaged by violence, its gorgeous embroideries obscured and soiled (7). 'This robe,' the poet notes, 'created by the sovereign industry of our predecessors, had already been damaged and pulled loose by violent hands, and several pieces violently torn from it, so that the upper part was darkened and all but a few of the *fleurs-de-lis* there were broken or sullied'

(7).[58] The destruction of the garment is such that the ancient figures that had once stood for knowledge and enlightenment are now torn asunder, so that 'only a few could be put together that carried any profitable meaning' (7). Chartier's work, written in the years immediately following the Treaty of Troyes (1420), looks back on the destruction of France, both on the field of battle at Agincourt, and as a result of the power struggles that had divided the court and kingdom. The broken figures on France's robe suggest not only the destruction of science and learning, but also an even more fundamental struggle to make sense of what has happened – a struggle not merely to interpret, but in the most rudimentary way to make meaning (that is, to write anything useful or 'profitable') in the wake of these traumatic events.

Chartier's imagery of his ravaged and despoiled nation resonates in significant ways with Shakespeare's representation, at the end of *Henry V*, of France as a neglected garden, particularly in the play's associations of a previously fertile France with the youthful princess Katherine. In *Henry V*'s final scene, the Duke of Burgundy delivers a speech to Henry V and his entourage in which he describes peace as 'naked, poor, and mangled' (5.2.34) and compares France to a garden that has run wild. Here, it is 'peace' that is personified, while the garden imagery works to feminize France to a somewhat different effect. 'Why', Burgundy asks, should not 'peace' – the 'nurse of arts, plenties, and joyful births' – 'put up her lovely visage' in France, the 'best garden of the world' (5.2.34–7)? Answering his own question, he continues:

> Alas, she hath from France too long been chased,
> And all her husbandry doth lie on heaps,
> Corrupting in its own fertility.
> Her vine, the merry cheerer of the heart,
> Unpruned dies; her hedges even-pleached,
> Like prisoners wildly overgrown with hair,
> Put forth disordered twigs; her fallow leas
> The darnel, hemlock and rank fumitory

Doth root upon, while that the coulter rusts
That should deracinate such savagery.

(5.2.38–47)

Upon this image he piles another, in the form of a meadow that once 'brought sweetly forth / The freckled cowslip, burnet and green clover' (5.2.48–9), but, 'wanting the scythe', now produces weeds: 'hateful docks, rough thistles, kecksies, burrs, / Losing both beauty and utility' (5.2.50, 52–3). Burgundy then extends the conceit to include all the vineyards of France, its fields, meadows and hedges, all of them growing 'to wildness' (5.2.55). From there, he turns to the 'sciences' that lie neglected, so that the children of the nation, lacking the kind of knowledge that 'should become our country' (5.2.58), grow instead

like savages, as soldiers will
That nothing do but meditate on blood,
To swearing and stern looks, diffused attire,
And everything that seems unnatural.

(5.2.59–62)

He draws his speech to a close just a few lines later, noting that they are all assembled there to negotiate a treaty so that 'gentle peace' might 'expel these inconveniences / And bless us with her former qualities' (5.2.65–7).

Burgundy's speech, which recalls, unmistakably, the garden scene in *Richard II*, compares France to an overgrown, untended garden, from which 'peace', once a careful nurse and now a poor naked woman, has been 'chased', her 'husbandry' neglected. His feminization of 'peace' and of France recalls the kinds of comparisons we have seen proposed above by Orléanist writers and, specifically, by Chartier. Richard Dutton points out that Burgundy's lengthy speech is a 'feature of the play for which Shakespeare had no sanction in his sources', which raises the tantalizing question of whether any of these French responses to

Agincourt were available to Shakespeare and influenced the composition of his play.[59] Burgundy appears briefly in the analogous scene of Shakespeare's source, the *Famous Victories*, but gives no such speech, merely swearing allegiance to the conquering English king. Holinshed makes Burgundy a prominent figure in the peace negotiations that resulted in the Treaty of Troyes, but does not put any speeches in his mouth. The connection of Burgundy's speech here with Chartier's writing is thus intriguing. Curry tells us that the *Quadrilogue invectif* was 'one of several French texts to be translated into English in the third quarter of the fifteenth century', but how widely did it circulate?[60] An attention to literary and historiographical materials produced in France in the aftermath of 1415, then, not only provides a strikingly different perspective that helps us to interrogate *Henry V*'s commitment to nationalism, but allows us to wonder whether any of these texts were available to Shakespeare or had an influence on what has come down to us as a quintessentially English play.

As this discussion has shown, French writers produced a considerable body of work in response to the Battle of Agincourt, much of it focused on working through the traumatic losses suffered on that fateful day in 1415. From the French chroniclers to literary figures such as Charles d'Orléans, Christine de Pizan and Alain Chartier, the writers I have discussed here offer a range of insights and perspectives that cast into sharp relief Shakespeare's manipulation of historical fact. Yet this study is only a beginning: there is much work still to be done, and further investigations into this fascinating but neglected corpus will help us better understand the complex legacy of Shakespeare's play.

9

Learning and Teaching Resources

Gillian Woods, with Laura Seymour

War criminal or national hero? Patriotic myth or deconstructed history? As a play which survives in two texts, and in which critics since Rabkin have found a double vision, *Henry V* lends itself well to debates that keep classrooms lively. This chapter suggests various ways of engaging students with the play's central features: genre, staging, character, language, gender and texts. Teachers may wish to focus on one particular concept or to mix and match the exercises and questions described in each section. The tasks presented are designed to open out independent critical investigations rather than to foreclose interpretation.

Staging

Since the play of *Henry V* is obsessed with its theatrical status, exploring the practicalities of staging provides a useful foothold for students. After all, this is a drama in which the central character performs a number of different roles and where an importunate Chorus constantly reveals the play's theatrical workings. The Prologue ushers the audience into the historical world by counter-intuitively drawing their attention to the present-day edifice of the playhouse: 'this unworthy scaffold', 'this cockpit', 'this wooden O' (Prologue 10–13). Engaging students with the question of how history plays were performed on the early modern stage in relation to *Henry V*'s metatheatrical glosses helps them to evaluate how theatricality conditions the meaning of history.

Numerous electronic resources are available to introduce students to the playhouses for which Shakespeare and his contemporaries wrote. The University of Victoria's *Early Modern Map of London* features an interactive digital edition of the 1561 woodblock map of London known as the Agas Map.[1] This website can be used to stress the significance of the location of theatres in the liberties and suburbs. Students may independently research questions such as, how near or far are the playhouses to the centre of the city? What other activities are possible in the neighbourhood of the playhouses? What sights might playgoers have passed as they journeyed to see a play? A briefer activity might focus specifically on the Curtain playhouse – where *Henry V* is generally believed to have been first performed – since the website includes a possible early image of the theatre and a mini-essay on its architecture, environs and use by various theatrical companies.[2] While archaeological excavations have suggested that the Curtain was rectangular, the Lord Chamberlain's Men's Globe theatre was famous as a 'wooden O' (Prologue 13).[3] An image of such a structure is available through the Museum of London Archaeology and Cloak and Dagger Studios' animation of the 1576 Shoreditch theatre.[4] Having seen the open-air structure and the proximity of stage to audience spaces, students can consider how the performance and reception of plays might differ in such a space from a modern theatre, where audiences sit in a darkened auditorium all facing the stage in one direction.⁵ The boundary between staged illusion and the real conditions of the early modern playhouse are extremely porous, and so it is not surprising that Renaissance play texts are metatheatrical. Informed by knowledge of early conditions, a close reading of the *Henry V* Prologue opens out questions about the extent to which the pleas for 'pardon' (Prologue 8) register humility (Shakespeare's company would shortly upgrade to the new Globe theatre across London), or conceal a brag (it is productive to add up the impact of the various Os in the Prologue and calculate the worth of a 'cipher' in a 'million' (Prologue 16–17)).⁶ Such discussion can focus on the larger problem that necessarily attends any consideration of staging in *Henry V*: what is the significance of such insistently metatheatrical devices in this particular play? How is history being shaped here, and how are the audience directed to think about the way it has been shaped?

The Prologue labels the play a 'history' (Prologue 32) and the theatrical associations of this genre can be illustrated by the opening to another Lord Chamberlain's Men play staged in the same year as *Henry V*. *A Warning for Faire Women* (1599) begins with an argument between personified representations of Tragedy, History and Comedy. History appears 'with Drum and Ensigne' and Tragedy complains about the racket:

>   peace with that drum:
> Downe with that Ensigne which disturbs our stage
> out with this luggage, with this fopperie,
> This brawling sheepeskin is intollerable.
>
>   (*A Warning for Faire Women*, A2r)

This depiction suggests the appeal of dramatized history centred on noise and combat. It can be set alongside Thomas Heywood's claims in *Apology for Actors* (1612) about the impact of watching 'domestic histories':

> [W]hat English blood seeing the person of any bold English man presented and doth not hugge his fame and hunnye at

his valor, pursuing him in his enterprise with his best wishes, and as beeing wrapt in contemplation, offers to him in his hart all prosperous performance, as if the Personator were the man Personated, so bewitching a thing is liuely and well spirited action, that it hath the power to new mold the harts of the spectators and fashion them to the shape of any noble and notable attempt.[7]

Heywood's assertions complicate any simplistic assumptions that open-air audiences remained too aware of the artifice of performance to buy into its illusion. History plays are here recorded as emotionally and even ideologically stirring: they fashion patriotic spectators. Of course, the bias of Heywood, himself a prolific playwright writing an 'Apology' or defence of drama, is also relevant here. Nevertheless, such extracts can be a useful way of highlighting the complexity of audience response, which can be as diverse as the people in it. Furnished with some contemporary accounts of staged histories, students are equipped to consider the slippery ways in which *Henry V* both satisfies and disappoints expectations.

Collecting references to sound effects (drum, alarum, flourish, trumpet, tucket, sennet, chambers) helps to pinpoint the way the play establishes its credentials as a 'history'. Individuals or groups of students can track sound effects, considering whether particular sounds are associated with certain actions or groups of characters, and what signifying work these effects are performing. It is helpful to discuss the visceral impact of loud noises (especially in an age that lacked the background hum of cars and aeroplanes), as well as to consider what actors might be doing at these moments, and how the audience's 'imaginary forces' are being utilized. While the sound effects are relatively specific, the stage directions are somewhat more generalized in terms of military action. For example, the closest the text comes to specifying staged violence is in its 'alarums' (battle calls), and its single instance of '*Excursions*' (4.4.0), which derives 'from the Latin *excurrere* ("the action of running out"), the military term for "an issuing forth against an enemy, a sortie" '. Alan C. Dessen and Leslie Thomson point out that it is difficult to attribute a specific action to 'excursion' in Renaissance texts, 'given that the direction almost invariably comes when the stage has just been cleared, probably as many soldiers as were available entered, performed some representative action, and exited; possibly they merely crossed over the stage as if going to battle'.[8] However, the permissiveness of these directions is itself revealing. *Henry V* does not stipulate staged combat between individual figures of the kind specified, for example, in *Richard III*: '*Enter Richard and Richmond, they fight. Richard is slaine*'.[9] By contrast, any staged fighting in *Henry V* is representative and surprisingly dispensable.

The siege at Harfleur (3.1) offers an opportunity to consider how use of stage space relates to the aural effects already detailed: what metonymic work is done by the '*scaling-ladders*' (3.1.0)? How can entrances and exits be handled in this scene (Henry comes out to start a siege, but then goes back in to undertake it)? Relatedly, the scene where Henry threatens the Governor of Harfleur reveals the referential possibilities of the stage space (the theatre's balcony as city walls; the doors or central opening as gates). It is worth pointing out that the Governor remains in possession of the '*gates*' (3.3.0) two scenes after Henry's army attempted to scale them: has the siege failed? Having scrutinized the possibilities of stage action, students might then consider the impact of Henry's language at the gates. Why might various images like the stirring phrase 'imitate the action of the tiger' (3.1.6) and the threats to 'Defile the locks of your shrill-shrieking daughters ... Your naked infants spitted upon pikes' (3.3.35–8) appear only verbally? Starting with the staged action before returning to the language helps students to recognize quite how graphic the language is, and how staged violence is strikingly unfixed.

Enumerating the specific expectations established by the Prologue and Chorus and what is actually delivered by the main action of the play then enables students to develop their understanding of how the play's theatricality relates to its attitude to history. Close readings of the notorious disjunctions between what is promised and what is shown help students to think about the different ways in which historical representation works. The Chorus at the head of Act 2 announces that 'all the youth of England are on fire' (2.0.1) and claims that we are going to be shown Southampton and then France; instead, the Act opens in London with the king's aging companions. Similarly, the Prologue collaborates with the audience, requiring them to use 'imaginary puissance' to see 'horses' and 'deck kings', and focus on 'two mighty monarchies' and the stuff of staged history (Prologue 19–34). However, instead of an international combat, the audience are first presented with a bathetic brawl between the comic Englishmen, Pistol and Nym, who draw their swords but are reconciled before duelling. Exploring the staging demands of *Henry V* entails thinking through the possible impact of what is *not* shown, as well as what is performed. This focus helps students to identify ways that the audience is involved in the play's interrogation of how history is made.

Genre

Focused attention on genre enables students to take their own informed position on the play's ideological strategies. As a history play, *Henry V* does not so much represent events from the historical past as demonstrate numerous ways of representing the past, revealing 'history' as an inescapably partial perspective.

Genre is inherently flexible: it offers a means of categorizing works of art according to structural and tonal features, but at the same time writers often produce meaning through flouting those 'rules' and confounding expectations. The First Folio's 'Contents' nicely illustrate the pragmatic nature of generic labels: why are some plays about the past called 'histories' but not others (*King Lear*, *Julius Caesar*, *Coriolanus* and so on)?[10] As a new genre that was developed in the Elizabethan period, the 'history play' lacks the structural form of classically derived genres like comedies and tragedies. Heywood declared, 'Comedies begin in trouble, and end in peace; Tragedies begin in calmes, and end in tempest', but the DNA of history plays is not so easy to detect.[11] Students might engage actively with this problem by producing a generic map of the play. Supply plot synopses and invite students to give a generic label to each scene. Revealingly different structures might emerge: four acts of episodic history followed by a romantic comedy conclusion; or scenes of military history framed by mythologizing/satirical choruses and interspersed with bathetically comic scenes of cowardice. Why are different generic readings possible? These maps can form the basis for a discussion of how and why history draws on other genres. For example, how are the political needs of the narrative met by the comedic emphasis on marriage in the last scene? Do the different generic elements of the play fuse together to produce a particular message about history, or create friction and a different kind of meaning?

At this point, students might question what 'history' means in the context of early modern culture. Oxford University's online Holinshed Project provides access to both the 1577 and 1587 texts of the *Chronicles* (Shakespeare seems to have used the later, fuller edition).[12] Comparative source work can risk aimless accounts of differences between one document and another. However, inviting students to consider how and why the chronicle and the play are differently framed gives them a direct understanding of how 'history' itself is conceptualized in plays and history books. It is also useful to explain the various ideas of historical causation circulating in the era: 'a Machiavellian universe, where the hand of God is absent or invisible' and in which the efforts of individuals determine the course of history, and a 'providential' design, which sees God plotting human history.[13] Both Holinshed and *Henry V* reveal that these apparently contradictory schemas often interacted in Renaissance historiography.

The theatrical appeal of 'history' could also be explored in the light of Nashe's description of plays which took stories, borrowed out of our English Chronicles,

> wherein our forefathers valiant acts (that haue [lain] long buried in rustie brasse, and worme-eaten bookes) are reuiued, and they themselues raised from the Graue of Obliuion, and brought to pleade their aged Honours in open presence: than which, what can be a sharper reproofe to these degenerate effeminate dayes of ours.[14]

Nashe's account provides a good opportunity to think through the relationship between history books (assumed to be 'worme eaten') and the (resurrectory) power of theatricality. As a writer, Nashe might have financial interest in asserting the patriotic value of theatrical history, but even if we do not accept that history plays did what he claimed, the idealized (or, since this is Nashe, perhaps ironic) response he pitches is itself revealing: the medieval past is more glorious than the Elizabethan present, and men can retool their masculinity by watching its enactment. Discussion of the extent to which *Henry V* fits this brief might be kept specific by comparing some of the rousing martial scenes with, say, the Archbishop of Canterbury's lengthy account of Salic Law (1.2.33–95), the shaky basis of Henry's claims on France and the means by which Canterbury intends to distract Henry from his seizure of Church lands. In the context of the kinds of expectations suggested by Nashe, students might debate whether Canterbury's speech works as 'a serious interpretation of history or a satire on a politician's use of history to establish the legitimacy of his claims'.[15] Indeed, to what extent does 'history' emerge in *Henry V* as a discourse used for particular ideological ends?

The play's generic structure is shaped by an awareness of the dynamics of temporality. When grappling with the way Shakespeare constructs his history, students might identify moments when characters reflect consciously on the passage of time. Some, like the Archbishop of Canterbury, use 'history' to advance their own ends. Others imagine the present or immediate future in terms of how it will seem when it has receded into the past. When seeking to inspire his vastly outnumbered troops to bravery, Henry asks them to think about how their deeds are going to be remembered in the future, actions which are somehow resistant to oblivion (4.3.44–60). The soldier Michael Williams projects still further forward to Judgement Day, when the dead common soldiers are reanimated in a Christian horror story: 'the King himself hath a heavy reckoning to make when all those legs and arms and heads chopped off in a battle shall join together at the latter day and cry all "We died at such a place"' (4.1.134–8). The audience are also drawn into the problems of temporality in the Epilogue, which sharply undercuts the final political and romantic union found in 5.2:

> Henry the Sixth, in infant bands crowned King
> Of France and England, did this king succeed,
> Whose state so many had the managing
> That they lost France and made his England bleed,
> Which oft our stage hath shown[.]
>
> (Epilogue 9–13)

This Epilogue locks the audience into a temporal paradox: we look forward in chronological time (beyond Henry V to the reign of his son) while looking backwards in theatrical time (to previous productions of the war-riven *Henry VI* plays), so that the bloodshed begins again and history takes on an inescapably cyclical shape. Discussing what it means to end the play with or without the Epilogue usefully returns students to the formal difficulties of the 'history' genre, which does not have an obvious end point.

Character

Actors and audiences approach plays through questions of character, but the concept of character varies considerably across time. *Henry V* focuses mainly on a single character: Henry. But that character's singularity is far from secure.

Seminar activities which analyse the part of Henry can dislodge anachronistic expectations of character and address central tensions in the play.

Before looking directly at Henry's part itself, it is worthwhile spending time discussing what 'character' means. Establish the students' latent associations with the term by having them quickly brainstorm their immediate responses to it. This activity can be followed by a brief discussion unpacking the significance of these various connotations, and starting to consider which might be relevant in the early modern period. Supplying students with early modern and critical descriptions of 'character' then affords a way of distinguishing between the idea of a representation and a real person, and working out historically appropriate definitions. The Lexicons of Early Modern English website is a great resource for contemporary definitions of the term.[16] For example, Thomas Cawdrey's definition of character as 'the fashion of a letter, a marke or stampe' (1604) can prompt a fruitful discussion of the word's etymology and the significance of character 'types'. Consideration of other relevant terms such as 'part', 'role' and 'subject' also helps to identify the various dimensions of what Simon Palfrey calls 'these speaking things': at once theatrical performances produced via scripts and actors, and signs of living beings with personalities and, it is sometimes implied, inner lives.[17]

Prepared with these definitions, students might begin to analyse Henry V's character, not to assess his personality, but rather to explore how the representation has been put together, and its implications. The Prologue almost immediately highlights a difficulty. He yearns for 'A kingdom' as a 'stage' and princely actors: 'Then should the warlike Harry, like himself, / Assume the port of Mars' (Prologue 5–6). Theatrical characterization is here described in terms of a simile: the actor/character is like the real Henry. However, in the context of the play's historical fiction, the precise terms of the simile are weirdly tautological: the character could be 'like himself'. Furthermore, Henry then turns out to be most like himself when he 'Assumes the port of Mars', that is, when he takes on the posture of the classical god of war and is therefore like someone else. Perhaps Henry *is* most 'like himself' in this mythical guise because this character is a kind of myth rather than a representation of a real person? These tricky descriptions sound an early warning about how hard it is to pin down the concept of 'Henry'. Students can be encouraged to interrogate these difficulties by following through other characterological similes in the play. What does it mean for Henry to tell the French messenger that he intends to 'keep my state, / Be like a king' (1.2.274–5)? How is the king's 'selfhood' and self-likenesses aligned when, towards the end of the play, Henry reveals to the common soldier Williams that 'It was our self thou didst abuse' (4.8.50) when he toured the camp in disguise? What about when Williams retorts, 'Your majesty came not like your self' and should therefore not take offence on account of that self (4.8.51)? Curiously, through being like himself, Henry's self seems to be splintered.

Graham Holderness's account of Henry's characterization offers a way of further analysing the role's multidimensional qualities. He points out that Henry speaks from a number of different positions at different moments in the drama: as a soldier, as a pragmatic and secular monarch and as a divine king or sovereign divinity. The role-playing is politically advantageous: 'By virtue ... of the complex and inclusive character Henry has established for himself, he is able to speak from different subject positions within this composite totality.'[18] One way of engaging students with this critical reading is to set individuals (or groups) different passages of the play with a view to analysing how Henry constructs his identity to match the occasion, adjusting his speech to suit his listeners. Especially telling extracts include 1.2.260–98 (dispatching the French ambassador); 3.3.1–43 (threatening the governor at the gates of Harfleur); 4.1.227–81 (soliloquizing on the eve of battle); 4.3.18–67 (rousing the troops prior to battle); and 5.2.98–277 ('wooing' Katherine). Students might consider how Henry labels himself in this scene. What is he aiming to do? What kind of language does he use (verse or prose, English or another language, monosyllabic or polysyllabic words, figurative or plain) and how does it match his purpose? When students compare their findings on different parts of the play, they pool together a range of evidence that points towards a complex picture. Such investigations can be taken still further through comparisons with other plays, such as Hal's soliloquy in *1 Henry IV*, where he explains that his prodigal role-playing is a political strategy; the opening to *1 Henry VI*, where Henry V is much celebrated, but appears as a corpse. At this point, it is also possible to address the polarizations in the critical debates about the play as idealizing and patriotic or myth-busting and anti-war. Armed with evidence from the play, students are well positioned to take their own view on these critical disputes.

This analysis of character is also a good jumping-off point for investigations of the ethics of the play. Sutherland and Watts's work, *Henry V: War Criminal?*, is a useful resource for sparking discussion here as they concisely set out the 'puzzle' of Henry's status as a supposedly noble paragon of kingly virtue and the fact that he facilitates and perpetrates several acts that can be called war crimes such as the retaliatory killing of the French prisoners.[19] In 2010, several US judges, led by Ruth Bader Ginsburg, subjected Shakespeare's character of Henry V to a mock trial in Washington, DC, and awarded large damages against Henry in favour of his French prisoners. A full seminar could be devoted to a similar kind of trial. Students might consider Henry's language in the speech before the siege of Harfleur (3.1) and the extent to which such threats constitute evidence of responsibility, especially given the disjunction between language and staged action in this play.

Alternatively, the problems of Henry's many-faced characterization might also be addressed by considering how modern actors and directors have attempted to give it coherence. Clips from, say, Olivier's 1944 film, Branagh's 1989 film and Sharrock's 2013 television film for the BBC's *Hollow Crown* series provide useful comparisons. Students might assess how each production responds to the complications of

Henry's characterization, and explore the different political contexts that might shape each film. Emma Smith's *King Henry V: Shakespeare in Production* provides an excellent model for analysing the way in which performers have dealt with and manipulated the play's ambiguities.[20]

Language

In a play that focuses so insistently on war, language functions as a weapon. *Henry V* sees characters manipulating, persuading, cajoling, exposing, condemning, threatening, inspiring, intimidating and seducing one another with their words. Students can be alerted to the verbal range and force of the play by encouraging them to look out for its different styles as they read the text. Instructing them to find examples of linguistic opposites can help them to engage with the play's dynamic language: verse and prose, English and French, 'standard' and dialect, elevated and everyday (colloquialisms and malapropisms). Jointly gathering ideas in class about which forms of language are associated with particular characters and/or situations lays a foundation for more advanced analysis.

Putting the play's language in its historical contexts then helps to unlock the linguistic politics of the drama. Henry V was the first king after the Norman Conquest to use English (rather than French) in his written administration. The British Library's online Learning English Timeline provides an image of one of Henry's English letters.[21] This document can prompt discussion about the role language plays in national identity and conquest, and the specific tensions between French and English in the medieval period. David Steinsaltz suggests that 'As the English nation is perpetually at war with the French, so must their languages be at war.' He also points out that one after-effect of the Norman Conquest was 'a thick stratum of French vocabulary' sedimenting within the English language, together with a native English sense that 'French words are arrogant, mannered, and even rude'.[22] The historical Henry V's use of English was politically astute. It is also worth noting that for many years following the Norman invasion, English was not thought to be rich or flexible enough to be a medium for great literature. But when Shakespeare wrote his play about the medieval past, Renaissance writers were making claims for the strengths of English. Thus Philip Sidney, noting that different styles of verse emphasized either the 'quantity of each syllable' or 'the sounding of the words, which we call rhyme', asserted:

> Truely the English, before any other vulgar language I know, is fit for both sorts: for, for the Ancient, the Italian is so full of Vowels, that it must euer be cu[m]bred with *Elisions*. The Dutch, so of the other side with Co[n]sonants, that they cannot yeeld the svveet slyding, fit for a Verse. The French, in his whole language, hath not one word, that hath his accent in the last silable, sauing two, called *Antepenultima*, and little more hath the Spanish: and therefore, very gracelesly may they vse *Dactiles*. The English is subiect to none of these defects.[23]

The explosion of literary creativity during the Renaissance has a patriotic thrust that is particularly relevant to *Henry V*. Being aware of this context helps students to understand the freighted nature of the play's diverse linguistics.

Of course, close analysis of those styles is essential to any study of the play's language. In the very first scene, Canterbury celebrates Henry's switch from youthful profligate to charismatic monarch as a linguistic victory (1.1.38–59). Students might analyse that speech to identify the variety of speaking styles Canterbury praises in Henry, and their effects. This exercise sets up broader questions about how effective language is in the play: at what moments are speakers able to influence their listeners? What kinds of things are listeners persuaded to do? At this point students might be reminded about the Renaissance imperative of eloquence, and why training in rhetoric (the art of persuasion) was seen to be an essential part of the education of future statesmen and diplomats. Providing students with lists of key rhetorical terms (which can be found glossed at the Silva Rhetoricae: Forest of Rhetoric website or in the pithily provocative definitions in Richard Lanham's *Handlist of Rhetorical Terms*) helps to engage them with the dynamics of rhetorical persuasion.[24] For example, speeches exemplifying different aspects of Henry's character (detailed above) might be revisited here, and looked at in relation to other attempts at manipulation (such as Canterbury at 1.2.183–221) or politically off-message language, such as Pistol's 'Eastcheap' idiom in 2.1, or Bates's and Williams's cynical prose in 4.1. In this exercise, students might identify examples of rhetorical techniques and other stylistic features and, crucially, the persuasive work performed by these techniques. Teachers who have access to Early English Books Online (EEBO) might also supply their students with 'The names of your figures Auricular' found in the final two pages of George Puttenham's *The Arte of English Poesie* (1589).[25] Puttenham's witty translations of classical terms help to isolate the mechanisms of each device. Thinking of *hyperbole* as '*the loud lier*' sheds interesting light on Henry's threat that the 'howls' of tortured women will 'break the clouds' (3.3.39–40) if the Governor does not open his gates; interpreting *climax* as '*the marching figure*' likewise illuminates the rhythm of 'Cry "God for Harry! England and Saint George!"' (3.1.34). When discussing students' findings, it is helpful to reflect on whether only formal or elevated language seems to be persuasive, or if there might be a strategy underpinning colloquial language too.

With their close-analysis muscles warmed up, students might then return to the ideological implications of the play's linguistic interactions. Steinsaltz's sensitive reading of the political connotations of word-roots can be used to prepare the ground for a research task. Students with access to the online *Oxford English Dictionary* (*OED*) might usefully investigate the etymology of the vocabulary used in various parts of the text.[26] Linguistic comparison of the dramatic St Crispin's Day speech (4.3.18–67) with that found in Holinshed (1587) is especially illuminating.[27] Etymological analysis of the vocabulary in the two speeches reveals that Shakespeare gave his Henry more Anglo-Saxon words than are found in the Holinshed report. What difference does this linguistic shift make? Fuller research projects might be developed with students exploring the roots of the vocabulary used by Henry at different moments of the play, and by other characters.

Of course not just French loanwords, but French itself, is a vocal presence in the play. Princess Katherine attempts to learn English in 3.4, a scene almost entirely conducted in French. Any student difficulties with the scene can be a pedagogical advantage. One way to pinpoint the theatrical impact of the 'foreign' material is to show a clip while withholding access to a translation. Ask the students to write down what they understand, in terms of words, plot and tone. The class can then discuss their varying experiences of the scene: what divisions in understanding are there between those who can and cannot speak French? How much of the scene is available to those who can't speak French? How might these experiences key into the play's investigation of national and linguistic conflict? Closer analysis of Katherine's unwittingly bawdy puns might draw on Juliet Fleming's discussion:

> It takes some time to unpack all the sexual puns uttered by the inadvertent Katharine. The first two words that she asks her teacher to translate, *le pied* and *la robe*, were used in England to mean respectively one who commits buggery (from pied, meaning variegated), and a female prostitute. *Foot* sounds to Katharine like *foutre* (to copulate), while *count* would have been recognized as *cunt* by the audience. *D'elbow* sounds like *dildo*, *neck* and *nick* were synonyms for *vulva*, and *sin* was a euphemism for fornication. Finally, *excellent* had lewd connotations, and was especially associated with buggery, as was *assez*, understood to mean ass-y enough.[28]

Informed by this glossary of Elizabethan smut, students are equipped to debate the relationship between language and power in this scene. What does Katherine's comically inexpert use of English do to her status here? What is the impact of the specifically sexualized humour? Does the scene encourage a sense of superiority in English audiences (even if they cannot understand the French)? A follow-up discussion asking similar questions of the concluding scene would consolidate this investigation. What terms are used to describe English and French in this scene? Who holds the power in this scene and how is it registered? What is the impact of Henry addressing Katherine as 'Kate'?[29] Does Katherine seem to capitulate or resist?

French is not the only challenger to English dominance in this play; the drama's linguistic registers are emphatically plural. Paola Pugliatti describes *Henry V* as presenting a 'polyphonic political picture'. She argues that,

> by deploying so explicit and endemic a plurilinguism, by crediting a number of social discourses and of political perspectives, the play foregrounds conflicts of interests and a variety of viewpoints ... the many disturbing and disuniting effects of many-voicedness are deployed in the play in which national unity is celebrated is, to say the least, noticeable.[30]

Students might test out this argument by tracing the impact of a particular dialect (Scottish, Irish or Welsh) through the play and exploring the extent to which these alternative voices decentre English. After all, Henry disguises himself as 'Harry le Roy', compounding an English nickname with a French title, only for Pistol to wonder if he is 'Cornish' and for Henry then to proclaim himself 'a Welshman' (4.1.49–52). English is a somewhat unstable concept in the drama. Gower is furious that Pistol 'dare not avouch in [his] deeds any of [his] words' and berates him for his linguistic chauvinism:

> You thought because [Fluellen] could not speak English in the native garb he could not therefore handle an English cudgel. You find it otherwise, and henceforth let a Welsh correction teach you a good English condition.
>
> (5.1.75–9)

Pistol's bragging idiom counterfeits English words, since his signifying boasts are not made sound by significant action. Instead, Welsh-English proves truer and 'English' (the language and the national character) is taught to Pistol by a Welshman. Such scenes provide good sources for debates about whether the multiple languages of the play undermine its rhetorical insistence on a unified 'brotherhood', or whether this heteroglossia shows that brotherhood to be strengthened by plurality.

Gender

The representation of 'brotherhood' is also essential to investigations of gender in *Henry V*. 'Gender' is etymologically related to 'genre', meaning 'kind' or 'sort'; both gender and genre are concerned with categorization. In *Henry V*, the connections formed between men help to forge a sense of a group or brotherhood, and thus undergird ideas about masculinity.

Before sending students in search of examples of these bonds in the play, it is useful to provide them with early modern ideas about masculinity. Bruce R. Smith's *Shakespeare and Masculinity* is a rich source of contextual information about contemporary masculine ideals (which are significantly plural). For example, his discussion of 'virtue' helpfully sets the scene for analyses of virility:

> In a sermon on chivalry preached before the Artillery Company of London in 1626 William Gouge laments that the English language, unlike Latin, has no way of distinguishing 'man' as a term for just any male (*homo*) from 'man' as the embodiment of virtue and prowess (*vir*):

Our English is herein penurious: it wanteth fit words to express this difference. We call all, whether mighty or mean *men*, yet sometimes this word *men* in our tongue hath his emphasis, as in ... 'They have played the *men*' ... The fact that *virtue* is derived from *vir* establishes a fundamental connection between masculinity and the conformity to ethical ideals.[31]

Ideal masculinity is both etymologically innate in *virile* men and a *virtue* that needs to be performed. Smith also points out that two distinct economic systems coexisted in Shakespeare's era: the feudal system in which one's status depended upon inheritance, and the newer capitalist system whereby one's acquisition of money enabled a man to reposition himself. These conditions set up questions that might productively illuminate *Henry V*: to what extent is masculinity a performed condition in the play? Is masculine honour associated with inherited nobility or individual action?

In order to answer these questions, students might identify and analyse examples of male–male bonds in the play. Examples found might then be grouped according to bonds which forge or cut across family, rank and nationality. Earlier work on language can be drawn upon to deepen analysis: do the play's masculine bonds emerge as meaningful ethical connections or are they a rhetorical strategy? Henry's claim that

> he today that sheds his blood with me
> Shall be my brother; be he ne'er so vile,
> This day shall gentle his condition

(4.3.61–3)

repays close attention. The *OED* unlocks the potentially unfortunate pun on 'vile' (an Anglo-Norman word) as 'of little account' (*OED a.* 5), 'physically repulsive' (*OED a.* 3.a.) and 'despicable on moral grounds' (*a.* 1). And 'gentle' in this speech enacts the very shift in meaning described by the dictionary: 'Well-born, belonging to a family of position; originally used synonymously with *noble*, but afterwards distinguished from it.' Putting this speech alongside Henry's post-battle question, 'What prisoners of good sort are taken, uncle?' (4.8.76), opens out space for interrogation of the extent to which Henry's promise is upheld. Judith Haber's work on 'Simile, Paternity, and Identity' also provides a provocative stimulus for discussion. She notes that Henry 'calls on his men to prove their legitimacy by acting just like their "war-proof" fathers (who are, in turn "like many Alexanders")', but argues that the play presents a 'constellation of inadequate, failed comparisons and similes'.[32] In considering this claim, students might debate how far the play's rhetoric is persuasive, even if not literally accurate.

Of course, masculinity takes its meaning in relation to femininity. But female characters in this play are few in number. As Jean E. Howard and Phyllis Rackin pointed out in the 1990s, *Henry V*, unlike the earlier *Henry VI* plays, denies women a place on the battlefield. Students engaged in extended investigations of gender in history plays could consider Joan la Pucelle and Margaret alongside the French Princess and Mistress Quickly (married in the interim between *2 Henry IV* and *Henry V*). Howard and Rackin contend that '[d]omesticated and dependent, the female characters in *Henry V* are both economically and sexually vulnerable'.[33] One way for students to investigate this argument is to look at what happens to female characters in the play, and to consider the rhetorical value of gendered language. What does it mean for Henry to threaten sexual violence at the gates of Harfleur (3.3.35)? How does that threat resonate with the play's final scene, where the action is sometimes described as 'wooing', but is sometimes called a 'symbolic rape'?[34]

Texts

Surviving as it does in two substantially different early printed forms (the 1600 Quarto and the 1623 Folio), *Henry V* also offers an opportunity for advanced students to investigate the slippery categories of 'text' and 'play'. Good facsimiles of these texts are now readily available thanks to two free, very user-friendly websites: The Bodleian First Folio and the British Library's Treasures in Full: Shakespeare in Quarto.[35] Andrew Gurr's affordable Cambridge edition of *The First Quarto of King Henry V* also means it is now possible to teach the Quarto *Henry V* as a stand-alone incarnation of the play.[36]

If students are new to textual history, the different physical formats of the two texts of *Henry V* offer striking comparisons. Images of the title page of the Quarto and some of the paratexts of the Folio (the title page, the contents and some of the prefatory addresses) provide useful material for a comparative exercise. While the Folio collection is named for its author and features a prominent woodcut image of him, Shakespeare's name does not appear on the Quarto. Instead, Quarto readers are told that the play '*hath bene sundry times playd by the Right honourable the Lord Chamberlaine his seruants*'. Thus the two texts invite discussion of the ways early modern plays were 'authorized' (a debate which can be extended by considering how the posthumous Folio constructs a narrative about the author in its prefatory verses and addresses). The Quarto advertises that the play includes Henry's '*his battell fought at Agin Court in France. Togither with Auntient Pistoll*' and students might reflect on what this blurb tells us about the early modern appeal of the play. The Database of Early English Playbooks (DEEP) enables further research here, since it features searchable information about the title pages of Renaissance drama.[37] Students can investigate other plays printed at the same time as the *Henry V* Quarto to build up a picture of how title pages marketed plays, what kinds of texts were in demand in this period, and how different theatrical companies responded to their competitors' repertoires.

Scholars tend to agree that the Folio text of *Henry V* was derived from Shakespeare's authorial manuscript. For many years, the 1600 text was dismissed as a 'bad' Quarto, but Andrew Gurr's edition argues to the contrary that this much shorter text show[s] radical corrections made to the F text either in the course of preparing the play for performance or during its first run on stage ... The speed with which it came to the press only a year after its first staging is a mark both of its proximity to the text performed by the company that owned it and its authority as an official version.[38]

This suggestion provides a good opportunity to invite students to deepen their understanding of what they consider the 'play' to be: is it the artistic vision created by an author, or, given its theatrical purpose, is it a performance? What happens if we cannot access with any certainty either the author's vision or a play's first performance? Since plays are often performed more than once in different settings (we know that *Henry V* was performed in a public theatre, and at the royal court on 7 January 1605), should we expect them to be subject to change?

The specific differences between the Quarto and Folio text mean that these more abstract ideas can be explored practically. Comparison exercises can easily be developed focusing on, for example, the two texts' openings (Q: A2r–Br; F: hr–h2v) or the different versions of the siege at Harfleur (Q: C2v–C3r; F: [h5r]–[h6r]). Missing from the Quarto are the Prologue and the whole first scene in which Canterbury explicitly says he will distract Henry from his plan to 'strip' the Church of 'temporal lands' given to the Church with talk of Salic Law (1.1.9–11). Similarly, the Quarto's depiction of the siege at Harfleur is greatly reduced: soldiers do not appear with '*scaling-ladders*' (3.1.0), Henry does not urge his men to return 'Once more unto the breach' (3.1.1) and the four captains do not debate 'What ish my nation?' (3.2.124). These cuts reflect a broader trend in the Quarto which is to dramatically reduce the Folio text: the Quarto is half the length, not least because the Prologue, Choruses and Epilogue have been removed and Henry's own speeches are shrunk to 50 per cent of their Folio size.[39] These differences afford a good opportunity to consolidate the analytical work done on the themes raised above. Students might evaluate Gurr's argument that the

Quarto represents a text 'corrected' for performance, and consider whether and how these cuts make the play more 'playable'. Similarly, the Quarto's truncated size provides a new perspective on language, characterization and history-making. Does the snappier action help to make the less wordy Henry seem 'braver' as Gurr suggests? What are the political implications of the topical comparison to the Earl of Essex in the Folio ([i6r]) and the absence of a such an allusion in the Quarto? More broadly, if the play does not feature a disjunctive Chorus, does Henry emerge as a more or less troublingly inconsistent character? What happens to the Folio text's self-conscious focus on how 'history' is not a direct window to the past, but a constructed narrative?

Henry V opens out fascinating questions about the actions staged in the 'wooden O' and the political contexts of playhouses and printing presses. A multifaceted and multilingual play that survives in multiple texts, it gives students lots of opportunities for exciting research and stimulating debate.

Resource list

Detailed surveys of the critical resources for *Henry V* are found in the chapters by James Mardock and Emma Smith above. Listed here are resources that support the specific pedagogical strategies detailed in this chapter.

Electronic resources (public)

The Bodleian First Folio, http://firstfolio.bodleian.ox.ac.uk/
The British Library: Learning English Timeline, http://www.bl.uk/learning/timeline/item126569.html?
The British Library Treasures: Shakespeare in Quarto, http://www.bl.uk/treasures/shakespeare/quartos.html
Database of Early English Playbooks (DEEP), http://deep.sas.upenn.edu/

The Holinshed Project, http://www.cems.ox.ac.uk/holinshed/index.shtml
Shakespearean London Theatres (ShaLT), http://shalt.dmu.ac.uk/
Silva Rhetoricae: The Forest of Rhetoric, http://rhetoric.byu.edu/
The Theatre, Shoreditch 1595, http://www.explorethetheatre.co.uk/

Electronic resources (subscription)

Early English Books Online (EEBO), https://eebo.chadwyck.com/home
Lexicons of Early Modern English (LEME), http://leme.library.utoronto.ca/ (quick lexicon searches are available to non-subscribers)
Oxford English Dictionary Online (OED), http://www.oed.com/

Staging

Aaron, Melissa D. 'The Globe and *Henry V* as Business Document'. *Studies in English Literature* 40, no. 2 (2000): 277–92.
Bowsher, Julian. *Shakespeare's London Theatreland: Archaeology, History and Drama.* London: Museum of London Archaeology, 2012.
Dessen, Alan C., and Leslie Thomson. *A Dictionary of Stage Directions in English Drama, 1580–1642.* Cambridge: Cambridge University Press, 1999.
Gurr, Andrew, and Mariko Ichikawa. *Staging in Shakespeare's Theatres.* Oxford: Oxford University Press, 2000.
Pollard, Tanya. *Shakespeare's Theater: A Sourcebook.* Oxford: Blackwell, 2004.

Genre

Danson, Lawrence. *Shakespeare's Dramatic Genres.* Oxford: Oxford University Press, 2000.
Hattaway, Michael, ed. *The Cambridge Companion to Shakespeare's History Plays.* Cambridge: Cambridge University Press, 2002.
Rackin, Phyllis. *Stages of History: Shakespeare's English Chronicles.* New York: Cornell University Press, 1990.
Smith, Emma, ed. *Shakespeare's Histories: A Guide to Criticism.* Oxford: Blackwell, 2003.

Character

Burns, Edward. *Character: Acting and Being on the Pre-Modern Stage*. Basingstoke: Macmillan, 1990.
Cloud, Random. '"The Very Names of the Persons": Editing and the Invention of Dramatick Character'. In *Staging the Renaissance*, edited by David Scott Kastan and Peter Stallybrass, 88–96. London: Routledge, 1991.
Holderness, Graham. *Shakespeare: The Histories*. Basingstoke: Palgrave, 1999.
Palfrey, Simon. *Doing Shakespeare*. London: Arden, 2005.
Palfrey, Simon, and Tiffany Stern. *Shakespeare in Parts*. Oxford: Oxford University Press, 2011.
Smith, Emma, ed. *King Henry V: Shakespeare in Production*. Cambridge: Cambridge University Press, 2002.

Language

Fleming, Juliet. 'The French Garden: An Introduction to Women's French'. *ELH* 56, no. 1 (1989): 19–51.
Lanham, Richard. *A Handlist of Rhetorical Terms: Second Edition*. Berkeley: University of California Press, 1991.
Maguire, Laurie E. '"Household Kates": Chez Petruchio, Percy, and Plantagenet'. In *Gloriana's Face: Women, Public and Private, in the English Renaissance*, edited by S. P. Cerasano and Marion Wynne-Davies, 129–65. Detroit: Wayne State University Press, 1992.
Pugliatti, Paola. 'The Strange Tongues of *Henry V*'. *Yearbook of English Studies* 23 (1993): 235–53.
Steinsaltz, David. 'The Politics of French Language in Shakespeare's History Plays'. *Studies in English Literature* 42, no. 2 (2002): 317–34.
Vickers, Brian, ed. *English Renaissance Literary Criticism*. Oxford: Oxford University Press, 2003.

Gender

Aughterson, Kate, ed. *Renaissance Woman: A Sourcebook*. London: Routledge, 1995.

Haber, Judith. '"I cannot tell wat is like me": Simile, Paternity, and Identity in *Henry V*'. *Shakespeare Studies* 41 (2013): 127–47.

Howard, Jean E., and Phyllis Rackin. *Engendering a Nation*. London: Routledge, 1997.

Smith, Bruce R. *Shakespeare and Masculinity*. Oxford: Oxford University Press, 2000.

Texts

Egan, Gabriel. *The Struggle for Shakespeare's Text: Twentieth-Century Editorial Theory and Practice*. Cambridge: Cambridge University Press, 2010.

Gurr, Andrew, ed. *The First Quarto of King Henry V*. Cambridge: Cambridge University Press, 2000.

Jowett, John. *Shakespeare and Text*. Oxford: Oxford University Press, 2007.

Maguire, Laurie. 'Shakespeare Published'. In *Shakespeare: An Oxford Guide*, edited by Stanley Wells and Lena Cowen Orlin, 582–94. Oxford: Oxford University Press, 2003.

Sangha, Laura, and Jonathan Willis. *Understanding Early Modern Primary Sources*. London: Routledge, 2016.

NOTES

Introduction

1 Shakespeare wrote two tetralogies (that is, two series of four plays): the so-called 'first tetralogy', written between 1592 and 1595, covers the reigns of Henry VI, Edward IV and Richard III (in four plays, *1 Henry VI*, *2 Henry VI*, *3 Henry VI*, *Richard III*); the 'second tetralogy', although written after the first one, covers the preceding reigns – those of Richard II, Henry IV and Henry V (again in four plays, *Richard II*, *1 Henry IV*, *2 Henry IV* and *Henry V*). For an overview of the controversy surrounding Shakespeare's putative authorship of the *Henry VI* plays, see Shakespeare, *King Henry VI, Part 1*, ed. Edward Burns (London: Arden Shakespeare, 2000), 73–84.

2 http://www.visitmonmouthshire.com/things-to-do/agincourt.aspx (accessed 18 July 2017).

3 See the official site for Agincourt 600 at http://www.agincourt600.com/agincourt–600-the-charity/ (accessed 19 July 2017).

4 A *gendarme* is a man-at-arms. http://france3-regions.francetvinfo.fr/hauts-de-france/azincourt-le-programme-des-commemorations-des–600-ans-de-la-bataille–831817.html (accessed 10 October 2017).

5 In Dan Spencer's account (from the University of Southampton), see https://www.futurelearn.com/courses/agincourt/0/steps/15340 (accessed 10 October 2017).

6 A bombard, in medieval warfare, is a canon or mortar used during sieges to throw stone balls to destroy enemies' walls.

7 See the exhibition catalogue, *D'Azincourt à Marignan. Chevaliers et bombardes, 1415–1515*, ed. Antoine Leduc, Sylvie Leluc and Olivier Renaudeau (Paris: Gallimard / Musée de l'Armée, 2015).

8   Quoted in Jean-Michel Déprats, 'A French History of *Henry V*', in *Shakespeare's History Plays: Performance, Translation and Adaptation in Britain and Abroad*, ed. A. J. Hoenselaars (Cambridge: Cambridge University Press, 2004), 75.

9   Cf. Hermann Ulrici, quoted in Matthew Woodcock, *Shakespeare: Henry V* (London: Palgrave Macmillan, 2008), 46–8.

10 The director was Jean-Louis Benoit. This was the first *recorded* professional performance.

11 E. M. W. Tillyard suggested that a young Shakespeare wrote this anonymous play. Other possible authors include the actor Richard Tarleton and the playwright Samuel Rowley. For a discussion of *The Famous Victories* and *Henry V*, see Janet Clare, 'Medley History: *The Famous Victories of Henry The Fifth* to *Henry V*', *Shakespeare Survey* 63 (2010): 102–13.

12 Annabel Patterson, *Reading Holinshed's Chronicles* (Chicago and London: University of Chicago Press, 1994), 3–31.

13 John Dennis was the first person to suggest that Shakespeare wrote *The Merry Wives of Windsor* at Elizabeth's behest: see John Dennis, *The Comical Gallant, or the Amours of Sir John Falstaffe* (London: A. Baldwin, 1702), sig. A2r. See also William Shakespeare, *A Most Pleasaunt and Excellent Conceited Comedie, of Syr John Falstaffe; and the Merrie Wiues of Windsor* (London: Arthur Johnson, 1602), title page.

14 See Maurice Morgann, *An Essay on the Dramatic Character of Sir John Falstaff* (London: T. Davies, 1777).

15 'Falstaff. A Symphonic Study in C minor, with two Interludes in A minor'. See Edward Elgar, 'Falstaff', *The Musical Times* 54, no. 847 (September 1913): 575–8.

16 Three quarto texts are extant, published in 1600 (Q1, or Q), 1602 (Q2) and 1619 (Q3 – with a title page deliberately misdated to 1608). In Duncan Salkeld's words, 'Q2 and Q3 are essentially reprints of Q1, with some corrections': Duncan Salkeld, 'The Texts of *Henry V*', *Shakespeare* 3, no. 2 (2007): 163.

17 The phrase 'bad quarto' was coined by A. W. Pollard in 1909: see A. W. Pollard, *Shakespeare Folios and Quartos: A Study in the Bibliography of Shakespeare's Plays, 1594–1685* (London: Methuen, 1909), 64–5.

18 Andrew Gurr, *King Henry V, New Cambridge Shakespeare* (Cambridge: Cambridge University Press, 1992; rev. 2005), 64. See also Andrew Gurr, *The First Quarto of King Henry V* (Cambridge: Cambridge University Press, 2000), 2.

19 Lukas Erne, *Shakespeare as Literary Dramatist* (Cambridge: Cambridge University Press, 2003), 230–2.

20 See Salkeld, 'Texts', 176.

21 Annabel Patterson, 'Back By Popular Demand: The Two Versions of *Henry V*', *Renaissance Drama* 19 (1988): 31–2.

22 Paul E. J. Hammer, 'Devereux, Robert, second earl of Essex (1565–1601)', *Oxford Dictionary of National Biography* (Oxford: Oxford University Press, 2004); online edn, October 2008, http://www.oxforddnb.com.ezproxy.library.wisc.edu/view/article/7565 (accessed 24 November 2017).

23 For the identification of Mountjoy, see Richard Dutton, '*The Famous Victories* and the 1600 Quarto of *Henry V*', in *Locating the Queen's Men, 1583–1603: Material Practices and Conditions of Playing*, ed. Helen Ostovich, Holger Schott Syme and Andrew Griffin (Farnham: Ashgate, 2009), 135–44.

24 For a detailed account of the play's multifaceted evocation of Essex, see Peter Lake, *How Shakespeare Put Politics on the Stage: Power and Succession in the History Plays* (New Haven, CT: Yale University Press, 2016), 382–97.

25 Maev Kennedy, 'Excavation finds early Shakespeare theatre was rectangular', *Guardian*, 17 May 2016, https://www.theguardian.com/culture/2016/may/17/curtain-excavation-early-shakespeare-theatre-rectangular-shoreditch (accessed 24 November 2017).

26 Ben Jonson, *Every Man In His Humour*, in *The Cambridge Edition of the Works of Ben Jonson*, ed. David Bevington, Martin Butler and Ian Donaldson, 7 vols (Cambridge: Cambridge University Press, 2012), 4.632, Prologue 15. Voltaire called *King Henry V*'s wooing scene, 'une des plus étranges scènes des tragédies de Shakespeare' ['one of the weirdest scenes in Shakespearean tragedy']: Voltaire, *Lettre de Mr de Voltaire à l'Académie Française lue dans cette Académie à la solemnité de la St. Louis le 25 Auguste 1776* (s.l.,1776), 10.

27 Erne, *Shakespeare*, 255.

28 Norman Rabkin, 'Rabbits, Ducks, and *Henry V*', *Shakespeare Quarterly* 28 (1977): 279.

Chapter 1

1 Edward Berry, 'Twentieth-Century Shakespeare Criticism: the Histories', in *The Cambridge Companion to Shakespeare Studies*, ed. Stanley Wells (Cambridge: Cambridge University Press, 1986), 255.

2 The full title of Q1 is *The Cronicle History of Henry the fift, With his battell fought at Agin Court in France. Togither with Auntient Pistoll.*

3 Alexander Leggatt, *Shakespeare's Political Drama: The Roman Plays and the History Plays* (New York: Routledge, 1988), 114.

4 Ben Jonson, *Every Man In His Humour*. In *The Cambridge Edition of the Works of Ben Jonson*, ed. David Bevington, Martin Butler and Ian Donaldson, 7 vols (Cambridge: Cambridge University Press, 2012), 4.632, Prologue 15.

5 Francis Beaumont and John Fletcher, *Dramatic Works*, ed. Fredson Bowers, 10 vols (Cambridge: Cambridge University Press, 1966–98), 3.167 (3.4.96–138). Fletcher may have derived his scene – in which characters wrangle over the legitimacy of a title in the purview of the Salic Law – from Shakespeare's source in Holinshed's chronicle, but it seems just as likely that the scene is an homage to the work of his dramatic collaborator.

6 For the controversy over competing stage depictions of Oldcastle, see Peter Corbin and Douglas Sedge (eds), *The Oldcastle Controversy* (Manchester: Manchester University Press, 1991); James J. Marino, *Owning William Shakespeare* (Philadelphia: University of Pennsylvania Press, 2011), 107–42; and especially James M. Gibson, 'Shakespeare and the Cobham Controversy' *Medieval and Renaissance Drama in England* 25 (2012): 94–132. For an argument for restoring the name Oldcastle to the character later known as Falstaff, as the Oxford Shakespeare did in 1986 with *1 Henry IV*, see Gary Taylor, 'The Fortunes of Falstaff', *Shakespeare Survey* 38 (1986): 85–100.

7   The Lord Chamberlain's Men, Shakespeare's company, was founded in 1594 under the patronage of Henry Carey, 1st Baron Hunsdon, the Lord Chamberlain, who was in charge of the Queen's entertainments. The company became The King's Men in 1603 when King James became the company's patron.

8   Andrew Gurr, *The Shakespearean Playing Companies* (Oxford: Clarendon Press, 1996), 288.

9   *King Henry V: Shakespeare in Production*, ed. Emma Smith (Cambridge: Cambridge University Press, 2002), 10.

10 The setting of the Quarto entirely as verse may simply be the result of printing-house expedience, but in comparison with the more familiar version of the play that keeps its classes segregated by speech, it does have critical implications. Alfred Hart, in *Stolne and Surreptitious Copies: A Comparative Study of Shakespeare's Bad Quartos* (Melbourne: Melbourne University Press, 1942), found the universality of the verse to be troubling – 'King, queen, cardinal, duchess, peer, soldier, lover, courtier, artisan, peasant, servant and child all speak alike' (104) – and perhaps class bias fed into his reading of Q as 'illiterate'. But we might just as easily see it as an attempt in Q to render the English as the more unified community that the Folio's choruses promise, but that the Folio play does not quite deliver.

11 Laurie Maguire gives an apt summation of the case against the eighteenth-century theories of textual transmission in *Shakespearean Suspect Texts: The 'Bad' Quartos and their Contexts* (Cambridge: Cambridge University Press, 1996), 7.

12 A. W. Pollard, *Shakespeare Folios and Quartos* (London: Methuen, 1909); see also A. W. Pollard and John Dover Wilson, 'Henry V (1600)', *Times Literary Supplement*, 13 March 1919, 134.

13 The 'New Bibliography' developed by and associated with W. W. Greg and R. B. McKerrow supplied the narrative of memorial reconstruction to explain the shorter quarto texts, and the theory became ubiquitous during the twentieth century. The earlier theory of playhouse piracy by a member of the audience – either transcribing or memorizing the play in order to profit from unauthorized printings – had been discarded by 1910, when Greg first proposed, in his edition of *The Merry Wives of Windsor*, that certain actors, having memorized their own parts

as well as many of their peers' lines, worked to reconstruct the plays from memory, and that the unauthorized versions they produced then served as the copy texts for the 'bad' quartos (*The Merry Wives of Windsor*, ed. W. W. Greg (Oxford: Clarendon Press, 1910)). From the passages that most closely paralleled those in the 'good' texts, Greg and later scholars who pursued this explanation found that they could identify the parts played by these memorial reconstructors, most of which seemed to be small parts likely to have been played by hirelings and not by the player-sharers (i.e. those actors with a financial stake in the textual property of the Lord Chamberlain's Men). The main logical problem with the memorial reconstruction model, as Maguire, among others, has pointed out, is that it can be used to explain nearly any textual problem at all (*Shakespearean Suspect Texts*, 5–6), but in the case of *Henry V*, it is also simply inadequate to explain several of the changes to the Q text.

14 Stanley W. Wells and Gary Taylor, *Modernizing Shakespeare's Spelling: With Three Studies of the Text of Henry V* (Oxford: Oxford University Press, 1979), 125. Despite the Folio having been printed much later, modern scholars now gravitate toward the opinion that the version of the play behind the F text came earlier, and that the Q text was cut down from this text, rather than the F text being expanded from the Quarto version. The reference in F's Act 5 Chorus to 'the general of our gracious empress' (5.0.30) has been read by almost all critics as a reference to the Earl of Essex; if this is correct, it would date the composition of the Folio version of the play between March and September of 1599, well before the printing of the Quarto. That interpretation of the Chorus's allusion has never been quite unanimous, however, and outlying scholar Steven Urkowitz has argued repeatedly since 1980 – starting with his *Shakespeare's Revision of* King Lear (Princeton, NJ: Princeton University Press, 1980) – that all of the earlier versions of plays that differ from their counterparts in the Folio represent earlier stages in Shakespeare's revising process, a consistent and continuous endeavor of expansion and artistic improvement. In this view, the 1600 Quarto might have been printed from the promptbook of a *Henry V* that had been performed in the 1590s and was no longer in use since Shakespeare had revised and expanded the

play. Urkowitz's model is appealing for its picture of an author humanized by his less-polished early drafts and deeply invested in the artistic quality of his plays.

15 Gary Taylor, 'Shakespeare's Leno: *Henry V* IV.V.14', *Notes and Queries* 224 (1979): 117–18.

16 Annabel M. Patterson, 'Back by popular demand: the two versions of *Henry V*', *Renaissance Drama* n.s. 19 (1988): 29–62, 39.

17 Taylor, *Modernizing*, 130.

18 In 1991, Kathleen Irace conducted an exhaustive examination of the memorial reconstruction theory and produced a narrative of actors who had taken part in the play producing a new text from their memory of performances of the longer, Folio-linked text. Despite being deliberate and linked to playhouse practice, Irace maintains that the changes these actors made, and the Quarto text itself, have no claim to authority and cannot 'communicate Shakespeare's intentions', but her conclusions – that such a shortened text must be a promptbook for a touring performance, that such performances must be inferior, and that such texts are by definition further removed from authorial intentions – are based on unsupportable assumptions. See Kathleen Irace, 'Reconstruction and Adaptation in Q *Henry V*', *Studies in Bibliography* 44 (1991): 249.

19 *Henry V*, ed. Gary Taylor (Oxford: Oxford University Press, 1982); *The First Quarto of King Henry V*, ed. Andrew Gurr (Cambridge: Cambridge University Press, 2000); *Henry V*, ed. James Mardock, Internet Shakespeare Editions, University of Victoria, 4 October 2013, http://internetshakespeare.uvic.ca/Library/Texts/H5/ (accessed 17 July 2017).

20 Quoted in *Eighteenth-Century Essays on Shakespeare*, ed. D. Nichol Smith, 2nd edn (Oxford: Clarendon Press, 1963), 86.

21 William Shakespeare, *The Plays of William Shakespeare*, ed. Samuel Johnson, 8 vols (London: J. and R. Tonson et al., 1765), 4.414.

22 Shakespeare, *Plays*, ed. Johnson, 4.450, 487.

23 Shakespeare, *Plays*, ed. Johnson, 4.397.

24 Shakespeare, *Plays*, ed. Johnson, 4.479.

25 Shakespeare, *Plays*, ed. Johnson, 4.441.

26 William Hazlitt, *Characters of Shakespeare's Plays* (London: R. Hunter and C. and J. Ollier, 1818), xviii.
27 A. W. Schlegel, *Lectures on Dramatic Art and Literature*, trans. John Black, 2 vols (London, 1815), 2.217.
28 Hazlitt, *Characters*, 210.
29 Hazlitt, *Characters*, 205.
30 Hazlitt, *Characters*, 203.
31 Hazlitt, *Characters*, 206, 205.
32 *The Romantics on Shakespeare*, ed. Jonathan Bate (Harmondsworth: Penguin, 1992), 11.
33 Thomas Carlyle, *On Heroes, Hero-Worship and the Heroic in History* (London: Chapman and Hall, 1841; repr. Lincoln: University of Nebraska Press, 1966), 110.
34 Hermann Ulrici, *Shakspeare's Dramatic Art* (London: Chapman Brothers, 1846), 379.
35 Ulrici, *Dramatic Art*, 377–8.
36 Ulrici, *Dramatic Art*, 379.
37 G. G. Gervinus, *Shakespeare Commentaries*, trans. F. E. Bunnett, 2 vols (London: Smith, Elder, & Company, 1863), 1.473.
38 Gervinus, *Commentaries*, 1.479, 480.
39 H. N. Hudson, *Shakespeare: His Life, Art, and Characters*, 4th edn, 2 vols (Boston: Ginn, Heath, 1898), 2.119. In 1896, F. S. Boas is still pursuing this line of moral defence. He argues that while the play suffers for its too-tight focus on one character, it presents a successful portrait of a 'peerless leader of men' who 'shows that his policy is to be swayed, not by Machiavellian canons of self-interest, but by principles of equity': *Shakspere and His Predecessors* (London: John Murray, 1896), 288, 281.
40 Edward Dowden, *Shakspere: A Critical Study of His Mind and Art*, 3rd edn (New York: Harper & Brothers, 1905), v.
41 Dowden, *Shakspere*, 163.
42 Dowden, *Shakspere*, 66 (Dowden's emphasis).
43 Dowden, *Shakspere*, 75.
44 Algernon Charles Swinburne, *A Study of Shakespeare* (London: Chatto and Windus, 1880), 112.

45 William Watkiss Lloyd, *Critical Essays on the Plays of Shakespeare* (London: G. Bell and Sons, 1875), 252.
46 Lloyd, *Essays*, 254.
47 Lloyd, *Essays*, 255.
48 Lloyd, *Essays*, 255.
49 Lloyd, *Essays*, 254.
50 Lloyd, *Essays*, 255–6.
51 L. C. Knights, 'How Many Children Had Lady Macbeth? An Essay in the Theory and Practice of Shakespeare Criticism', in *Explorations* (New York: New York University Press, 1964), 15–54. Bradley had not posed the question that provided Knights with his facetious title, but the essay mocked the sort of questions Bradley did pose (such as 'Where was Hamlet at the time of his father's murder?'), considered by Knights irrelevant to criticism of the plays Shakespeare actually wrote.
52 A. C. Bradley, 'The Rejection of Falstaff', in *Oxford Lectures on Poetry*, 2nd edn (Glasgow: Glasgow University Press, 1909), 254.
53 Bradley, 'Rejection', 258.
54 Bradley, 'Rejection', 260.
55 A. P. Rossiter, 'Ambivalence: The Dialectic of the Histories', in *Angel with Horns, and Other Shakespeare Lectures*, ed. Graham Storey (London: Longman, 1961), 57.
56 Gerald Gould, 'A New Reading of *Henry V*', *English Review* 29 (1919): 42–55.
57 Gould, 'New Reading', 50.
58 Gould, 'New Reading', 42, 46.
59 Harold C. Goddard, *The Meaning of Shakespeare*, 2 vols (Chicago: University of Chicago Press, 1960), 1.218.
60 Goddard, *Meaning*, 231, 242.
61 Goddard, *Meaning*, 261–6.
62 For Una Ellis-Fermor, in *The Frontiers of Drama* (London: Methuen, 1945), Henry is destroyed as an individual by his constant performance of kingship: 'never off the platform' and 'never alone', his individual selfhood is 'utterly eliminated, sublimated... there is no Henry, only a king' (45–7).

63 Norman Rabkin, 'Rabbits, Ducks, and *Henry V*', *Shakespeare Quarterly* 28 (1977): 279.

64 Rabkin, 'Rabbits, Ducks', 296.

65 Rabkin, 'Rabbits, Ducks', 295.

66 Larry Champion, *Perspective in Shakespeare's English Histories* (Athens: University of Georgia Press, 1980); Phyllis Rackin, *Stages of History: Shakespeare's English Chronicles* (London: Routledge, 1990); Claire McEachern, *The Poetics of English Nationhood, 1590–1612* (Cambridge: Cambridge University Press, 1996).

67 John Stuart MacKenzie, *Arrows of Desire: Essays on Our National Character and Outlook* (London: Allen & Unwin, 1920), 43.

68 John C. McCloskey, 'The Mirror of All Christian Kings', *Shakespeare Association Bulletin* 19 (1944): 36.

69 Gervinus, *Commentaries*, 1.487.

70 G. Wilson Knight, *The Olive and the Sword: A Study of England's Shakespeare* (London: Oxford University Press, 1944), 4.

71 William Shakespeare, *Henry V*, ed. John Dover Wilson (Cambridge: Cambridge University Press, 1947), xxxiv.

72 E. M. W. Tillyard, *Shakespeare's History Plays* (London: Chatto & Windus, 1942), 320–1.

73 Lily B. Campbell, *Shakespeare's 'Histories': Mirrors of Elizabethan Policy* (San Marino, CA: Huntington Library Press, 1947), 15.

74 Campbell, *Shakespeare's 'Histories'*, 125.

75 Campbell, *Shakespeare's 'Histories'*, 268–71.

76 Reprinted in Stephen Greenblatt, *Shakespearean Negotiations* (Berkeley: University of California Press, 1988), 41.

77 Greenblatt, *Negotiations*, 58.

78 Greenblatt, *Negotiations*, 51.

79 Greenblatt, *Negotiations*, 63.

80 Greenblatt, *Negotiations*, 61.

81 Jonathan Dollimore and Alan Sinfield, 'History and Ideology: the instance of *Henry V*', in *Alternative Shakespeares*, ed. John Drakakis (London: Methuen, 1985), 206–27, 210–11.

82　Dollimore and Sinfield, 'Instance of *Henry V*', 215.

83　Dollimore and Sinfield, 'Instance of *Henry V*', 226.

84　Dollimore and Sinfield, 'Instance of *Henry V*', 217–18.

85　Graham Bradshaw, *Misrepresentations: Shakespeare and the Materialists* (Ithaca, NY: Cornell University Press, 1993), 85.

86　Bradshaw, *Misrepresentations*, 112.

87　*Presentist Shakespeares*, ed. Hugh Grady and Terence Hawkes (London: Routledge, 2007), 3.

88　Jonathan Dollimore and Alan Sinfield, 'History and Ideology, Masculinity and Miscegenation', in *Faultlines: Cultural Materialism and the Politics of Dissident Reading*, ed. Alan Sinfield (Oxford: Clarendon Press, 1992), 109–42.

89　Lance Wilcox, 'Katherine of France as Victim and Bride', *Shakespeare Studies* 17 (1985): 61–76; Jean Howard and Phyllis Rackin, *Engendering a Nation: A Feminist Account of Shakespeare's English Histories* (London: Routledge, 1997). For a more recent account of the relationship between homosociality and rape in the play, see Christian M. Billing, *Masculinity, Corporality and the English Stage 1580–1635* (Farnham: Ashgate, 2008), 84.

90　David J. Baker, '"Wildehirissheman": Colonialist Representation in Shakespeare's *Henry V*', *English Literary Renaissance* 22 (1992): 37–61; Michael Neill, 'Broken English and Broken Irish: Nation, Language and the Optic of Power in Shakespeare's Histories', *Shakespeare Quarterly* 45 (1994): 18–22; Andrew Murphy, 'Shakespeare's Irish History', *Literature and History* 5 (1996): 38–59.

91　Lisa Hopkins, 'Welshness in Shakespeare's English Histories', in *Shakespeare's History Plays: Performance, Translation and Adaptation in Britain and Abroad*, ed. A. J. Hoenselaars (Cambridge: Cambridge University Press, 2004), 60–74; Philip Schwyzer, *Literature, Nationalism, and Memory in Early Modern England and Wales* (Cambridge: Cambridge University Press, 2004).

92　James Shapiro, 'Revisiting *Tamburlaine*: *Henry V* as Shakespeare's Belated Armada Play', *Criticism* 31 (1989): 351–66, and James Shapiro, *1599: A Year in the Life of William Shakespeare* (London: Faber & Faber, 2005); Joel Atman, '"Vile

Participation": The Amplification of Violence in the Theater of *Henry V*', *Shakespeare Quarterly* 42 (1991): 1–32; Nick de Somogyi, *Shakespeare's Theatre of War* (Aldershot: Ashgate, 1998).

93 Camille Wells Slights, 'The Conscience of the King: *Henry V* and the Reformed Conscience', *Philological Quarterly* 80 (2001): 37–55; Michael Davies, 'Falstaff's Lateness: Calvinism and the Protestant Hero in *Henry V*', *Review of English Studies* n.s. 56 (2005): 351–78; Phebe Jensen, *Religion and Revelry in Shakespeare's Festive World* (Cambridge: Cambridge University Press, 2008); David Womersley, *Divinity and State* (Oxford: Oxford University Press, 2010).

Chapter 2

1 See *Shakespeare's Globe Rebuilt*, ed. James Ronald Mulryne and Margaret Shewring (Cambridge: Cambridge University Press, 1997).

2 See for instance Stephen Orgel's influential study, *Impersonations: The Performance of Gender in Shakespeare's England* (Cambridge: Cambridge University Press, 1996).

3 See Christie Carson, 'Mark Rylance, *Henry V* and "Original Practices" at Shakespeare's Globe: History Refashioned', in *Filming and Performing Renaissance History*, ed. Mark Thornton Burnett and Amanda Streete (London: Palgrave Macmillan, 2011), 127–45.

4 Paul Taylor, 'Theatre: *Henry V* / *The Winter's Tale*, The Globe, London', *The Independent*, 8 June 1997, http://www.independent.co.uk/arts-entertainment/theatre-henry-v-the-winters-tale-the-globe-london–1255060.html (accessed 17 September 2017).

5 Taylor, 'Theatre'.

6 See *La vie du roi Henry V*, ed. Gisèle Venet, trans. Jean-Michel Déprat, Folio Théâtre (Paris: Gallimard, 1999), 397.

7 Robert Migliorini, 'Henry V prend ses quartiers à Vincennes La pièce de Shakespeare, créée au festival d'Avignon cet été, est jouée pendant deux mois au théâtre de l'Aquarium, dans la mise

en scène de Jean-Louis Benoit', *La Croix*, 8 January 2000, https://www.la-croix.com/Archives/2000-01-08/Henry-V-prend-ses-quartiers-a-Vincennes-La-piece-de-Shakespeare-creee-au-festival-d-Avignon-cet-ete-est-jouee-pendant-deux-mois-au-theatre-de-l-Aquarium-dans-la-mise-en-scene-de-Jean-Louis-Benoit-_NP_-2000-01-08-99161 (accessed 17 October 2017).

8 See William Shakespeare, *King Henry V*, ed. Andrew Gurr (Cambridge: Cambridge University Press, 1992), 220–1.

9 Philip Sidney, *The Defence of Poesie* (London: William Ponsonby, 1595), sig. H4r.

10 Ben Jonson, *Volpone*, ed. Richard Dutton, in *The Cambridge Edition of the Works of Ben Jonson*, ed. David Bevington, Martin Butler and Ian Donaldson, 7 vols (Cambridge: Cambridge University Press, 2012), 3.44, lines 30–2.

11 Ben Jonson, *Every Man In His Humour* (F), ed. David Bevington, in *The Cambridge Edition of the Works of Ben Jonson*, edited by David Bevington, Martin Butler and Ian Donaldson, 7 vols (Cambridge: Cambridge University Press, 2012), 4.631, line 9.

12 Sidney, *Defence*, sig. H4r. See also Francisco Robortello, *Aristotelis poeticam explicationes* (Florence: Lorenzo Torrentino, 1548), an influential reinterpretation of Aristotle's *Poetics* for the humanists in Europe.

13 Ben Jonson, *Every Man Out Of His Humour*, ed. Randall Martin, in *The Cambridge Edition of the Works of Ben Jonson*, ed. David Bevington, Martin Butler and Ian Donaldson, 7 vols (Cambridge: Cambridge University Press, 2012), 1.273, lines 262–3; Jonson, *Every Man In His Humour*, ed. Bevington, 4.632, line 15.

14 Terry Hands, quoted in *Political Shakespeare: New Essays in Cultural Materialism*, ed. Jonathan Dollimore and Alan Sinfield (Manchester: Manchester University Press, 1985), 175.

15 Michael Pennington, quoted in James N. Loehlin, *Shakespeare in Performance: Henry V* (Manchester: Manchester University Press, 1997), 112.

16 *The Cronicle History of Henry the fift, With his battell fought at Agin Court in France. Togither with Auntient Pistoll* (London: Thomas Millington and John Busby, 1600).

17 *King Henry V: Shakespeare in Production*, ed. Emma Smith (Cambridge: Cambridge University Press, 2002), 196–7.

18 'If you be not too much cloyed with fat meat, our humble author will continue the story with Sir John in it', although his death was already planned: 'Falstaff shall die of a sweat' (*2 Henry IV*, Epilogue, 26–30).

19 Gurr, *King Henry V*, 44.

20 Ben Jonson, 'To the Memory of my Belovèd, The Author Master William Shakespeare And What He Hath Left Us', ed. Colin Burrow, in *The Cambridge Edition of the Works of Ben Jonson*, ed. David Bevington, Martin Butler and Ian Donaldson, 7 vols (Cambridge: Cambridge University Press, 2012), 5.638–42, line 43.

21 John Dryden, *Of Dramatick Poesie, An Essay* (London: Henry Herringman, 1668), 39.

22 Dryden, *Of Dramatick Poesie*, 29.

23 Samuel Pepys, *Diary of Samuel Pepys*, ed. Ernest Rhys and Richard Garnett, 2 vols (London: J. M. Dent, 1906), 1.510. See also entry for 28 December 1666, 2.156.

24 See Denis Lagae-Devoldère, '"New Rights We Grant Not, But the Old Declare": *le Henry V* de Roger Boyle (1664), ou Shakespeare "restauré"', *Études Épistémè* 14 (2008), http://journals.openedition.org/episteme/726 (accessed 12 December 2017).

25 Lagae-Devoldère, 'New Rights We Grant Not', notes 11 and 12.

26 Aaron Hill, *King Henry the Fifth: Or the Conquest of France, By the English. A Tragedy* (London: for W. Chetwood and J. Watts, 1723), Preface to the Reader, n.p.

27 Hill, *King Henry the Fifth*, Epilogue spoken by Mrs Oldfields (the actress playing Katherine): quoted in Loehlin, *King Henry V*, 17.

28 See *A compleat history of the trials of the rebel lords in Westminster-Hall; and the rebel officers and others concerned in the Rebellion in the year 1745, at St. Margaret's-Hill, Southwark* (London, 1746).

29 Loehlin, *King Henry V*, 17. Lagae-Devoldère also argues for the reciprocity of politics and aesthetics in the making of new

30 The Frenchwomen's confusion in this scene is in part explained by the fact that the word *'baiser'* in French means both to kiss and to have sex.
31 See Gurr, *King Henry V*, 44.
32 Kean was apparently 'unable to remember more than four consecutive lines'. Loehlin, *King Henry V*, 19.
33 Smith, *King Henry V*, 18.
34 Loehlin, *King Henry V*, 19; Smith, *King Henry V*, 22.
35 Quoted in Smith, *King Henry V*, 2.
36 Quoted in Loehlin, *King Henry V*, 20, from John William Cole, *The Life and Theatrical Times of Charles Kean* (1859).
37 Quoted in Smith, *King Henry V*, 26, from *Shakespeare's Play of King Henry the Fifth, Arranged for Representation at the Princess's Theatre, With Historical and Explanatory Notes by C. Kean* (1859).
38 Charles Calvert's production of the play was performed in The Prince's Theatre in Manchester in 1872, and eventually toured in America. Cf. Richard Foulkes, 'Charles Calvert's *Henry V*', *Shakespeare Survey* 41 (1989): 23–35.
39 George Bernard Shaw, *Our Theatres in the Nineties*, 3 vols (London: Constable and Company, 1931), 2.134.
40 Cf. Gerald Gould: 'the play is ironic' (1919), quoted in Smith, *King Henry V*, 45.
41 *Birmingham Gazette* (1946), quoted in Smith, *King Henry V*, 58.
42 Quoted in *The Royal Shakespeare Company's Production of 'Henry V' for the Centenary Season at the Royal Shakespeare Theatre*, ed. Sally Beauman (Oxford: Pergamon Press, 1976), 14.
43 Loehlin, *King Henry V*, 110.
44 Smith, *King Henry V*, 73.
45 The choice of the First World War rather than the Second World War was perhaps dictated by the fact that there is greater pathos attached in the collective imagination to the image of young men in the trenches.
46 Quoted in Smith, *King Henry V*, 92.

47 Susannah Clapp, 'Cry "God for Chelsea, England and Saint Kev!"', *Observer*, 3 September 2000, https://www.theguardian.com/theobserver/2000/sep/03/features.review47 (accessed 16 September 2017).

48 Michael Billington, '*Henry V*', *Guardian*, 4 May 2003, https://www.theguardian.com/stage/2003/may/14/theatre.artsfeatures2 (accessed 14 September 2017).

49 Billington, '*Henry V*', 4 May 2003.

50 Michael Billington, '*Henry V*', *Guardian*, 8 November 2007, https://www.theguardian.com/stage/2007/nov/08/theatre (accessed 14 September 2017).

51 Billington, '*Henry V*', 8 November 2007.

52 This production followed a version of the play performed in York in October 2015, which had an all-female cast. See Charles Hutchinson, 'Claire Morley leads York Shakespeare Project cast in all-female staging of Henry V at First World War munitions factory', *York Press*, 14 October 2015, http://www.yorkpress.co.uk/news/13845703.Claire_Morley_leads_York_Shakespeare_Project_cast_in_all_female_staging_of_Henry_V_at_First_World_War_munitions_factory/ (accessed 1 December 2017).

53 Michael Billington, '*Henry V* Review: An Astonishing Gender-Switched Reinvigoration', *Guardian*, 23 June 2016, https://www.theguardian.com/stage/2016/jun/23/henry-v-review-open-air-theatre-regents-park (accessed 14 September 2017).

54 Susannah Clapp, 'Henry V Review – If Shakespeare Had Done Brexit', *Observer*, 3 July 2016, https://www.theguardian.com/stage/2016/jul/03/henry-v-open-air-regents-park-review-michelle-terry (accessed 15 September 2017).

55 Billington, '*Henry V* Review'.

56 Billington, '*Henry V* Review'.

57 José Axelrad mentions a production of *Henry V* in 1963 at the Comédie de l'Ouest (Rennes, France) in 'Shakespeare's Impact Today in France', *Shakespeare Survey* 16 (1963): 56, without further details.

58 *The Oxford Companion to Shakespeare*, ed. Michael Dobson and Stanley Wells (Oxford: Oxford University Press, 2001,

2015), 573. Pictures of this staging can be found online at http://www.rideaudebruxelles.be/fantomas/22/662 (accessed 15 September 2017).

59 Nicholas Grene, *Shakespeare's Serial History Plays* (Cambridge: Cambridge University Press, 2002), 33.

60 Quoted in Grene, *Serial*, 34.

61 Quoted in Grene, *Serial*, 35. See Robert K. Sarlos, 'Dingelstedt's Celebration of the Tercentenary: Shakespeare's Histories as Cycle', *Theatre Survey* 5, no. 2 (1964): 117–31.

62 Jürgen Walderman, 'Dingelstedt, Shakespeare und Weimar', *Shakespeare Jahrbuch* 55 (1919): 75–85.

63 Loehlin, *King Henry V*, 147.

64 *Shakespeare on the German Stage, Volume 2, The Twentieth Century*, ed. Wilhelm Hortmann (Cambridge: Cambridge University Press, 1998), 122.

65 See Anon., 'ZADEK: Falscher Held', *Der Spiegel* 12/1964 (18 March 1964), http://www.spiegel.de/spiegel/print/d–46163513.html (accessed 15 September 2017).

66 Smith, *King Henry V*, 65.

67 Ben Brantley, 'Shakespeare's Take On the Game of Thrones', *New York Times*, 6 November 2016, https://www.nytimes.com/2016/11/05/theater/review-shakespeares-take-on-the-game-of-thrones.html (accessed 15 October 2017).

68 See https://www.stbernards.org/page/shakespeare-play (accessed 13 October 2017).

69 V. E. C. Manders, 'Shakespeare at St. Bernard's', *Shakespeare Quarterly* 2 (1951): 123.

70 Louis Marder, 'History Cycle at Antioch College', *Shakespeare Quarterly* 4 (1953): 58.

71 See the online company history, http://babeswithblades.org/about/company-history/ (accessed 28 September 2017).

72 Lauren Whalen, 'Henry V (Babes With Blades Theatre)', *Chicago Theater Beat*, 17 March 2017, http://chicagotheaterbeat.com/2017/03/17/henry-v-review-babes-with-blades/ (accessed 15 October 2017).

73 Whalen, 'Henry V (Babes With Blades Theatre)'.

74 Neil Genzlinger, 'Two Islands Are a Stage, and All Are Actors', *New York Times*, 12 July 2011, http://www.nytimes.com/2011/07/13/theater/reviews/henry-v-new-york-classical-theater-review.html (accessed 15 October 2017).

75 Julia Furlan, 'New Yorkers Take the Boat to France With Henry V', WNYC Online, 8 July 2011, http://www.wnyc.org/story/145085-new-yorkers-take-boat-france-henry-v (accessed 27 September 2017).

76 Loehlin, *King Henry V*, 156. See also Frank Rich, 'Henry V Takes Field in Central Park', *New York Times*, 6 July 1984, http://www.nytimes.com/1984/07/06/arts/stage-henry-v-takes-field-in-central-park.html?pagewanted=all (accessed 15 September 2017).

77 Rich, 'Henry V'.

78 Caldwell Titcomb, 'Anti-War "Henry V" Is Fascinating Failure', *Harvard Crimson*, 30 June 1969, http://www.thecrimson.com/article/1969/6/30/anti-war-henry-v-is-fascinating-failure/ (accessed 15 October 2017).

79 See Titcomb, 'Anti-War'.

80 See Titcomb, 'Anti-War'.

81 See J. L. Styan, *The Shakespeare Revolution: Criticism and Performance in the Twentieth Century* (Cambridge: Cambridge University Press, 1977), 187.

82 Robert K. Brady, 'International Notes: Malaya', *Shakespeare Survey* 7 (1954): 113.

83 See the company's website, https://popupglobe.com.au/about/overview/ (accessed 27 September 2017).

84 On its home page, the company advertises that 'This is Shakespeare like it's 1614': see https://popupglobe.com.au (accessed 27 September 2017).

85 See R. H. Thomson's 2009 interview of Christopher Plummer for the Theatre Museum Canada, https://www.youtube.com/user/THEATREMUSEUMCANADA/featureda (accessed 27 September 2017).

86 See http://www.nntt.jac.go.jp/english/productions/detail_009693.html (accessed 27 September 2017).

87 James Pickford, 'RSC to Translate All Shakespeare's Plays Into Mandarin', *Financial Times*, 28 October 2016, https://www.ft.

com/content/dcb5bab8–99dc–11e6–8f9b–70e3cabccfae (accessed 15 October 2017).

Chapter 3

1 Hugh Grady and Terence Hawkes, 'Introduction: Presenting Presentism', in *Presentist Shakespeares*, ed. Hugh Grady and Terence Hawkes (London and New York: Routledge, 2007), 5.
2 William Shakespeare, *Henry V*, ed. Gary Taylor (Oxford: Oxford University Press, 1982), 1.
3 Mackubin T. Owens, 'Shakespeare was no Pacifist', *Ashbrook Center Editorial* (November 2002), http://ashbrook.org/publications/oped-owens–02-shakespeare/ (accessed 17 July 2017).
4 Gary Taylor, 'Cry Havoc', *Guardian*, 5 April 2003.
5 *Henry V, War Criminal? & Other Shakespeare Puzzles*, ed. John Sutherland and Cedric Watts (Oxford: Oxford University Press, 2000), 115–16.
6 Scott Newstrom, 'Right Pitches Dubya as Henry V', *Alternet* (2003), http://www.alternet.org/story/16025/right_pitches_dubya_as_henry_v (accessed 17 July 2017).
7 David Coleman, 'Ireland and Islam: Henry V and the "War on Terror"', *Shakespeare* 4 (2008): 169.
8 Coleman, 'Ireland', 172, 178.
9 Mary Polito, '"Warriors for the Working Day": Shakespeare's Professionals', *Shakespeare* 2 (2006): 2.
10 Polito, 'Warriors', 8.
11 Norman Rabkin, 'Rabbits, Ducks, and *Henry V*', *Shakespeare Quarterly* 28 (1977): 279.
12 Tom McAlindon, 'Natural Closure in *Henry V*', *Shakespearean International Yearbook 3: Where are we now in Shakespearean Studies?* (2003): 156.
13 McAlindon, 'Natural', 168.
14 Malcolm Pittock, 'The Problem of *Henry V*', *Neophilologus* 93 (2009): 177.

15 Pittock, 'Problem', 190.

16 Bradley Greenburg, '"O for a muse of fire": Henry V and plotted self-exculpation', *Shakespeare Studies* 36 (2008): 183–5.

17 Dennis Kezar, 'Shakespeare's Guilt Trip in *Henry V*', *MLQ: Modern Language Quarterly* 61 (2000): 460–1.

18 John S. Mebane, '"Impious War": Religion and the Ideology of Warfare in Henry V', *Studies in Philology* 104 (2007): 251–2.

19 Mebane, 'Impious', 256.

20 Mebane, 'Impious', 258.

21 Mebane, 'Impious', 265.

22 David Womersley, *Divinity and State* (Oxford: Oxford University Press, 2010), 328–9. For other versions of this critical history, see James D. Mardock's chapter in the present volume, and Matthew Woodcock, *Shakespeare: Henry V* (Basingstoke: Palgrave Macmillan, 2008).

23 Womersley, *Divinity*, 1.

24 Womersley, *Divinity*, 338.

25 Womersley, *Divinity*, 330.

26 Camille Wells Slights, 'The Conscience of the King: Henry V and the Reformed Conscience', *Philological Quarterly* 80 (2001): 38.

27 Slights, 'Conscience', 41.

28 Slights, 'Conscience', 52.

29 Maurice Hunt, 'The "Breaches" of Shakespeare's *The Life of King Henry the Fifth*', *College Literature* 41 (2014): 8.

30 Hunt, 'Breaches', 15.

31 Hunt, 'Breaches', 18.

32 Maurice Hunt, 'Brothers and "Gentles" in *The Life of King Henry the Fifth*', *Comparative Drama* 49 (2015): 80.

33 Hunt, 'Brothers', 90.

34 Christopher Dowd, 'Polysemic Brotherhoods in *Henry V*', *Studies in English Literature* 50 (2010): 341.

35 Dowd, 'Polysemic', 351.

36 Jeffrey Knapp, *Shakespeare's Tribe: Church, Nation, and Theater in Renaissance England* (Chicago and London: University of Chicago Press, 2002), 17.

37 Knapp, *Tribe*, 19.
38 Knapp, *Tribe*, 119, 127.
39 Knapp, *Tribe*, 131–2.
40 Ken Jackson and Arthur F. Marotti, 'The Turn to Religion in Early Modern English Studies', *Criticism* 46 (2004): 179.
41 Matthew J. Smith, 'The Experience of Ceremony in *Henry V*', *SEL: Studies in English Literature* 54 (2014): 403.
42 Smith, 'Experience', 414.
43 Smith, 'Experience', 417.
44 Alison Thorne, '"Awake Remembrance of These Valiant Dead": *Henry V* and the Politics of the English History Play', *Shakespeare Studies* 30 (2002): 164.
45 Thorne, 'Awake', 172.
46 Anja Müller-Wood, 'No Ideology without Psychology: the Emotional Effects of Shakespeare's *Henry V*', *Style* 46, no. 3 (Fall 2012): 356.
47 Müller-Wood, 'No Ideology', 369–70.
48 Cedric Watts, 'Henry V's Claim to France: Valid or Invalid', in *Henry V, War Criminal? & Other Shakespeare Puzzles*, ed. John Sutherland and Cedric Watts (Oxford: Oxford University Press, 2000), 124–5.
49 Richard Hillman, *Shakespeare, Marlowe, and the Politics of France* (Basingstoke: Palgrave, 2002), 188.
50 Vimala C. Pasupathi, 'Coats and Conduct: The Materials of Military Obligation in Shakespeare's *Henry IV* and *Henry V*', *Modern Philology* 109 (2012): 348.
51 Eric Pudney, 'Mendacity and Kingship in Shakespeare's *Henry V* and *Richard III*', *European Journal of English Studies* 19 (2015): 163.
52 Pudney, 'Mendacity', 173.
53 Carrie Pestritto, 'Outlooks on Honor in *Henry V* and *Julius Caesar*', *Connotations* 17 (2007): 64.
54 Rita Banerjee, 'The Common Good and the Necessity of War: Emergent Republican Ideals in Shakespeare's *Henry V* and *Coriolanus*', *Comparative Drama* 40 (2006): 31.
55 Banerjee, 'Common', 34.

56 Cyndia Clegg, 'Feared and Loved: *Henry V* and Machiavelli's Use of History', *Ben Jonson Journal* 10 (2003): 179–207.

57 Hugh Grady, *Shakespeare, Machiavelli, and Montaigne: Power and Subjectivity from 'Richard II' to 'Hamlet'* (Oxford: Oxford University Press, 2002), 204.

58 Alison A. Chapman, 'Whose Saint Crispin's Day Is It? Shoemaking, Holiday Making, and the Politics of Memory in Early Modern England', *Renaissance Quarterly* 54 (2001): 1482.

59 Adrian Poole, 'The Disciplines of War, Memory and Writing: Shakespeare's *Henry V* and David Jones's *In Parenthesis*', *Critical Survey* 2 (2010): 91–104.

60 Jerry Brotton, 'Shakespeare's Turks and the Spectacle of Ambivalence in the History Plays', *Textual Practice* 28 (2014): 521–2.

61 Brotton, 'Turks', 531, 533–4.

62 Benedict S. Robinson, 'Harry and Amurath', *Shakespeare Quarterly* 60 (2009): 401.

63 Robinson, 'Harry', 403–4.

64 Robinson, 'Harry', 416.

65 Robinson, 'Harry', 422.

66 Alison Walls, 'French Speech as Dramatic Action in Shakespeare's *Henry V*', *Language and Literature* 22 (2013): 129.

67 Philip Searjeant, 'Ideologies of English in Shakespeare's *Henry V*', *Language and Literature* 18 (2009): 26.

68 Searjeant, 'Ideologies', 29.

69 Searjeant, 'Ideologies', 41.

70 John Kerrigan, 'Oaths, Threats and *Henry V*', *Review of English Studies* 63 (2012): 570.

71 Kerrigan, 'Oaths', 562.

72 Jonathan Baldo, '"Into a Thousand Parts": Representing the Nation in *Henry V*', *English Literary Renaissance* 38 (2008): 55–6.

73 Baldo, 'Thousand', 76.

74 Evelyn Tribble, 'Where Are the Archers In Shakespeare?', *English Literary History* 82 (2015): 789–91.

75 Tribble, 'Archers', 804.

76 Tribble, 'Archers', 807.

77 Tribble, 'Archers', 809.

78 Lucy Munro, 'Speaking History: Linguistic Memory and the Usable Past In the Early Modern History Play', *Huntington Library Quarterly* 76 (2013): 523.

79 Munro, 'Speaking', 538–9.

80 H. Austin Whitver, 'Materiality of Memory in Shakespeare's Second Tetralogy', *Studies in English Literature* 56 (2016): 287.

81 Whitver, 'Materiality', 300–1.

82 Isabel Karremann, *The Drama of Memory in Shakespeare's History Plays* (Cambridge: Cambridge University Press, 2015), 125.

83 Karremann, *Drama*, 152.

84 Meghan C. Andrews, 'Gender, Genre, and Elizabeth's Princely Surrogates in *Henry IV* and *Henry V*', *Studies in English Literature* 54 (2012): 377.

85 Andrews, 'Gender', 383.

86 Andrews, 'Gender', 389, 386, 389.

87 Corinne S. Abate, '"Once More Unto the Breach": Katharine's Victory in *Henry V*', *Early Theatre* 4 (2001): 74.

88 Abate, 'Once', 79.

89 Abate, 'Once', 82.

90 Judith Haber, '"I Cannot Tell Wat Is Like Me": Simile, Paternity and Identity in *Henry V*', *Shakespeare Studies* 41 (2013): 127.

91 Haber, 'Simile', 138–9.

92 Sarah Werner, 'Firk and Foot: The Boy Actor in *Henry V*', *Shakespeare Bulletin* 21 (2003): 19–27.

93 Drew Daniel, '*King Henry V*: Scambling Harry and Sampling Hal', in *Shakesqueer: A Queer Companion to the Complete Works of Shakespeare*, ed. Madhavi Menon (Durham, NC, and London: Duke University Press, 2011), 123, 125.

94 Duncan Salkeld, 'The Texts of *Henry V*', *Shakespeare* 3 (2007): 162.

95   Lukas Erne, *Shakespeare as Literary Dramatist* (Cambridge: Cambridge University Press, 2003), 220.

96   Erne, *Shakespeare*, 226–7.

97   Cyrus Mulready, 'Making History in Q *Henry V*', *English Literary History* 43 (2013): 480.

98   Mulready, 'Making', 492, 499.

99   Richard Dutton, '"Methinks the Truth Should Live From Age to Age": The Dating and Contexts of *Henry V*', *Huntington Library Quarterly* 68 (2005): 184.

100 Dutton, 'Methinks', 188.

101 Linda Charnes, 'Anticipating Nostalgia: Finding Temporal Logic in a Textual Anomaly', *Textual Cultures* 4 (2009): 80.

102 James N. Loehlin, *Henry V* (Manchester: Manchester University Press, 1997); *King Henry V: Shakespeare in Production*, ed. Emma Smith (Cambridge: Cambridge University Press, 2002).

103 *Shakespeare on Screen: The Henriad*, ed. Sarah Hatchuel and Nathalie Vienne-Guerrin (Rouen: Publications des Universités de Rouen et du Havre, 2008), 285–6.

104 Deborah Vukovitz, 'Shakespeare on Film: *Henry V* Rendered in Music', *Shakespeare Bulletin* 21 (2003): 42–5; José Ramón Díaz-Fernández, 'The Henriad On Screen: An Annotated Filmo-Bibliography', in *Shakespeare on Screen*, ed. Hatchuel and Vienne-Guerrin, 269–348.

Chapter 4

1   See Norman Rabkin, 'Rabbits, Ducks, and *Henry V*', *Shakespeare Quarterly* 28 (1977): 279–96. See also Norman Rabkin, *Shakespeare and the Problem of Meaning* (Chicago: University of Chicago Press, 1981), 34.

2   Alexander Leggatt, *Shakespeare's Political Drama* (London: Routledge, 1988), 114.

3   Peter B. Erickson, '"The Fault/My Father Made": The Anxious Pursuit of Heroic Fame in Shakespeare's *Henry V*', *Modern Language Studies* (1979–80): 13; Stephen Greenblatt, 'Invisible

Bullets: Renaissance Authority and its Subversion, *Henry IV* and *Henry V*', in *Political Shakespeare: Essays in Cultural Materialism*, ed. Jonathan Dollimore and Alan Sinfield (Manchester: Manchester University Press, 1985), 42; Sidney Shanker, *Shakespeare and the Uses of Ideology* (Paris: Mouton, 1975), 71.

4 Pauline Kiernan, *Shakespeare's Theory of Drama* (Cambridge: Cambridge University Press, 1996), 147–8.

5 My italics.

6 My italics.

7 James Hirsh, 'Shakespeare's Stage Chorus and Olivier's Film Chorus', in *Shakespeare on Screen: The Henriad*, ed. Sarah Hatchuel and Nathalie Vienne-Guerrin (Rouen: Publications des universités de Rouen et du Havre, 2008), 169–92.

8 Stephen M. Buhler, 'Text, Eyes, and Videotape: Screening Shakespeare Scripts', *Shakespeare Quarterly* 46 (1995): 240.

9 See Stanley Wells, 'The Canon in the Can', *Times Literary Supplement*, 10 May 1985, 522; Graham Holderness, 'Boxing the Bard: Shakespeare and Television', in *The Shakespeare Myth*, ed. Graham Holderness (Manchester: Manchester University Press, 1991), 173–89.

10 Holderness, 'Boxing', 181.

11 Kenneth Branagh, *Henry V: A Screen Adaptation* (London: Chatto & Windus, 1989), 12.

12 Kenneth Branagh, *Beginning* (London: Chatto & Windus, 1989), 141.

13 Mera J. Flaumenhaft, 'Three Views of *Henry V*: Shakespeare, Olivier, and Branagh', in Mera J. Flaumenhaft, *The Civic Spectacle: Essays on Drama and Community* (Lanham, MD: Rowman & Littlefield, 1994), 148. Branagh actually designated Picasso's *Guernica* as his favourite painting during an interview with Laurent Tirard, 'Branagh Côté Jardin', *Studio* 123 (1 July 1997): 78–83.

14 Branagh, *Beginning*, 229.

15 Chris Fitter, 'A Tale of Two Branaghs: *Henry V*, Ideology and the Mekong Agincourt', in *Shakespeare Left and Right*. ed. Ivo Kamps (London: Routledge, 1991), 270.

16 Kenneth Branagh, 'Unpublished Screenplay and Storyboard of *Henry V*', Renaissance Film Company Archive, located at the Kenneth Branagh Archive, Queen's University, Belfast (October 1998), 2, 27.

17 Branagh, *Henry V: A Screen Adaptation*, 15.

18 *Mise-en-abyme*, a French term derived from heraldry, designates a formal technique in which an image contains a smaller copy of itself. A film-within-a-film is an example of *mise-en-abyme* as the film being made (or shown) within the film refers to the real film being made.

19 Note that in the first version of Branagh's screenplay, an allusion to the execution of the prisoners was retained in lines delivered by soldier Gower. After discovering the murdered boys, Gower says, 'wherefore the King most worthily hath caused every soldier to cut his prisoner's throat' (4.7.8–10). See 'Unpublished Screenplay', 81. The fact that Branagh eventually decided to cut this line as well is symptomatic of his desire to protect Henry's heroic status.

20 Interviewed by Gary Crowdus, 'Sharing an Enthusiasm for Shakespeare: An Interview with Kenneth Branagh', *Cineaste* 24 (1998): 39.

21 See Elizabeth Marsland, 'Updating Agincourt: The Battle Scenes in Two Film Versions of *Henry V*', in *Modern War on Stage and Screen/Der Moderne Krieg auf die Buhne*, ed. Wolfgang Görtschacher and Holger Klein (Lewiston, NY: Edwin Mellen, 1997), 18.

22 Michael Hattaway, 'Shakespeare's Histories: the Politics of Recent British Productions', in *Shakespeare in the New Europe*, ed. Michael Hattaway, Boika Sokolova and Derek Roper (Sheffield: Sheffield Academic Press, 1994), 364.

23 Ian Aitken, 'Formalism and Realism: *Henry V* (Laurence Olivier, 1944; Kenneth Branagh, 1989)', *Critical Survey* 3 (1991): 265; Curtis Breight, 'Branagh and the Prince, or a "Royal Fellowship of Death"', *Critical Quarterly* 33 (1991): 96.

24 Samuel Crowl, 'Fathers and Sons: Kenneth Branagh's *Henry V*', in *Shakespeare Observed: Studies in Performance on Stage and Screen* (Athens: Ohio University Press, 1992), 172.

25 Warren Chernaik, 'The Death of Bardolph: Branagh and Olivier Rewrite *Henry V*', in *Shakespeare on Screen*, ed. Hatchuel and Vienne-Guerrin, 165.

26 Ramona Wray, 'Hegemonic Masculinity, the Roman Epic and Kenneth Branagh's *Henry V*', in *Shakespeare on Screen*, ed. Hatchuel and Vienne-Guerrin, 224.

27 Jonathan Hart, 'Shakespeare's *Henry V*: Towards the Problem Play', *Cahiers Elisabéthains* 42 (1992): 33.

28 See Sarah Hatchuel, '"Into a Thousand Parts Divide One Man": Dehumanised Metafiction and Fragmented Documentary in Peter Babakitis' *Henry V*', in *Screening Shakespeare in the Twenty-First Century*, ed. Mark Thornton Burnett and Ramona Wray (Edinburgh: Edinburgh University Press, 2006), 150.

29 See Burhan Wazir, 'Docu-dramas Set to Storm the Screens: Viewers Lap Up Mix of Fact and Fiction', *Observer*, 18 May 2003, https://www.theguardian.com/media/2003/may/18/broadcasting.uknews (accessed 2 December 2017).

30 Hatchuel, 'Thousand', 152.

31 See the Internet Movie Database (IMDb), 'Frequently Asked Questions for *Henry V* (2007): How is this film different from older screen adaptations of Henry V', http://www.imdb.com/title/tt1261975/faq (accessed 2 December 2017).

32 David Livingstone, 'Silenced Voices: A Reactionary Streamlined *Henry V* in *The Hollow Crown*', *Journal of University of Lodz (Multicultural Shakespeare: Translation, Appropriation and Performance)* 12 (2015): 87–100.

33 Mariangela Tempera, '"Only About Kings": References to the Second Tetralogy in Film and Television', in *Shakespeare on Screen*, ed. Hatchuel and Vienne-Guerrin, 234.

34 Tempera, 'Only About Kings', 261.

35 Craig Dionne, 'The Shatnerification of Shakespeare: *Star Trek* and the Commonplace Tradition', in *Shakespeare after Mass Media*, ed. Richard Burt (Basingstoke: Palgrave, 2002), 173–91.

36 See the chapter on 'microadaptations' in Shannon Wells-Lassagne, *Television and Serial Adaptation* (London: Routledge, 2017), 63–87.

Chapter 5

1. William Hazlitt, *The Round Table & Characters of Shakespear's Plays* (London: J. M. Dent, 1817; repr. 1951), 285.
2. Hazlitt, *Round*, 289.
3. William Shakespeare, *King Henry V*, ed. T. W. Craik, Arden Shakespeare, Third Series (London: Routledge, 1995), 71.
4. A. C. Bradley, 'The Rejection of Falstaff', in *Oxford Lectures on Poetry*, 2nd edn (Glasgow: Glasgow University Press, 1909), 256.
5. Bradley, 'Rejection', 257.
6. Bradley, 'Rejection', 257.
7. William Shakespeare, *Henry V*, ed. J. H. Walter, Arden Shakespeare, Second Series (London: Methuen, 1954), xxii. Cf. also Zdeněk Stříbrný, '*Henry V* and History', in *Shakespeare in a Changing World*, ed. Arnold Kettle (New York: International Publishers, 1964), 90.
8. Shakespeare, *Henry V*, ed. Walter, xxix.
9. Jonathan Dollimore and Alan Sinfield, 'History and Ideology: the Instance of *Henry V*', in *Alternative Shakespeares*, ed. John Drakakis, 2nd edn (London: Routledge, 2002), 216.
10. Dollimore and Sinfield, 'History', 219.
11. Stephen Greenblatt, 'Invisible Bullets: Renaissance Authority and its Subversion, *Henry IV* and *Henry V*', in *Political Shakespeare: New Essays in Cultural Materialism*, ed. Jonathan Dollimore and Alan Sinfield (Manchester: Manchester University Press, 1985), 28.
12. Greenblatt, 'Invisible', 28–9.
13. See Stephen Greenblatt, *Shakespearean Negotiations: The Circulation of Social Energy in Renaissance England* (Berkeley: University of California Press, 1988). His introductory chapter, 'The Circulation of Social Energy', is followed by a revised version of the essay on 'Invisible Bullets'. The passage quoted above remains (39), although it jars considerably with the claim, 'if I wanted to hear the voice of the other, I had to hear my own voice' (20).
14. See Gary Taylor, 'The Fortunes of Oldcastle', *Shakespeare Survey* 38 (1985): 85–100. Taylor's claim is that Shakespeare had

originally intended to use the name 'Oldcastle' but, under pressure from the influential Cobham family to whom the Protestant martyr Sir John Oldcastle was related, changed the speech-prefix to 'Falstaff'. In the *Oxford Shakespeare* (1989), and on the basis of this argument, the name 'Oldcastle' replaces 'Falstaff', although it must be emphasized that no manuscript detailing this change *nor* any early edition of the plays in the second tetralogy exists that contain the speech-prefix 'Oldcastle'. Sophisticated and plausible though Taylor's historical argument may be, it rests on a traditional version of the well-known 'intentional fallacy' that claims to be able to locate the writer's *intention* beneath the surface of the text.

15 Taylor, 'Fortunes', 98.
16 Taylor, 'Fortunes', 96.
17 See Richard Wilson, *Secret Shakespeare: Studies in Theatre, Religion and Resistance* (Manchester: Manchester University Press, 2004), 62, 290.
18 See especially, Andrew Gurr, '*Henry V* and the Bees' Commonwealth', *Shakespeare Survey* 30 (1977): 61–72.
19 See Michael Davies, 'Falstaff's Lateness: Calvinism and the Protestant Hero in *Henry IV*', *Review of English Studies* n.s. 56 (2005): 351–78, in which 'Shakespeare's great Harry is clearly a hero of this Essexian apocalyptic mould, imbued with the "true fortitude" of the noble, godly, Protestant warrior' (375).
20 Anon., *The Famous Victories of Henry V*, ed. John Jowett (Manchester: Malone Society, 2007), v.
21 Anon., *Famous*, ed. Jowett, xxii.
22 See John Drakakis, 'Shakespeare as Presentist', *Shakespeare Survey* 66 (2013): 182–3.
23 Edward Hall, *The Union of the Two Noble Families of Lancaster and York* (London: Richard Grafton, 1548), fol. rrriiii.
24 Hall, *Union*, fol. rrriiii.
25 Hall, *Union*, fol. rli.
26 Hall, *Union*, fol. li.
27 Shakespeare, *Henry V*, ed. Craik, 376.
28 Gurr, '*Henry V* and the Bees' Commonwealth', 72.

29 Jean Bodin, *On Sovereignty*, ed. and trans. Julian H. Franklin (Cambridge: Cambridge University Press, 1992; repr. 2007), 49. Cf. also Carl Schmitt, *Political Theology: Four Chapters on the Concept of Sovereignty*, trans. George Schwab (Chicago: University of Chicago Press, 2005), 8–9.

30 Christopher Marlowe, *The Jew of Malta*, ed. N. W. Bawcutt (Manchester: Manchester University Press, 1978), 62–3. All citations are from this edition.

31 Nicholas Machiavelli, *Nicholas Machiavel's Prince* (London: Will Hills, 1640), 119–20.

32 Jacques Derrida, *The Beast and the Sovereign*, trans. Geoffrey Bennington, 2 vols (Chicago: University of Chicago Press, 2009), 1.140.

33 Machiavelli, *Nicholas Machiavel's Prince*, sig. A4r. Although 1640 was the date of *The Prince*'s first English publication, it is generally thought that Machiavelli's text circulated widely in translation during the late sixteenth century. Compare also Friar Laurence's words in Shakespeare's *Romeo and Juliet*, 'Virtue itself turns vice, being misapplied, / And vice sometime by action dignified' (2.3.17–18).

34 This essay was included in the 1985 edition of *Political Shakespeare*, ed. Dollimore and Sinfield, 18–47. Its reappearance in Greenblatt, *Negotiations*, 21–65, alters, extends and clarifies parts of the earlier publication.

35 Greenblatt, *Negotiations*, 22.

36 Greenblatt, *Negotiations*, 27.

37 Greenblatt, *Negotiations*, 63.

38 Greenblatt, *Negotiations*, 65.

39 Graham Holderness, *Shakespeare's History* (Dublin: Gill and Macmillan, 1985), 137.

40 Slavoj Žižek, *The Sublime Object of Ideology* (London: Verso, 1989), 28.

41 Žižek, *Sublime*, 32.

42 Žižek, *Sublime*, 32–3.

43 Žižek, *Sublime*, 33.

44 Jean Calvin, *Institutes of the Christian Religion*, ed. John T. McNeill, 2 vols (Philadelphia: Westminster Press, 1960), 1.600.

45 Calvin, *Institutes*, ed. McNeill, 1.595.
46 Peter Sloterdijk, *Critique of Cynical Reason*, trans. Michael Eldred (London: Verso, 1988), 26.
47 Sloterdijk, *Critique*, 32.
48 Sloterdijk, *Critique*, 32.
49 See Calvin, *Institutes*, ed. McNeill, 1.195–6.
50 The idea behind the concept of 'the fortunate fall' is that the disobedience of Adam and Eve sets mankind on a path that leads ultimately through repentance to redemption by the intercession of Christ.
51 Sloterdijk, *Critique*, 28–9.
52 Alan Sinfield, *Literature in Protestant England 1560–1660* (London: Croom Helm, 1983), 8–9.
53 See William Shakespeare, *Henry V*, ed. Gary Taylor (Oxford: Oxford University Press, 1982), 216, and Shakespeare, *Henry V*, ed. Craik, 271. See also, Shakespeare, *Henry V*, ed. Walter, 102, where the lines appear without quotation marks.
54 Davies, 'Falstaff's Lateness': 375.

Chapter 6

1 Excluding stage directions and speech prefixes, the 1600 Quarto text, entitled *The Cronicle History of Henry the fift, With his battell fought at Agin Court in France. Togither with Auntient Pistoll*, includes twenty-three occurrences of the word 'England' and thirteen of the word 'English'. *The Life of Henry the Fift*, as printed in the 1623 Folio, includes fifty occurrences of 'England', forty-four of 'English', and four combined of 'Englishman' or 'Englishmen' (excluding stage directions and speech prefixes). It also contains Shakespeare's only use of the word 'Englishwoman'. These words surface more in *The Life of Henry the Fift* than in any other play by Shakespeare. Perhaps the finest appropriation of this play for the purposes of patriotism is Laurence Olivier's 1944 film version, which was dedicated to the 'Commandos and Airborne Troops of Great Britain, the spirit of whose ancestors it has humbly attempted to recapture'.

2   James Shapiro, *1599: A Year in the Life of William Shakespeare* (London: Faber & Faber, 2005), 104.

3   All references, unless otherwise specified, are to William Shakespeare, *King Henry V*, ed. T. W. Craik (London: Arden Shakespeare, 1995), which bases itself on the Folio text.

4   Shakespeare, *Henry V*, ed. Craik, 132. Andrew Gurr's gloss of 'imperial' is more apropos: '"Empire" meant absolute sovereignty': William Shakespeare, *King Henry V*, ed. Andrew Gurr (Cambridge: Cambridge University Press, 1992), 78.

5   Shakespeare was writing plays at a time when 'the British overseas empire remained a nascent phenomenon'. See John Kerrigan, *Archipelagic English: Literature, History, and Politics 1603–1707* (Oxford: Oxford University Press, 2008), 50.

6   Roger Mason, 'Scotching the Brut: Politics, History and National Myth in Sixteenth-Century Britain', in *Scotland and England, 1286–1815*, ed. Roger Mason (Edinburgh: John Donald Publishers, 1987), 69.

7   See *Statutes of the Realm*, ed. Alexander Luders et al., 11 vols (London: Dawsons, 1810–28), 3.427.

8   Richard Helgerson, *Forms of Nationhood: The Elizabethan Writing of England* (Chicago: University of Chicago Press, 1992), 4. Some of the 'Elizabethan' writers studied by Helgerson – Drayton, Shakespeare, Speed – also made signal contributions to the Jacobean writing of Britain.

9   On Shakespeare's turn from matters English to British, see Kerrigan, *Archipelagic English*, 14; Neil Rhodes, 'Wrapped in the Strong Arms of the Union: Shakespeare and King James', in *Shakespeare and Scotland*, ed. Willy Maley and Andrew Murphy (Manchester: Manchester University Press, 2004), 37; and Christopher Wortham, 'Shakespeare, James I and the Matter of Britain', *English* 45 (1996): 97–122. 'There is little celebration,' Wortham writes, 'of England and Englishness in Shakespeare's plays written after the accession of James VI of Scotland to his English throne as James I in 1603' (Wortham, 'Shakespeare', 97).

10 Benedict Anderson, *Imagined Communities: Reflections on the Origin and Spread of Nationalism*, rev. edn (London: Verso, 1991), 19, 7.

11 Shakespeare's Henry may at times be '*England*' in speech prefixes in the Folio, but just how English was the historical King Henry V? According to Anderson, 'there has not been an "English" dynasty ruling in London since the eleventh century (if then)' (Anderson, *Imagined Communities*, 21). Anderson voices a peculiarly modern scepticism about national origins; later in this essay I will suggest that Shakespeare's play does something similar.

12 Anderson, *Imagined Communities*, 7.

13 Helgerson, *Forms of Nationhood*, 10. 'Blood relations at the end of the play are a matter of marriages and dynasties, not of the blood shed by brothers in arms' (Shakespeare, *King Henry V*, ed. Gurr, 36).

14 Helgerson, *Forms of Nationhood*, 195.

15 David Baker captures the play's dynastic/national inbetweenness nicely: 'The place of *Henry V*. . . is *both* a royal demesne, stretched loosely across the British Isles, *and* the spatially distinct and regulated domain that we have now come to think of as a nation': David J. Baker, *Between Nations: Shakespeare, Spenser, Marvell, and the Question of Britain* (Stanford, CA: Stanford University Press, 1997), 63. What I wish to suggest is that the play's representation of England's 'porous and indistinct' borders owes much to the issue of Elizabeth's foreign successor (Anderson, *Imagined Communities*, 19).

16 Thomas Nashe, *Pierce Penilesse His Supplication to the Diuell* (London: John Busbie, 1592), sig. F3v.

17 'The constitutional status of the English king's continental possessions varied, but the most recent recension of English claims was contained in the Treaty of Troyes (1420). In accordance with its terms, the infant Prince Henry succeeded as Henry VI to the crown of England on the death of his father, Henry V, in August 1422 and to the crown of France on the death of his maternal grandfather, King Charles VI, two months later, thus creating a dual monarchy. Subsequently, Henry VI was crowned king of England at Westminster in 1429 and king of France in Paris in 1431': Steven G. Ellis, 'From Dual Monarchy to Multiple Kingdoms: Unions and the English State, 1422–1607', in *The Stuart Kingdoms in the Seventeenth Century: Awkward Neighbours*, ed. Allan I. MacInnes and Jane Ohlmeyer (Dublin: Four Courts Press, 2002), 42.

18 After the English victory at Agincourt, Henry traces the route back home: 'And then to Calais, and to England then' (4.8.126). Five references to Calais surface in the play, and it could be argued that these references serve as an unsettling reminder of the loss of England's French territories.

19 Jonathan Baldo, 'Wars of Memory in *Henry V*', *Shakespeare Quarterly* 47, no. 2 (1996): 137.

20 Both Queen Elizabeth I and King James I retained France in their official titles; however, they were both monarchs of France in name only.

21 Ellis, 'From Dual Monarchy', 39.

22 Ellis, 'From Dual Monarchy', 39.

23 Ellis, 'From Dual Monarchy', 38.

24 Ellis, 'From Dual Monarchy', 38.

25 Ellis, 'From Dual Monarchy', 38. Ellis notes that 'no Tudor monarch ever visited Ireland or Scotland (notwithstanding the 'Rough Wooing' of Protector Somerset in the 1540s). For the most part, they confined themselves to their royal palaces and houses concentrated in south-east England' (Ellis, 'From Dual Monarchy', 45).

26 By no means do I wish to downplay the Welsh presence in the histories: 'Welsh characters and locales feature even more frequently in [Shakespeare's] plays than does contemporary Italy.' Willy Maley and Philip Schwyzer, 'Introduction: A Welsh Correction', in *Shakespeare and Wales: From the Marches to the Assembly*, ed. Willy Maley and Philip Schwyzer (Farnham: Ashgate, 2010), 2.

27 Ellis, 'From Dual Monarchy', 38.

28 Anon., *The Famous Victories of Henry the Fifth: Containing the Honourable Battell of Agin-court: As it was plaide by the Queenes Maiesties Players* (London, 1598), sig. D2r. This idea is then revised in the play by the Lord of Oxford: 'He that wil Scotland win, must first with France begin', adding 'I thinke it best first to inuade France, / For in conquering Scotland, you conquer but one, / And conquere France and conquere both' (sig. D2v).

29 The speech is attributed to Ely in the Folio.

30 In the 1600 Quarto version of the play, Canterbury does say 'your *England*' (sig. A3r).

31 Grandpré uses 'island' adjectivally when he refers to the English army as 'Yon island carrions' (4.2.38).
32 Andrew Murphy, *But the Irish Sea Betwixt Us: Ireland, Colonialism, and Renaissance Literature* (Lexington: University of Kentucky Press, 1999), 114.
33 Shakespeare, *The Cronicle History of Henry the fift*, sig. A3r.
34 'Davy Gam, cited as one of the English dead at Agincourt, was a leading Welsh soldier' (Shakespeare, *King Henry V*, ed. Gurr, 68).
35 In the First Folio, the three non-English captains are given ethnically specific speech prefixes. The English captain, Gower, is designated by his name ('*Gower*'), but repeatedly we find Fluellen given the speech prefix '*Welch*', and Macmorris (also 'Makmorrice' and 'Mackmorrice') and Jamy ('Jamy' and 'James') given the respective speech prefixes '*Irish*' and '*Scot*'. See *The First Folio of Shakespeare: The Norton Facsimile*, ed. Charlton Hinman, 2nd edn (New York: Norton, 1996), TLN 1186–1258 (TLN refers to Hinman's 'through line number' referencing system).
36 Jean Howard and Phyllis Rackin, *Engendering a Nation: A Feminist Account of Shakespeare's English Histories* (London: Routledge, 1997), 4.
37 Jonathan Baldo, for example, refers to 'the British army at Agincourt', 'British yeoman', 'British dead' and even 'the British nation': Jonathan Baldo, '"Into a Thousand Parts": Representing the Nation in *Henry V*', *English Literary Renaissance* 38 (2008): 56, 79, 81.
38 We do find the French character 'Britaine' and the speech prefix '*Brit.*' in the First Folio (see, for example, the dialogue in 3.5). Some modern editors emend this character's name to Brittany, since he is presumably connected to an area that is now in northern France.
39 Claire McEachern, *The Poetics of English Nationhood, 1590–1612* (Cambridge: Cambridge University Press, 1996), 107.
40 Like Shapiro, Christopher Highley accepts that 'the General' refers to Essex and, therefore, reads the play as a reflection on Elizabeth's Irish wars. 'In *Henry V*,' Highley writes, 'Shakespeare's misgivings about Essex together with an awareness of burgeoning public alarm at the war in Ireland

produce a skeptical counter-discourse about English expansionism within the British Isles.' Christopher Highley, *Shakespeare, Spenser, and the Crisis in Ireland* (Cambridge: Cambridge University Press, 1997), 135–6.

41 See, for example, Warren Smith, 'The *Henry V* Choruses in the First Folio', *Journal of English and Germanic Philology* 53 (1954): 38–57, and Richard Dutton, '"Methinks the Truth Should Live From Age to Age": The Dating and Context of *Henry V*', *Huntington Library Quarterly* 68 (2005): 173–204. We know that the play was performed in the summer of 1599. What we do not know is which version was performed – that is, which parts were included and excluded.

42 Shakespeare, *King Henry V*, ed. Gurr, 4.

43 Shakespeare, *King Henry V*, ed. Gurr, 4.

44 Rhodes, 'Wrapped in the Strong Arms of the Union', 49.

45 John Savile's 'Salutatorie' poem to James highlights Ireland's less-than-smooth incorporation into James's composite monarchy: 'Irefull cold *Ireland*, cease from thy rage at last, / To yeeld subjection to thy King make hast, / Sound out Saint *Patricke*, Scotland Saint *Andrew* sing / King *James* is Englands, Scotlands, Fraunce, Irelands king.' John Savile, *King Iames His Entertainment at Theobalds: With His Welcome to London, Together with a Salutatorie Poem* (London: T. Este, 1603), sig. C3v.

46 Michael Neill, *Putting History to the Question: Power, Politics and Society in Renaissance Drama* (New York: Columbia University Press, 2000), 358. Neill's 'Gallicized' should read 'Gaelicized'.

47 Edmund Spenser, for instance, speaks of those Anglo-Norman colonists in Ireland who have 'degenerated and grown almost mere Irish': Edmund Spenser, *A View of the Present State of Ireland*, ed. W. L. Renwick (London: Scholars Press, 1934), 62.

48 In the 'list of roles' for his edition of the play, T. K. Craik glosses 'BRITAIN' as 'John de Montfort (d. 1442), Duke of Bretagne (Brittany)': Shakespeare, *Henry V*, ed. Craik, 117.

49 Shakespeare, *The Cronicle History of Henry the fift*, sig. C4r.

50 Savile, *King Iames His Entertainment at Theobalds*, sig. C3r.

51 Henry Spelman, 'Of the Union', in *The Jacobean Union: Six Tracts of 1604*, ed. Bruce Galloway and Brian Levack (Edinburgh: Scottish Historical Society, 1985), 170.

52 Philip Schwyzer, *Literature, Nationalism, and Memory in Early Modern England and Wales* (Cambridge: Cambridge University Press, 2004), 127. McEachern describes Fluellen 'as the favored subcultural exponent, with an authority both guaranteed and subordinated by an ethnic kinship to Henry himself': McEachern, *The Poetics of English Nationhood*, 107. Any 'ethnic kinship' in the play is invented; however, the Tudor monarchy's Welsh descent was real.

53 Rhodes, 'Wrapped in the Strong Arms of the Union', 48.

54 One pro-union tract, for example, states 'Behold how we are joyned, God, Nature, & Time, have brought us together, and so miraculously, if we observe the revolutions of time, as me thinketh the very words after the consummation of a marriage, shall not bee unproperly used, *Those whome God hath joyned together, let no man separate.*' See William Cornwallis, *The Miraculous and Happie Union of England and Scotland* (London: Edward Blount, 1604), sig. D1r.

Chapter 7

1 Robert Fletcher, *The Nine English Worthies* (London: John Jarrison the younger, 1606), 19. See also Nick de Somogyi, 'Fletcher, Robert (*fl.* 1581–1606)', *Oxford Dictionary of National Biography*, http://www.oxforddnb.com.janus.biu.sorbonne.fr/view/article/9741 (accessed 1 September 2016).

2 Fletcher, *English Worthies*, 49.

3 See Edward Hall's *Chronicle Containing the History of England*, quoted in Tom McAlindon, *Shakespeare's Tudor History: A Study of* Henry IV, Parts 1 and 2 (Aldershot: Ashgate, 2001), 206, 25n.

4 William Hazlitt, *Characters of Shakespeare's Plays*, ed. J. H. Lobban (Cambridge: Cambridge University Press, 1908), 156.

5 Lorna Hutson, 'Imagining Justice: Kantorowicz and Shakespeare', *Representations* 106 (2009): 118–42.

6 See Ernst Kantorowicz, *The King's Two Bodies: A Study in Medieval Political Theology* (Princeton, NJ: Princeton University Press, 1957, 2016), 24–41.

7   Kantorowicz, *The King's Two Bodies*, 119.
8   Kantorowicz, *The King's Two Bodies*, 135.
9   Kevin Sharpe, *Reading Authority and Representing Rule in Early Modern England* (London: Bloomsbury, 2013), 116.
10 James VI and I's Divine Right theory was affected by his strict Calvinistic upbringing and did not favour much sense of magic or mystique of the king's body. Stephen Brogan notes that James was at first sceptical of thaumaturgy and refused to practise it, but then changed his mind and began to touch people with scrofula within a few months of the start of his reign. Brogan explains this change as a sort of Protestant reframing of the ceremony. See Stephen Brogan, *The Royal Touch in Early Modern England: Politics, Medicine and Sin* (Rochester, NY: Boydell, 2015), 69–70.
11 On the association between rhetoric and the law, see *Rhetoric and the Law in Early Modern Europe*, ed. Victoria Kahn and Lorna Hutson (New Haven, CT: Yale University Press, 2001), especially Barbara J. Shapiro's chapter on 'Classical Rhetoric and the English Law of Evidence', 54–72.
12 This bringing forth of evidence was termed 'the circumstances', defined by Lorna Hutson as 'in a specific, technical sense... the rhetorical topics or "places" from which many different kinds of argument of proof were drawn': see Lorna Hutson, *Circumstantial Shakespeare* (Oxford: Oxford University Press, 2015), 1. This type of rhetoric is satirized in Armado's letter in the first scene of *Love's Labour's Lost*. William C. Carroll has discussed the relation of Armado's copious rhetoric to legalese, identifying his style as the 'who-what-where approach'. See William C. Carroll, *The Great Feast of Language in Love's Labour's Lost* (Princeton, NJ: Princeton University Press, 1976), 48.
13 See Jurgis Baltrusaitis, *Anamorphoses. Les perspectives dépravées* (Paris: Flammarion, 1984), 90–112.
14 Patricia Parker, *Shakespeare from the Margins: Language, Culture, Context* (Chicago: University of Chicago Press, 1996), 165.
15 William Shakespeare, *Henry V*, ed. J. H. Walter, Arden Shakespeare, Second Series (London: Methuen, 1954; repr. 1990), 31, 20n.
16 William Shakespeare, *King Henry V*, ed. T. W. Craik, Arden Shakespeare, Third Series (London: Routledge, 1995), 37.

17 Joseph M. Lenz, 'The Politics of Honor: The Oath in *Henry V*', *Journal of English and Germanic Philology* 80, no. 1 (1981): 1.

18 Parker, *Margins*, 14.

19 See *OED* discipline *n.* I and II.

20 Michel Foucault, *Discipline and Punish: The Birth of the Prison*, trans. Alan Sheridan (New York: Vintage Books, 1975; repr. 1995), 45.

21 Conal Condren, 'Understanding Shakespeare's Perfect Prince: Henry V, the Ethics of Office and the French Prisoners', *Shakespearean International Yearbook 9, Special Section, South African Shakespeare in the Twentieth Century*, ed. Laurence Wright (Farnham: Ashgate, 2009): 204. Theodor Meron, *Henry's Wars and Shakespeare's Laws: Perspectives on the Law of War in the Later Middle Ages* (Oxford: Clarendon Press, 1993), 170.

22 Gentili, in *De jure belli* ('On the law of war', first published in 1589 and dedicated to the Earl of Essex), strongly criticized Henry. See Christopher N. Warren, '*Henry V*, Anachronism, and the History of International Law', in *The Oxford Handbook of English Law and Literature, 1500–1700*, ed. Lorna Hutson and Bradin Cormack (Oxford: Oxford University Press, 2017), 717.

23 Joan Fitzpatrick, *Shakespeare and the Language of Food: A Dictionary* (London: Continuum, 2011), 85.

24 On the character of Thersites in Shakespeare's play, see Robert Kimbrough, 'The Problem of Thersites', *Modern Language Review* 59, no. 2 (1964): 173–6.

25 See Shakespeare, *Henry V*, ed. Craik, 162, note to line 77.

26 Tonio Hölscher, 'Images of War in Greece and Rome: Between Military Practice, Public Memory, and Cultural Symbolism', *Journal of Roman Studies* 93 (2003): 8.

27 See Jean-Pierre Vernant, 'A "Beautiful Death" and the Disfigured Corpse in Homeric Epic', in *Mortals and Immortals, Collected Essays*, ed. Froma I. Zeitlin (Princeton, NJ: Princeton University Press, 1991), 63.

28 See Henry Peacham, *Minerva Britanna* (London: by Wa. Dight, 1612), 17.

29 Charles Russell Stone, *From Tyrant to Philosopher-King: A Literary History of Alexander the Great in Medieval and Early Modern England* (Turnhout: Brepols, 2013), 219.

30 Judith Mossman, 'Henry V and Plutarch's Alexander', *Shakespeare Quarterly* 45, no. 1 (1994): 58.

31 This accumulation of royal figures could be reminiscent of the multitude of counterfeit kings in *1 Henry IV*. They also make it difficult to define and distinguish kingship on the stage. David Scott Kastan has pointed to the relation between 'counterfeiting' and 'miming majesty' in that play, and the implication this has on the nature of kingship. David Scott Kastan, 'Proud Majesty Made a Subject: Shakespeare and the Spectacle of Rule', *Shakespeare Quarterly* 37, no. 4 (1986): 459–75.

32 The same thing could be said of Homeric characters. In the Oxford edition of the play, Gary Taylor draws attention to Chapman's possible influence on *Henry V*, a possibility he justifies through the reference to Essex, Chapman's main dedicatee, as well as several verbal parallels and situations. However, Taylor is careful to reject the idea that *Henry V* would be 'epic' more than 'dramatic' because of those parallels: Shakespeare, *Henry V*, ed. Gary Taylor (Oxford: Oxford University Press, 1982), 54–5.

33 Niccolò Machiavelli, *The Prince*, ed. Quentin Skinner and Russell Price (Cambridge: Cambridge University Press, 1988; repr. 2003), 62.

34 In the 1685 English translation of the text, entitled *The Courtiers Manual Oracle, or, The Art of Prudence*, maxim 130 is translated as 'To doe, and make it appear'. The beginning of the text stresses the importance of appearances over substance: 'Things go not for what they are, but for what they appear to be. To know how to doe, and to know how to shew it, is a double knowledge. What is not seen, is as if it had no being': Baltasar Gracián y Morales, *The Courtiers Manual Oracle* (London: Abel Swalle, 1685), 124.

35 *La Vie du roi Henri V*, ed. Gisèle Venet, trans. Jean-Michel Déprats (Paris: Gallimard, 1999), 25–6.

36 See Jonathan Dollimore and Alan Sinfield, 'History and Ideology: The Instance of *Henry V*', in *Alternative Shakespeares*, ed. John Drakakis (London: Routledge, 1985; repr. 2002),

209–30. The word 'trunk' could also be an echo of Falstaff's 'trunk of humours' in *1 Henry IV*, 2.4.437.

37 Sarah Covington, *Wounds, Flesh and Metaphor in Seventeenth-Century England* (New York: Palgrave Macmillan, 2008), 105.

38 Sarah Covington sees a change in the seventeenth century: 'a particular kind of ambivalence attached itself to the warrior's battered flesh, which was damaged by devastating weaponry and sacrificed for a not always heroic war': Covington, *Wounds*, 84.

39 Foucault, *Discipline*, 164.

40 As Neil Jamieson has pointed out, 'for privileged members of an aristocratic elite, violence was not only allowed but in certain circumstances positively encouraged as a means of winning and protecting their honour'. See Neil Jamieson, '"Sons of Iniquity": The Problem of Unlawfulness and Criminality Amongst Professional Soldiers in the Middle Ages', in *Outlaws in Medieval and Early Modern England: Crime, Government and Society c. 1066–c.1600*, ed. John C. Appleby and Paul Dalton (Farnham: Ashgate, 2009), 92.

41 Jamieson, 'Sons', 125.

42 Dollimore and Sinfield, 'History and Ideology', 229.

43 E. F. J. Tucker, 'Legal Fiction and Human Reality: Hal's Role in *Henry V*', *Educational Theatre Journal* 26, no. 3 (1974): 309.

44 Peter B. Erickson, '"The Fault / My Father Made": The Anxious Pursuit of Heroic Fame in Shakespeare's *Henry V*', *Modern Language Studies* 10, no. 1 (1979–80): 14.

45 On *copia* and fame, and this particular passage, see Laetitia Coussement-Boillot, *Copia et cornucopia. La poétique shakespearienne de l'abondance* (Bern: Peter Lang, 2008), 22.

Chapter 8

1 I am grateful to Deanne Williams and David Goldstein for their advice and help with this chapter. I will use 'Agincourt' throughout the chapter, because that is how the place (and battle) has come to be known in English since the Middle Ages, although 'Azincourt' is the accurate French spelling.

2   Philippe Contamine, *Azincourt* (Paris: Gallimard, 1964).
3   For historical studies of the battle and the Hundred Years' War, see for instance Juliet R. V. Barker, *Agincourt: The King, The Campaign, The Battle* (London: Folio Society, 2016); *The Battle of Agincourt*, ed. Anne Curry and Malcolm Mercer (New Haven, CT: Yale University Press, 2015); and R. C. Ambühl, *Prisoners of War In the Hundred Years War* (Cambridge: Cambridge University Press, 2013).
4   *The Battle of Agincourt: Sources and Interpretations*, ed. Anne Curry (Woodbridge, Suffolk, and Rochester, NY: Boydell Press, 2000), 2. To date, most of the scholarship on the French literary responses to Agincourt is author-specific or deals with the longer period of the Hundred Years' War. Nevertheless, see Anne Curry, *Agincourt* (Oxford: Oxford University Press, 2015); M. J. Ailes, 'Literary Responses to Agincourt: the Allegories of *La Pastorale* and *Le Quadrilogue invectif*', *Reading Medieval Studies* 41 (2015): 1–20; A. E. B. Coldiron, *Canon, Period, and the Poetry of Charles of Orléans: Found in Translation* (Ann Arbor: University of Michigan Press, 2000); *Charles d'Orléans in England, 1514–1440*, ed. Mary-Jo Arn (Cambridge: D. S. Brewer, 2000); *Healing the Body Politic: The Political Thought of Christine de Pizan*, ed. Karen Green and Constant J. Mews (Turnhout: Brepols, 2005); Tracy Adams, *Christine de Pizan and the Fight for France* (University Park: Pennsylvania State University Press, 2014); and *Chartier in Europe*, ed. Emma Cayley and Ashby Kinch (Cambridge: D.S. Brewer, 2008).
5   In France, Agincourt has most often been discussed in larger studies on the Hundred Years' War, but the 2015 anniversary has spawned several collective and single-authored volumes focusing on the battle itself. For overall studies, see for instance Philippe Contamine, *La Guerre de Cent Ans* (Paris: Presses universitaires de France, 2002); Philippe Contamine, *Guerre, État et société à la fin du Moyen Âge: études sur les armées des rois de France, 1337–1494*, 2 vols (Paris: Editions de l'Ecole des hautes études en sciences sociales, 2003, 2004 (1972)); and Boris Bove, *Le temps de la guerre de Cent Ans, 1328–1453* (Paris: Belin, 2009). For specific studies of the battle, see for instance Dominique Paladhile, *Azincourt, 1415* (Paris: Perrin, 2015), and Valérie Toureille, *Le drame d'Azincourt: histoire d'une étrange défaite* (Paris: Albin Michel, 2015).

6 There are significant disagreements about the number of deaths (see Curry, *Sources and Interpretations*, 11–13). The Religieux of Saint-Denis claims 4,000 French dead; other important chroniclers, including Monstrelet, Waurin and Le Fèvre, say the number was 10,000 or more. Shakespeare's play claims 10,000 dead on the French side (4.8.81–101) and just 29 English soldiers (4.8.103–6). The language of this scene, and the numbers of English dead, suggest Shakespeare's direct indebtedness to the account in Holinshed's *Chronicles* (1587).

7 Marie's husband, Jean de Bourbon, was captured at Agincourt and died in England in 1434; her son, Charles d'Artois, Count of Eu, was also captured and only released (four years after her death) in 1438; Philip of Nevers, her son-in-law, was killed on the battlefield.

8 Her cousins, Anthony of Burgundy, Duke of Brabant, and Charles d'Albret, Count of Dreux, were killed. Most sources suggest Harcourt was taken prisoner. See Christine de Pizan, *The Epistle of the Prison of Human Life with An Epistle to the Queen of France and Lament on the Evils of the Civil War*, ed. and trans. Josette A. Wisman (New York: Garland Publishing, 1984), xxii.

9 On the dislocation and confusion that followed the battle, see Curry, *Agincourt*, 68.

10 For some, though, a decision not to name the battle might be political: pro-Burgundian French chronicle sources claim that Henry V named the battle after the nearby castle at Azincourt (Curry, *Sources and Interpretations*, 1, n. 1).

11 [Michel Pintoin], *Chronique du Religieux de Saint-Denys, Contenant le Règne de Charles VI, de 1380 à 1433*, trans. M. L. Bellaguet, 6 vols (Paris: Crapelet, 1844), vol. 5, 557. (The author has been identified as Michel Pintoin (*c.* 1349–1421), a monk affiliated with the Abbey of Saint-Denis in Paris.)

12 Pizan, *Prison of Human Life*, ed. Wisman, 3, 4. See also Curry, *Sources and Interpretations*, 345. Curry cites the work of an early sixteenth-century French chronicler, Philippe de Vigneulles of Metz, who reported that 'the battle was popularly called *la malheureuse journée*' (345, n. 107). Chartier does mention Agincourt once by name in the other work I discuss here, the *Quadrilogue invectif* (1422).

13 Charles d'Orléans, 'Ballade LXXXIV' (Curry, *Sources and Interpretations*, 354, translated from *Charles d'Orléans, Poésies*, ed. Pierre Champion, 2 vols (Paris: [s.n.] 1923–7), 1.135).

14 See *Le journal d'un bourgeois de Paris, 1405–1449*, ed. Alexandre Tuetey (Paris: H. Champion, 1881). See also Curry, *Sources and Interpretations*, 358 (who translates from *Le Jouvencel par Jean de Bueil, suivi du commentaire de Guillaume Tringant*, 2 vols (Paris: Société de l'Histoire de France, 1887, 1889), 2.62–3).

15 On the queen's role in the power struggle, see Tracy Adams, '*Moyennerresse de traicte de paix*: Christine de Pizan's Mediators', in *Healing the Body Politic*, ed. Green and Mews, 177–200.

16 See Emily J. Hutchison, 'The Politics of Grief in the Outbreak of Civil War in France, 1407–1413', *Speculum* 91, no. 2 (April 2016): 422–52.

17 In her *Epistle to the Queen of France*, Christine pleads with Isabeau to 'hear the complaints and pitiful regrets of the suffering and suppliant French people' and to 'procure and obtain peace soon between these two princes of the same blood'. She warns, moreover, citing Luke 2.7, that a 'kingdom divided within itself will be destroyed'. Pizan, *Prison*, ed. Wisman, 73. On the circulation of Christine's works in England, see Stephanie Downes, 'A "Frenche booke called the Pistill of Othea": Christine de Pizan's French in England', in *Language and Culture in Medieval Britain: The French of England c.1100–1500*, ed. Jocelyn Wogan-Browne et al. (York: York Medieval Press, 2009), 457–68.

18 Curry, *Sources and Interpretations*, 340.

19 *Chronique du Religieux de Saint-Denys*, 5.543. My translation.

20 Curry, *Sources and Interpretations*, 333.

21 Pizan, *Prison*, ed. Wisman, xvii.

22 Holinshed, *The Third Volume of Chronicles* (London, 1586), 572. The 'duke' here is Philip the Good, Duke of Burgundy from 1419 until his death in 1467.

23 Curry, *Agincourt*, 72.

24 These entries cover the period leading up to the Treaty of Troyes and Henry's marriage to Katherine. See *Journal*, ed. Tuetey, 124, 127–9, 135, 139.

25 *Journal*, ed. Tuetey, 129. There is text missing from both extant manuscripts just prior to this passage, but he seems to be talking about the English here. He might also be referring to the Armagnac 'traitors' who had just assassinated the Duke of Burgundy.
26 Curry, *Agincourt*, 71. See especially *Chronique du Religieux de Saint-Denys*, 5.557.
27 Curry, *Agincourt*, 71.
28 Curry, *Agincourt*, 71. For more detailed discussion, see *Chronique du Religieux de Saint-Denys*, 5.557.
29 Jean Le Fèvre, *Chronique de Jean Le Fèvre, Seigneur de Saint-Remy*, ed. François Morand, 2 vols (Paris: Renouard, 1876), 1.245–6. Curry explains that Le Fèvre was 'a non-combattant who accompanied the English as a heraldic observer from Harfleur to the battle' (Curry, *Agincourt*, 73).
30 Curry, *Agincourt*, 72.
31 Curry, *Agincourt*, 72, 75.
32 Curry, *Sources and Interpretations*, 333.
33 Curry, *Sources and Interpretations*, 338.
34 Curry, *Sources and Interpretations*, 338–9.
35 Coldiron, *Canon*, 1.
36 Coldiron, *Canon*, 25.
37 'Scez tu dont vient ton mal, a vray parler? / Congnois tu point pourquoy es en tristesse?' Orléans, 'Complainte I', *Poésies*, ed. Champion, 1.259.
38 'Ton grant ourgueil, glottonie, peresse, / Couvoitise, sans justice tenir, / Et luxure, dont as eu abondance, / Ont pourchacié vers Dieu de te punir, / Trescretien, franc royaume de France!' Orléans, 'Complainte I', *Poésies*, ed. Champion, 1.259. Coldiron notes that although Charles's 'political poems do not appear in parallel English versions', a copy of 'Complainte I' appears in a royal manuscript that was owned by Henry VII and Henry VIII: Coldiron, *Canon*, 27, a nd n. 39.
39 Orléans, 'Ballade LXXXIV', *Poésies*, ed. Champion, 1.135.
40 Pizan, *Prison*, ed. Wisman, 3.
41 Pizan, *Prison*, ed. Wisman, 3.

42 Louise d'Arcens, 'Petit estat vesval: Christine de Pizan's Grieving Body Politic', in *Healing the Body Politic*, ed. Green and Mews, 201–26, 214. Christine lost her father sometime between 1385 and 1389, and her husband in 1389: Pizan, *Prison*, ed. Wisman, xiii–xiv.

43 d'Arcens, 'Petit', 215.

44 Pizan, *Prison*, ed. Wisman, 3.

45 For a good reading of Katherine's significance in *Henry V*, see Corinne S. Abate, '"Once More Unto the Breach": Katherine's Victory in *Henry V*', *Early Theatre* 4 (2001): 73–85. Also relevant is Elizabeth Pentland, '"I cannot speak your England": French women in *King John* and *Henry V*', *Early Modern Literary Studies (EMLS), Special Issue* 27, *European Women in Early Modern Drama* (2017), ed. Ema Vyroubalová and Edel Semple, https://extra.shu.ac.uk/emls/journal/index.php/emls/article/view/380/288 (accessed 18 February 2018).

46 Pizan, *Prison*, ed. Wisman, 21. Christine is referring to the popular *Vita Secundi Philosophi*, or *Life of the Philosopher Secundus*. Shakespeare, as we know, makes a punning reference to the Diet of Worms in *Hamlet* (4.3.19–30), but in *1 Henry IV* the phrase food 'for worms' is also invoked by the future Henry V as he stands over the body of Hotspur, whom he has just killed in battle (5.4.85–6).

47 Pizan, *Prison*, ed. Wisman, 23.

48 Basil of Caesarea, or Basil the Great (*c.* 330–79), was bishop of Caesarea in Cappadocia (Asia Minor, or what is now eastern Turkey) and a leading figure in the early Christian Church.

49 See Alain Chartier, *The Poetical Works of Alain Chartier*, ed. J. C. Laidlaw (Cambridge: Cambridge University Press, 1974), 32, 33.

50 Curry, *Sources and Interpretations*, 345.

51 Curry, *Sources and Interpretations*, 346.

52 Chartier, *Poetical Works*, ed. Laidlaw, 35.

53 Curry, *Sources and Interpretations*, 346.

54 Curry describes the *Quadrilogue* as 'a political treatise rather than a literary work': Curry, *Sources and Interpretations*, 349. For a useful reading of the work as allegory, see Ailes, 'Literary Responses': 1–20.

55 Curry, *Sources and Interpretations*, 345. In *The Consolation of Philosophy*, Philosophy appears to the writer as a 'woman of majestic countenance', whose clothing 'had been darkened in color somewhat by neglect and the passage of time' and whose robe has been torn 'by the hands of violent men': Boethius, *The Consolation of Philosophy*, trans. Richard Green (New York: Macmillan 1962), 4.

56 Alain Chartier, *Le Quadrilogue invectif*, ed. E. Droz (Paris: Honoré Champion, 1923), 5. My translation.

57 Chartier's reference to the 'disloyalty' of some subjects may point generally to the French civil wars, but it is probably a partisan dig at John the Fearless, Duke of Burgundy, who did not fight at Agincourt and who prevented his son from taking part as well. After John's assassination in 1519, his son entered into an alliance with England, supporting the Treaty of Troyes (1520), which had the effect of disinheriting the Dauphin and securing an English succession to the French throne.

58 Chartier's phrasing follows Boethius very closely here.

59 Richard Dutton, '"Methinks the truth should live from age to age": The Dating and Contexts of *Henry V*', in *The Uses of History in Early Modern England*, ed. Paulina Kewes (San Marino, CA: Huntington Library Press, 2006), 186.

60 Curry, *Sources and Interpretations*, 349.

Chapter 9

1 Available at https://mapoflondon.uvic.ca/ (accessed 13 July 2017).

2 See also Julian Bowsher, *Shakespeare's London Theatreland: Archaeology, History and Drama* (London: Museum of London Archaeology, 2012), 62–7.

3 See Maev Kennedy, 'Excavation Finds Early Shakespeare Theatre Was Rectangular', *Guardian*, 17 May 2016, https://www.theguardian.com/culture/2016/may/17/curtain-excavation-early-shakespeare-theatre-rectangular-shoreditch (accessed 13 July 2017).

4 See http://www.explorethetheatre.co.uk (accessed 13 July 2017).

5 Further explorations of the nature of early modern playhouses could be productively keyed to the Shakespearean London Theatres (ShaLT) website, which hosts a number of videos and audio lectures by leading academics, as well as details for walks around the historical sites of Renaissance playhouses, http://shalt.dmu.ac.uk/ (accessed 13 July 2017).

6 See Melissa D. Aaron, 'The Globe and *Henry V* as Business Document', *Studies in English Literature* 40 (2000): 277–92. Questions of performance are further complicated by the existence of the 1600 Quarto, which is discussed later in this chapter.

7 Thomas Heywood, *An Apology for Actors* (London: Nicholas Okes, 1612), sig. [B4r].

8 Alan C. Dessen and Leslie Thomson, *A Dictionary of Stage Directions in English Drama, 1580–1642* (Cambridge: Cambridge University Press, 1999), 84.

9 William Shakespeare, *Mr. William Shakespeares Comedies, Histories, & Tragedies* (London: William Jaggard et al., 1623), sig. t2v.

10 Available at http://firstfolio.bodleian.ox.ac.uk/ (accessed 13 July 2017).

11 Heywood, *Apology*, sig. Fv.

12 Available at http://www.cems.ox.ac.uk/holinshed/index.shtml (accessed 13 July 2017).

13 Phyllis Rackin, *Stages of History: Shakespeare's English Chronicles* (New York: Cornell University Press, 1990), 55.

14 Thomas Nashe, *Pierce Penilesse his Supplication to the Diuell* (London: John Busbie, 1592), sig. F3r. Thomas Heywood's similar claims, cited in the 'Staging' section above, might also be useful in this exercise.

15 Lawrence Danson, *Shakespeare's Dramatic Genres* (Oxford: Oxford University Press, 2000), 109.

16 Available at http://leme.library.utoronto.ca/ (accessed 14 July 2017).

17 Simon Palfrey offers a sophisticated but accessible account of characters in *Doing Shakespeare* (London: Bloomsbury, 2005), 171–290.

18 Graham Holderness, *Shakespeare: The Histories* (Basingstoke: Palgrave, 1999), 150.

19 See John Sutherland and Cedric Watts, *Henry V, War Criminal? & Other Shakespeare Puzzles* (Oxford: Oxford University Press, 2000).

20 See *King Henry V: Shakespeare in Production*, ed. Emma Smith (Cambridge: Cambridge University Press, 2002).

21 Available at http://www.bl.uk/learning/timeline/item126569.html (accessed 14 July 2017).

22 David Steinsaltz, 'The Politics of French Language in Shakespeare's History Plays', *Studies in English Literature* 42 (2002): 318, 319.

23 Philip Sidney, *An Apologie for Poetrie* (London: Henry Olney, 1595), sig. L2r.

24 Available at http://rhetoric.byu.edu/ (accessed 14 July 2017); Richard Lanham, *A Handlist of Rhetorical Terms*, 2nd edn (Berkeley: University of California Press, 1991).

25 George Puttenham, *The Arte of English Poesie* (London: Richard Field, 1589), sigs. Mmr–v. EEBO is available at http://eebo.chadwyck.com/home (accessed 14 July 2017).

26 Available at http://www.oed.com/ (accessed 14 July 2017).

27 This speech is available at Oxford University's Holinshed Project, http://english.nsms.ox.ac.uk/holinshed/texts.php?text1=1587_5158 (accessed 14 July 2017).

28 Juliet Fleming, 'The French Garden: An Introduction to Women's French', *ELH* 56 (1989): 45.

29 This question is brilliantly answered in Laurie E. Maguire, '"Household Kates": Chez Petruchio, Percy, and Plantagenet', in *Gloriana's Face: Women, Public and Private, in the English Renaissance*, ed. S. P. Cerasano and Marion Wynne-Davies (Detroit: Wayne State University Press, 1992), 129–65.

30 Paola Pugliatti, 'The Strange Tongues of *Henry V*', *Yearbook of English Studies* 23 (1993): 237, 242.

31 Bruce R. Smith, *Shakespeare and Masculinity* (Oxford: Oxford University Press, 2000), 42.

32 Judith Haber, '"I cannot tell wat is like me": Simile, Paternity, and Identity in *Henry V*', *Shakespeare Studies* 41 (2013): 139.

33 Jean E. Howard and Phyllis Rackin, *Engendering a Nation* (London: Routledge, 1997), 206.

34 Howard and Rackin, *Engendering*, 214.
35 Available at http://firstfolio.bodleian.ox.ac.uk/ and http://www.bl.uk/treasures/shakespeare/henry5.html (accessed 14 July 2017).
36 William Shakespeare, *The First Quarto of King Henry V*, ed. Andrew Gurr (Cambridge: Cambridge University Press, 2000).
37 Available at http://deep.sas.upenn.edu/ (accessed 14 July 2017).
38 Andrew Gurr, 'Introduction', in Shakespeare, *First Quarto*, ed. Gurr, 1.
39 Shakespeare, *First Quarto*, ed. Gurr, 1–11.

BIBLIOGRAPHY

All references to Shakespeare's plays are to the Arden Shakespeare, Third Series, unless otherwise noted.

Aaron, Melissa D. 'The Globe and *Henry V* as Business Document'. *Studies in English Literature* 40, no. 2 (2000): 277–92.

Abate, Corinne S. '"Once More Unto the Breach": Katharine's Victory in *Henry V*'. *Early Theatre* 4 (2001): 73–85.

Adams, Tracy. '*Moyennerresse de traicte de paix*: Christine de Pizan's Mediators'. In *Healing the Body Politic: The Political Thought of Christine de Pizan*, edited by Karen Green and Constant J. Mews, 177–200. Turnhout, Belgium: Brepols, 2005.

Adams, Tracy. *Christine de Pizan and the Fight for France*. University Park: Pennsylvania State University Press, 2014.

Ailes, M. J. 'Literary Responses to Agincourt: the Allegories of *La Pastorale* and *Le Quadrilogue invectif*'. *Reading Medieval Studies* 41 (2015): 1–20.

Aitken, Ian. 'Formalism and Realism: *Henry V* (Lawrence Olivier, 1944; Kenneth Branagh, 1989)'. *Critical Survey* 3, no. 3 (1991): 260–8.

Altman, Joel. '"Vile Participation": The Amplification of Violence in the Theater of *Henry V*'. *Shakespeare Quarterly* 42, no. 1 (1991): 1–32.

Ambühl, R. C. *Prisoners of War In the Hundred Years War*. Cambridge: Cambridge University Press, 2013.

Anderson, Benedict. *Imagined Communities: Reflections on the Origin and Spread of Nationalism*, rev. edn. London: Verso, 1991.

Andrews, Meghan C. 'Gender, Genre, and Elizabeth's Princely Surrogates in *Henry IV* and *Henry V*'. *Studies in English Literature* 54, no. 2 (2012), 375–99.

Anon. *The Famous Victories of Henry the Fifth, Containing the Honourable Battell of Agin-Court: As It Was Plaide by the Queenes Maiesties Players*. London: Thomas Creede, 1598.

Anon. *The Famous Victories of Henry V*. Edited by John Jowett. Manchester: Malone Society, 2007.
Anon. 'ZADEK: Falscher Held'. *Der Spiegel* 12 (18 March 1964). Available at http://www.spiegel.de/spiegel/print/d-46163513.html (accessed 15 September 2017).
Arn, Mary-Jo, ed. *Charles d'Orléans in England, 1514–1440*. Cambridge: D. S. Brewer, 2000.
Axelrad, José. 'Shakespeare's Impact Today in France'. *Shakespeare Survey* 16 (1963): 53–6.
Baker, David J. '"Wildehirissheman": Colonialist Representation in Shakespeare's *Henry V*'. *English Literary Renaissance* 22, no. 1 (1992): 37–61.
Baker, David J. *Between Nations: Shakespeare, Spenser, Marvell, and the Question of Britain*. Stanford, CA: Stanford University Press, 1997.
Baldo, Jonathan. 'Wars of Memory in *Henry V*'. *Shakespeare Quarterly* 47, no. 2 (1996): 132–59.
Baldo, Jonathan. '"Into a Thousand Parts": Representing the Nation in *Henry V*'. *English Literary Renaissance* 38, no. 1 (2008): 55–82.
Balstrusaitis, Jurgis. *Anamorphoses. Les perspectives dépravées*. Paris: Flammarion, 1984.
Banerjee, Rita. 'The Common Good and the Necessity of War: Emergent Republican Ideals in Shakespeare's *Henry V* and *Coriolanus*'. *Comparative Drama* 40, no. 1 (2006): 29–49.
Barker, Juliet R. V. *Agincourt: The King, The Campaign, The Battle*. London: Folio Society, 2016.
Bate, Jonathan, ed. *The Romantics on Shakespeare*. Harmondsworth: Penguin, 1992.
Beauman, Sally, ed. *The Royal Shakespeare Company's Production of 'Henry V' for the Centenary Season at the Royal Shakespeare Theatre*. Oxford: Pergamon Press, 1976.
Beaumont, Francis, and John Fletcher. *Dramatic Works*. Edited by Fredson Bowers. 10 vols. Cambridge: Cambridge University Press, 1966–98.
Belleval, René de. *Azincourt*. Paris: Dumoulin, 1865.
Berry, Edward. 'Twentieth-Century Shakespeare Criticism: the Histories'. In *The Cambridge Companion to Shakespeare Studies*, edited by Stanley Wells, 249–56. Cambridge: Cambridge University Press, 1986.

Billing, Christian M. *Masculinity, Corporality and the English Stage 1580–1635*. Farnham: Ashgate, 2008.
Billington, Michael. '*Henry V*'. *Guardian*, 4 May 2003. Available at https://www.theguardian.com/stage/2003/may/14/theatre.artsfeatures2 (accessed 14 September 2017).
Billington, Michael. '*Henry V*'. *Guardian*, 8 November 2007. Available at https://www.theguardian.com/stage/2007/nov/08/theatre (accessed 14 September 2017).
Billington, Michael. '*Henry V* Review: An Astonishing Gender-Switched Reinvigoration'. *Guardian*, 23 June 2016. Available at https://www.theguardian.com/stage/2016/jun/23/henry-v-review-open-air-theatre-regents-park (accessed 14 September 2017).
Boas, F. S. *Shakspere and His Predecessors*. London: John Murray, 1896.
Bodin, Jean. *On Sovereignty*. Edited and translated by Julian H. Franklin. Cambridge: Cambridge University Press, 1992; repr. 2007.
Bodleian Library. *The Bodleian First Folio*. Available at http://firstfolio.bodleian.ox.ac.uk/ (accessed 13 July 2017).
Boethius. *The Consolation of Philosophy*. Translated by Richard Green. New York: Macmillan 1962.
Bove, Boris. *Le temps de la guerre de Cent Ans, 1328–1453*. Paris: Belin, 2009.
Bowsher, Julian. *Shakespeare's London Theatreland: Archaeology, History and Drama*. London: Museum of London Archaeology, 2012.
Boyle, Roger. *The history of Henry the Fifth. And The tragedy of Mustapha, son of Solyman the Magnificent. As they were acted at his Highness the Duke of York's Theater*. London: for Henry Herringman, 1668.
Bradley, A. C. 'The Rejection of Falstaff'. In *Oxford Lectures on Poetry*, 247–73. 2nd edn. Glasgow: Glasgow University Press, 1909.
Bradshaw, Graham. *Misrepresentations: Shakespeare and the Materialists*. Ithaca, NY: Cornell University Press, 1993.
Brady, Robert K. 'International Notes: Malaya'. *Shakespeare Survey* 7 (1954): 113.
Branagh, Kenneth. *Beginning*. London: Chatto & Windus, 1989.
Branagh, Kenneth. *Henry V: A Screen Adaptation*. London: Chatto & Windus, 1989.

Branagh, Kenneth. 'Unpublished Screenplay and Storyboard of *Henry V*'. Renaissance Film Company Archive, located at the Kenneth Branagh Archive, Queen's University Belfast (October 1998).

Brantley, Ben. 'Shakespeare's Take On the Game of Thrones'. *New York Times*, 6 November 2016. Available at https://www.nytimes.com/2016/11/05/theater/review-shakespeares-take-on-the-game-of-thrones.html (accessed 15 October 2017).

Breight, Curtis. 'Branagh and the Prince, or a "Royal Fellowship of Death"'. *Critical Quarterly* 33, no. 4 (1991): 95–111.

Brigham Young University. *Silva Rhetoricae: Forest of Rhetoric*. Available at http://rhetoric.byu.edu and http://www.csudh.edu/ccauthen/350S11/ethosdef.htm (accessed 14 July 2017).

British Library. *Learning English Timeline*. Available at http://www.bl.uk/learning/timeline/item126569.html (accessed 14 July 2017).

British Library. *Treasures in Full: Shakespeare in Quarto*. Available at http://www.bl.uk/treasures/shakespeare/henry5.html (accessed 14 July 2017).

Brogan, Stephen. *The Royal Touch in Early Modern England: Politics, Medicine and Sin*. Rochester, NY: Boydell, 2015.

Brotton, Jerry. 'Shakespeare's Turks and the Spectacle of Ambivalence in the History Plays'. *Textual Practice* 28, no. 3 (2014): 521–38.

Bueil, Jean de, comte de Sancerre. *Le Jouvencel par Jean de Bueil, suivi du commentaire de Guillaume Tringant*. 2 vols. Paris: Sociéte de l'Histoire de France, 1887–9.

Buhler, Stephen M. 'Text, Eyes, and Videotape: Screening Shakespeare Scripts'. *Shakespeare Quarterly* 46, no. 2 (1995): 236–44.

Calvin, Jean. *Institutes of the Christian Religion*. Edited by John T. McNeill. 2 vols. Philadelphia: Westminster Press, 1960.

Campbell, Lily B. *Shakespeare's 'Histories': Mirrors of Elizabethan Policy*. San Marino, CA: Huntington Library Press, 1947.

Carlyle, Thomas. *On Heroes, Hero-Worship and the Heroic in History*. London: Chapman and Hall, 1841; Lincoln: University of Nebraska Press, 1966.

Carroll, William C. *The Great Feast of Language in Love's Labour's Lost*. Princeton, NJ: Princeton University Press, 1976.

Carson, Christie. 'Mark Rylance, *Henry V* and "Original Practices" at Shakespeare's Globe: History Refashioned'. In *Filming and Performing Renaissance History*, edited by Mark Thornton

Burnett and Amanda Streete, 127–45. London: Palgrave Macmillan, 2011.

Cayley, Emma, and Ashby Kinch, eds. *Chartier in Europe*. Cambridge: D. S. Brewer, 2008.

Champion, Larry. *Perspective in Shakespeare's English Histories*. Athens: University of Georgia Press, 1980.

Chapman, Alison A. 'Whose Saint Crispin's Day Is It? Shoemaking, Holiday Making, and the Politics of Memory in Early Modern England'. *Renaissance Quarterly* 54, no. 4 (2001): 1467–94.

Charnes, Linda. 'Anticipating Nostalgia: Finding Temporal Logic in a Textual Anomaly'. *Textual Cultures: Texts, Contexts, Interpretations* 4, no. 1 (2009), 72–83.

Chartier, Alain. *Le Quadrilogue invectif*. Edited by E. Droz. Paris: Honoré Champion, 1923.

Chartier, Alain. *The Poetical Works of Alain Chartier*. Edited by J. C. Laidlaw. Cambridge: Cambridge University Press, 1974.

Chernaik, Warren. 'The Death of Bardolph: Branagh and Olivier Rewrite *Henry V*'. In *Shakespeare on Screen: The Henriad*, edited by Sarah Hatchuel and Nathalie Vienne-Guerrin, 157–69. Rouen: Publications des Universités de Rouen et du Havre, 2008.

Clapp, Susannah. 'Cry "God for Chelsea, England and Saint Kev!"'. *Observer*, 3 September 2000. Available at https://www.theguardian.com/theobserver/2000/sep/03/features.review47 (accessed 16 September 2017).

Clapp, Susannah. 'Henry V Review – If Shakespeare Had Done Brexit'. *Observer*, 3 July 2016. Available at https://www.theguardian.com/stage/2016/jul/03/henry-v-open-air-regents-park-review-michelle-terry (accessed 15 September 2017).

Clare, Janet. 'Medley History: *The Famous Victories of Henry The Fifth* to *Henry V*'. *Shakespeare Survey* 63 (2010): 102–13.

Clegg, Cyndia Susan. 'Feared and Loved: *Henry V* and Machiavelli's Use of History'. *Ben Jonson Journal* 10 (2003): 179–207.

Coldiron, A. E. B. *Canon, Period, and the Poetry of Charles of Orléans: Found in Translation*. Ann Arbor: University of Michigan Press, 2000.

Coleman, David. 'Ireland and Islam: *Henry V* and the "War on Terror"'. *Shakespeare* 4, no. 2 (2008): 169–80.

Condren, Conal. 'Understanding Shakespeare's Perfect Prince: Henry V, the Ethics of Office and the French Prisoners'. In *The Shakespearean International Yearbook 9. Special Section, South*

African Shakespeare in the Twentieth Century, edited by Laurence Wright, 195–213. Farnham: Ashgate, 2009.

Contamine, Philippe. *Azincourt*. Paris: Gallimard, 1964.

Contamine, Philippe. *La Guerre de Cent Ans*. Paris: Presses universitaires de France, 2002.

Contamine, Philipe. *Guerre, État et société à la fin du Moyen Âge: études sur les armées des rois de France, 1337–1494*. 2 vols. Paris: Editions de l'Ecole des hautes études en sciences sociales, 2003, 2004 (1972).

Corbin, Peter, and Douglas Sedge, eds. *The Oldcastle Controversy*. Manchester: Manchester University Press, 1991.

Cornwallis, William. *The Miraculous and Happie Union of England and Scotland*. London: Edward Blount, 1604.

Coussement-Boillot, Laetitia. *Copia et cornucopia. La poétique shakespearienne de l'abondance*. Bern: Peter Lang, 2008.

Covington, Sarah. *Wounds, Flesh and Metaphor in Seventeenth-Century England*. New York: Palgrave Macmillan, 2008.

Crowdus, Gary. 'Sharing an Enthusiasm for Shakespeare: An Interview with Kenneth Branagh'. *Cineaste* 24, no. 1 (1998): 34–41.

Crowl, Samuel. *Shakespeare Observed: Studies in Performance on Stage and Screen*. Athens: Ohio University Press, 1992.

Crunelle-Vanrigh, Anny. '*Henry V* as a Royal Entry'. *Studies in English Literature* 47, no. 2 (2007): 355–77.

Curry, Anne, ed. *The Battle of Agincourt: Sources and Interpretations*. Woodbridge and Rochester, NY: Boydell Press, 2000.

Curry, Anne. *Agincourt*. Oxford: Oxford University Press, 2015.

Curry, Anne, and Malcolm Mercer, eds. *The Battle of Agincourt*. New Haven, CT: Yale University Press, 2015.

Daniel, Drew. '*King Henry V*: Scambling Harry and Sampling Hal'. In *Shakesqueer: A Queer Companion to the Complete Works of Shakespeare*, edited by Madhavi Menon, 121–9. Durham, NC, and London: Duke University Press, 2011.

Danson, Lawrence. *Shakespeare's Dramatic Genres*. Oxford: Oxford University Press, 2000.

d'Arcens, Louise. 'Petit estat vesval: Christine de Pizan's Grieving Body Politic'. In *Healing the Body Politic: The Political Thought of Christine de Pizan*, edited by Karen Green and Constant J. Mews, 201–26. Turnhout: Brepols, 2005.

Davies, Michael. 'Falstaff's Lateness: Calvinism and the Protestant Hero in *Henry V*'. *Review of English Studies* 56, no. 225 (2005): 351–78.

Dennis, John. *The Comical Gallant, or the Amours of Sir John Falstaffe*. London: A. Baldwin, 1702.

Déprats, Jean-Michel. 'A French History of *Henry V*'. In *Shakespeare's History Plays: Performance, Translation and Adaptation in Britain and Abroad*, edited by A. J. Hoenselaars, 75–91. Cambridge: Cambridge University Press, 2004.

Derrida, Jacques. *The Beast and the Sovereign*. Translated by Geoffrey Bennington. 2 vols. Chicago: University of Chicago Press, 2009.

Dessen, Alan C., and Leslie Thomson. *A Dictionary of Stage Directions in English Drama, 1580–1642*. Cambridge: Cambridge University Press, 1999.

Díaz-Fernández, José Ramón. 'The Henriad On Screen: An Annotated Filmo-Bibliography'. In *Shakespeare on Screen: The Henriad*, edited by Sarah Hatchuel and Nathalie Vienne-Guerrin, 269–348. Rouen: Publications des Universités de Rouen et du Havre, 2008.

Dionne, Craig. 'The Shatnerification of Shakespeare: *Star Trek* and the Commonplace Tradition'. In *Shakespeare after Mass Media*, edited by Richard Burt, 173–91. Houndmills: Palgrave, 2002.

Dobson, Michael, and Stanley Wells, eds. *The Oxford Companion to Shakespeare*. Oxford: Oxford University Press, 2001, 2015.

Dollimore, Jonathan, *Political Shakespeare: New Essays in Cultural Materialism*, edited by Jonathan Dollimore and Alan Sinfield, 18–48. Manchester: Manchester University Press, 1985.

Dollimore, Jonathan, and Alan Sinfield. 'History and Ideology: the Instance of *Henry V*'. In *Alternative Shakespeares*, edited by John Drakakis, 206–27. London, Methuen, 1985. 2nd ed. London, Routledge, 2002.

Dollimore, Jonathan, and Alan Sinfield. 'History and Ideology, Masculinity and Miscegenation'. In *Faultlines: Cultural Materialism and the Politics of Dissident Reading*, edited by Alan Sinfield, 109–42. Oxford: Clarendon Press, 1992.

Dowd, Christopher. 'Polysemic Brotherhoods in *Henry V*'. *Studies in English Literature* 50, no. 2 (2010): 337–53.

Dowden, Edward. *Shakspere: A Critical Study of His Mind and Art*, 3rd edn. New York: Harper & Brothers, 1905.

Downes, Stephanie. 'A "Frenche booke called the Pistill of Othea": Christine de Pizan's French in England'. In *Language and Culture in Medieval Britain: The French of England c.1100–1500*, edited by Jocelyn Wogan-Browne et al., 457–68. York: York Medieval Press, 2009.

Drakakis, John. *Alternative Shakespeares*. London: Methuen, 1985; Routledge, 2002.

Drakakis, John. 'Shakespeare as Presentist'. *Shakespeare Survey* 66 (2013): 177–87.

Dryden, John. *Of Dramatick Poesie, An Essay*. London: Henry Herringman, 1668.

Dutton, Richard. '"Methinks the Truth Should Live from Age to Age": The Dating and Contexts of *Henry V*'. *Huntington Library Quarterly* 68, nos 1–2 (2005): 173–204.

Egan, Gabriel, et al. *Shakespearean London Theatres (ShaLT)*. Available at http://shalt.dmu.ac.uk/ (accessed 13 July 2017).

Elgar, Edward. 'Falstaff'. *Musical Times* 54, no. 847 (September 1913): 575–8.

Ellis, Steven G. 'From Dual Monarchy to Multiple Kingdoms: Unions and the English State, 1422–1607'. In *The Stuart Kingdoms in the Seventeenth Century: Awkward Neighbours*, edited by Allan I. MacInnes and Jane Ohlmeyer, 37–48. Dublin: Four Courts Press, 2002.

Ellis-Fermor, Una. *The Frontiers of Drama*. London: Methuen, 1945.

Erickson, Peter B. '"The Fault/My Father Made": The Anxious Pursuit of Heroic Fame in Shakespeare's *Henry V*'. *Modern Language Studies* 10, no. 1 (1979–80): 10–25.

Erne, Lukas. *Shakespeare as Literary Dramatist*. Cambridge: Cambridge University Press, 2003.

Farmer, Alan B., and Zachary Lesser. *Database of Early English Playbooks*. Available at http://deep.sas.upenn.edu/ (accessed 14 July 2017).

Fitter, Chris. 'A Tale of Two Branaghs: *Henry V*, Ideology and the Mekong Agincourt'. In *Shakespeare Left and Right*, edited by Ivo Kamps, 259–75. London: Routledge, 1991.

Fitzpatrick, Joan. *Shakespeare and the Language of Food: A Dictionary*. London: Continuum, 2011.

Flaumenhaft, Mera J. *The Civic Spectacle: Essays on Drama and Community*. Lanham, MD: Rowman & Littlefield, 1994.

Fleming, Juliet. 'The French Garden: An Introduction to Women's French'. *English Literary History* 56, no. 1 (1989): 19–51.
Fletcher, Robert. *The Nine English Worthies*. London: John Jarrison the younger, 1606.
Foucault, Michel. *Discipline and Punish: The Birth of the Prison*. Translated by Alan Sheridan. New York: Vintage Books, 1975, 1995.
Furlan, Julia. 'New Yorkers Take the Boat to France With Henry V'. WNYC Online, 8 July 2011. Available at http://www.wnyc.org/story/145085-new-yorkers-take-boat-france-henry-v (accessed 27 September 2017).
Genzlinger, Neil. 'Two Islands Are a Stage, and All Are Actors'. *New York Times*, 12 July 2011. Available at http://www.nytimes.com/2011/07/13/theater/reviews/henry-v-new-york-classical-theater-review.html (accessed 15 October 2017).
Gervinus, G. G. *Shakespeare Commentaries*. Translated by F. E. Bunnett. 2 vols. London: Smith, Elder, & Company, 1863.
Gibson, James M. 'Shakespeare and the Cobham Controversy'. *Medieval and Renaissance Drama in England* 25 (2012): 94–132.
Goddard, Harold C. *The Meaning of Shakespeare*. 2 vols. Chicago: University of Chicago Press, 1960.
Gould, Gerald. 'A New Reading of *Henry V*'. *English Review* 29 (1919): 42–55.
Gracián y Morales, Baltasar. *The Courtiers Manual Oracle*. London: Abel Swalle, 1685.
Grady, Hugh. *Shakespeare, Machiavelli, and Montaigne: Power and Subjectivity from 'Richard II' to 'Hamlet'*. Oxford: Oxford University Press, 2002.
Grady, Hugh, and Terence Hawkes, eds. *Presentist Shakespeares*. London: Routledge, 2007.
Green, Karen, and Constant J. Mews, eds. *Healing the Body Politic: The Political Thought of Christine de Pizan*. Turnhout: Brepols, 2005.
Greenblatt, Stephen. 'Invisible Bullets: Renaissance Authority and its Subversion, *Henry IV* and *Henry V*'. In *Political Shakespeare: New Essays in Cultural Materialism*, edited by Jonathan Dollimore and Alan Sinfield, 18–47. Manchester: Manchester University Press, 1985; Ithaca, NY: Cornell University Press, 1994.
Greenblatt, Stephen. *Shakespearean Negotiations: The Circulation of Social Energy in Renaissance England*. Berkeley: University of California Press, 1988.

Greenburg, Bradley. '"O for a Muse of Fire": Henry V and Plotted Self-Exculpation'. *Shakespeare Studies* 36 (2008): 182–206.

Grene, Nicholas. *Shakespeare's Serial History Plays*. Cambridge: Cambridge University Press, 2002.

Gurr, Andrew. '*Henry V* and the Bees' Commonwealth'. *Shakespeare Survey* 30 (1977): 61–72.

Gurr, Andrew. *The Shakespearean Playing Companies*. Oxford: Clarendon Press, 1996.

Haber, Judith. '"I Cannot Tell Wat Is Like Me": Simile, Paternity and Identity in *Henry V*'. *Shakespeare Studies* 41 (2013): 127–47.

Hall, Edward. *The Union of the Two Noble Families of Lancaster and York*. London: Richard Grafton, 1548.

Hammer, Paul E. J. 'Devereux, Robert, second earl of Essex (1565–1601)'. In the *Oxford Dictionary of National Biography*. Oxford: Oxford University Press, 2004. Available online at http://www.oxforddnb.com.ezproxy.library.wisc.edu/view/article/7565 (accessed 24 November 2017).

Hart, Alfred. *Stolne and Surreptitious Copies: A Comparative Study of Shakespeare's Bad Quartos*. Melbourne: Melbourne University Press, 1942.

Hart, Jonathan. 'Shakespeare's *Henry V*: Towards the Problem Play'. *Cahiers Elisabéthains* 42 (1992): 17–35.

Hatchuel, Sarah. '"Into a Thousand Parts Divide One Man": Dehumanised Metafiction and Fragmented Documentary in Peter Babakitis' *Henry V*'. In *Screening Shakespeare in the Twenty-First Century*, edited by Mark Thornton Burnett and Ramona Wray, 146–62. Edinburgh: Edinburgh University Press, 2006.

Hatchuel, Sarah, and Nathalie Vienne-Guerrin, eds. *Shakespeare on Screen: The Henriad*. Rouen: Publications des Universités de Rouen et du Havre, 2008.

Hattaway, Michael. 'Shakespeare's Histories: the Politics of Recent British Productions'. In *Shakespeare in the New Europe*, edited by Michael Hattaway, Boika Sokolova and Derek Roper, 351–69. Sheffield: Sheffield Academic Press, 1994.

Hazlitt, William. *The Round Table & Characters of Shakespear's Plays*. London: J. M. Dent, 1817, 1951.

Hazlitt, William. *Characters of Shakespeare's Plays*. London: R. Hunter and C. and J. Ollier, 1818.

Hazlitt, William. *Characters of Shakespeare's Plays*. Edited by J. H. Lobban. Cambridge: Cambridge University Press, 1908.

Hedrick, Donald. 'Advantage, Affect, History, *Henry V*'. *PMLA* 118, no. 3 (2003): 470–87.
Helgerson, Richard. *Forms of Nationhood: The Elizabethan Writing of England*. Chicago: University of Chicago Press, 1992.
Helmbold, Anita. '"Take a Soldier, Take a King": The (In)Separability of Conflict in Branagh's *Henry V*'. *Literature/Film Quarterly* 33, no. 4 (2005): 280–9.
Heywood, Thomas. *An Apology for Actors*. London: Nicholas Okes, 1612.
Highley, Christopher. *Shakespeare, Spenser, and the Crisis in Ireland*. Cambridge: Cambridge University Press, 1997.
Hill, Aaron. *King Henry the Fifth: Or the Conquest of France, By the English. A Tragedy*. London: for W. Chetwood and J. Watts, 1723.
Hillman, Richard. *Shakespeare, Marlowe, and the Politics of France*. Basingstoke: Palgrave, 2002.
Hirsh, James. 'Shakespeare's Stage Chorus and Olivier's Film Chorus'. In *Shakespeare on Screen: The Henriad*, edited by Sarah Hatchuel and Nathalie Vienne-Guerrin, 169–92. Rouen: Publications des Universités de Rouen et du Havre, 2008.
Holderness, Graham. *Shakespeare's History*. Dublin: Gill and Macmillan, 1985.
Holderness, Graham. 'Boxing the Bard: Shakespeare and Television'. In *The Shakespeare Myth*, edited by Graham Holderness, 173–89. Manchester: Manchester University Press, 1991.
Holderness, Graham. *Shakespeare: The Histories*. Basingstoke: Palgrave, 1999.
Holinshed, Raphael. *Chronicles of England, Scotlande, and Irelande*. [London]: John Harison et al., 1587.
Hölscher, Tonio. 'Images of War in Greece and Rome: Between Military Practice, Public Memory, and Cultural Symbolism'. *Journal of Roman Studies* 93 (2003): 1–17.
Hopkins, Lisa. 'Welshness in Shakespeare's English Histories'. In *Shakespeare's History Plays: Performance, Translation and Adaptation in Britain and Abroad*, edited by Ton Hoenselaars, 60–74. Cambridge: Cambridge University Press, 2004.
Hortmann, Wilhelm, ed. *Shakespeare on the German Stage. Volume 2: The Twentieth Century*. Cambridge: Cambridge University Press, 1998.
Howard, Jean E., and Phyllis Rackin. *Engendering a Nation: A Feminist Account of Shakespeare's English Histories*. London: Routledge, 1997.

Hudson, H. N. *Shakespeare: His Life, Art, and Characters*, 4th edn. 2 vols. Boston: Ginn, Heath, 1898.

Hunt, Maurice. 'The "Breaches" of Shakespeare's *The Life of King Henry the Fifth*'. *College Literature* 41, no. 4 (2014): 7–24.

Hunt, Maurice. 'Brothers and "Gentles" in *The Life of King Henry the Fifth*'. *Comparative Drama* 49, no. 1 (2015): 71–93.

Hutchinson, Charles. 'Claire Morley leads York Shakespeare Project cast in all-female staging of Henry V at First World War munitions factory'. *York Press*, 14 October 2015. Available at http://www.yorkpress.co.uk/news/13845703.Claire_Morley_leads_York_Shakespeare_Project_cast_in_all_female_staging_of_Henry_V_at_First_World_War_munitions_factory/ (accessed 1 December 2017).

Hutchison, Emily J. 'The Politics of Grief in the Outbreak of Civil War in France, 1407–1413'. *Speculum* 91, no. 2 (April 2016): 422–52.

Hutson, Lorna. 'Imagining Justice: Kantorowicz and Shakespeare', *Representations* 106 (2009): 118–42.

Hutson, Lorna. *Circumstantial Shakespeare*. Oxford: Oxford University Press, 2015.

Internet Movie Database (IMDb). 'Frequently Asked Questions for *Henry V* (2007)'. Available at http://www.imdb.com/title/tt1261975/faq (accessed 2 December 2017).

Irace, Kathleen. 'Reconstruction and Adaptation in Q *Henry V*'. *Studies in Bibliography* 44 (1991): 228–53.

Jackson, Ken, and Arthur F. Marotti. 'The Turn to Religion in Early Modern English Studies'. *Criticism* 46, no. 1 (2004): 167–90.

Jamieson, Neil. '"Sons of Iniquity": The Problem of Unlawfulness and Criminality Amongst Professional Soldiers in the Middle Ages'. In *Outlaws in Medieval and Early Modern England: Crime, Government and Society c. 1066–c.1600*, edited by John C. Appleby and Paul Dalton, 91–110. Farnham: Ashgate, 2009.

Jensen, Phebe. *Religion and Revelry in Shakespeare's Festive World*. Cambridge: Cambridge University Press, 2008.

Jonson, Ben. *Every Man In His Humour* (F). Edited by David Bevington. In *The Cambridge Edition of the Works of Ben Jonson*, edited by David Bevington, Martin Butler and Ian Donaldson. Volume 4. 7 vols. Cambridge: Cambridge University Press, 2012.

Jonson, Ben. *Every Man Out Of His Humour*. Edited by Randall Martin. In *The Cambridge Edition of the Works of Ben Jonson*, edited by David Bevington, Martin Butler and Ian Donaldson. Volume 1. 7 vols. Cambridge: Cambridge University Press, 2012.

Jonson, Ben. 'To the Memory of my Belovèd, The Author Master William Shakespeare And What He Hath Left Us'. Edited by Colin Burrow. In *The Cambridge Edition of the Works of Ben Jonson*, edited by David Bevington, Martin Butler and Ian Donaldson. Volume 5. 7 vols. Cambridge: Cambridge University Press, 2012.

Jonson, Ben. *Volpone*. Edited by Richard Dutton. In *The Cambridge Edition of the Works of Ben Jonson*, edited by David Bevington, Martin Butler and Ian Donaldson. Volume 4. 7 vols. Cambridge: Cambridge University Press, 2012.

Kahn, Victoria, and Lorna Hutson, eds. *Rhetoric and the Law in Early Modern Europe*. New Haven, CT: Yale University Press, 2001.

Kantorowicz, Ernst. *The King's Two Bodies: A Study in Medieval Political Theology*. Princeton, NJ: Princeton University Press, 1957, 2016.

Karremann, Isabel. *The Drama of Memory in Shakespeare's History Plays*. Cambridge: Cambridge University Press, 2015.

Kastan, David Scott. 'Proud Majesty Made a Subject: Shakespeare and the Spectacle of Rule'. *Shakespeare Quarterly* 37, no. 4 (1986): 459–75.

Kennedy, Maev. 'Excavation Finds Early Shakespeare Theatre Was Rectangular'. *Guardian*, 17 May 2016. Available at https://www.theguardian.com/culture/2016/may/17/curtain-excavation-early-shakespeare-theatre-rectangular-shoreditch (accessed 24 November 2017).

Kerrigan, John. *Archipelagic English: Literature, History, and Politics 1603–1707*. Oxford: Oxford University Press, 2008.

Kerrigan, John. 'Oaths, Threats and *Henry V*'. *Review of English Studies* 63, no. 261 (2012): 551–71.

Kezar, Dennis. 'Shakespeare's Guilt Trip in *Henry V*'. *MLQ: Modern Language Quarterly* 61, no. 3 (2000): 431–61.

Kiernan, Pauline. *Shakespeare's Theory of Drama*. Cambridge: Cambridge University Press, 1996.

Kimbrough, Robert. 'The Problem of Thersites'. *Modern Language Review* 59, no. 2 (1964): 173–6.

Knapp, Jeffrey. *Shakespeare's Tribe: Church, Nation, and Theater in Renaissance England*. Chicago and London: University of Chicago Press, 2002.

Knight, G. Wilson. *The Olive and the Sword: A Study of England's Shakespeare*. London: Oxford University Press, 1944.

Knights, L. C. 'How Many Children Had Lady Macbeth? An Essay in the Theory and Practice of Shakespeare Criticism'. In *Explorations*. New York: New York University Press, 1964.

Lagae-Devoldère, Denis. '"New Rights We Grant Not, But the Old Declare": *le Henry V* de Roger Boyle (1664), ou Shakespeare "restauré"'. *Études Épistémè* 14 (2008). Available at http://episteme.revues.org (accessed 13 September 2017).

Lake, Peter. *How Shakespeare Put Politics on the Stage: Power and Succession in the History Plays*. New Haven, CT: Yale University Press, 2016.

Lancashire, Ian, ed. *Lexicons of Early Modern English*. Available at http://leme.library.utoronto.ca/ (accessed 14 July 2017).

Lanham, Richard. *A Handlist of Rhetorical Terms*. 2nd edn. Berkeley: University of California Press, 1991.

Leduc, Antoine, Sylvie Leluc and Olivier Renaudeau, eds. *D'Azincourt à Marignan. Chevaliers et bombardes, 1415–1515*. Paris: Gallimard / Musée de l'Armée, 2015.

Le Fèvre, Jean. *Chronique de Jean Le Fèvre, Seigneur de Saint-Remy*. Edited by François Morand. 2 vols. Paris: Renouard, 1876.

Leggatt, Alexander. *Shakespeare's Political Drama: The Roman Plays and the History Plays*. New York: Routledge, 1988.

Lenz, Joseph M. 'The Politics of Honor: The Oath in *Henry V*'. *Journal of English and Germanic Philology* 80, no. 1 (1981): 1–12.

Livingstone, David. 'Silenced Voices: A Reactionary Streamlined *Henry V* in *The Hollow Crown*'. *Journal of University of Lodz (Multicultural Shakespeare: Translation, Appropriation and Performance)* 12 (2015): 87–100.

Lloyd, William Watkiss. *Critical Essays on the Plays of Shakespeare*. London: G. Bell and Sons, 1875.

Loehlin, James N. *Shakespeare in Performance: Henry V*. Manchester: Manchester University Press, 1997.

Luders, Alexander, et al., eds. *Statutes of the Realm*. 11 vols. London: Dawsons, 1810–28.

Machiavelli, Niccolò. *The Prince*. Edited by Quentin Skinner and Russell Price. Cambridge: Cambridge University Press, 1988, 2003.

Machiavelli, Nicholas. *Nicholas Machiavel's Prince*. London: Will Hills, 1640.

MacKenzie, John Stuart. *Arrows of Desire: Essays on Our National Character and Outlook*. London: Allen & Unwin, 1920.
Maguire, Laurie E. '"Household Kates": Chez Petruchio, Percy, and Plantagenet'. In *Gloriana's Face: Women, Public and Private, in the English Renaissance*, edited by S. P. Cerasano and Marion Wynne-Davies, 129–65. Detroit: Wayne State University Press, 1992.
Maguire, Laurie E. *Shakespearean Suspect Texts: The 'Bad' Quartos and their Contexts*. Cambridge: Cambridge University Press, 1996.
Maley, Willy, and Philip Schwyzer, eds. *Shakespeare and Wales: From the Marches to the Assembly*. Farnham: Ashgate, 2010.
Manders, V. E. C. 'Shakespeare at St. Bernard's'. *Shakespeare Quarterly* 2 (1951): 123–6.
Marder, Louis. 'History Cycle at Antioch College'. *Shakespeare Quarterly* 4 (1953): 57–8.
Marino, James J. *Owning William Shakespeare*. Philadelphia: University of Pennsylvania Press, 2011.
Marlowe, Christopher. *The Jew of Malta*. Edited by N. W. Bawcutt. Manchester: Manchester University Press, 1978.
Marsland, Elizabeth. 'Updating Agincourt: The Battle Scenes in Two Film Versions of *Henry V*'. In *Modern War on Stage and Screen/ Der Moderne Krieg auf der Buhne*, edited by Wolfgang Görtschacher and Holger Klein, 5–19. Lewiston, NY: Edwin Mellen, 1997.
Mason, Roger. 'Scotching the Brut: Politics, History and National Myth in Sixteenth-Century Britain'. In *Scotland and England, 1286–1815*, edited by Roger Mason, 60–84. Edinburgh: John Donald Publishers, 1987.
McAlindon, Tom. *Shakespeare's Tudor History. A Study of* Henry IV, Parts 1 and 2. Aldershot: Ashgate, 2001.
McAlindon, Tom. 'Natural Closure in *Henry V*'. *Shakespearean International Yearbook 3: Where Are We Now In Shakespearean Studies?* (2003): 156–71.
McCloskey, John C. 'The Mirror of All Christian Kings'. *Shakespeare Association Bulletin* 19 (1944): 36–40.
McEachern, Claire. *The Poetics of English Nationhood, 1590–1612*. Cambridge: Cambridge University Press, 1996.
Mebane, John S. '"Impious War": Religion and the Ideology of Warfare in *Henry V*'. *Studies in Philology* 104, no. 2 (2007): 250–66.

Meron, Theodor. *Henry's Wars and Shakespeare's Laws: Perspectives on the Law of War in the Later Middle Ages*. Oxford, Clarendon Press, 1993.

Migliorini, Robert. 'Henry V prend ses quartiers à Vincennes La pièce de Shakespeare, créée au festival d'Avignon cet été, est jouée pendant deux mois au théâtre de l'Aquarium, dans la mise en scène de Jean-Louis Benoit'. *La Croix*, 8 January 2000. Available at https://www.la-croix.com/Archives/2000-01-08/Henry-V-prend-ses-quartiers-a-Vincennes-La-piece-de-Shakespeare-creee-au-festival-d-Avignon-cet-ete-est-jouee-pendant-deux-mois-au-theatre-de-l-Aquarium-dans-la-mise-en-scene-de-Jean-Louis-Benoit-_NP_-2000-01-08-99161 (accessed 17 October 2017).

Morgann, Maurice. *An Essay on the Dramatic Character of Sir John Falstaff*. London: T. Davies, 1777.

Mossman, Judith. 'Henry V and Plutarch's Alexander'. *Shakespeare Quarterly* 45, no. 1 (1994): 57–73.

Müller-Wood, Anja. 'No Ideology without Psychology: the Emotional Effects of Shakespeare's *Henry V*'. *Style* 46, nos 3–4 (2012): 355–77.

Mulready, Cyrus. 'Making History in Q *Henry V*'. *English Literary History* 43, no. 3 (2013): 478–513.

Mulryne, James Ronald, and Margaret Shewring, eds. *Shakespeare's Globe Rebuilt*. Cambridge: Cambridge University Press, 1997.

Munro, Lucy. 'Speaking History: Linguistic Memory and the Usable Past In the Early Modern History Play'. *Huntington Library Quarterly* 76, no. 4 (2013), 519–40.

Murphy, Andrew. 'Shakespeare's Irish History'. *Literature and History* 5, no. 1 (1996): 38–59.

Murphy, Andrew. *But the Irish Sea Betwixt Us: Ireland, Colonialism, and Renaissance Literature*. Lexington: University of Kentucky Press, 1999.

Museum of London Archaeology and Cloak and Dagger Studios. *The Theatre*. Available at http://www.explorethetheatre.co.uk (accessed 13 July 2017).

Nashe, Thomas. *Pierce Penilesse His Supplication to the Diuell*. London: John Busbie, 1592.

Neill, Michael. 'Broken English and Broken Irish: Nation, Language and the Optic of Power in Shakespeare's Histories'. *Shakespeare Quarterly* 45, no. 1 (1994): 18–22.

Neill, Michael. *Putting History to the Question: Power, Politics and Society in Renaissance Drama*. New York: Columbia University Press, 2000.
Newstrom, Scott. 'Right Pitches Dubya as Henry V'. *Alternet* (2003). Available at http://www.alternet.org/story/16025/right_pitches_dubya_as_henry_v (accessed 17 July 2017).
Orgel, Stephen. *Impersonations: The Performance of Gender in Shakespeare's England*. Cambridge: Cambridge University Press, 1996.
Orléans, Charles d'. *Charles d'Orléans, Poésies*. Edited by Pierre Champion. 2 vols. Paris: n.p., 1923–7.
Owens, Mackubin T. 'Shakespeare was no Pacifist'. Ashbrook Center Editorial (November 2002). Available at http://ashbrook.org/publications/oped-owens-02-shakespeare/ (accessed 17 July 2017).
Oxford English Dictionary. Oxford: Oxford University Press, 2017. Available at http://www.oed.com/ (accessed 14 July 2017).
Oxford University. Holinshed Project. Available at http://www.cems.ox.ac.uk/holinshed/index.shtml (accessed 13 July 2017).
Paladhile, Dominique. *Azincourt, 1415*. Paris: Perrin, 2015.
Palfrey, Simon. *Doing Shakespeare*. London: Bloomsbury, 2005.
Parker, Patricia. *Shakespeare from the Margins: Language, Culture, Context*. Chicago: University of Chicago Press, 1996.
Pasupathi, Vimala C. 'Coats and Conduct: The Materials of Military Obligation in Shakespeare's *Henry IV* and *Henry V*'. *Modern Philology* 109, no. 3 (2012): 326–51.
Patterson, Annabel M. 'Back By Popular Demand: the Two Versions of *Henry V*'. *Renaissance Drama* 19 (1988): 29–62.
Patterson, Annabel M. *Reading Holinshed's Chronicles*. Chicago and London: University of Chicago Press, 1994.
Peacham, Henry. *Minerva Britanna*. London: by Wa. Dight, 1612.
Pentland, Elizabeth. '"I Cannot Speak Your England": French Women in *King John* and *Henry V*'. *Early Modern Literary Studies, Special Issue 27: European Women in Early Modern Drama* (2017). Edited by Ema Vyroubalová and Edel Semple. Available at https://extra.shu.ac.uk/emls/journal/index.php/emls/article/view/380/288 (accessed 18 February 2018).
Pepys, Samuel. *Diary of Samuel Pepys*. Edited by Ernest Rhys and Richard Garnett. 2 vols. London: J. M. Dent, 1906.

Pestritto, Carrie. 'Outlooks on Honor in *Henry V* and *Julius Caesar*'. *Connotations* 17, no. 1 (2007): 61–7.

Pickford, James. 'RSC to Translate All Shakespeare's Plays Into Mandarin'. *Financial Times*, 28 October 2016. Available at https://www.ft.com/content/dcb5bab8-99dc-11e6-8f9b-70e3cabccfae (accessed 15 October 2017).

[Pintoin, Michel.] *Chronique du Religieux de Saint-Denys, Contenant le Règne de Charles VI, de 1380 à 1433*. Translated by M. L. Bellaguet. 6 vols. Paris: Crapelet, 1839–52.

Pittock, Malcolm. 'The Problem of *Henry V*'. *Neophilologus* 93, no. 1 (2009): 175–90.

Pizan, Christine de. *The Epistle of the Prison of Human Life; with, An Epistle to the Queen of France; and, Lament on the Evils of the Civil War*. Edited and translated by Josette A. Wisman. New York: Garland Publishing, 1984.

Polito, Mary. '"Warriors for the Working Day": Shakespeare's Professionals'. *Shakespeare* 2, no. 1 (2006), 1–23.

Pollard, A. W. *Shakespeare Folios and Quartos: A Study in the Bibliography of Shakespeare's Plays, 1594–1685*. London: Methuen, 1909.

Pollard, A. W., and John Dover Wilson. '*Henry V* (1600)'. *Times Literary Supplement*, 13 March 1919.

Poole, Adrian. 'The Disciplines of War, Memory and Writing: Shakespeare's *Henry V* and David Jones's *In Parenthesis*'. *Critical Survey* 22, no. 2 (2010): 91–104.

Pudney, Eric. 'Mendacity and Kingship in Shakespeare's *Henry V* and *Richard III*'. *European Journal of English Studies* 19, no. 2 (2015): 163–75.

Pugliatti, Paola. 'The Strange Tongues of *Henry V*'. *Yearbook of English Studies* 23 (1993): 235–53.

Puttenham, George. *The Arte of English Poesie*. London: Richard Field, 1589.

Rabkin, Norman. 'Rabbits, Ducks, and *Henry V*'. *Shakespeare Quarterly* 28, no. 3 (1977): 279–96.

Rabkin, Norman. *Shakespeare and the Problem of Meaning*. Chicago: University of Chicago Press, 1981.

Rackin, Phyllis. *Stages of History: Shakespeare's English Chronicles*. New York: Cornell University Press, 1990.

Rhodes, Neil. 'Wrapped in the Strong Arms of the Union: Shakespeare and King James'. In *Shakespeare and Scotland*,

edited by Willy Maley and Andrew Murphy, 37–52. Manchester: Manchester University Press, 2004.
Rich, Frank. 'Henry V Takes Field in Central Park'. *New York Times*, 6 July 1984. Available at http://www.nytimes.com/1984/07/06/arts/stage-henry-v-takes-field-in-central-park.html?pagewanted=all (accessed 15 September 2017).
Robinson, Benedict S. 'Harry and Amurath'. *Shakespeare Quarterly* 60, no. 4 (2009): 399–424.
Robortello, Francisco. *Aristotelis poeticam explicationes*. Florence: Lorenzo Torrentino, 1548.
Rossiter, A. P. 'Ambivalence: The Dialectic of the Histories'. In *Angel with Horns, and Other Shakespeare Lectures*, edited by Graham Storey, 40–57. London: Longman, 1961.
Salkeld, Duncan. 'The Texts of *Henry V*'. *Shakespeare* 3, no. 2 (2007): 161–82.
Sarlos, Robert K. 'Dingelstedt's Celebration of the Tercentenary: Shakespeare's Histories as Cycle'. *Theatre Survey* 5, no. 2 (1964): 117–31.
Savile, John. *King Iames His Entertainment at Theobalds: With His Welcome to London, Together with a Salutatorie Poem*. London: T. Este, 1603.
Schlegel, A. W. *A Course of Lectures on Dramatic Art and Literature*. Translated by John Black. 2 vols. London: Baldwin et al., 1815.
Schmitt, Carl. *Political Theology: Four Chapters on the Concept of Sovereignty*. Translated by George Schwab. Chicago: University of Chicago Press, 2005.
Schwyzer, Philip. *Literature, Nationalism, and Memory in Early Modern England and Wales*. Cambridge: Cambridge University Press, 2004.
Seargeant, Philip. 'Ideologies of English in Shakespeare's *Henry V*'. *Language and Literature* 18, no. 1 (2009): 25–44.
Shakespeare, William. *The Cronicle History of Henry the fift, With his battell fought at Agin Court in France. Togither with Auntient Pistoll*. London: Thomas Millington and John Busby, 1600.
Shakespeare, William. *A Most Pleasaunt and Excellent Conceited Comedie, of Syr John Falstaffe; and the Merrie Wiues of Windsor*. London: Arthur Johnson, 1602.
Shakespeare, William. *Mr. William Shakespeares Comedies, Histories, & Tragedies*. London: William Jaggard et al., 1623.

Shakespeare, William. *The Plays of William Shakespeare*. Edited by Samuel Johnson. 8 vols. London: J. and R. Tonson et al., 1765.

Shakespeare, William. *The Merry Wives of Windsor*. Edited by W. W. Gregg. Oxford: Clarendon Press, 1910.

Shakespeare, William. *Henry V*. Edited by John Dover Wilson. Cambridge: Cambridge University Press, 1947.

Shakespeare, William. *Henry V*. Edited by J. H. Walter. Arden Shakespeare, Second Series. London: Methuen, 1954.

Shakespeare, William. *Henry V*. Edited by Gary Taylor. Oxford: Oxford University Press, 1982.

Shakespeare, William. *William Shakespeare: The Complete Works*. Edited by Stanley Wells and Gary Taylor. Oxford: Clarendon Press, 1986.

Shakespeare, William. *King Henry V*. Edited by Andrew Gurr. New Cambridge Shakespeare. Cambridge: Cambridge University Press, 1992, 2005.

Shakespeare, William. *King Henry V*. Edited by T. W. Craik. Arden Shakespeare, Third Series. London: Routledge, 1995.

Shakespeare, William. *The First Folio of Shakespeare: The Norton Facsimile*. Ed. Charlton Hinman. 2nd edn. New York: Norton, 1996.

Shakespeare, William. *Henry V*. Edited by Gisèle Venet. Translated by Jean-Michel Déprat. Folio Théâtre. Paris: Gallimard, 1999.

Shakespeare, William. *La Vie du roi Henri V*. Edited by Gisèle Venet. Translated by Jean-Michel Déprats. Folio Théâtre. Paris: Gallimard, 1999.

Shakespeare, William. *The First Quarto of King Henry V*. Edited by Andrew Gurr. New Cambridge Shakespeare. The Early Quartos. Cambridge: Cambridge University Press, 2000.

Shakespeare, William. *King Henry VI, Part 1*. Edited by Edward Burns. Arden Shakespeare, Third Series. London, Routledge, 2000.

Shakespeare, William. *Romeo and Juliet*. Edited by René Weis. Arden Shakespeare, Third Series. London: Bloomsbury, 2012.

Shakespeare, William. *Henry V*. Edited by James D. Mardock. Internet Shakespeare Editions. University of Victoria. 4 October 2013. Available at http://internetshakespeare.uvic.ca/Library/Texts/H5/ (accessed 17 July 2017).

Shakespeare, William. *King Henry IV, Part 2*. Edited by James C. Bulman. Arden Shakespeare. Third Series. London: Bloomsbury, 2016.

Shanker, Sidney. *Shakespeare and the Uses of Ideology*. Paris: Mouton, 1975.

Shapiro, Barbara J. 'Classical Rhetoric and the English Law of Evidence'. In *Rhetoric and the Law in Early Modern Europe*, edited by Victoria Kahn and Lorna Hutson, 54–72. New Haven, CT: Yale University Press, 2001.

Shapiro, James. 'Revisiting *Tamburlaine*: Henry V as Shakespeare's Belated Armada Play'. *Criticism* 31, no. 4 (1989): 351–66.

Shapiro, James. *1599: A Year in the Life of William Shakespeare*. London: Faber, 2005.

Sharpe, Kevin. *Reading Authority and Representing Rule in Early Modern England*. London: Bloomsbury, 2013.

Shaw, George Bernard. *Our Theatres in the Nineties*. 3 vols. London: Constable and Company, 1931.

Sidney, Philip. *An Apologie for Poetrie*. London: Henry Olney, 1595.

Sidney, Philip. *The Defence of Poesie*. London: William Ponsonby, 1595.

Sinfield, Alan. *Literature in Protestant England 1560–1660*. London: Croom Helm, 1983.

Slights, Camille Wells. 'The Conscience of the King: *Henry V* and the Reformed Conscience'. *Philological Quarterly* 80, no. 1 (2001): 37–55.

Sloterdijk, Peter. *Critique of Cynical Reason*. Translated by Michael Eldred. London: Verso, 1988.

Smith, Bruce R. *Shakespeare and Masculinity*. Oxford: Oxford University Press, 2000.

Smith, D. Nichol, ed. *Eighteenth-Century Essays on Shakespeare*. 2nd edn. Oxford: Clarendon Press, 1963.

Smith, Emma, ed. *King Henry V: Shakespeare in Production*. Cambridge: Cambridge University Press, 2002.

Smith, Matthew J. 'The Experience of Ceremony in *Henry V*'. *SEL: Studies in English Literature, 1500–1900* 54, no. 2 (2014): 401–21.

Smith, Warren. 'The *Henry V* Choruses in the First Folio'. *Journal of English and Germanic Philology* 53 (1954): 38–57.

Somogyi, Nick de. *Shakespeare's Theatre of War*. Aldershot: Ashgate, 1998.

Somogyi, Nick de. 'Fletcher, Robert (*fl.* 1581–1606)'. In *Oxford Dictionary of National Biography*. Available at http://www.oxforddnb.com.janus.biu.sorbonne.fr/view/article/9741 (accessed 1 September 2016).

Spelman, Henry. 'Of the Union'. In *The Jacobean Union: Six Tracts of 1604*, edited by Bruce Galloway and Brian Levack, 161–84. Edinburgh: Scottish Historical Society, 1985.

Spenser, Edmund. *A View of the Present State of Ireland*. Edited by W. L. Renwick. London: Scholars Press, 1934.

Steinsaltz, David. 'The Politics of French Language in Shakespeare's History Plays'. *SEL: Studies in English Literature, 1500–1900* 42, no. 2 (2002): 317–34.

Stone, Charles Russell. *From Tyrant to Philosopher-King: A Literary History of Alexander the Great in Medieval and Early Modern England, Cursor Mundi* 19. Turnhout: Brepols, 2013.

Stříbrný, Zdeněk. '*Henry V* and History'. In *Shakespeare in a Changing World*, edited by Arnold Kettle. New York: International Publishers, 1964.

Styan, J. L. *The Shakespeare Revolution: Criticism and Performance In The Twentieth Century*. Cambridge: Cambridge University Press, 1977.

Sutherland, John, and Cedric Watts. *Henry V, War Criminal? & Other Shakespeare Puzzles*. Oxford: Oxford University Press, 2000.

Swinburne, Algernon Charles. *A Study of Shakespeare*. London: Chatto and Windus, 1880.

Taylor, Gary. 'Shakespeare's Leno: *Henry V* IV.V.14'. *Notes and Queries* 26, no. 2 (1979): 117–18.

Taylor, Gary. 'The Fortunes of Oldcastle'. *Shakespeare Survey* 38 (1985): 85–100.

Taylor, Gary. 'Cry Havoc'. *The Guardian*, 4 April 2003. Available at https://www.theguardian.com/stage/2003/apr/05/theatre.classics (accessed 2 December 2017).

Taylor, Peter. 'Theatre: *Henry V / The Winter's Tale*, The Globe, London'. *The Independent*, 8 June 1997. Available at http://www.independent.co.uk/arts-entertainment/theatre-henry-v-the-winters-tale-the-globe-london–1255060.html (accessed 17 September 2017).

Tempera, Mariangela. '"Only About Kings": References to the Second Tetralogy in Film and Television'. In *Shakespeare on*

Screen: The Henriad, edited by Sarah Hatchuel and Nathalie Vienne-Guerrin, 169–92. Rouen: Publications des Universités de Rouen et du Havre, 2008.

Thorne, Alison. '"Awake Remembrance of These Valiant Dead": *Henry V* and the Politics of the English History Play'. *Shakespeare Studies* 30 (2002): 162–87.

Tillyard, E. M. W. *Shakespeare's History Plays*. London: Chatto & Windus, 1942.

Tirard, Laurent. 'Branagh Côté Jardin'. *Studio* 123 (1 July 1997): 78–83.

Titcomb, Caldwell. 'Anti-War "Henry V" Is Fascinating Failure'. *Harvard Crimson*, 30 June 1969. Available at http://www.thecrimson.com/article/1969/6/30/anti-war-henry-v-is-fascinating-failure/ (accessed 15 October 2017).

Toureille, Valérie. *Le drame d'Azincourt: histoire d'une étrange défaite*. Paris: Albin Michel, 2015.

Tribble, Evelyn. 'Where Are the Archers In Shakespeare?'. *English Literary History* 82, no. 3 (2015): 789–814.

Tucker, E. F. J. 'Legal Fiction and Human Reality: Hal's Role in *Henry V*', *Educational Theatre Journal* 26, no. 3 (1974): 308–14.

Tuetey, Alexandre, ed. *Le Journal d'un bourgeois de Paris, 1405–1449*. Paris: H. Champion, 1881.

Ulrici, Hermann. *Shakspeare's Dramatic Art*. London: Chapman Brothers, 1846.

University of Victoria. *Early Modern Map of London*. Available at https://mapoflondon.uvic.ca/ (accessed 13 July 2017).

Urkowitz, Steven. *Shakespeare's Revision of* King Lear. Princeton, NJ: Princeton University Press, 1980.

Venet, Gisèle. *Leçon littéraire sur* Henry V *de Shakespeare*. Paris: Presses Universitaires de France, 2000.

Vernant, Jean-Pierre. *Mortals and Immortals, Collected Essays*. Edited by Froma I. Zeitlin. Princeton, NJ: Princeton University Press, 1991.

Voltaire. *Lettre de Mr de Voltaire à l'Académie Française lue dans cette Académie à la solemnité de la St. Louis le 25 Auguste 1776*. s.l., 1776.

Vukovitz, Deborah. 'Shakespeare on Film: *Henry V* Rendered in Music'. *Shakespeare Bulletin* 21, no. 1 (2003): 42–5.

Walderman, Jürgen. 'Dingelstedt, Shakespeare und Weimar'. *Shakespeare Jahrbuch* 55 (1919): 75–85.

Walls, Alison. 'French Speech as Dramatic Action in Shakespeare's *Henry V*'. *Language and Literature* 22, no. 2 (2013): 119–31.

Warren, Christopher N. '*Henry V*, Anachronism, and the History of International Law'. In *The Oxford Handbook of English Law and Literature, 1500–1700*, edited by Lorna Hutson and Bradin Cormack, 709–27. Oxford: Oxford University Press, 2017.

Watts, Cedric. 'Henry V's Claim to France: Valid or Invalid'. In *Henry V, War Criminal? & Other Shakespeare Puzzles*, edited by John Sutherland and Cedric Watts, 117–25. Oxford: Oxford University Press, 2000.

Wazir, Burhan. 'Docu-dramas Set to Storm the Screens: Viewers Lap Up Mix of Fact and Fiction'. *Observer*, 18 May 2003. Available at https://www.theguardian.com/media/2003/may/18/broadcasting.uknews (accessed 2 December 2017).

Wells, Stanley. 'The Canon in the Can'. *Times Literary Supplement*, no. 4284 (10 May 1985): 522.

Wells, Stanley W., and Gary Taylor. *Modernizing Shakespeare's Spelling: With Three Studies of the Text of Henry V*. Oxford: Oxford University Press, 1979.

Wells-Lassagne, Shannon. *Television and Serial Adaptation*. London: Routledge, 2017.

Werner, Sarah. 'Firk and Foot: The Boy Actor in *Henry V*'. *Shakespeare Bulletin* 21, no. 4 (2003): 19–27.

Whalen, Lauren. 'Henry V (Babes with Blades Theatre)'. *Chicago Theater Beat*, 17 March 2017. Available at http://chicagotheaterbeat.com/2017/03/17/henry-v-review-babes-with-blades/ (accessed 15 October 2017).

Whitver, H. Austin. 'Materiality of Memory in Shakespeare's Second Tetralogy'. *Studies in English Literature* 56, no. 2 (2016): 285–306.

Wilcox, Lance. 'Katherine of France as Victim and Bride', *Shakespeare Studies* 17 (1985): 61–88.

Wilson, Richard. *Secret Shakespeare: Studies in Theatre, Religion and Resistance*. Manchester: Manchester University Press, 2004.

Womersley, David. *Divinity and State*. Oxford: Oxford University Press, 2010.

Woodcock, Matthew. *Shakespeare: Henry V*. Basingstoke and London: Palgrave Macmillan, 2008.

Wortham, Christopher. 'Shakespeare, James I and the Matter of Britain'. *English* 45 (1996): 97–122.

Wray, Ramona. 'Hegemonic Masculinity, the Roman Epic and Kenneth Branagh's *Henry V*'. In *Shakespeare on Screen: The Henriad*, edited by Sarah Hatchuel and Nathalie Vienne-Guerrin, 209–32. Rouen: Publications des Universités de Rouen et du Havre, 2008.

Wright, Thomas, ed. *Political Poems and Songs Relating to English History, Composed During the Period from the Accession of Edward III to that of Richard III*. 2 vols. London: Longman, 1859–61.

Žižek, Slavoj. *The Sublime Object of Ideology*. London: Verso, 1989.

INDEX

Abate, Corinne 96–7, 292n.
Agincourt 600 3
Agincourt, Battle of xii, xv, 2, 3, 4, 9, 10, 17, 20, 23, 24, 25, 26, 33, 41, 43, 51, 55, 58, 60, 61, 70, 71, 77, 80, 87, 89, 93, 94, 103, 104, 106, 107, 108, 109, 113, 114, 123, 132, 137, 149, 150, 154, 161, 168, 169, 175, 176, 201–20, 280n., 281n., 287–93n.
Aitkin, Ian 111
Alexander the Great 53, 195–7, 240
Althusser, Louis 43, 144
Altman, Joel 46
Andrews, Meghan C. 95–6
Ascham, Roger 94
Augustine, Saint 212, 214
Avignon Festival xvi, 5, 49, 54, 258–9n.
Azincourt 2, 3, 201, 287n., 288n., 289n.

Babakitis, Peter xvi, 102, 113–17
Babes With Blades (theatre company) xvi, 69
Baker, David J. 45, 90, 279n.
Baldo, Jonathan 93, 162, 281n.
Banerjee, Rita 89

Bardolph (character) 6, 11, 60, 61, 62, 83, 84, 85, 105, 110, 115, 118, 145, 147, 186, 189, 190, 191, 193
Bates (character) 36, 82, 123, 150–1, 152, 168, 235
Battle of Agincourt *see* Agincourt, Battle of
Battle of Crécy *see* Crécy, Battle of
Beckett, Samuel 88
Benoit, Jean-Louis xvi, 49, 248n.
Berry, Duke of 208, 211
Berry, Edward 19, 22, 38, 45
Berry, Marie de, Duchess of Auvergne and Berry 202, 211, 212, 215
Billington, Michael 64
Black Prince, Edward, the xii, 160–1, 176
Blount, Charles, Lord Mountjoy 10, 99, 171, 249n.
Bodin, Jean 136, 150
Boer War 59
Boethius 12, 216, 217, 293n.
Bogdanov, Michael 13, 16, 62–3, 66, 72, 102, 112–13, 120
Boyd, Michael 64
Boydell Shakespeare Gallery xv

INDEX

Boyle, Roger, Lord Orrery xiv, 14–15, 55
Bradley, A. C. 6, 29, 34–5, 36, 38, 126–7, 255n.
Bradshaw, Graham 44
Branagh, Kenneth xv, xvi, 3, 13, 53, 62, 100, 102, 104, 107–12, 113, 115, 118, 232, 271n., 272n.
  Love's Labour's Lost 113
  Much Ado About Nothing 113
  Thor 118
Breight, Curtis 111
Britain/British 3, 4, 13, 17, 19, 49, 57, 61, 62, 66, 71, 72, 77, 105, 107, 114, 121, 124, 125, 156–79, 277–83n.
Brooks, Richard 122
Brotton, Jerry 90–1
Brutus/Brute (founder of Britain) 167, 174
Buhler, Stephen 105
Burgtheater, Vienna 66
Burgundy (character) 9, 99, 174, 218–20
Burgundy, Anne of 55
Burgundy, Duke of xiii, 204, 205, 220, 290n., 291n., 293n.
Bush, George W. 77, 121

Calais 162, 164, 280n.
Calvert, Charles 58–9, 261n.
Calvin, John (Jean) 16, 46, 143–4, 284n.
Cambridge (character) xii, 42, 84, 145–6, 147, 192
Campbell, Lily B. 40–1

Canterbury (character) 9, 11, 12, 14, 22, 24, 26, 33, 37, 41, 52, 85, 134–5, 139, 141–2, 143, 144, 157, 159, 160, 165–6, 167–8, 172, 184–6, 199, 228, 234, 235, 242, 281n.
Carlyle, Thomas 30, 137
Catherine of Valois xii 117
Cawdrey, Thomas 230
Champion, Larry 38
Chapman, Alison 90
Charles VI of France xii, xiii, 2, 203, 204, 209, 279n.
Charles VII of France xiii, 2, 133
Charnes, Linda 99
Chartier, Alain 17, 202, 203, 204–5, 215–20, 289n., 293n.
Chernaik, Warren 112
Churchill, Winston 105
Clegg, Cyndia 89–90
Cockerell, Toby 48
Coke, Sir Edward, Speaker of the House of Commons 93
Coldiron, Anne 209–10, 291n.
Coleman, David 15, 77–8
Coleridge, Samuel Taylor 30
Collins, Lieutenant-Colonel Tim 77, 78
Condren, Conal 190
Costner, Kevin 121
Covent Garden xv, 57
Covington, Sarah 198, 287n.
Craik, T. W. 126, 157, 170, 187, 282n.
Crécy, Battle of 161

Crimean War 76
cultural materialism 19, 40, 43–4
Cunningham, David L. 121
Curry, Anne 201, 206, 216, 220, 289n., 291n., 292n., 293n.
Curtain Theatre, Shoreditch 10, 222

Daniel, Drew 97
Daniel, Samuel 195
Daniels, Ron 63
Dauphin (character) 12, 24, 25, 61, 71, 106, 173, 198, 204, 205, 206–7, 211, 293n.
Davies, Michael 46, 155, 275n.
Davies, Oliver Ford 120
DEEP (Database of Early English Playbooks) 241, 243
Dekker, Thomas 22–3, 90
Delacrote Theater, Central Park 70
Deloney, Thomas 90
Dench, Judi 106
Derrida, Jacques 97, 138
Dessen, Alan C. 225, 244
Devereux, Robert, 2nd Earl of Essex 9–10, 39, 43, 50, 90, 96, 99, 131, 170–1, 243, 252n., 275n., 281n., 285n., 286n.
Díaz-Fernández, José Ramón 100
digital scholarship 97, 222, 227, 233, 235, 243–4
Dingelstedt, Franz 65–6
Divine Right of Kings 16, 129, 134, 147, 154, 155, 183, 284n.

Dollimore, Jonathan 43, 45, 127–8
Doran, Gregory 14, 102, 119–20
Dover 164
Dowd, Christopher 84
Dowden, Edward 32, 33, 39
Doyle, Patrick 100, 111
Drakakis, John 7, 16, 80, 186
Drury Lane xv, 55
Dryden, John 54–5
Dutton, Richard 99, 219, 249n.

Edict of Nantes 88
Edinburgh Festival 73
Edward III xii, 2, 159, 160, 176
Elgar, Edward 6
Elizabeth I xiii, xiv, 6, 9, 40, 96, 99, 131, 157, 162, 171, 177, 248n., 279n., 280n.
Ellis, Steven 163–4, 279n., 280n.
Ellis-Fermor, Una 37, 255n.
Ely (character) 9, 11, 12, 14, 24, 26, 33, 41, 52, 85, 134, 142, 143, 160, 185–6, 280n.
Elyot, Sir Thomas xiii, 78, 94
England xii–xiv, 1, 2, 5, 7, 10, 17, 18, 20, 31, 40, 43, 55, 67, 72, 73, 82, 88, 93, 96, 103, 104, 105, 109, 113, 116, 119, 123, 138, 156–9, 161–9, 171, 173–9, 180, 191, 194, 199, 203, 205, 207, 209, 213, 226, 229, 235
English Channel 2, 3, 4, 65, 113, 164, 210

English identity/Englishness 17, 20, 30, 32, 41, 57, 65, 66, 73, 84, 90, 92, 105, 132–3, 156–79, 199, 205–6, 209–10, 223–4, 227–8, 237–8

English language 4, 15, 16, 18, 27, 42, 49, 57, 73, 84, 92, 94–5, 97, 122, 123, 125, 160, 177–8, 185, 187, 188, 191, 201, 220, 221, 225, 232, 233–8, 239, 240, 243, 245

English Shakespeare Company 62, 112

Erickson, Peter B. 199

Erne, Lukas 8, 11, 98

Etienne, Claude 65

Exeter (character) 62, 134, 154, 160, 194, 208

Falklands War 13, 49, 61–3, 109, 112–13

Falstaff (character) 6, 9, 11, 22, 23, 28, 29, 31, 34–5, 36, 42, 46, 53–4, 99–100, 110, 118, 120, 127, 130, 145, 147, 187, 193, 250n., 260n., 275n., 287n.

The Famous Victories of Henry V xiv, 5, 8, 22, 23, 25, 26, 131, 133, 161, 165, 220, 248n., 280n.

Fer, Monsieur Le (character) 103, 108

First Folio xiv, 7–11, 13, 23–7, 49–50, 52, 54, 60, 97–100, 131, 148, 156, 157, 159, 167, 170, 171, 172, 174, 176, 178, 186, 226, 240–3, 251n., 252n., 253n., 277n., 279n., 280n., 281n.

First World War 38, 59, 63, 66, 81, 109, 261n.

Flaumenhaft, Mera J. 109

Fleming, Juliet 236, 245

Fletcher, John 22, 158, 250n.

Fletcher, Robert 180–1

Fluellen (character) 17, 24, 41, 45, 53, 84, 90, 110, 154, 167, 169, 171–2, 176–7, 187, 188–91, 195, 238, 281n., 283n.

Ford, John 122

Foucault, Michel 42, 43, 79, 140, 189–90, 198

Fougières, Gallois de 3

French king (character) 161, 175–6, 177–8

French queen (character) 24, 178

Fuseli, Henry xv

Garrick, David xv, 57

Gaunt, John of (character) 164, 166

George II (British king) 57

George III (British king) 54

Gervinus, G. G. 31–2, 39, 254, 256

Giles, David 102, 107

Ginsburg, Ruth Bader 232

Globe Theatre, Southwark xiv, 10, 18, 47–8, 63, 72, 105, 110, 131, 148, 155, 222, 223, 244

Godard, Jean-Luc 123

Goddard, Harold C. 36–7

Gould, Gerald 35–6, 37, 39, 41
Governor of Harfleur (character) 118, 225, 231, 235
Gower (character) 84, 110, 169, 195, 197, 237–8, 272n., 281n.
Gracian, Baltasar (Gracián y Morales, Baltasar) 197, 286n.
Grady, Hugh 75, 89–90
Green, Dorothy 59
Greenblatt, Stephen 42–3, 128–9, 140–1, 274n.
Greenburg, Bradley 79
Gregory, Miles 72
Grey (character) 84, 145–6, 147, 192
Grossman, David 122
Guienne, Duke of 204, 208
Gulf War 121
Gurr, Andrew 8, 11, 22–3, 27, 50, 135, 171, 241, 242, 243, 244, 246, 278n.
Gwillim, David 107

Haber, Judith 97, 240, 246
Hall, Edward 63
Hall, Peter 60, 63
Hands, Terry 14, 52, 60, 61
Hanmer, Thomas 27
Harcourt, Jean VII d' 202, 289n.
Hardy, Robert 106, 107
Harfleur, Siege of xii, 2, 9, 21, 24, 26, 56, 58, 76–7, 79, 83, 105, 107, 108, 113, 118, 119, 120, 122, 123, 168, 196, 204, 225, 231, 232, 240, 242, 291n.
Hassell, Alex 120
Hastie, Robert xvi, 64–5, 101
Hatchuel, Sarah 13, 14, 16, 100
Hattaway, Michael 111, 244
Hawkes, Terence 75
Hayes, Michael 102, 106
Hazlitt, William 29–30, 31, 32, 33, 34, 35, 38, 39, 40, 81, 126, 181, 182, 191, 200
Helgerson, Richard 158, 159, 278n., 279n.
Helmbold, Anita 100
Henri IV of France 39, 88
Henry IV (Henry Bolingbroke) xii, xiv, 7, 131–2, 133, 136, 148, 182, 186, 247n.
Henry V xii, xiii, 2–3, 5, 19–20, 23, 55, 95, 132, 180–1, 191, 202–9, 210, 233–4
  as Prince Hal 32, 36, 42, 54, 61, 69, 77, 96, 107, 120, 127, 138, 139, 141–4, 185, 187, 190, 193, 195, 197, 232
  evaluations of character 5–7, 8–9, 12–13, 15, 16, 17, 18, 20–2, 26–46, 48, 49, 52, 53–4, 59, 60–5, 70, 78–86, 89, 91, 97, 100, 104, 107, 110–11, 112, 114–16, 118, 120, 126–7, 150–5, 175–7, 181–3, 190, 195–200, 229–33, 235
Henry VI xiii, 2, 37, 56, 60, 67, 117, 162, 177, 213, 247n., 279n.
Henry VII xiii, 177, 291n.
Henry VIII xiii, 158, 162, 291n.
Henry Percy (Harry Hotspur) xii, 186, 197, 292n.

INDEX

Henry, Prince of Wales (son of James VI and I) 180–1, 195
Heywood, Thomas 223–4, 227, 294n.
Hiddleston, Tom xvi, 117, 118
Hill, Aaron xiv, 15, 53, 55–6, 260n.
Hillman, Richard 88
Holbein, Hans 184–5
Holderness, Graham 107, 141, 231, 245
Holinshed, Raphael 5, 23, 103, 132, 140, 169, 205, 208, 220, 227, 236, 244, 250n., 289n.
The Hollow Crown xvi, 102, 117–19, 232–3
Holly, Ellen xv
Hölscher, Tonio 194–5
Hooks, Robert xv
Hopkins, Lisa 45
Horsley, Owen 73–4
Hove, Ivo van 67–8
Howard, Jean 95, 169, 240, 246
Hudson, H. N. 32, 254n.
Hugo, François-Victor xv, 65
Hundred Years' War xii, 2–3, 288–9n.
Hunt, Maurice 82–4
Hurt, John 117, 119
Hutson, Lorna 182, 198, 284n.
Hytner, Nicholas 64

imperial/imperialism 35, 74, 104, 117, 148, 157–64, 278n.
Iraq War 64, 76–7, 114–15, 117, 121
Ireland/Irish 5, 9–10, 15, 17, 24, 26, 43, 45, 50, 76, 77–8, 90, 92, 99, 131, 157, 162–4, 168–73, 176, 179, 237, 280n., 281n., 282n.
Isabeau, Queen 204, 290n.
Ivic, Christopher 16–17

Jackson, Ken 85–6
Jacobi, Derek 108, 109
James VI and I xiv, 22–3, 99, 162, 163, 170, 171, 174, 175, 177, 179, 195, 251n., 278n., 280n., 282n., 284n.
Jamy (character) 23, 24, 26, 84, 99, 169, 171, 189, 281n.
Jensen, Phebe 46
Joan of Arc (Joan la Pucelle) xiii, 2, 240
Johnson, Samuel 27–9, 34, 37
Jones, David 90
Jonson, Ben 11, 50, 51, 54
  Every Man In His Humour 22, 52
  Every Man Out of His Humour 51–2
Judgement Day 82, 229

Kahn, Michael 71
Kantorowicz, Ernst 182
Karremann, Isabel 95
Katherine de Valois (character) xv, 15, 21, 27, 48, 49, 55, 56–7, 64, 91, 96–7, 111, 123, 147, 155, 177, 178, 188, 212, 215, 218, 231, 236–7, 257n., 260n., 290n., 292n.

INDEX

Kean, Charles xv, 58, 261n.
Kean, Edmund 53, 57
Kemble, J. P. xv, 53, 57, 58
Kerrigan, John 92, 278n.
Kezar, Dennis 79–80
Kline, Kevin 70
Knapp, Jeffrey 84–5, 86
Knight, G. Wilson 39
Knights, L. C. 34, 255n.

Laidlaw, J. C. 216
Langham, Michael xv, 73
Lanham, Richard 235, 245
Leggatt, Alexander 20, 103
Lenz, Joseph M. 188, 190
Lester, Adrian xvi, 64
Le Tourneur, Pierre xv
Lindtberg, Leopold 66
Lloyd, W. W. 33–4, 35
Loehlin, James 66, 100, 261n.
Lord Chamberlain's Men 10, 22, 99, 222, 223, 241, 251, 252
luggage boys 60, 62, 117, 190

McAlindon, Tom 78–9
McCloskey, John C. 38
McDiarmid, Ian 61–2, 104
McEachern, Claire 169, 283n.
Machiavelli, Niccolò/Machiavellianism 21, 32, 33, 37, 78, 80, 83, 84, 89–90, 114, 118, 129, 136, 137–40, 143, 144, 197, 227, 254n., 276n.
MacKenzie, John Stuart 38
Macmorris (character) 24, 26, 45, 84, 92, 169, 171, 172–3, 176, 189, 281n.

Macready, William 53, 58
Mardock, James D. 7, 8, 14, 15, 49, 75, 78, 86, 90, 243, 266n.
Marignano (Battle of) 4
Marlowe, Christopher 94
  Jew of Malta 138
  Tamburlaine 91
Marotti, Arthur F. 85–6
Marshall, Penny 120–1
Mason, Roger 158
Mebane, John S. 80–1
Meron, Theodor 190
Miller-Blaise, Anne-Marie 5, 13, 14–15, 16
Monmouth (town in Wales) xii, 3, 53, 176
Montaigne, Michel de 83
Montrose, Louis 96
Morgann, Maurice 6, 28–9, 34
Mossman, Judith 196
Müller-Wood, Anja 87
Mulready, Cyrus 98–9
Munday, Anthony 22
Munro, Lucy 94–5
Murphy, Andrew 45, 90
Musée de l'Armée 4

Napoleon Bonaparte 29, 57–8, 81
Nashe, Thomas 161, 227–8
nationalism 8–9, 13, 29, 91–2, 95, 103, 104, 117, 120, 144, 154, 160, 199, 220, 283n.
Neill, Michael 45, 90, 172
new criticism 36
new historicism 19, 40, 41–4, 85, 128–9

New National Theatre, Tokyo 73
New York Classical Theater 69–70
Nine Years' War 157
Noble, Adrian 61–2, 104, 110, 118–19
Normans/Norman Conquest 163, 172, 173–5, 233–4, 239, 282n.
Nunn, Trevor 5
Nym (character) 62, 83, 84, 145, 186–7, 191–3, 226

Oldcastle, Sir John 22, 23, 130, 250n., 274–5n.
Olivier, Laurence xv, 3, 13, 16, 39, 48, 53, 59, 63, 65, 102, 104–6, 107–8, 110, 112, 113, 116, 120, 127, 232, 277n.
Olivier, Richard 48–9
O'Neill, Hugh, 2nd Earl of Tyrone 9, 45
Open Air Theatre, Regent's Park xvi, 64–5, 101
Orléans, Charles d' 17, 202, 203, 204, 205, 208, 209–10, 216, 220

pacifism 59, 66, 80
Palfrey, Simon 230, 245
Parker, Patricia 82–3, 186
Pasupathi, Vimala C. 88–9
Patterson, Annabel 9, 26
Peacham, Henry 195
Pennington, Michael 52, 62, 112
Pentland, Elizabeth 17, 292n.
Pepys, Samuel 55

Percy, Henry *see* Henry Percy
Pestritto, Carrie 89
phenomenology 86–7
Philip IV of France 159
Pistol (character) 167, 176, 186–7, 189, 191–4, 197, 226, 235, 237–8
Pittock, Malcolm 79
Pittsburgh Public Theater 72
Pizan, Christine de 17, 202, 203, 204, 205, 210–15, 217, 220, 290n., 292n.
Plutarch 196
Poel, William 47, 59
Polito, Mary 78
Poole, Adrian 90
Pop-Up Globe 72
presentism 15, 44, 75–8, 99–100
Preston, Carrie 121
providence/providential history 7, 16, 40, 142–3, 147, 154, 155, 164, 209, 227
Pudney, Eric 89
Pugliatti, Paola 237, 245

Quickly, Mistress Nell, the Hostess (character) 6, 9, 62, 186–7, 191, 193–4, 240

Rabkin, Norman 12, 37–8, 78–80, 82–3, 84, 100, 103, 221
Rackin, Phyllis 38, 45, 95, 169, 240, 244, 246
Rambures (character) 166
Rehmani, Sabaa 116
Religieux of Saint-Denis 203, 204, 205, 206, 207–8, 209, 210, 215, 289n.

Rice, Hayley xvi, 69
Richard II xii, 7, 15, 16, 33, 81, 95, 129, 131, 133, 147, 186, 247n.
Richard III xiii, 60, 66, 67, 112, 247n.
Robinson, Benedict S. 91–2
Roman 41, 89, 172, 189, 192
Romantics/Romanticism 5, 29, 30, 57, 254n.
Rossiter, A. P. 35, 36
Rouen (Siege of) xii
Royal Shakespeare Company xv, 3, 13–14, 60, 63–4, 72, 73, 102, 104, 108, 119–20
Royal Society of Antiquaries 58, 175
Rylance, Mark 48, 63

Salic Law 22, 36, 77, 95, 99, 134, 157, 172, 184, 186, 228, 242, 250n.
Salisbury (character) 154
Salkeld, Duncan 98, 248n.
Savile, John 174–5, 282n.
Schlegel, A. W. xv, 29, 30, 65
Schwyzer, Philip 45–6
Scotland/Scottish xiv, 5, 17, 23, 56, 99, 121, 157, 162–3, 164–8, 169, 171, 175, 177–9, 189, 237, 278n., 280n., 281n., 282n.
Scroop, Lord (character) 36, 55, 84, 145, 146, 147, 192, 194
Searjeant, Philip 92
Second World War xv, 3, 39, 59, 65, 105, 121, 261n.

Seven Years' War 57
Seymour, Laura 18
Shakespeare Festival, Stratford, CT 71
Shakespeare Festival, Stratford, Ontario 73
Shakespeare Ladies' Club 57
Shakespeare, William
  Antony and Cleopatra 192, 195
  Coriolanus 89, 198, 226
  Hamlet xiv, 59, 73, 83, 98, 110, 112, 196, 197, 213, 255n., 292n.
  Julius Caesar xiv, 89, 226
  King Henry IV, Parts 1 and 2 xiv, 6, 12, 22, 28, 31, 32, 35, 37, 53, 57, 66, 88, 96, 106, 107, 117, 120, 122, 127, 128, 129, 130, 134, 136, 186, 187, 190, 194, 197, 232, 240, 247n., 250n., 260n., 275n., 286n., 287n., 292n.
  King Henry VI, Parts 1, 2 and 3 31, 60, 73, 91, 106, 229, 232, 240, 247n.
  King Henry VIII 179
  King Lear 73, 226, 252n.
  Love's Labour's Lost 113, 196, 284n.
  A Midsummer Night's Dream 96, 118, 79
  Richard II xiv, 13, 50, 66, 88, 106, 117, 127, 129, 136, 148, 164, 186, 219, 247n.
  Richard III 13, 60, 66, 67, 73, 89, 106, 112, 123, 183, 225, 247n.

Titus Andronicus 94, 113, 118
Troilus and Cressida 192, 193, 195
Shakespeare's Globe (modern theatre) 47–8, 63
Shanghai Dramatic Art Center 73–4
Shapiro, James 46, 157, 171
Sharpe, Kevin 183
Sharrock, Thea 102, 117, 232
Sher, Antony 120
Shrewsbury, Battle of xii
Sidney, Sir Henry 92
Sidney, Sir Philip 50, 51, 234
Simpson, Richard 39, 41
Sinfield, Alan 43, 45, 127–8, 151
Singapore Arts Theatre 72
Sir John Oldcastle see Oldcastle, Sir John
Slights, Camille Wells 46, 82
Sloterdijk, Peter 144, 154
Smales, Maggie xvi
Smith, Bruce R. 238–9, 246
Smith, Emma 7, 10, 15, 16, 23, 57, 63, 66, 100, 233, 243, 244, 245
Smith, Matthew J. 86–7
Somme, Battle of the 76
Somogyi, Nick de 46
Spanish Armada 4, 39, 46, 158
Spelman, Henry 175
Squire, William 106
Steinsaltz, David 233–4, 235, 245
Stone, Charles Russell 195
Suffolk (character) 154

Sukic, Christine 17, 147
Sutherland, John 77, 232
Swinburne, A. C. 33

Taylor, Gary 25–7, 76, 77, 130, 274–5n., 286n.
Taylor, Paul 48–9
Taymor, Julie 113, 118
Tempera, Mariangela 120, 122–3
Terry, Michelle xvi, 64–5
tetralogy
    first 3, 60, 130, 247n.
    second 1, 4, 6–7, 60, 88, 95, 96, 117, 120, 127, 129, 130–1, 137, 139, 247n., 275n.
Thatcher, Margaret 13, 16, 49, 62, 111, 112
Théâtre du Nouveau Monde 73
Theobald, Lewis 99–100
Thomson, Leslie 225, 244
Thorne, Alison 87
Tillyard, E. M. W. 30, 40–1, 44, 127, 248n.
Treaty of Troyes *see* Troyes, Treaty of
Treaty of Vervins, *see* Vervins, Treaty of
Tribble, Evelyn 93–4
Troyes, Treaty of xii, 2, 205, 218, 220, 279n., 290n., 293n.
Tucker, E. F. J. 199
Tudor, Owen 55, 177
Tudor dynasty/myth xiii, 40–1, 46, 163, 177, 182

Ulrici, Hermann 30–1

Venet, Gisèle 5, 13, 14–15, 16, 197–8
Vernant, Jean-Pierre 195
Vervins, Treaty of 88
Vienne-Guerrin, Nathalie 100
Vietnam War 70–1, 109
Voltaire 11, 65, 249n.
Vukovitz, Deborah 100

Wales/Welsh 5, 17, 26, 45–6, 53, 157, 161–4, 166–8, 169, 172, 176–7, 179, 180, 195, 237–8, 280n., 281n., 283n.
Walls, Alison 92
Walter, J. H. 127, 186–7
Wanamaker, Sam 47
Warburton, William 27
Warchus, Matthew 63
Warren, Christopher 191
Wars of the Roses xiii, 53–4, 56, 60, 62, 102, 112

Watts, Cedric 77, 88, 232
Weimar Theatre 65–6
Welles, Orson xv
Werner, Sarah 97
Westmorland (character) 24, 165
Whedon, Joss 118, 123
Whitvers, H. Austin 95
widows 93, 117, 207–8, 211, 215
Williams, Michael (character) 11, 21, 33, 42, 44, 77, 82, 83, 93, 105, 124, 150–2, 169, 175, 188, 190–1, 229, 231, 235
Wilson, John Dover 37, 39–40
Womersley, David 46, 81–2, 86
Woods, Gillian 18

York (character) 118, 154

Zadek, Peter 66–7, 68
Žižek, Slavoj 141–3

www.ingramcontent.com/pod-product-compliance
Lightning Source LLC
Chambersburg PA
CBHW052143300426
44115CB00011B/1500